PIECES OF
SOAP

—— essays by ——

STANLEY
ELKIN

SIMON & SCHUSTER

New York   London   Toronto   Sydney   Tokyo   Singapore

SIMON & SCHUSTER
Simon & Schuster Building
Rockefeller Center
1230 Avenue of the Americas
New York, New York 10020

SIMON & SCHUSTER and colophon are registered
trademarks of Simon & Schuster Inc.
Designed by Caroline Cunningham and Marc Strang
Manufactured in the United States of America

1   3   5   7   9   10   8   6   4   2

Library of Congress Cataloging-in-Publication Data
Elkin, Stanley, date
Pieces of soap : essays / by Stanley Elkin.
p.   cm.
I. Title.
PS3555.L47P5   1992
813'.54—dc20   91-37973
CIP

ISBN: 0-671-73442-3

Portions of this book were previously published.

"Performance and Reality" originally appeared in *Grand Street*, Summer 1983.
"Plot" originally appeared in *Sub-Stance* 27, 1980.
"Acts of Scholarship" originally appeared in *Chicago*, September 1987.

(Credits continue on page 336.)

To Joan

CONTENTS

INTRODUCTION

"THE MAGIC KINGDOM"—AS STANLEY ELKIN ONCE CALLED A fictional Disney World—would do as a name for Elkin's rich, wonderful, and grotesque America. The world seen through Elkin's eyes has a carnival-rough shine—barkers, who are as much curators as pitchmen, outclaiming each other's sideshows, entrances hiding funhouse mirrors and tilting floors, even the eerie glide into dark pools. Though it's not the world you and I may live in, it bears a resemblance—suspicious and even insulting we say, trying to retain our self-respect—to our world, where we hang on to our pitiful gentilities and amenities. Elkin's world, comic though it is, has let down all the bars of shame and modesty; in it, pity and terror, translated into mockery and savagery, hold center stage. In his foreword to the Thunder's Mouth Press edition of *Criers and Kibitzers, Kibitzers and Criers* he tells how and why he adopted his naked bravado and the ostentation of his style:

> I'm trying to tell what turned me. Well, delight in language as
> language certainly. (I'd swear to that part.) But something less de-

lightful, too. It was that nothing very bad had happened to me yet.
(I was a graduate student, protected, up to my ass in the ivy.) My
daddy's rich and my ma is good lookin'. Then my father died in
1958 and my mother couldn't take three steps without pain. Then
a heart attack I could call my own when I was thirty-seven years
old. Then this, then that. Most of it uncomfortable, all of it boring.
I couldn't run, I couldn't jump. Because, as the old saying *should*
go, as long as you've got your health you've got your naïveté. I lost
the one, I lost the other, and maybe that's what led me toward
revenge—— a writer's revenge, anyway, the revenge, I mean, of
style.

The naked truth, streaking past in the athletic marathon of style, is
what the spectator in Stanley Elkin's Magic Kingdom gets to see.

When I first knew Stanley at Smith, we shared an office and a
typewriter. Stanley wrote in the morning; I came in after lunch. When
I came in, I would find in the typewriter a version of life that I read,
each day, with a weirder and weirder sensation of déjà-non-vu; that
is, we would all—Stanley, his wife, Joan, and I—have taken our boys,
Philip and David, to some one of the desolate entertainments offered
by our rural surroundings (a State Fair, an ox-pulling contest), and
there it would be in Stanley's typing, our Sunday. I had lived it, yes,
but I hadn't seen it. It was, on Stanley's page, lit up in Day-Glo colors,
the oxen more Hardyesque, the drivers great Paul Bunyans, the arena
almost a bullring, the crowd almost Madrileños. The prizes glittered,
the earth heaved in mighty dust, the sun stood still over the Homeric
exploits, and the Pindaric ode had nothing on the Elkinic essay. Why,
our Sunday excursion rivaled anything Ulysses had run into. I was
Stanley's slave forever. The Magic Kingdom had gained another citizen.

Go to California with him ("An American in California"), but be
sure, as he keeps reminding himself, to come back to the States afterwards. And while you're there, remember you've gone along with
(his word) a cripple—Stanley has multiple sclerosis—and you find
yourself taking your chances with slippery bathrooms and no grab bars.
You also take your chances with the Reagans at the Beverly Hilton;
elsewhere ("At the Academy Awards") you encounter ceremonial seating and disco parties as seen by a man who (four months before his

second heart bypass) wonders why the PR person on the phone calls him "Stanley" and "not Your Mortalityship or your Woundship."

It is death and wounds that give Stanley Elkin's prose its bite and edge, that confer on his world its lurid charms and its shoddy airs. On the other hand it's Elkin's gusto ("my bobby-soxer heart") that gives his world its celebratory openhandedness, its lavish buoyancy. And it's his air of telling all—*does* he tell all? he'll never tell—that promises new shocks per page.

The page-turners: How does a Chicago boy wanting to lose his virginity find a whorehouse in Kankakee? What happens to a soldier fleeing AWOL down a mountain so he can read Thomas Mann? What sort of a shirt do you wear to hear T. S. Eliot read? Will Stanley dare to drive his motorcycle or will he move it into the living room as a planter? But Stanley isn't only the inspired voyeur of American culture or the hero of his own amazed, amplified, airwave talk show. Those (as his critics like to say) are his *shticks*, and he slips as easily into them as into his tuxedo ("My Tuxedo: A Meditation"); his Pagliaccio clown suit alternates with his ancient Mariner weeds. The rhetoric of his spiel comes from his worship of the sales pitch—after all, wasn't his father Coro's man in the Midwest?—but the salesman (like the franchiser, the bail bondsman, his novelistic alter egos) is only a front for the artist. He's almost too shy to say so (it's easier, in America, to own up to being a tax evader than an artist), but every so often the truth will out. In Stanley's story "The State of the Art," God is asked why he made creation. Was it out of goodness?

> *Goodness?* No. It was Art. It was always Art. I work by the contrasts and metrics, by the beats and silences. It was all Art. *Because it makes a better story is why.*

That's Elkin's icy defense of the law of evolving inner being, obeyed by every work of art worthy of the name.

And Stanley Elkin—when he's not being the anthropologist of our postmodern tribal life—is a great theorist of fiction. Try his gruesome nugget on plot. Or his fantastic Faulknerian tour-de-force, "What's in a Name," such a deadpan history of fraud, arson, and exploitation that when he acknowledged there wasn't a word of truth in any of it,

I felt betrayed. The best of all the theory pieces is "The Rest of the Novel," Elkin's hymn to fiction, its

> . . . compounding stress level, . . . some taut, tauter, tautest, up-taut crescendo of din and skirmish growing and exploding like a bolero from the lull of apparent quiescence to the ripsnorting reality of a disturbed perturbation that lurks just fractions of fractions be-neath the papered-over calm of surface.

And that's only about the pacing; there's also the content, the plot—

> . . . cautionary, purposeful pain (because the *Book of Job* is the only book), God testing men's waters, as if this is the day the Lord has made in order to break your bones, in order to cheat you and mug you and play you for a fool and leave you for dead bleeding in the street (or why are the table stakes of dramatic prose such high ones)?

There are stylists who forget they're supposed to be rewriting the *Book of Job* and tragedians who forget that without style there's no tragedy. His Woundship's duels with reality are stylishly and revenge-fully conducted, all the way. Stanley has a caricaturist's eye, wickedly aimed, and he catches the buffoonish gestures of his America with a blend of the disgusted and the enchanted. Our Daumier, he can sketch Dr. Kinsey or a flamenco dancer with equal expressiveness, throwing in for good measure his mythologized St. Louis, its Third Tuesdays, its Insight Lady, its Mondrian grid. And his soaps.

The soaps ("Pieces of Soap") are special. Because his father brought home ("stole," says Elkin) soaps from the hotels he stayed in, Stanley collects stolen soaps. At first modestly arrayed in bathroom baskets, the soaps have overflowed into panniers, hampers, bins. After years of collections and contributions of soap, Stanley (second-bypass Stan-ley) is haunted by the specter of mortality, and he starts *using the soap.* It's a ritual to prolong existence: As long as the soaps last, so will Stanley. One could say that the hoarded global noticings of the Elkin eye—from the baffled first glimpses of high life under his father's tutelage down to yesterday's jaundiced glances at the Reagans—are the stored-up soaps of his imagination, the lacerating wherewithal of his intelligence. Every time he writes something—using up the soap, as it were—another piece of twentieth-century life is installed in a display case. When people coming after us want to know what we were like, they can read Elkin's time capsules.

The English essay was once sedate, instructive, moral, and civilized; then it became Romantic, anguished, and hallucinatory; it even took on rant and satire. The Elkin essay, while knowing all these modes, is also a creature of its own exotic playfulness, animated by dismayed delight in seeing and naming the most secret desires, vanities, and revulsions. Window-shopping in Stanley Elkin's essays, we can see life's dreck and dross but also its pure gold of pain, affection, and hilarity. Like the soap baskets, the Elkin genius has a mythical inexhaustibility. Anything—the Newberry Library, a novelty company's catalogue—is enough to set off its rocketing energies. It takes us through space in long loop-the-loops all its own; and when it sets us down, we feel, wistfully, our own diminished and grounded base state. Luckily, we have only to turn the page—turn the page, O reader— to be launched on one more ride.

Helen Vendler
Cambridge, Massachusetts

PART ONE

PERFORMANCE
AND
REALITY

THERE IS IN LITERATURE AN ELEMENT OF WHAT I SHALL CALL "crossover." In primitive form it is often little more than echo, or allusion, and is borrowed from one thing and imposed on another for what might almost be homeopathic reasons, growing a sort of interest, as money grows interest—lump-sum momentum like a chain letter no one has broken.

We frequently see the crossover in story titles. E. M. Forster writes *A Room with a View*, *A Passage to India*; Bob Coover *"The Cat in the Hat for President."* Joan Didion calls her novel *A Book of Common Prayer*, Thornton Wilder his play *The Skin of Our Teeth*. Indeed, it isn't only authors who consciously mine the allusive, magical properties inherent in prior names—inherent *after* the fact—history itself does it. "World War Two" is a crossover, catchy as a tune. Not sequential convenience, mind you, though that's certainly part of it, but actual art. So artful and catchy, in fact, that the one on the drawing boards, if it ever happens, will be called "World War Three."

Writers of advertising copy and the editors of popular magazines are perhaps the most expert, certainly the most self-conscious, practitioners of this form—and it *is* a form—with its values of pun and slogan. It would be an interesting exercise to examine the titles of the news articles in just one issue of *Time* magazine. I'm too lazy to take the trouble, and too troubled to take the pains, but if I were a better person and had the character for it, I'm certain that what I would find would be a kind of cornucopia of recombinant and essentially *literary* elements—in-jokes for outsiders.

But whether the source is literary or idiomatic—usually it's idiomatic—the intended effect, when it is not merely cute, is always the same—new wine in old bottles, some recycled but incremental and compounded sense of the world, the lifting of one occasion to enhance another.

Some years ago, to no one's particular notice, I thought to call a collection of bits and pieces from my previous books *Stanley Elkin's Greatest Hits*. I thought it an inspired title. The model was from the recording industry, an allusion to what, in America, has become almost a genre—*Wayne Newton's Greatest Hits, Elvis's* . . . : the habit of reissuing in a new package the popular but out-of-print blockbuster golds and platinums of established stars. Often these anthology recordings are promoted in TV commercials with the note, like a surgeon general's disclaimer on a package of cigarettes, that it's not available in stores.

My intentions had been honorable. That is, like all honorable intentions, they were born out of frustration and despair. All I've ever wanted, as I tell my friends, is to be rich and famous and to live forever without pain. My title, I felt, was pure crossover ironic, not in the least cute, pure art. I have no greatest hits of course, no golds, no platinums, none of the fabulous and rare ores, elements, and alchemicals of the Las Vegans; in me metallurgy reduced to mere spin-off, simple dross. Anticipating, I even tried to make the case with my publisher that we should use the other crossover phrase as well and display prominently on the jacket the fact that the book was "Not Available in Stores." An in-joke for an outsider. For me, I mean.

To this point, at least, I've been talking only along the fringes of art and fiction, my notion of crossover simplistic—allusions, slogans, and puns, statutory miles from my argument. But even allusions, slogans, and puns with their pentimento, almost geological, layers and palimpsest arrangements, do in primary colors what good fiction with its infinite palette must always try to do.

• • •

Let me tell you about the flamenco dancer.

The flamenco dancer sits in the café against the whitewashed walls, slouched in his wooden chair. While the women dance, a guitar player, his feet oddly stolid and flatfoot on the small platform, leans his ear against the back of his instrument as if he is tuning it. Another gazes impassively across the fretted fingerboard of his guitar as though he were blind. The family—it is impossible to know relationships here, to distinguish husbands from brothers, sisters from wives—a mysterious consanguinity undefined as the complicated connections in circus; only the standing, hand-clapping man in the suit, shouting encouragement like commands, seems in authority here, or the woman, her broad, exposed back and shoulders spilling her gown like the slipped, toneless flesh of powerful card players. Even the slouching brother? husband? nephew? son? is attentive but demure, the women's hair pulled so tightly into their comb tiaras you can see the deep, straight furrows of their scalps. Their arrhythmic clapping is not so much on cue as beside it, beneath it, random as traffic, signaled by some private, internal urging like spontaneous pronouncement at a prayer meeting. Yes. Like testimony, like witness. Except for this—the finger snapping, the hand claps never synchronous as applause, the occasional gutturals of the men and the abrupt chatter of the women like a musical gossip— they do not seem absorbed, or even very interested, their attention deflected, thrown as the voice of a ventriloquist, loss of affect like a dominant mood. Inside the passionate music and performance they are rigid, distracted as jugglers. The men and women, patient in their half circle of chairs as timid Johns, polite whores in a brothel, seem even less aware of each other than they are of the performers, kinship and relationship in abeyance, whatever of love that connects them dissolved, intimacy stoicized, the curious family in the cavelike room suddenly widowed, suddenly widowered, orphaned, returned to some griefless condition of independence.

And now the *bailora* completes her turn. Like some human beast, she seems to rise from the broad, tiered flounces of her costume as from a package of waves at a shoreline, the great, fabric petals of her long train swirled, heaped as seawater at her feet, her immaculate ass, hips, thighs, and tits a lesson in the meaty rounds of some mythic geometry, her upper arms spreading from her shoulders like wings, angled to her forearms, her forearms angled to her wrists, her wrists and hands and fingers and long Latin nails a squared circle of odd, successive dependencies, the stiff, queer displacement of the askew fingers like some hoodoo signal to charm the bright arrogance of the dance.

The man in the suit—when did the cigarette, burned out now, only a dead ash longer than the intact paper that supports it, go into his lips?—beats an asyndeton, paratactic, ungrammatical applause. It is that same deliberate offbeat accompaniment that earlier had almost but not quite violated the heel clicks and toe taps of the *bailora*. No matter how studiously the audience in the café tries to keep up with it, they cannot fall in with this artful dodger.

Now the flamenco dancer rises from his chair. Slim and grave as a bullfighter he moves in his gypsy silks and gabardines, his trapezist's *pasodoble* entrances and heroics. Alone, it is as if he marches in a procession, deadpan as a saint, solemn as Jesus. He looks like a condemned man leading an invisible party of executioners and priests to his gallows, the host at his own murder feast. There is nothing epicene or hermaphroditic in his bearing, yet he could almost be the embodiment of some third sex, or no, some sexual specialist, a fucker of virgins, say, of nymphets and schoolgirls and all the newly menstrual. In his tight, strange clothing, the trousers that rise above the waist and close about his spine, the small of his back, the narrow jacket and vest that just meet them, leaving off exactly where the trousers begin, not a fraction of an inch of excess material, sausaged into his clothes as the girls' hair had been into their comb tiaras, the bulge of his genitals customized, everything, all, all bespoke, fitting his form, seamless as apple peel, the crack in his ass, the scar on his hip, he seems dressed, buttocks to shoulders, in a sort of tights, some magic show-biz gypsy latex.

And now he is in position on the platform, conducted there by the asyncopatic hand claps of the man in the suit.

At first he appears the perfect flamenco analogue of a bullfighter. If the women, with their elaborate hand and arm movements, had seemed to flourish banderillas and brandish lances, the flamenco dancer with his minimal upper-body gestures and piledriver footwork, seems to wield capes, do long, stationary passes, slow-motion veronicas, outrageous down-on-one-knee *rodillas*. Indeed, with his furious heel-toe, heel-toe momentum, he seems at times to be the actual bull itself, pawing the ring of platform in flamenco rage. Bullfighter *and* bull, as the dancing woman had seemed an extension of the actual sea.

This is what the flamenco dancer looks like.

He has the face of a cruel, handsome Indian and looks insolent as a man in a tango. There are layers of indifference on his face like skin, like feature itself, some fierce inappetency and a listlessness so profound that that itself might almost be his ruling passion, some smoky nonchalance of the out-of-love. Not cold, not even cool, for these words at least suggest an *idea* of temperature, and the flamenco dancer seems to have been born adiabatic, aseptic. What, on someone else's face, might look like sneer, snarl, contempt, may, on his, signify no more than the neutral scorn and toughness on the face of a bulldog.

Now the flamenco dancer is possessed by his *duende*, his musical *dybbuk*. His is *jondo*, profound—death, anguish, tragedy. The larger issues. (Music is hard. In prose, music is very hard to do, unconvincing as lyrics, a cappella on a page. Avoid trying to render music. Avoid the sensations of orgasm. Steer clear of madmen as protagonists, and likewise eschew a writer as a hero of the fiction. And it's swimming at your own risk in the stream of consciousness. "Knowing believes before believing remembers," says Faulkner in a Joe Christmas section in *Light in August*. What the hell does that mean?) And the guitarist is singing his serious *soleares*, calling his *cante* like a ragman, whining his tune like a cantor. *Davvening* despair.

> *I am no longer what I was* [he sings,
>   calls, whines, *davvens*]
> *now will I be aga-ain*
> *I am a tree of sadness*
> *in the shadow of a waa-aall* . . .

> *A woman was the cause*
> *of my first downfall;*
> *there is no perdition in the world*
> *that is not caused by women* . . .

> *In the neighborhood of Triana*
> *there is neither pen nor ink*
> *with which to write my mother,*
> *whom I haven't seen for* . . . *ye-ars.*

"*¡Olé!*"s pour in from the satellite performers half an orbit behind the flamenco dancer. "*¡Olé!*"s like an agreement, a deal, an oral handshake, a struck bargain. The done/done arrangements of serious negotiation.

And now it happens. Just now. The flamenco dancer is doing a particularly difficult riff. This murderous tango of a man whose body is one taut line of mood, who, touched at one end of that body should, by the laws of physics if not the conventions of his trade, like the strings on the musician's guitar, vibrate at the other, but whose art it is to defy physics, to drive his feet like pistons without ruffling a ruffle of his shirt, who *does* that, whose ruling second skin of costume, revealing still that inch and a half of scar, the material caught in it, in the *scar*, the magic show-biz gypsy latex, stuck there like the long, dark vertical of a behind snagged in the pants of a fat man rising from a chair on a hot day, does not, does *not*, display a single qualm of muscle, not one quiver, tremor, shiver, flutter, not one shake, not even his trousers which, snug as they are from mid-thigh to the small of the back, are cut like normal men's beneath that and actually hang like a gaucho's in a sort of a flare below the knee, not even his damn trousers jump! It is as if *he* is the ventriloquist (you must come back; you must return and use everything; you must use up your material; you must move the furniture around); it is as if *he* is the ventriloquist, only what he throws is not his voice but his feet, his shoe leather; it is as if *he* is the ventriloquist, has exactly on the physical plane the ventriloquist's schizophrenic detachment, straight man and comic all together all at once, only it ain't only his lips that don't move, it's *everything!* His hands are stilled, his calves are quiet, his knees, the ruffles on his shirt, *all* his torso, and it's as if he really *is* detached, actually separated from the interests of his body, only his feet going on about their business like steps drawn on a dance chart.

Except, as I say, now it happens. This dark fandango of a fellow is grinning. He is grinning; not smiling, grinning; not pleased as punch; probably not even happy; but grinning, *grinning*. And not *just* grinning, not simple human cheer or the Cheshire risibles of pleased teeth, but the original, paradigmatic, caught-out, pants down, caught-in-the-act, shit-eating smirk of grin itself!

Because that is how the flamenco dancer must be rendered, I think. A man who never grins, whose profession it is to keep a straight face, who earns his bread by artful scorn, whose squared back, poseur, gypsy bearing is by ordinary the stately four-four time of toreros and graduating seniors, must be shown with his face naked, his bared teeth and grinning lips like private parts. There must be crossover, what joke writers call the "switch." There must, that is, be a grafting of one condition upon another, the episodic or eventful equivalencies of pun and slogan, the schizophrenic tensions and torsions—though unless he's a minor character the flamenco dancer may not be mad, recall— of all discrepant allegiance.

It's like this. A flamenco dancer, a tinker, a tailor, a candlestick maker, any human being, cannot be shown in fiction without quirk, wrinkle, slippage—the fall, I mean, from the photographic, all, I mean, the strictly realistic and correct dictionary parameters and ideals of grace. Which explains whiskey priests, golden-heart whores, hung-over surgeons, cowardly soldiers, misers who tithe, mercenaries who develop some long-haul loyalty they cannot understand or even very definitively or coherently explain. "A man," Hemingway's dying Harry Morgan says in *To Have and Have Not*, "one man alone ain't got. No man alone now. No matter how a man alone ain't got no bloody fucking chance." Which explains, that is, all driven stereotype and fictional cliché. But the instincts of the cliché are correct; only the judgment of the writer is flawed, his critical lapse of recognition, maybe his reading habits. He is like the writer of mystery stories pursuing the idiosyncratic as relentlessly as ever his amateur detective pursued any murderer.

But I'm not talking about the idiosyncratic so much as I am about the strange—the flat-out, let-stand, mysterious. If there can be no flamenco dancer without that shit-eating grin, neither ought there to be any of the tight hospital corners of explanation. In James Agee's *A Death in the Family* there occurs perhaps one of the strangest ghost stories I've ever read. Jay, the father, has just been buried. The family returns to the house after the funeral. Here Agee discharges point of view into the disparate consciousnesses of a handful of characters. Upstairs the mother senses a presence in the room—that of her dead husband. Simultaneously, in another part of the house, their little boy feels that his father's spirit has suddenly returned. Still another relative hears an odd noise, looks around, sees nothing but is convinced that Jay has returned from the dead to comfort his mourners. Each character is certain that Jay has come back, is with them again, but, not wanting to upset the others who might not understand, decides to say nothing about the visitation. Agee never explains the startling conviction of reunion each has experienced. Indeed, he never even alludes to it.

Or Anthony Powell. In his novel *From a View to a Death*, Powell draws a tight and quite conventional picture of the middle professional class. Mrs. is sixtyish, a bit dowdy, a touch past it but still civilized. Mr. is a professional soldier, a major, retired. They live an uncomplicated home life in a genteel but ordinary house a few miles from town. They drink sherry, they take the *Times*. And one morning his wife goes into town to do some shopping. I don't have the book in front of me, but this, at least approximately, is what happens. "You'll be all right, dear?" "Oh, yes, I'll read I should think." "Is there anything you need?" "Cigarettes. I require cigarettes." "What, don't you have *cigarettes*?" "Well I thought I did, but it appears I've run out." "I'll bring some from Scrapple." "Most kind. Most decent." "It's on my way. It isn't as if it wasn't on my way." "Most considerate." "And I did wish to see Scrapple. Ask after his wife." "Mnn." "What's that, dear?" "My book. I can't seem to find that book I was reading." "What, the one about the campaigns?" "Yes, the campaign one, that's it." She sees the book and brings it to him. "Oh," she says, "that sunlight! Much too bright on the page." "Yes. It is rather. Yes." "Shall I draw the drapes then? You could switch on the lamp." "Most thoughtful. Yes." And she draws the drapes and the major thanks her, and they kiss good-bye, and she goes out to start the car. He hears it start up and listens to her drive off and rises from the chair beside which the lamp is now burning. He puts the book about the campaigns on the seat of the wing chair so that he won't misplace it again and walks into another room. When he returns he is dressed in his wife's clothes, even her makeup, even her hat. He sits back down in the chair and reads the book about the campaigns by the light of the lamp in the drape-drawn room. That is the end of the chapter. Powell never mentions the major's transvestism again. Though we see him again. And each time we do, *each time*, observing him closely now, astonished by him, gradually taken with an apparently decent man, we think: This fellow dresses up in women's clothes; he likes to put on a girdle; he enjoys the brace of a brassiere, the squeeze of a pump. There is that faintly geological feel of crossover, character layered as a cake.

Not the idiosyncratic, not the strange, maybe not even the myste-

rious, finally, so much as the queer, protuberant salience of the
obliquely sighted. What the periscope saw, what goes on in the corner
of the eye, talking pictures in the kaleidoscope, an eye staring back at
you, weeping, through the keyhole, the application of a close but
possibly afflicted vision, as if writers were color-blind, say, or mental.
Because the flamenco dancers and the ghosts and the British majors
(ret.) are all used up. We endanger a species simply by mentioning
it. So not the idiosyncratic, strange, or mysterious, or even that queer
protuberant salience of the obliquely sighted; maybe only surprise.
Which I take to be some flipped-coin mix—flipped-coin because it
can go either way—of the ordinary in league with the exotic, the
strange displacements of the ordinary. The flamenco dancers and
ghosts and majors retired are all used up, but we can never be quit of
them, or they of us. We must wring them dry as a sheet, put usurer's
pressures on them, dun them with obligation, hit them when they're
down. And, using surprise, surprise always in some un-Hitchcockian
way so that surprise is not ever expected, not ever the form itself that
is, not ever looked for, some logical, non-*Jaws*ian sense of the thing.
Not Boo! from a closet or Happy Birthday! from pals. Surprise inevitable as verdict, ordered as law.

I went to the Metropolitan Museum of Art. It was one of those fine,
rare spring days in New York when optimism flows like an energy,
when, mysteriously, there is a kind of astonishing democracy in the
air, the pollen count zero and the ego and envy in abeyance, not even
coveting my neighbor's wife, not coveting at all, giving everyone the
benefit of the doubt, *this* old Scrooge, better than Christmas; not "You,
boy! You know the poulterer on the High Street? Fetch a goose, I'll
write you into the will!" Because you figure he doesn't need it, convinced everyone is a personage anyway, the pimply fellow in dirty
jeans, the bag lady, the Howard Hughes type fishing coins from the
gutter—— all, all personages, all upperly mobile and down from the
three-million-buck co-ops across Fifth Avenue, out for a breath of air,
a touch of art. Your eye out for Kissinger, your eye out for Jackie.
On Eighty-first Street, personages were sprawled on the museum
steps eating hot dogs, knotted saltbread, sipping soda. Two vendors,
their marvelous wagons with their clever compartments like trick drawers in a desk, about twelve feet apart, cry "Hot dogs, hog dogs here,"

more to each other than to their customers. They do a brisk business and seem terribly amused, as if all that's at stake is the side bet they have down on who will turn over the most saltbread today.

I schlepp up the steps, pulling myself along by the railing, this privileged Porgy for whom even the bag ladies get out of the way. I climb half a mile of stairs. (I *love* art!)

Schoolkids, cross-legged on the floor, civil and serious, snug and curiously private in this public place, copy masterpieces into their sketchbooks. Joan has organized a wheelchair. I wave to the toddlers in strollers. "Hi kids," I say, amusing myself that I know what each is thinking, struggling to say. Not "Hey look at the cripple," but "Mommy, Mommy, there goes the biggest toddler in the goddamn world!" I'm having a marvelous time, my heart in high for once. Everywhere people back from the gift shop carry Metropolitan Museum shopping bags like so much artistic grocery, and I have, in this perfect temperate zone with its ideal temperature and humidity designed for canvas and pigment, a sense of some best-foot-forward, good-willed world, as if Philanthropy were an actual order of actual politics, as much a rule of reign as the dynasties and kingdoms and tribes whose artifacts and paintings and sculptures seem somehow the place's generative treasury, not a repository of art at all but native wealth, natural resource, like Saudi oil, Zimbabwe chrome, Argentine beef. So close to the source of things, I am close to tears. It could be the giant toddler is simply overtired, on the edge of crankiness, tantrum. But nah, nah, his heart's in high, overwhelmed by the good order and best behavior of the citizens of this good country, the schoolgirls seated cross-legged on the floor, concentrating, intense, their lower lips in their teeth to get a line just right, to catch it on the tip of their drawing pens and hold it there, balancing, balancing, careful, gentle as people in bomb squads, till they can thrust it safely onto the drawing pad and be rid of it. (I will tell you something secret about myself. It's none of your business, but I don't much care for music, the classics I mean, the high symphonies and opera styles, yet whenever I go to a concert I weep. It's the cooperation that gets me every time, that dedicated sense of the civil—not the music but the musicians, the useless fiction of harmony they perpetuate. It is this that gets me now.)

Did I tell you that it is Saturday? It is Saturday, and scattered among the lovers and schoolkids, the Fifth Avenue co-op owners, the freelance tour guides and museum guards and gift-shop marketers and

toddlers—use it; use it up—the retired majors and flamenco dancers—
are fathers and sons, fathers and daughters. The children—use it; use
it up—have lunched on vendor hot dogs and have mustard on their
chins, the corners of their lips, bits of saltbread like a light seasoning
in the wrinkles of their clothes. The kids are oddly solicitous and gaze
where their dads direct their attentions with a courteous, leashed patience, not bored but the opposite, concentrating—use it; use it up—
working hard as those schoolgirls cross-legged on the floor, intense
themselves, as nervous about line, but it's their own expressions they're
perfecting, that they must balance even longer than that memory on
the tip of that drawing pen, hold and hold like a smile for an old-time
photograph, breathing of course, even talking, giving and taking, ex-
changing ideas, opinion, but everything controlled as the climate in
this place, and suddenly I recognize these kids. They are Saturday's
children, and they are here by court order, by official decree, sentenced
by a judge and their own mixed loyalties, serving their time like good
cons, and the fathers, too, sneaking a glance at their watches, wondering if it's time yet to go to the museum restaurant, time to get out
altogether, figuring how much time it will take up to get a cab to the
Russian Tea Room, how long the wait will be, how fast the service,
which movie to take the kid to, when it gets out, timing what's left of
the morning, the long afternoon, doing in their heads all the sums of
visitation, rehearsing the customs of custody.

And I get an idea for a story. Perhaps it was my private joke in the
wheelchair that set it off, my vision of myself as a giant toddler; perhaps
it was all this, well, *behaving*, this sedate and serious steady-state
attention I feel all about me, the suspicion, grown now to conviction,
that no one is having a very good time; certainly my sudden awareness
of the divorced fathers and their children, doing God knows what sums
of custody in *their* heads, had the most to do with it, but I have an
idea for a story.

It's this.

Julian's—I even have the name—parents are divorced when Julian
is eleven years old, and Julian's mother gets custody. The court grants
Julian's father liberal visitation privileges—weekends, of course, certain specified holidays, Julian's birthday in even-numbered years. And
Julian will spend at least one month of his summer vacation with his
dad.

Only when the story opens Julian is thirty-two years old, his mother and father in their early fifties, and Julian is dutifully waiting for his father's Saturday visit. Nothing, absolutely nothing, is wrong with Julian. Though he still lives at home, he has grown up to be an intelligent, healthy young man, decently employed, still single but ordinarily sexed, not particularly fixated on either his mother or his dad. The story will concern itself with their afternoon, Julian's and his father's, with the mutual anxieties both have about these visits, anxieties not all that different from the anxieties of the parents and children doing those secret sums of custody in their heads. Perhaps they will visit the Metropolitan, certainly they will go to the Russian Tea Room, where their order will be taken by the man in the suit. I expect they will have the conversation fathers and sons usually have on such occasions, the father discreetly pressing Julian for information about his mother, and Julian politely resisting, reluctant to be either go-between or honest broker, and both, from time to time, glancing at their watches.

The story is not yet written, or even begun, but I am satisfied that it satisfies my criteria, that it has all the elements—— the shit-eating grin on the flamenco dancer's face, the idiosyncratic, the strange, the mysterious, the queer protuberant salience of the obliquely sighted, crossover, and what the periscope saw, surprise, and all the rest of these strange displacements of the ordinary.

PLOT

SUPPOSE WE DO THIS. SUPPOSE WE TAKE FOR OUR SITUATION A bank robbery, and suppose, to remain within clear, clean lines, we decide it shall be a one-man job—nothing elaborate, no *Rififi* complications, no electronics genius sent from far, no big-deal Indy wheelman, no demolitions expert who can blow up Fort Knox or a box of Kleenex or take the crabgrass off your lawn without disturbing the zoysia, no safecracker with the sensitized fingers of a concert pianist who has never thrown a punch because his hands are his fortune—and no mastermind. Just a guy, a dropout with the drop on the teller and one hand on the arm roughly of the pregnant lady in front of him in line. A meanish fellow in need of money, a man of no particular charm who will kill the woman when her usefulness as a hostage has ended and abandon her body in another state, who will not even stop the car when he shoots her, not because he hasn't the imagination to elicit last words, and not even because he is unwilling to hear her plead, but because a shot on the highway in a closed car at fifty-five miles an hour will make even less noise than a shot in the woods, and perhaps, too, he is not a good marksman and even *he* can't miss the immense close-range target she makes beside him.

His problem, as I see it, is this: He must dispose of her body before he stops to fill up or to pee or pay a toll or look for a place where the truckdrivers eat. (Well there might be other problems, too, of course. Hadn't some witness taken down his license plate in the parking lot? The woman was pregnant, terrified, hard to negotiate into his car. Wouldn't she have slowed him down enough for someone to get a make on him or at the very least on his car? Perhaps. But our man has not thought about this very much. He's no TV crook with a large wardrobe and a larger manner. Like the poor who can least afford to, he trusts to luck, plays life by ear. He is not dashing or devil-may-care so much as disappointed by plans—merely chronically impatient at one end of things so that he must be massively patient at another. That's the breaks, he thinks, and is broken. Maybe he doesn't even *need* money. He doesn't need it for an operation. Hospitals will *give* you operations. He doesn't need it for his "habit." Drugs are for suckers, they make him nervous, they give him rash. He doesn't need it for a down payment on a house in a nice part of town. He's got itchy feet and has always hankered to live west, to see the mountains, the ocean, border towns where the cowboys lope. He doesn't need it for clothes and he doesn't need it for food, for luxuries that are inaccessible only because they have never been imagined or for necessities. Necessities are cheap, easily come by. Even the poor live in America. He needs it because he needs it. I mean because he *wants* it—and he wants it because other men have wanted it, and he does not have the character to do without what other men will not do without. Finally, he needs it because money is the single necessity that is *not* cheap.) So here's this dead woman beside him. He's surprised there's so much blood. It flows from her nipple like you were letting in a tub from her. He's not a reflective man but he thinks there's so much blood because she was pregnant. They double their blood when they're pregnant. Hasn't he heard that somewhere? This disgusts him, the notion that some of the blood might be her kid's. And there's some like slime around. He wants her out of his car. There's too much traffic now to stop and just dump her out. Where'd the goddam traffic come from?

Then he sees the big sign: Rest Area, 2 Miles. Then the other one: Rest Area, 1 Mile. He slows down and gets over on his right to scout if any cars have pulled into the area. He sees one. A couple is eating its lunch at a picnic table. He speeds up momentarily, then brakes abruptly and enters the access road at fifty-three miles an hour, the gravel popping against his car like shrapnel. He gets out on his side and walks around behind the car to the passenger side. The husband smiles and welcomes him vaguely. He smiles back and approaches the picnic table. "Driving so long," he says, "got to stretch my legs."

The husband glances at his out-of-state license. He says, "You can make good time on these interstates, but they sure can hypnotize you. It's good they have these rest areas."

"It is," he says and he takes his gun out of his pocket and shoots the man in the face. Then he shoots the man's wife. He has pressed the gun directly into their flesh because he thinks this will muffle the report. The reason he has shot the man first—he'd actually thought this one out and despite the fact that given his druthers he'd have chosen not to kill either of them (he feels some small pleasure in his reasoning)—is that surprise is a terrific advantage and he doesn't want to give the man too much time to react. He can always take care of the wife, he feels. He's a male-chauvinist-pig murderer. He steals their lunch—— fried chicken, coleslaw, potato salad, Cokes in cans. To tell the truth, he's on a diet but it's difficult to watch what you eat when you're on the road. He starts back to his car. He means to pull the dead woman out of the front seat and leave her there. Then he thinks: Jesus, am I stupid? They could be looking for my car. I'll take theirs. And that's what he does.

Now suppose we do this. Suppose, for the sake of argument, that we introduce stream-of-consciousness into our tale, that we finesse, as one erases a tape, whatever minimal body of ideas we had permitted the bank robber in our initial account and substitute other, even nobler ones. Say we give him a memory, say we give him a past. Say at the same time that we do not change a single thing in the chronology of his day. He still grabs the woman, still demands money of the teller, still has trouble pushing his hostage into the car, still gets out of town, still shoots his passenger, still is unhappy with the blood, still sees the sign for the rest area, still has that moment of indecision when he comes to the turnoff and finds that it's inhabited, still enters the access road, still gets out of his car, still approaches the husband and wife when the man smiles, still initiates the same conversation, still listens to the same reply, still makes his own reply, and still shoots first the husband, then the wife, takes their lunch, and trades in his car for theirs. Instead of each of these events posing problems, however, instead of each action being a specific if not very clever solution to those problems, suppose we just leave them to be events, individually articulated phenomena, as snow falling in Kansas is one phenomenon and a man buying a ticket on the London Underground is another. It's too late, of course. You'll have seen that. Getting the money requires taking the hostage. Taking the hostage requires getting rid of the hostage. Getting rid of the hostage requires killing the innocent couple at the picnic area. We have loosed a great universal principle on our story—— THAT THERE BE NO WITNESSES. It's a bloodbath but other people have died for principle before ever our husband and wife did. Still, even if it is too late, I ask you to accept as arbitrary what I've already admitted to be a closed circle of inevitable logic. For this I am prepared to fill in lacunae, to plant a new consideration for each one I've taken away, like a responsible forester in the state of Maine.

He walks into the bank and stands in line in front of the third teller's cage. He glances at the brass nameplate but the name doesn't register. He thinks, I shall have to write Gloria. Our last communication was not satisfactory. Neither of us is good on the phone. Perhaps it has something to do with the time difference. When it's nine o'clock here it's only just six there. Dinnertime. Gloria just back from the office preparing her widow's supper, opening cans, mashing tuna, slicing in eggs, chips of celery, as one deals a hand of solitaire. Spooning dollops of mayonnaise and vaguely worried about the mercury count. I call, threatening love, boasting love on a full stomach, in my pajamas. "What did you do today?" "Nothing. The usual." "Is Holmes back?" "Guevada's plane was grounded in San Diego. He couldn't get to Honolulu for his address. They wired that they'd put it back to the last day of the conference. Holmes was supposed to fly out after the morning meeting, but he was scheduled to introduce Guevada. I suppose he felt he had to stay over." "Is it tough for you in the office?" "No." "You're irritable." "I'm tired." "I love you." "Yes. That's fine." "Have you eaten?" "I'm doing a tuna salad." "Go out to a restaurant, why don't you?" "I wouldn't know what to order. I'd order tuna salad." Not our ages nor our circumstances—— only the time difference. My noon, her morning; my evening, her afternoon; my night, her evening; my dawn, her night. Coming at each other across zones of irreconcilable mood.

He grabs the pregnant woman for his hostage, pulling her out of line with a rough tug beside him, and wonders what has become of the summer house, if clotted oil like savage footprints march the beach. He thinks of the greasy grains of sand in his bathing trunks, the sun's and summer's gravel that he used to pick from his testicles and thighs like a sort of lice, patient at his harvest as a kindly ape. Suddenly he wants seersucker on him like a pediatrician in a small town. He wants his throat mounted in a white collar and a tie like a dagger. He recalls the scent of Lifebuoy soap, the red bar like a portion of rich fish, and shoves the pregnant woman into his automobile. When he shoots her in Ohio he remembers the arcane word for secretary that has been on the tip of his tongue all morning. It is "amanuensis." Sheila always said she was a private amanuensis to a big corporation lawyer in Albany. Only Sheila said "barrister." How did it go? "I am private amanuensis to a top-drawer corporation barrister in the capital of the Empire State," she would explain seriously to people who asked about her. She typed all his business epistles personally, she said. The odd thing was that she was so tall. He understood pretentiousness only in the short. Was this a sort of prejudice? he wondered.

He sees the second sign: Rest Area, 1 Mile. The brass nameplate, wide and high as a dollar, said "Mrs. Peterssen," two esses.

Dauff, back from Europe, was very excited. He had a cause—drip-dry clothing: "They don't have the facilities for dry cleaning," he explains. "Oh sure in the big cities they have them, but even there they have to use the old Bellen machines. It's very expensive. The sons of bitches practically invented sheep but they can't clean wool. Drip-dry's the answer. And you save on your overage if you go by plane. The new fibers are very lightweight. The average suitcase—I'm talking about fully packed—weighs fourteen pounds less than it did a dozen years ago. You want to know something else? People don't appreciate this. They're in the dark about this. Christ, I ought to be the one to do that *Europe on Ten Dollars a Day* thing, I know so much about it—What's the chief disadvantage of the new drip-dry fabrics? Tell me that."

The husband bites into a chicken thigh and waves at him.

"Dauff, what are the broads like?"

"Never mind the broads. What's the chief disadvantage of the new polyesters and synthetics? Are you prepared to tell me?"

"Driving so long," he tells the man, "got to stretch my legs."

"I give up," I said.

"That they don't hold a crease! That you take 'em out of the dryer you look like you slept in 'em!"

"You can make good time on these interstates, but they sure can hypnotize you. It's good they have these rest areas."

"Well, there you are." I told Dauff.

"Where are you? *Where? Here* it's a disadvantage. There it's an advantage. Do you see how subtle? Do you follow this?" He was so excited he was jumping up and down. At the top of the arc of his jump he wasn't quite as tall as Sheila, I noticed.

"It is," he tells the husband.

"Here what's a disadvantage is an advantage over there. It's a topsy-turvy world. You always look creased. They don't know you're an American. You look like one of *them. You get their rates wherever you go!"*

He shoots first the husband, then the wife. He takes their lunch and steals their car. For a moment, in the rearview mirror, slumped over their paper plates, dead at their lunch, the couple look exactly as if they are pronouncing a sort of nearsighted grace. But he isn't looking. He doesn't see this. He is thinking of Magda and the big game.

Something is radically wrong with our plot. There is a touch of the two-headed Russian mutt about it—— as though we had transplanted Steve Canyon's brains onto Popeye's neck. No. The analogy is off-center, little better than the plot. Discrepancies between body and spirit are not only acceptable in fiction, they are often poignant. What we have in the second version of the plot is a discrepancy between consciousness and situation. What's been transplanted is one character's consciousness onto another character's circumstances, a shuffled memory and will, like Gloria's widowed afternoon and her caller's evening, fiction's mad-scientist effect, fiction's freak show. The first plot was merely weak, the second fake. What's wrong with our character in the second plot is not the fact that he's a bank robber and a coward who uses a pregnant lady for a hostage, not his bad driving, nor the circumstance that he's murdered three innocent people and stolen two lunches. Nobody's perfect. No. What's wrong with him is that he doesn't pay attention! That he's careless. I mean that he doesn't *care*. That there is a hideous failure of affect between mind and body, circumstance and concern, technique and spirit. That he's cut loose from time, severed from space, divided inexcusably from his own best interests.

One could object then, I suppose, that *that's* the plot, and to a certain extent the objection is reasonable, for plot, after all, is everywhere. A condition almost of grammar itself, it comes, as it were, with the territory of personality, pronouns, and proper names. Yet we ought, I think, to look to our clichés and take them more seriously. Art imposes order. Everyone knows this. Like a kind of magnet it arranges life's iron filings into lovely patterns, into superb cat's cradles of the sweetest geometry. But the essence of these orderings—in fiction at least—is character, and character is *not* everywhere. It grows in and from choice, from choice's predispositions and predilections. Various as snowflake, it is never for one individual what it is for another. Only what engines it is the same. Here is character's oxygen cycle: Vague desire becomes specific desire, specific desire becomes will, will becomes decision, decision action, action consequence. Consequence is either acceptable or unacceptable. If it's acceptable the chain stops, if unacceptable it begins all over again. But *always*, peeking over the will's shoulder—to pick up just one element in the chain—is the character's brooding, critical, and *concerned* presence. Plot is simply the unity between what character desires and how it seeks to satisfy those desires. It is a closed community of intention that can be dissolved only by success or resignation. And here's an elemental ground rule of plot. There may be no good losers in fiction. All characters are essentially sore losers. And even resignation, which occurs with increasing incidence in fiction, is lousy losing. The character would have his life otherwise. That he consents to his fate is an aspersion on his energy, not his values, only the will crying uncle.

But it's too narrow a view finally. What happens in so solipsistic an account to surprise, maunderings, meanderings, abrupt turnings and reversals, all plot's fancy footwork, its slitherings and hairpin squiggles like an ancient river in Texas or bad handwriting in a Slavic tongue?

Say this. Say plot is a merging of two positions: What I want and what wants me. Obsession on the one hand, resistance on the other—fiction's Charley Atlasness, its isometric essence. Plot's soul is double then. What the character wants to happen and what he does *not* want to happen. Order and process arise from the first principle, and plot's good fun, its suspense and excitement and surprise, from the second, each hand striving to be uppermost. I don't just mean conflict though, I mean *fleshed* conflict. Plot must have its reasons. Indeed, it *is* its reasons. What Aristotle calls "soul," I would call *bipartisan* soul, split theme. Motive must exist on both sides, the character's and the world's. Plot would be the sum of these disparate motives.

It will not do, I think, for the image of the dead couple slumped over their picnic as in prayer to appear momentarily in the rearview mirror of the speeding car seeking its reentry onto the interstate. It will not do, that is, unless the killer sees it first, or his Nemesis does.

Plot is people. *But it is never other people.*

ACTS
OF
SCHOLARSHIP

It's always seemed to me that the act of scholarship has something to do with an abeyant condition of time, like sleep, say, or the opposite of any cliché pressure—all the famous, bloated old formulas of anxiety and danger. Seconds like minutes, minutes like hours, hours hanging on like eternities. Because where *does* the time go? When we read. When we paint or make music, when we grow in our gardens or work our woods. Say when we pray. Say, I mean, when we forget ourselves and have returned to us—not grinding our teeth or playing with our hair, not biting our nails or worrying flesh like a doodle—a state of grace; our hearts, I mean, on hold, the participatory oblivion of one's engaged attentions as solid and efficient as meshed gears.

Pure—forget tenure, the pressure to publish—axless virtue I mean. Old advertent, meticulous heed; all old Magic Marker'd focus. Man learning, concentrate and contemplative as a babe. The act of scholarship, the calling of books. I'm a Ph.D. myself (University of Illinois, 1961; "Religious Symbolism in the Novels of William Faulkner"), but sometimes I think there *are* no subjects, that the humanities exist only in the imagination of the humanist, that there is no history, only historians, no painting, only painters, no philosophy, only philosophers. Perhaps there is not even mathematics, only mathematicians, no physics, only physicists, no economics, only money, no medicine, only cancer. Only what kills us, you see, only what we have in the bank or see from our room, the light we read by but not the electricity. The world is an abstraction for most of us. We are *so* ignorant. *I* am.

What I'm driving at, of course, is an idea of immensity, looking for a way to convey my sense—I suspect everyone's sense—of our astonished solipsism, that frightful moment when we look up and discover that we are flying solo in the universe. There's too much, too much to know, too much planet, too much everything like so many bumper crops of the possible. (The world has more news than is fit to print and backs up on our lawn and in our lives like so many papers we'll never get to.)

And this—the unknowableness of the world—it seems to me, is what scholars know, why they cut the universe up into little pieces and take small bites.

First of all, we have to distinguish between the scholar doing research and the scholar loose in the world, between books, articles, monographs; teaching his classes; gone fishing.

So then. A scholar in the carrel—this is my memory talking, the gone old days in my own carrel—is one sort of fellow. As innocent of venality as someone who's just made love is of lust. What a sweetheart the scholar on the job in pursuit of his subject. What a pussycat and honeybunch. What a jolly good fellow, what an eye apple, what a peach. What cream in what coffee! On time's smooth roll, as forgetful of himself as your kid asleep, the fact of raptness on him like a vision in the cross hairs of a saint. Like your kid asleep, indeed. Yes. Never so manly as at work, never less the preener, coxcomb, fop. Never, that is, less the so-and-so or S.O.B. His audience? It might as well be lint, flowers, stone, the teeth in combs. Animal, vegetable, or mineral, or the black holes in the sky. His audience the page he writes on, the number-two pencil she uses. And probably never so happy. No, never. Happier than when giving to charity or doing good deeds. Happier, for that matter, than when being praised. (Being praised is moving; it gives you goose bumps, lumps your throat, and wets your eyes, but it can't make you happy, not in the tall, astronaut-heightened, empyrean ways.) Homework. Life as homework!

Which brings us to the scholar's other state—— the scholar *not* studying. Caught in some bear trap of ego, some Sing Sing of self, doing time in his personality, solitary confined in his character. Look at him, miles beyond the twelve-mile limit of his ordinary range. In some town off the turnpike, say, in a library in some community college seeking guarantees of his existence in the card catalogue, the day made or broken depending upon whether his books are among the holdings. But not enough merely to be included; actually taking the call number down in his head, bouncing it silently on the tongue, so that he looks like a nibbler or a reader of lips who moves *his* lips when he reads. See him, patrolling the stacks, sidling the shelves, this guerrilla of culture, some sharpshooter's instinct for the spine of his book, coming up on it like an Indian, appraising the condition of its spine like a Dutchman a diamond, knowing without even removing the book from the shelf the number of times it's been taken out, or how long it's been allowed to stand like milk in the sunshine, whether it's spoiled, whether it's turned, knowing but having to see anyway, sliding the book out, opening it from the back, from the right, in some orthodoxy of obsession, noting on the card in the envelope pasted on the inside of the rear board how many times it's circulated, doing this absurd bookkeeping, a bookkeeper, a balancer of his own book, and wondering if his odometer will be turned back, if he'll *ever* be re-bound.

C. P. Snow liked to talk about the two Cultures. Alarmed by the distance humanists and scientists put between one another, by the scientific illiteracy of the liberally educated, and by poetic tone deafness in the laboratory, Lord Snow wrote his famous essay decrying this mutual ignorance. We were growing apart, he said. Competence in one area usually bespoke incompetence in the other, though the suggestion was always there that it was the humanists who had blinked first, that the language of technology, if not superior to iambic pentameter, was at least more rigorous. Your traditionally well-rounded man could not roll downhill. The curriculum would have to be overhauled. Those already out of school would have to catch up, take crash courses in physics, hydraulics, recover the natural laws, learn light, article themselves to matter, gravity, trajectory, the stars. For their part, the scientists would practice metaphor and urban planning, would get by heart the heart.

But I've already said. Two cultures? *Two?* There are two thousand. Two million. Too many.

And oh, oh, the bicameral mind, the chambered competencies, the left hand that doesn't know what the right hand is up to. Biology damns us, seals us off, apartheids our will, and sends us to spend our life in some South Africa of the soul. Giving with one chromosome what it takes away with the other. Am I athletic? Then I can't read sheet music. Can I read sheet music? I can't follow a recipe. Or I follow a recipe but am a bad driver. I'm a good driver but can't carry a tune. I carry a tune but pick rotten wallpaper. My wallpaper's sound but I can't tell a joke. I tell fine jokes but get lost in a forest. I find my way home but I can't get French. My French is pure but I don't know trees. I know all trees but I can't nail wood. I nail wood great but don't like fruit. I *adore* fruit but I'm allergic.

For all gifts are Indian finally, and each of us lives the negotiated life, traffic'd, transacted, haggled and higgled, trading up, trading down, offering bullish hopes in bearish circumstances. "Look what they gave me for the cow," says Beanstalk Jack to the poor widow, his mom, and shows her his garish, shining beans like some savage hick primping dime-store beads and factory feathers on real estate no longer in the family.

No one's to blame, no one, not even ourselves. Who, ourselves? *Ourselves?* Who'd cut the best deal we could, who'd buy cheap and sell dear and grow tall and push up the whitest teeth and run fleet miles and squeeze the bejesus out of the other guy's hand when we're introduced and get the girls and have big houses in the best neighborhoods of the finest cities and claim the prizes and give that dollar to research that breaks the cancer code? Or settling for less, say, all we'd want would be to live forever without pain? *Ourselves?* Get outta here.

What's done is done by nature, by the parameters of condition, by genetics and God. I'm left-handed not right, a man not a woman. Do I know my antiques? I can't ride a horse. Am I psychic? Heights give me the willies. Could I learn lines in a play? I don't hold my liquor, my children are spoiled. I'm worthless on skis, I can't pick good wines. I'll wash, you dry.

And oh, oh, the *more*-than-bicameral culture, its sealed rooms and mazed space like a Pharaoh's tomb.

As if the curricula could ever be changed. As if we wouldn't go

BOOM in the crash course. And we might as well make three wishes, and we might as well say prayers.

Because the secret of life is . . . come closer . . . the secret of life is to specialize.

The Newberry Library, at 60 West Walton Street on Chicago's Near North Side, is the stone-gray color of a blackboard and looks like a Romanesque cave, the kind of place the Dead Sea Scrolls might have been stashed. Which, to get my own act of scholarship—right off the Newberry's fact sheet—out of the way, would be outside the purview of a collection whose particular speciality is, as we scholars say, well, Western Civ.

Most of the Newberry's 1.4 million volumes, 5 million manuscript pages, and 60,000 historic maps relate to the Italian Renaissance, English Renaissance literature, the histories of music, cartography, printing, and railroads; sixteenth- and seventeenth-century American history, American Indian history, Brazilian and Mexican, the American West; calligraphy, philology, bibliography, midwestern American literature, and extensive holdings in local and family history and genealogy. It is privately funded and its books, maps, and manuscripts—valued at about $300 million—are noncirculating, but it's essentially a public library. The Newberry, equal to if not greater than the best independent research libraries in the United States—the Folger in Washington, the Huntington in California, the Morgan in New York, and the Research Division of the New York Public Library—has the broadest special collections and, except for the New York Public Library, more books than any of the other thirteen most important unaffiliated research libraries in the country. It has an endowment of about $30 million, and gives away about $350,000 to $400,000 a year in fellowships for scholars to come to Chicago to work at the Newberry, and spends an additional $600,000 or so to add to its collections. It sponsors research projects and administers courses in the Newberry's Lyceum Seminars. From 9,000 to 10,000 people a year use the library.

Here are four of them.

Jean Gottlieb is sixty-three, trim, with short gray hair, and rather elegant. She is a Newberry Library Fellow and is preparing a checklist for the library on Renaissance science.

"My field is actually eighteenth-century English drama. At least that's what I got my Ph.D. in at the University of Chicago. My specialty was textual studies and bibliography. I began working on the checklist as a result of an exhibit I helped to assemble about the influence of Giordano Bruno—an Italian Hermeticist and mystic—on Sir Philip Sidney and his literary circle. The exhibit was a sort of crossover between literature and science. I knew nothing about the history of science at that point, but Allen Debus, a historian of science, gave me a list of perhaps 100 books that were in the Newberry. He said he thought there were quite a few more books besides those he'd used for his research and that it would be a good idea to write an article about the hidden science in this humanistic collection. I started looking. We knew there was quite a bit about witchcraft because William Frederick Poole, the Newberry's first librarian, was very interested in it, and along with that came alchemy and so on. But then, as I began to read in the field of early science, I found all kinds of things that no one really knew were here—books on botany, books on anatomy with magnificent illustrations that had been classified as the history of printing.

"I've been working on this on and off for about ten years, and in the last two or three I've been working on it almost constantly, and I've now got a list of about 2,500 titles, science books I've found here that were written between about 1470 and 1750. I don't go beyond 1750 because then science becomes a much more cut-and-dried and less humanistic discipline. In a sense, the nature of this work is deflection because my first obligation is to make a decision about what constitutes science for this period. Well, for me it's not going to be architecture, it's not going to be military science in the sense of the deployment of troops. I'm looking for humanistic science, I'm looking for a science that's kind of hidden—Phineas Fletcher's anatomical/allegorical poem about the human body, "The Purple Island"; works that discuss the Creation and attempt to reconcile the biblical account with, let's say, Copernican astronomy; attempts to explain life and death, the growth of plants, the change of seasons.

"I read in all the volumes to the best of my limited ability. I had high-school Latin, which, with a dictionary, is standing me in good stead now. I can handle French, Italian, Spanish, English. I get Heinz Bluhm, a colleague here, or someone on the staff who speaks German, to help me with any German translations. My plan is to examine every book on this list.

"I'm making more of a checklist, really, than a bibliography because I'm not giving collations or the typography of the books and all that sort of thing. I'm simply going to give the author, title, publication information, and something about what each of the 2,500 books is about.

"I'm an unaffiliated Fellow here at the Newberry. They give me a carrel and use of the facilities, but basically I'm sponsoring myself. I've thought about stopping the work to attempt to get a grant but decided I'd rather finish the work. I've written a couple of short articles describing what's in the collection in a sort of overview and naming a few of the more unusual or distinguished books, and I've had expressions of interest from a lot of historians of science who are surprised that anything is here and are eager to know what all else is, and the Newberry is interested in publishing the checklist when it's finished. I'd love to be sponsored, but I don't really want to take the time to try, so I'm just swinging along with this on my own. As I say, the last three years I've worked on it full-time. Before that I had other jobs and would come in on Saturdays, or late in the afternoon, or on holidays, and work when I could.

"There's a lot of interest in the history of science as a humanistic discipline, in returning it to the place it really belongs, which is as part of the history of society, the history of the arts, the history of civilization. Alchemical symbolism played a big part in the work of people like Miró, for example—— the symbols for things like mercury. Alexander probably had an astrologer; and King Rudolf, who was a contemporary of Kepler, was very interested in astrology, as was Kepler, as was Newton. Superstition has discredited a lot of things that were really parts of science and were believed in and were seen as legitimate expressions of how the world came to be the way it is, how it got its curly tail.

"God created the universe so man could make sense of it. I mean, isn't that why He put man here—why, Garden of Eden or no Garden of Eden, He didn't put any restrictions on man about how he should find out? Now, the Church got nervous about that, of course, but the development of the first notions that there was order and number *supposedly* came from the Egyptians, and when the Renaissance Italians picked up on that, they had this bright idea about the importance of the universe and man's place in it and how it was all an arcane, very obscure, very mystical kind of symbolical business run by a series of mystical numbers, and there were certain ways you could ask it questions and receive answers to all things. The purpose of the universe was to be perfect, as the purpose of the triangle was to be the perfect shape, and the purpose of gold to be the perfect metal, and mathematics and geometry the perfect disciplines to take you into the meaning of the universe.

"It's astonishing to me that people we revere as scientists—I guess Isaac Newton is the prime example—were very much interested in alchemical activity, and while they might not have believed you could turn lead into gold, there were many other things you could learn along the way that would be useful to mankind. What the alchemists *really* did was to search for ways to understand the human body. It was a long time before people understood that disease was an entity in itself that came from outside. They didn't really see disease as something else. Their effort was to try chemicals they thought would affect the humors, and since all chemicals had a certain humoral quality to them—some were hot and dry, some were cold and wet, some were cold and dry, and so on—they would use these in conjunction with the diagnosis of an individual's condition to attempt to ameliorate it. Urine and pulse were two of the ways in which diagnoses were made. The whole way the medical lineup worked was quite different then. An apothecary examined the urine and pulse and would sometimes call in the physician. The physician consulted his books and never touched the patient. The surgeon did all the whacking and hacking. It was in the late fifteenth century that the first anatomical books began to appear and that people began to look at the world in a way that is perhaps more congenial to our way of thinking—the world as something to be seen, as opposed to something that was just there or some extension of one's self.

"It's fascinating stuff. I mean we've only been talking about medicine. I haven't talked about astronomy, I haven't talked about mathematics. You began by asking me about alchemy. I got off the track. I said the nature of this work is deflection, maybe the nature of all scholarship is—a sort of paper trail to reality and truth.

"Generally I'm here every day now. I get here when the library opens and stay till fairly late in the afternoon. I examine the books on my list alphabetically. I look at maybe ten to twelve books a day. If I find a book and I'm not really sure whether it's science or not, I can look in one of my reference books. If I still don't have a clue, if I'm not sure whether it's talking about something that's more theological than scientific—sometimes it's hard to tell—I'll look in one of the bibliographies I have in my carrel, and, well, sometimes I just have to make a judgment call. There's a book by a man named du Bartas that is really theological. He's not included in a lot of the science bibliographies I look at, but I'm going to put him in.

"I really started *looking* at books and stopped hunting for more a year ago last June, so it's taken me this long to do A and B and start C.

"This is a daunting job, and a humbling job, and nobody told me to do it. I decided that I wanted to, so I have no one to blame but myself. That's what keeps me sane. Not being affiliated means that I am really a part of this library family, and this library family has been very good to me. I have no other loyalties. I wouldn't mind being affiliated, but if I were I would probably have to hurry this up, I think."

Mary Quinlan-McGrath is a dark, slim woman with cropped hair and looks as if she is in her early thirties. She seems athletic, like someone on a track team, say, limber on the scaffolds she must climb to examine and photograph the frescoes in the tall Renaissance rooms she studies as an art historian. Currently she is at the Newberry working on a guide to the Villa Farnesina.

"The Villa Farnesina is a wonderful villa on the Tiber in Rome. It was built by Baldassare Peruzzi for Agostino Chigi in the early sixteenth century. I came upon it almost by accident. I knew Raphael's *Galatea* was there, and his Cupid and Psyche frescoes. My sister and I were just leaving Rome that day, and we took a quick cab ride from the Vatican to look at it. We were there all alone, without guards really. It was just closing, and I think whoever was supposed to be taking care of it had left early. We walked from room to room.

"The place is almost unvisited even though it has those Raphaels and the Peruzzi frescoes and other very famous Renaissance artists.

"My particular line is to try to recapture what the artists were thinking, by reading texts of the period. I don't know why some art historians don't like to get into literary texts. They don't mind doing all kinds of document work, but they don't like to sit down and read the Ovids and Virgils.

"Because of the wonderful Renaissance collection here at the Newberry, I was able to, well, decode the frescoes on the vault of the garden loggia ceiling. I had to get into these awful Renaissance astrology texts because I knew the ten Peruzzi panels I was interested in had to do with the patron's—Chigi's—birthday, but I couldn't figure out what the rest of them were. I looked into antique Renaissance astrological, astronomical—it all meant the same thing then—texts to try to see if there was any correlation between the subject matter of the paintings and the texts. Well, I finally found a passage in Aratus that seemed very closely related, and I started reading Renaissance commentaries on how you worked out a horoscope in the Renaissance, and I figured out that what the other frescoes referred to wasn't Chigi's birth but the time of his conception. Once I had figured that out, it explained other parts of the villa too.

"I sent an article to the *Journal of the Warburg and Courtauld Institutes,* and they wrote back saying they'd just had a request to publish a document from Siena. They'd found Chigi's exact birth date in the baptismal records, and the time of day he was born, and told me that I was twenty minutes off!

"Chigi was a little bit like the Renaissance popes, I think, in the sense that he had to create great works in order to be remembered. I'm not sure he trusted in his lineage, and it's always seemed to me that the villa itself, with all its elaborate paints, was to speak for him. And you see the first vault that was built? *It was his horoscope!*

"The art historian's fallback position is often that something is decorative. And the panels in the Villa Farnesina *are* decorative, there's no doubt about it, but why would you have this sort of specificity? Chigi had two long poems commissioned to celebrate his villa, one in 1511, and the other, probably also written in 1511 but published in 1512, to carry on his name. If you think about it, most of the poems about antiquity speak about ruins. What they knew about ancient Rome, which they adored, was now mostly a sheep pasture. So when Chigi had his villa built he made damn sure that the poems told about the villa, because the poets assumed, and he probably did, too—they say it over and over again—that the villa would turn to dust but the poems would remain. Well, the villa is glorious, and people visit it, but there are perhaps only half a dozen copies of the poems in existence.

"I feel in some way that I'm communicating with the dead, that they're not dead. These frescoes are in an important villa. They've been written about since 1550 and never entirely understood. Astrological and astronomical degrees don't deviate, the planets don't deviate, the stars don't deviate. When you're onto something that's more than a confluence of coincidences, you feel the documents and paintings and poetry are telling you things. People live through their work. Chigi's work—he was a banker; he had great mining operations, shipping operations—was his villa, and he lives on through it. Those who come to it will ask, as I did, what the painting on the ceilings mean. I suppose I feel I'm speaking for them, speaking for those people who are dead.

"You know, when Machiavelli was sent into exile, even though it was only to a place outside Florence, he still felt his exile. He no longer had political prestige, he no longer had position, and he described his life as that of a peasant among other peasants, stopping at the inn and chatting with whoever happened to be around. But he says that at night, at night he went into his study, dressed in his best clothes, and read the ancients. He just sat there reading them. Well, that's how *I* feel. I come here and read the ancients."

Paul Saenger, pale, thin, vaguely professorial, in his early forties, has sharp angular features and dark, graying hair. Like most people at the Newberry, he wears glasses.

"I am the curator of rare books and collection development coordinator, so I'm responsible for acquisitions. Probably the most important part of our effort comes in the reading of antiquarian catalogues and contact with rare-book dealers. I spend six weeks a year in Europe. There are certain antiquarian book fairs I'd like to go to, but in general I find it more useful to visit book dealers in their shops, because when they go to a book fair they take only a small percentage of their stock. It's a fraternal kind of relationship, friendly and amicable, yet there's a certain gamesmanship involved. . . .

"Our budget is about $600,000 a year and we try to spend at least 60 percent of it on antiquarian material. We try to devote a significant part of this to buying materials that are sources for the past and as close as possible to their original state. Our concern is as much with the artifact itself as with the text. That's why we exist. Many advanced graduate students start studying medieval history, Renaissance history, the history of early modern Europe and have never seen what a letter or a document looked like in the age of Louis XIV. And there are many quite well established scholars who are really uncomfortable with original source material. One of the underlying truths about the library is that the text itself is not sufficient. By collecting material in its original state, the Newberry keeps scholarship honest. Even for a text that is printed and well known, the manuscripts and early printed editions remain important for the integrity of the text.

"For example, in antiquity, texts were transcribed without word separation. A completely accurate edition of Tacitus would be *scriptura continua*, without separation, without punctuation. People read aloud in antiquity—I happen to be working on this subject just now—to keep information in their minds while they unraveled it. Oral expression, the *sound* of prose, was very important. The kind of reference reading important to us, consulting, looking for information, starting in the middle of a book, finding your way in a volume you haven't read end to end, was not a habit of ancient Rome. It was the medieval period that changed our notion of reading.

"The New Testament had divisions that facilitated consultation, but the Old Testament didn't receive standard divisions until the twelfth century. Throughout the Middle Ages our distinction of verses in the Bible didn't exist; names of characters were not set off in the plays of antiquity; the convention of writing with capitals didn't begin until the eighth and ninth centuries. Medieval readers themselves had a sense that texts were being corrupted. Scribes got proper names wrong, misunderstood them, or confused them with words or parts of words. And so you found this impulse to divide script into words, to use different signs that would complement word separation, like the capitalization of proper names. Another aspect of writing associated with the development of word separation is the hyphen at the end of a line. The hyphen shows continuity and is a change in mentality in the eleventh century—accent marks, diacritical marks, grammatical marks were added by a reader trying to elucidate a text. At the time, scribes did not put these in, but it's common to find them worked into medieval texts, even into early printed books, especially books in monastic libraries. The monks went through them word for word and repunctuated, accented words, and added things like hyphens at the end of lines. It wasn't the printer who did this; it was the reader. This adds great historical value and often lowers the cost of a book. That's why the Newberry is lucky, because our values are not necessarily the values of the marketplace. In the world of rare books, what is prized is a clean copy because collectors like that, whereas the book that's been annotated, reworked, even if it's just a clarification of a grammatical meaning, tells you something about the mentality that it survives. Last summer, in France, we bought a printed book of Franciscan piety mixed with annotations. Even if we had had the same printed book, we would have bought the volume.

"People who come to the library are attracted to our medieval manuscripts because they're the most beautiful, but there are other books, quite humble in appearance, even ugly, that are significant because they offer insights into the very notion of reading.

"I'm convinced it leads to a more profound understanding to see the way a text was presented to people who were contemporary. A dramatic example would be St. Thomas. If one reads St. Thomas in a Modern Library edition, one gets a great deal, but one loses a great deal. One doesn't understand how the text was presented in the fourteenth century. In general, pages weren't numbered before the sixteenth century. I would say that of all manuscripts from the fifteenth century and earlier, fewer than 15 percent have numeration on the folios. Chapters and distinctions within the chapter preceded numeration. That's why St. Thomas is organized in terms of parts. It's cross-referenced, a very sophisticated form of text division. That's a Christian contribution, a redefining of books into substructures. At the end of the Middle Ages people got fed up with this system. It was too complex, and they went to a direct numbering of the leaves, to a number system based on the physical properties of a book rather than on its intellectual division. And that's a *very* important change.

"I showed a famous French scholar some of our new acquisitions and tried out some of my theories on him. 'Well,' he said, 'the trouble with you, Saenger, is that you only buy books to conform with your thesis!'

"Well, that's not true. I have to be very careful of that."

Heinz Bluhm is an energetic, pleasant, courteous, perhaps even courtly seventy-nine-year-old man who looks a couple of decades younger. His parents emigrated from Germany in 1925 when he was seventeen. He did his graduate work at the University of Wisconsin and earned his Ph.D. in 1932, doing a dissertation on Goethe's literary reception in England. For thirty-one years he taught at Yale, and now, years past retirement, he still teaches the Goethe course at Boston College to classes of at least one hundred seniors. Professor Bluhm first came to the Newberry thirty years ago. Though today he has on a suit and tie, I'm told that he usually comes to the library wearing slacks, a sport shirt, and sneakers. His speech is lightly accented with a sort of gentle German burr.

"I had been in England as a Guggenheim Fellow, and in Cambridge I was told that there was a copy of the famous 1534 Miles Coverdale Bible at the Newberry Library, so I decided I would stop in Chicago and look at it. I did. Then I usually ask the *good* question: 'Do you have anything in German literature?' And the lady in charge of the rare-book room said, 'Yes, we have the papers of Goethe's daughter-in-law, Ottilie von Goethe.' My interest, of course, was aroused. She showed me six *immense* boxes filled with her diaries and letters, the engagement letters between Goethe's son, August, and Ottilie, and also letters and diaries of Goethe's grandchildren.

"I was invited back for the summer to start editing the Ottilie von Goethe papers, which I did, and they are published in six volumes. It took eight years to publish the six volumes, and then, a few weeks ago, I received another batch from Weimar—since I'm apparently the one who is most knowledgeable about the Goethe family at this stage of the game, they probably sent it to me rather than to one of their own people, or to my colleagues at Harvard, who would like to do it—which no one knew anything about, and so I was asked to come back to try to integrate the new material with the old. We had certain lacunae toward the end of her life. There's something in 1854 and then there's a gap. Now I have those of 1862, which I am deciphering. (She has an *awful* hand.) I came three weeks ago and brought the Xerox copies with me from Boston. To my great surprise and astonishment, I found that there are about seventy-five pages of material from Ottilie's diary during the last six years of her father-in-law's life. Of course, Goethe's diaries have been published and are available, so I can now make the comparison between what she reports and what the old man reports. And she reports many things that he *didn't* report, so I get some real insight into what life was like in the Goethe house. There were many problems. She entertained very loudly, so Goethe occasionally had to send a servant up to say, 'Please. Be quiet. I'm writing a few more lines of the second part of *Faust.*'

"Is there anyone more significant in modern literature? Remember Carlyle? 'The spirit of the world has entrusted more to this man than to any other mortal!' The author of *Faust*, the author of *Wilhelm Meister*. Magnificent. The monarch of letters . . . A model life, in the sense that it was given to intellectual pursuits. And he is a *modern* man. I know no one else I would be able to put into that class. It's claimed that only Leonardo da Vinci was able to survey the intellectual world as Goethe was. Presumably Goethe was the last who could still survey the entire field of human knowledge. He guided A. R. Hohlfeld, my mentor at Wisconsin, through ninety years of his life, and he's guided me, so far, through seventy-nine.

"Though, as a matter of fact, my real work now is on Luther. To try to understand what he would have done if he had been faced with the Bible as a human document. But Luther is greater than the Lutherans. The dogma doesn't make sense. His reason rejected Christianity 100 percent, but he said 'Since God revealed himself in the Bible, I sacrifice my reason.'

"I read his sermons, the most wonderful sermons ever given. There must be at least a thousand of them. Have you seen the Weimar edition of Luther? It's 110 folio volumes. You know, there's a marvelous story how it began. After Germany was victorious over France in the Franco-Prussian War—1870 to '71—the German emperor, William I, was going to offer something to both churches, the Roman Catholic and the Lutheran. 'Because you have prayed for me, German arms have won over France,' something of that sort. And so he said, 'You can ask me for whatever you want,' and the Catholics said, 'We would like to see the Cathedral of Cologne finished.' That was a *tremendous* expense. You see, it was just an unfinished Gothic building. And so it was finished at the expense of His Imperial Majesty. And the Lutherans said, 'We want the greatest edition that any human being ever received. We would like that done for Martin Luther.' And so the emperor said yes, and this edition was finished in 1983, a hundred years after it was begun. One hundred ten folio volumes. I have been an adviser, but I am not an editor. They use only Europeans for that, but I am doing something else.

"I have four research assistants in Boston. We are compiling an *index verborum* of Luther's German works. Not every word is understood, and even the great Grimm's dictionary doesn't work and so from 1946 to 1967—which was twenty-one years—this was started at Yale. Then that fund was exhausted, and a friend of mine at Boston College heard of this and said, 'You know, I think the Jesuits at Boston College would help you if you're willing to leave Yale.' Of course it was a difficult decision, but I said, 'If I can finish this *index verborum* I'll go there.' So I went. With a certain reserve. I wasn't quite sure. But I'm so devoted to Luther that I couldn't let him down.

"And the Jesuits have lived up to every word. Oh, yes, I must tell you this, the Jesuits have given me a whole house for an office, so my research assistants are able to work there, and the living room is part of my library—which is *immense*, about 15,000 books—and the sun porch, which they've also taken over, and the whole dining room is filled with index cards in wonderful steel cabinets. (At the beginning every word was written out on a three-by-five card.) The project is finished. It took another fifteen years. Now we are in the process of getting it ready for publication. But we've only reached the letter G.

"Here in Chicago I get up at six. I shower and shave—that's all. And I don't dress until I'm ready to go. I have no breakfast and I have no lunch. At 6:15 I'm at my desk. I read a chapter of the Bible. At this time I'm on Isaiah. Then I read half a book of Homer—the *Iliad*. Then I read a little Hegel. A little Immanuel Kant. At eight I get dressed and leave at 8:15 and am here at 8:28 and have to wait, because they don't admit us until 8:30. So at 8:30 I'm here and I go upstairs, but I'm not admitted to Special Collections because that doesn't open until nine. So I go to my carrel and read a sermon of Luther's. And then I move over to Special Collections. Then I start to work on Ottilie von Goethe, deciphering the manuscripts. So I'm here, and then I work till 12:00 with a coffee break at ten o'clock. If I don't show up, my colleagues are angry with me upstairs, so I have to be there at the dot of ten, because they take fifteen minutes, sometimes twenty when the conversation gets too good. At 12:00 I go back to my room. I don't really know what I do. I stay home for just a few minutes. Then I take my daily constitutional to the Goethe Institute and look at *The New York Times* and one or two other periodicals. And then I go upstairs to the public library just to see what's new—they have a shelf of new books—and I come back here to the Newberry usually by two or so. But today I went to the Art Institute because, you know, scholars are not the world's richest people, and Tuesdays are free admission. On Thursdays I sometimes go to the Field Museum because that's their free day. And then I'm back here. I have to turn in my manuscripts at 4:30. I leave at 5:00 because Special Collections closes at 5:00. So I go for another long walk, and I get my meal. I have a couple of favorite restaurants by this time. Then I go for another little walk. It's about 8:30. And then I stay up until midnight, reading.

"I read Schiller, especially the treatises on aesthetics, which are some of the greatest ever written. I read Schopenhauer, Nietzsche. Thomas Mann's diaries are in the midst of publication, and even now there are six volumes out and they've reached only 1947 and he lived to 1955. And these are *immense* volumes. I'll read those for a solid hour or so, since I knew him personally. I'm waiting to find the reference where he mentions me, but that won't be until 1952.

"I have no objection to my life, none whatsoever. I've found it interesting. And I'm reappointed for next year, so Faust will have another turn."

I feel like crying.

Because Jean Gottlieb chips away at her ABC's and Quinlan-McGrath decodes the interior decoration in an early sixteenth-century house. Because Linda P. Austern wonders about the relation of music to the English Renaissance controversy on women is why. Because Hal Barron studies half a century of rural life in the United States is. Because Winstanley Briggs learns about *le Pays des Illinois* and Christine Clark-Evans considers language in Diderot, while Elistine P. Holly gets up early black Chicago musicians. And Dan Katz, Johannes de Muris's *Libellus cantus mensurabilis*. And Ahmad Y. Majdoubeh works on the Orientalism of Washington Irving. And Mary Odem is interested in adolescent sexuality in America between 1880 and 1930, and Philippe Forêt in mapping the Great Wall of China. While Elaine Kruse studies divorce in Paris from 1792 to 1804. While William Hawk traces Matinnecock tribal history. While Rima Schultz regards the role of the businessman in the settlement of the West, and Gail Geiger, art and spirituality in Renaissance Florence.

Because Nancy L. Hagedorn is finding out about Indian interpreters among the Iroquois is why; because Roger Schlessinger is an expert on André Thevet is. And meanwhile, meanwhile, Jo Mano contemplates the significance of water symbolism in fifteenth- and sixteenth-century maps.

And who shapes curiosity? And who customizes interest? And what whets these sweet-toothed, busybodied, any-old-topic tropisms? Who seeds our brains like clouds? What triggers this itch, hey?

THE LAW
OF
AVERAGE

THERE USED TO BE MOVIES, I RECALL THE PREMISE, ABOUT PEOPLE so average you could make money off them. You spread different jellies on their toast and watched expectantly to see which one made them smile; you dipped assorted flavors into their ice-cream cones and held your breath until they licked and went yum-yum. Sometimes you ran them for president. They were blessed by the law of averages, kissed in their cradle by the Witch of the Typical. Attention corrupted, and somewhere along the line they lost it. Broken, they went home to Kansas.

What do I know? When I read Robert and Helen Lynd's *Middletown* for a freshman sociology course in college, I thought Middletown was somewhere in Connecticut. I also read *Babbitt* that year and had the idea that Zenith was in Connecticut, too. Connecticut—that's where the action was, where the boobs spoke only to the hicks and the hicks spoke only to the rubes.

Now I'm told—I live in St. Louis—that I'm the rube, a middle American, stripped of ethnicity, some rude, rawboned WASP of a thing. McDonald's has my number. Baskin-Robbins does—my tastes paced off like land worked over by the surveyors, my habits known, my mating dance noted as choreography, my heart an open book, all my affiliations and sympathies plumbed, my market researched. I am computer linked. (My junk mail, for example. The guys in the other party have written me off. How do they know I'm for gun control? How do they know I'd like to save the whale? Who told them my common causes?)

As the population shifts, as the Sun Belt is let out, there are fewer people in fewer places I can patronize. I may not say, as New Yorkers or folks in L.A. say to me, "Why do you live there? What do you do there? Are there escalators? Is there color TV? Do you live indoors? Do you get weather? Are the cats and dogs tame?"

When I was young, people believed in the exotic more. It was a staple of double bills, the travelogue common as the cartoon or the coming attraction. Margaret Mead took anthropology to the South Seas. Now, of course, the South Seas are paved, darkest Africa lighted bright as Broadway, and it's America all over the place. Even in America it's America, and the exotic is as endangered as Poland. How you gonna keep 'em down on the farm after they've seen the moon? (Indeed, how you even gonna get 'em to *look* at the moon after they've seen the rings of Saturn, Mars's red ice and ruby distances?) Name three astronauts who've gone the distance. Ah, but I can't, though I could tell you the explorers. (Who explores today? No one. Well, sure, geologists with their oil sticks poked in the earth to see whether the planet is down a quart. But no one else, no one else, exploration taken over by technologists, by NASA. Houston control on the blower to its men in the moon buggy, feeding remotely controlled direction— "Hang a left at the Sea of Dreams, a right at the Marsh of Sleep. It's a straight shot to the Crater of Plinius. You can't miss it." Explorers? They could be Sunday drivers.)

So we turn inward, inward, looking for the center. Pay dirt, mother lode, and the gift of truth. And even Middletown never got as far as Connecticut. It's Muncie, Indiana, taking the fall for America. Common denominator our rule of thumb, our weight and our measure. The documentary as picture book, family album.

Joe Loewenstein, a colleague of mine, has pointed out the strange format of the TV quiz show "Family Feud." Contestants score points not when their answers are true but when they conform to answers supplied in advance by the audience. Truth by consensus, by statistical decree. They grade on the curve, boring as a poll. Because polls *are* boring. One is not unmoved by the issues but by the numbers, all interest residing in how one's opinions stack up, whether one is in the majority or the minority, attention riveted—the word's too strong— not even, exactly, on the self but on some *version* of the self, the projected, extrapolated self, the self as it occurs, say, in horoscopes in the newspaper, in insurance underwriters' charts listing ideal weights for some highly invisible categorized population—I am male, large- framed, six foot one, fifty-one, and overweight—as it flirts above or below the median income for a family of four, bottom-line stuff from the Census Bureau—the price of my house, the number of rooms there . . .

So, if I have difficulty watching "Family Feud," I could look at Peter Davis's "Middletown" series forever.

Because persons—the proper study of mankind is "persons"—is where the action finally is, and I could exist happily ever after in sidewalk-café connection to the world, satisfied with my Peeping Tom appetites and privilege, my Via Veneto vision dear to me as curiosity, pleasant as overhearing the neighbors, as reading their mail or knowing their portfolios. What a show such as "Middletown" does, what tele- vision at its best does, is to supply one with ringside license, snug as my parking space for the handicapped, and permit one to pig out on details. (In the first episode, "The Campaign," about a 1979 mayoralty race in Muncie, I saw the Republican hostess beam, pushing her goodwill, some lasered love intense as a handshake in Rush Week, while her Democratic counterpart, perhaps needing the work more, is a little embarrassed by it all.) And if it's not sociology, and I don't know if it is or it isn't, it's something better than sociology. It's voy- eurism lifted perhaps to art, certainly to superior home movies, some one-on-one with strangers, a thing done with mirrors, like the viewing rooms at police lineups, the self safe and distanced behind the arras, privy, protected as a Polonius guaranteed immunity. Excitement risk- less as a home video game, bloodless as a good coup. Because we love these facts, these details dense with other peoples' specific gravity, and the charm of such programs is precisely the charm of history. The feast of the judgmental it affords—details, gossip, the aloof stance of God.

'Middletown' Dates

1924—New York sociologists Robert and Helen Lynd go to Muncie, Indiana; begin to study it.

1929—*Middletown*, the Lynds' name for Muncie, is published; becomes classic sociological text.

1937—Robert Lynd publishes update on first study, called *Middletown in Transition*.

1976—Theodore Caplow, of the University of Virginia, and research team begin third Muncie study, known as *Middletown III*.

1977—Muncie is setting for *Close Encounters of the Third Kind*, although location photography is done elsewhere.

1979—Filmmaker Peter Davis begins shooting six nonfiction films in Muncie, to be aired in 1982 on public TV as "Middletown."

1982—First volume of Caplow study is published (in April) as *Middletown Families: 50 Years of Change and Continuity*.

WHAT'S IN A NAME? (The 1987 Elizabeth and Stewart Credence Memorial Lecture)

PROFESSOR ADAMS, THANK YOU FOR YOUR KIND INTRODUCTION. You're very generous.

Chancellor Jones, Dean Smith, members of the faculty, students, ladies and gentlemen . . .

As Professor Adams has already told you, my name is Stanley.

Could you be mugged by a Stanley? Could a Stanley rape you? Tops, I might molest your kid, but *you'd* never know it, and neither would she. What, a little suntan lotion rubbed along the bottom of her swimsuit like a piping of frosting around a birthday cake? What, a spot of spilled tea on the sunsuit, my finger in the bespittled hand-kerchief moist from what it wouldn't even occur to you was drool before it was saliva, and vigorously brushing across what won't be breasts for another half dozen years yet, my grunt the two- or three-tone gutteral hum of deflection, nervous and oddly dapper as the tugs, pats, and twitches of a stand-up comic, distracting as the shot cuffs of magicians and cardsharps, all random melody's tangential rove? Because how could you ever even guess at my intentions and interiors, my inner landscapes and incisor lusts, the thickening at my throat like hidden shim, the ponderous stirrings of my ice-floe blood, deep as resource, buried as oil in my gnarled and knotty groin, my clotted sexual circuits? Could put it past you plenty, believe me, holding the kid's shoulder, the little girl's, for the leverage, drawing her within the fork of my white old thighs, a pervert like a master artisan, fixing her there like a piece of carpentry. Or violating her in absentia, my eyes on her kindergarten picture, my snoot in her laundry, in her eight-year-old grimes. All contacts troubled, gone off, amok but deceptive, accidental, clever as a pickpocket's.

Protected by reputation, see, my triumph of the human spirit, that heart of gold that I don't possess but people attribute to me anyway, mistaking cholesterol for karats, hypertension for love, innocence by association, by stereotype, dismissing me finally, all the world waving me through Customs like that guy in the audience at the nightclub whose lap the chanteuse sits in, kissing his bald spot, pinching his cheek, and telling folks what a good sport he is, leading the applause.

Protected finally by all my grotesque cuddlies— the limp, the cane, my toothless, grampsy ways, my fatty's belly and threatless aura, my ducky's waddle and feeble's klutz, my *Stanleyness* on me like a wimp heraldrics. Hey, I'm kidding. Only offering credential here, only flashing badge, showing my hand, franked under the ultraviolet like a kid's at the dance.

Stanley is as Stanley does and you are what you're called.

Stanley is your brother-in-law, your C.P.A., your cousin in Drapes. He collects stamps, washes his car, belongs to Triple A, and keeps a weather eye on the gas mileage. He is, that is, as all of us are, the fiction of his sound, all his recombinant glottals, labials, fricatives, and plosives. He's his flaps and trills. He's his spirants, I mean. He is, I mean, the vibrations of his name.

For great characters demand great names. (Of writers I admire, only Henry James—itself a fine name—lumbers his characters with bad ones. I'm thinking of Henrietta Stackpole, I'm thinking of Ralph Touchett, of Fleda Vetch and Milly Theale. I'm thinking of Madam Merle, of Casper Goodwood, Pansy Osmond, and Hyacinth Robinson. I'm thinking of Margaret Thatcher.) Here's a roll call for you. Beowulf and the Wife of Bath. King Lear but not Titus Andronicus. Hamlet but not Garp. Snow White, Pinocchio, and Mary Poppins but not Cinderella. Peter Pan but not Captain Hook. R2D2, Hans Solo, C3PO, and Obie wan Kenobie but not Princess Leia. Leopold Bloom but not Stephen Daedalus. (Who can explain it, who can tell you why? Fools give you reasons, wise men never try. Rodgers and Hammerstein but not Weber and Rice.) Harry Morgan, Harry Bailey, Harry Angstrom, Harry Lime. J.R. Phil Esterhaus. Babbit. Mr. Toots. John Jarndyce. Mr. Tulkinghorn. Flem Snopes. Will Varner. V. K. Ratliff. Dick Diver, Jay Gatsby. My Uncle Toby. Dorothea Brooke and Mr. Casaubon. Jiminy Cricket. Tom Jones, Humphrey Clinker. Hazel Motes. Becky Sharp. Captain Dobbin like a reliable horse. Emma Bovary, Emma Woodhouse, Julian Sorel. Swann and the Guermantes. Vautrin. Hans Castorp. Levin. Father Zossima. Bartleby. Hester Prynne and Arthur Dimmesdale. Angel Clare. Old Goriot, Elizabeth Bennett and her four sisters. All the not-to-be-pronounced names of God.

I want to speak to you this evening about Louis Paul Pelgas, the first Director of Admissions at any school in the Thirteen Colonies Conference, but before I begin it will be necessary to provide you with some sometimes dense, and often apparently trivial, historical background.

Clifton College is, as many of you know, a small liberal arts college in what are, quite literally, the outer edges of Pennsylvania. It is out of the way even for Norbiton, Pennsylvania, even for Chapel County. Look at a map. Surrounded on two sides by West Virginia in the extreme southwestern corner of what—it's that close to the West Virginia line, that close to the Ohio one—is referred to by its inhabitants as the "state" rather than the "commonwealth" of Pennsylvania (possibly to lend a little aura of the average to what is uncompromisingly an atypical part of the nation), Norbiton, like a heel in an old shoe, exactly snugs the perfect right angle in the tight corner where its western and southern borderlines meet.

This tiny portion of Pennsylvania had been unofficially a "state" since antebellum days when, feeling itself both physically and spiritually closer to the gravitational pull—Chapel County was the only county in Pennsylvania where it was legal to keep slaves although, due to the impossibility of cultivating crops in its harshly alkaline soil, except for the handful of "house niggers," exchanged as a sort of gag gift between one local merchant and another, there was never any appreciable slave population there—of its Virginian and West Virginian anti-abolitionist neighbors than it was to Harrisburg, three hundred fifty-seven miles distant, or Philadelphia three hundred sixty-nine miles off, or even to Pittsburgh, which though less than one hundred miles away was, for eighty of those hundred, accessible only through what John James Audubon himself has described in his notes as ". . . wilderness so cluttered and remote that its very sky is uninhabitable by the birds of the air, wilderness so cluttered and remote that that sky is itself wilderness." "A dry hole," he remarks in an 1847 journal entry, "which for all its varied vegetation, succulent berries, meaty nuts, and abundant fruit, is as zoologically lifeless as the moon. I cannot sketch there. My inks, oils, and watercolors go off like stale milk and lose their ability to congeal or adhere to paper. My pencil leads liquefy and my lines melt and run. There is a liquorish rifeness in the air so profound it lasts the autumn and can burn holes in the snow, or make—so viable is the half-life of the fermented spirits of all its fierce flora, its growth and undergrowth, its leaves and barks—an illusion of its 'frozen' streams and lakes, of ice apparently two and even three inches thick which is not only impossible to stand up on but worth your hat to set down on its obdurate-seeming surface. It is a wilderness so impregnable that no jack rabbit, dog, possum, coon, turkey, or even insect, let alone any animal as fragile and exotic as a bird, could possibly get close enough to it to thrive."

Nor is any of this typical John Audubon hyperbole. After a failed late-nineteenth-century attempt to survey the thousand or so square miles of this "queer, thick country"—Audubon's phrase—Phil and Pembler Roberts released foxes, dogs, and other small mammals at the margins of The Thicket. ("The Thicket" at the Chapel County end, but called "The Woody" at the Pittsburgh one, recalls Pembler Roberts's famous comment: "Viewing the unspoiled, unnibbled trees, leaves, and grasses in 'The Thicket' is as different from viewing them in 'ordinary' nature, a sylvan woodland or forest, say, as gazing at the defined, beautifully articulated stars in the country is from looking up at them in town.") Seeing them founder and return to their release points, they seemed, in Phil Robert's analogy, "like confused, guilty hunting dogs who have lost the scent." (The experiment has been successfully repeated for seventeen years in Professor Roger Barr's Psychology 101 classes. Julia Rayburton, while still a junior at Clifton College, devised a variant of the Pembler and Barr experiments. Wishing to test the very letter of Captain Audubon's 1847 journal entry, Ms. Rayburton stood at the edge of The Thicket—now, with the advent of bulldozers, trenchers, and the introduction of other heavy earth-moving equipment, reduced to a plot no larger than a decent-sized park in a medium-sized city—and scattered kernels of white corn, the favored food of all agrarian birds, into it in full view of three hungry bluejays who'd been kept in cages and deprived of food for more than eight hours. The jays, who had carefully and even rather slavishly followed the short trajectory of the corn—Rayburton is left-handed but tosses corn with her right hand—were unable to retrieve any of the kernels. They flew up and around but never entered the air space above "The Thicket," thus offering proof of Professor Barr's speculations regarding "Density theory," the psychological-cum-sociological postulate that "All bodies repudiate areas smaller than the space required to provide their egress." The implications this has for America's crowded prison system are, of course, immense. Professor Barr's and Julia Rayburton's findings have already been cited in four court rulings and are *sub judice* in who knows how many more.)

If this isolated and somewhat remarkable edge of the commonwealth had unofficially chosen to think of itself as a state since, you'll recall, the mid-nineteenth century, it ought to be said that no one really knows why the citizens of Chapel County preferred one designation over another. (What's in a name, eh?) Even as late as 1837, when Chapel and Green counties split off from each other (for reasons, incidentally, that had more to do with the close identification of The Thicket with the town of Norbiton than they did with slaver or anti-slaver sentiments), the term *commonwealth*, not *state*, was the legal nomenclature in each of the seventeen articles of incorporation. In fact, Chapel County has only *officially* been designated part of the "state of Pennsylvania" since Maurdon Legurney, both mayor of Norbiton and County Supervisor, was chosen to represent Chapel County at the Pennsylvania Constitutional Convention of 1878, about a year after the Congress of the recently Reunited States of America had put an end to the period of Reconstruction. The Convention, referred to in the newspapers of the day—even Horace Greeley sent a correspondent to cover it for the old *New York World-Examiner*—as "The New Reconstruction," was convened at the instigation of the people of Chapel County but was equally the brainchild of Legurney's political protégé, Governor Lamar White, a native of Norbiton who, when Legurney put his name into nomination at the Democratic Convention in St. Louis in 1882, was the first politician ever referred to as a "favorite son," though his family had removed from Norbiton when White was only two years old.

Reconstruction had been, of course, a time of ad hoc law, a period of makeshift legislation when some of the most bizarre laws in the history of this or any other nation were passed, almost, it seemed, as a kind of willed whim. It's largely forgotten now, but from 1865 to 1877, when this odd chapter in our history closed, Congress forbade the raising of orchids and carnations. It prohibited the sale of calves' liver in quantities under three pounds and made it a federal offense, punishable by a mandatory seven years in prison, for women to fish from a pier. The statute was vaguely worded, perhaps deliberately, and in the five years it was on the books, no one was actually sent to prison. Ironically, it was the vagueness and unenforceability of the law that gave rise, during the period, to its public flouting and introduced the term *fishwife* into the American vocabulary. (Less whimsical, but far more dangerous, was a peculiar law of evidence introduced just after the Civil War. This, of course, was the infamous "Mixed Race Witness Rule" which, when crimes were alleged against persons of one race by persons of another, made it obligatory for prosecutor and defense alike to produce witnesses of *both* races to the crime. The rule was obviously directed against the defeated South—it did not apply in nonslave states on the dubious grounds that Negroes were less populous in the North—by a piqued, if victorious, Union. What is perhaps more astonishing than the rule itself is the fact that during the dozen years before its repeal, it was five times sent up to the Supreme Court for "challenging" and five times adjudged constitutional!)

As indicated earlier, the Pennsylvania Constitutional Convention was convened in 1878 by a governor who, though he'd been a mere toddler when he left and had never been back, was born in Norbiton. As also indicated, this was barely a year after the nation had junked the notion of Reconstruction, the queer period of back-scratch law when all that was necessary to get a law passed was a quorum of cronies who would do unto each other what they would have each other do unto them. As in all periods to which there is an inevitable reaction, that reaction, when it finally came, was a lulu. What were demanded now were unarbitrary and entirely righteous rules of order, logic, and sequentiality— a return, if you will, to 1837, when Chapel County quietly signed seventeen articles of incorporation, each of which designated the new county as continuing to belong to the "Commonwealth" rather than to the "*State* of Pennsylvania." (That people in Chapel County held slaves was merely a fact of home rule, of little more significance at the time, really, than the local option that governs the sale of alcohol or is responsible for the blue laws.)

Now, however, there was, at least on the parts of the people of Chapel County, Governor White, and Maurdon Legurney, White's political guru and hand-picked emissary from Chapel County to the Pennsylvania Constitutional Convention, a reaction to the reaction to the reaction. If America wanted sequentiality again, some apostolic succession of convention and right reason, Chapel County, on the very verge of The Thicket, that then still one thousand square miles of all waivered, rebuffed, exempt, and repudiate Nature's lush and pointless, extended bramble, wanted, yearned for, and actually *demanded* the return of the random, even if they had to invent a legitimate, legal, due-processed pandect of *de jure* and prescribed code under the fiction of a rigged Constitutional Convention.

Here's what happened:

The people of Chapel County got to Maurdon Legurney, Maurdon Legurney got to Lamar White, and Governor White got a Constitutional Convention for his commonwealth, which was in all respects (save for that first cause like a wicked itch that convened it in the first place), splendid, making Pennsylvania a paradigm of justice and good sense that became a model of high democracy. With this exception— the little legalistic eye-teaser buried in the middle of chapter VII, article 42, section 12, subsection 9, paragraph 19, line 5: "All territory south of 79°, 30' longitude, 39°, 45' latitude, and north of 80°, 30' longitude, 40°, 45' latitude, and all peoples residing within said territory, shall henceforth, to the contrary notwithstanding, upon receipt of a vote of the majority in any constitutionally convened poll or public plebiscite as defined in chapter III, article 18, section 34, paragraph 1, line 1, not to be interpreted as incorporating the provisions of chapter IV, article 9, paragraph 1, line 16, in accordance with the doctrine, '*inclusio unuis est exclusio alterius*,' have the right to designate itself, and themselves citizens *of*, in perpetuity, subject to no contingent remainders or to conditional limitations or any other encumbrances, the State of Pennsylvania."

What, quite simply, this did was permit Norbiton, Pennsylvania, and all of Chapel County, and *only* Norbiton and *only* Chapel County, since only Norbiton and Chapel County were to the south and north of all those degrees like a temperate zone, and all those minutes like so many conveniently bunched quarters of an hour, all that mathematical, seaborne geography of that inland commonwealth, to (once the plebiscite passed) unsubjugate themselves to all the laws then on the books, and all the laws that might henceforth be written to join them, of that only *Commonwealth* of Pennsylvania!

I've already told you. The soil was alkaline. They were only local merchants, only small businessmen. But what Maurdon Legurney, Governor White, and the people of Chapel County had given themselves up to was the return of the random, permission to wallow in muddle and romp in their carefully legislated labyrinthine, skimble-skamble, higgledy-piggledy, helter-skelter, harum-scarum anarchy.

They opened whorehouses and nobody came.

They beat their horse stables into gaming casinos, and their horses stood in the rain while the local merchants stood high and dry inside, forlorn at the craps tables, which, despite all the spit, polish, elbow grease, and good honest effort that the remaining house niggers now emancipate-proclamated into ordinary domestics at the stroke of the presidential pen could put into them, still smelled faintly of crap. And nobody came.

"I tell you, boys," Legurney, back from all he'd accomplished for them at the Constitutional Convention at the capitol in Harrisburg, told them, "the world's our oyster. Norbiton, Pennsylvania, could be a regular Sin City, U.S.A. It's just too bad we're so far off the beaten track."

"Think of it, boys," said Oldham Broom, a pretty fair country tailor in his time, but now the kingpin numbers runner for all Chapel County, or, more precisely, numbers walker, or, yet more precisely still, not numbers runner, or walker, or any kind of numbers mover at all, or even just any common, ordinary, garden-variety arithmetician, but full-fledged Theoretical Mathematician, each day drawing the lottery and picking what would have been the winning combinations if only somebody had put down the two, four, six bits or buck other side of the ante, and solemnly contemplating the mysterious and elegant laws of chance, "double sixes three days running. What do you suppose the odds against something like *that* are?"

"It's just too bad we're so far off the beaten track." Maurdon Legurney said.

And at first moved their stills out from their old hole-and-corner hiding places into direct sunlight, and then—advertising was coming into its own about then—out onto the public sidewalks, and then, if they were tipsy enough from sampling their own brew, or maybe even just still sober enough to manage it, might carry a few bottles over to the empty Norbiton jail and offer to put them up against the sheriff's own, going from tipsy to cockeyed, cockeyed to maudlin, and maudlin to philosophical over the course of another slow, businessless, lazy afternoon.

"Folks in this part of the state couldn't get themselves arrested if they tried," Ed Flail, former operator of Norbiton's leading dry-goods store and now one of the town's most prominent dealers in stolen goods, remarked to Sheriff Leon Edgers.

"That's a fact," agreed Billy Slipper, poacher, sports fisherman, and hunter out-of-season of other people's trout and game.

And got an Amen from the county's rustlers, pimps, pickpockets, and other scoundrels.

Because it was true, Crime *didn't* pay. Not in Norbiton, not in Chapel County.

They were sitting on the porch of the Norbiton Inn. Maurdon Legurney, now a broken and melancholy man, nominal lame-duck Mayor, and County Supervisor with just a scant five-and-a-half years left to run on one or the other of his overlapping terms, started to say, "I tell you, boys, it's just too bad we're so . . ." But they didn't want to hear it.

"Again with the beaten track," Ed Flail said.

"Yeah, shut up about that damn beaten track already," Sheriff Edgers told His Honor.

But it was true. They were. And who knew this better than Legurney himself, who had not only been to the capitol in Harrisburg within the year but had come back from it as well, making not the giant but expeditious swing from Norbiton at the bottom, western limits of Pennsylvania, the one hundred miles up to Pittsburgh, and then, by rail, from Pittsburgh on a more or less straight easterly shot to Harrisburg two-thirds across the commonwealth, but the long, piecemeal, switchbacked, drawn out, up-hill-and-down-dale, down-hill-and-up-dale, zigzag journey through woodland and across farms where there were no roads, an honest-to-God, on-foot trespasser slash poacher far from the beaten and unbeaten tack either when he wasn't an out-and-out,

horsebackride-hitchhiking beggar? Practically slaloming himself the
length and breadth of the all-but-Commonwealth-of-Pennsylvania. A
Pennsylvania that, near where he was was still only this fits-and-starts
civilization, borrowing even its place-names from all the tamed cities
and myths of place, towns, and villages tinier than towns, tinier than
villages, calling themselves Paris, Rome, London, Vienna, calling
themselves Athens, Cairo, Istanbul, even Chicago. The better part of
two entire weeks until he even got to the part where the spur started
where you waited for the freight train that brought you to the whistle
stop that took you to the place where if you managed to get there by
a Tuesday you had only to wait till Thursday or Friday till you could
catch the train to Harrisburg.

So it was true. Off the beaten track. Off the beaten path. Off, for
all practical purposes, the goddamn compass itself. So they knew that,
who were only these local merchants and small businessmen and
gentlemen alkaline farmers. Whose feathered, attenuate world had
been shaped, though they'd forgotten this, were too close to it, who
couldn't see the forest for the trees or any of those one thousand or so
thorny square miles of difficult bramble that somebody on the Norbiton
side had once thought to call The Thicket. (Which hadn't been sur-
veyed, hadn't been mapped, and which, for all any of them knew,
might contain, somewhere within its tough terrains lost, fabled cities
of the Indians, tall mountains, vast deserts, gritty sand dunes, deep
inland seas.) Suddenly reminded only then, by Legurney's lugubrious
account of his long and epic but boring odyssey, despondent, failed,
and failing criminals manque on the porch of the Norbiton Inn. And
who (the fellow who suddenly reminded them lost, too) mentioned
that he'd heard tell that, speaking of Pittsburgh, it was an oddity of
geographical history that though they was off the beaten track now, in
the old days a right smart of folks had come down all the way from
Philadelphia and Harrisburg and the Poconos and just all over, even
from out of state, to see it.

"Speaking of Pittsburgh?"

"Well from all over except Pittsburgh."

"*Except* Pittsburgh."

"Well they had their *own* half. Where'd they get any call to go
traipsing all over hell and gone if all they wanted to look at The Woody
was to—"

"The Woody?"

"Well ain't that what they call it up there? I thought they called it by a different name. I thought they called it The Woody."

"Yeah? Well?"

"Well, all I was going to say was that if they wanted to see it, all they ever had to do was just turn their heads back over their shoulders and there she'd be."

And someone else remembered that Norbiton had been practically a boom town in those days, and that wasn't it funny the way things changed, that why even this porch we're standing on wasn't always the porch of just any old country inn but was part of a regular hotel.

"The Hotel Norbiton?"

"Thicket House," said Oldham Broom, who till now hadn't opened his mouth.

"Oh yeah, Thicket House. I recollect hearing talk of that now."

And then all of them began to pitch in with their memories. And collectively remembered that The Thicket had been a sight, even a tourist attraction, years before there was a railroad in Pennsylvania, let alone national or state parks.

"Commonwealth parks," Billy Slipper said.

"Yeah," said Ed Flail, "commonwealth parks."

Somebody remembered reading somewhere that the first picture postcard was of The Thicket and someone else that the first hotel in America named for its view, or proximity to a point-of-interest was in 1792 when Thicket House was built. They recalled all manner of things.

It was Maurdon Legurney himself who recalled all the old talk about slaves in The Thicket.

"Maurdon!" Sheriff Edgers said.

"Gettysburg's only the largest and most famous of Pennsylvania's battlefields," Legurney said.

"Maurdon!" the sheriff said.

"Shit," Legurney said, "if the citizens of a community ain't entitled to the use of their own legatee'd and birthrighted natural resources, I'd like to know who is then?"

"Maurdon, damn it to hell, shut up."

"Well who? Who is?"

"I'm warning you, Maurdon," the sheriff told his mayor. "Maurdon, I'm warning you."

"Why'd God put it here then? Can somebody tell me that? Why'd the good Lord give us a sense of humor to appreciate it in the first place? Why'd—"

"Maurdon, I'm not telling you again!"

"—He teach folks to plant and farm or dig up all the precious metals deep down in the mines? Why'd He stock the rivers and seas with fish and give us our rifles and our shells and our abiding, manly instinct to hunt?"

"Maurdon—"

"He makes some good points there, Leon," Ed Flail said.

"It's briars, goddamn it!" Legurney went on. "It's all pins-and-needled, barbed-wired, saw-toothed, razor's edgery. It's all spiked, prickly and pointy, stinging bristliosity. And what don't bite, nail, and sharp you to death would rash your skin clear off your bones. Because what ain't briars is all itchweed, poison oak and poison ivy, poison sumac allergens!

"Why'd He inspire us to come up with chapter VII, article 42, section 12, subsection 9, paragraph 19, line 5, and all the godgiven, goddamn, chickenshit, loophole rest of it?"

"What? the sheriff asked. "What's that?"

"What if it is tacky? What if it is? Because if we ain't subject to the strict letters of the laws of the Commonwealth, we ain't liable to being sued neither, Leon."

"Aw, Maurdon," the sheriff said. "Maurdon, aww."

So the whorehouses came down, and the stills were silenced, and all the energies of the people of Chapel County were redirected into beating the old Norbiton Inn back into its original avatar. It became Thicket House again.

The Thicket opened for business in the spring of 1881. It had taken two-and-a-half years to build the thirty-seven miles of great wooden wall, the wide, tall-planked platform, accessible by ladder, that rose around the perimeter of The Thicket and sent off cantilevered shoots deep into that queer and lifeless jungle.

They came from all over the Commonwealth, from Ohio and West Virginia and Maryland and up and down the entire eastern seaboard, from Kentucky and the border states and the states of the Confederacy that was, and from the west and even from foreign lands, and it became, you might say, America's first theme park.

The people of Chapel County were famous for their sense of humor, those gag-gift slaves they had once exchanged with each other, the "house niggers" whose trust they'd patiently cultivated in the years immediately preceding the Civil War, the abolitionist sympathies they faked, the underground railroad mythology they perpetuated.

"Follow," they'd said, drawing a slave aside and whispering to him, pointing to The Thicket and seducing him with the dream of freedom, "the drinking gourd!" And steer or lead him in the direction of the infrequent, illusory clearing or occasional false trail.

Or *I* say they'd say. As I've attributed to Legurney and Slipper and Oldham Broom and Sheriff Leon Edgers and the others *most* of the dialogue I've put down here. Because, except for Audubon's journal entries and Phil and Pembler Roberts's remarks, which are documented, we'll never really know who actually said what. The beginnings of a conspiracy are often smoky and seldom known, and all this was over one hundred years ago. But we know who was there and, because of the attendant publicity, have a pretty good idea of their personalities. The New York, Wheeling, Philadelphia, Harrisburg, and even Pittsburgh papers tell us what happened. So it had to be *something* like the way I've put it down. It had to be.

The rest is quickly told.

After the sawmill went up and the logging teams arrived, after the estimated million trees had been cut down, and the two-and-a-half years of construction was completed, and The Thicket officially opened, and the public came to climb the ladders that led to the exalted overview atop the high planks set on a wooden scaffolding like the jerrybuilt crisscrosses of condemnation, the thirty-seven miles of braided grid like a rough cat's cradle of loosely crocheted timber, after the first tentative, trepidatious, dread weight they put on the reinforced railing, after their first rubberneck gawk, *after the first remains of the runaways had been spotted*—remember: There were no signposts to lead them to them, no plaques; the carpenters who were the first to walk these planks, or get any sort of view at all from them, never told what they'd seen, and anyway it was advertised in the newspapers as a sort of "treasure hunt" even though there was no treasure, no prize, and all it really ever was was only this crazy sort of bird-watching— not clumps of the skeletal dead—or at least nor ordinarily—although there is the odd photograph of dead slaves huddled together for warmth or comfort or solace, embracing each other in loving, awful, open death, their twining elbows and ulnas, their backbones and collarbones, their flanges and humeruses, their scapulas, their sternums, their rib cages, their carpals and frontals, their cheekbones just touching—home at last the house niggers—*after* all this, they waited for more than two years—this would have been the summer of 1883— letting word of mouth do its job, the reports in the press, suckering them in, building the tip, specific about the summer—timing was everything—because they had to choose a season not just when the park was sure to be crowded—the idea of the two-week paid vacation had begun to catch on at about the same time that work was begun on the great wooden wall—but a time when the weather was dependable, when they could rely upon the long spells of hot, dry weather, when the rain, if it came, was likely to be the sort of fierce, brief deluge of which all traces are gone one or two hours after it has ceased.

They kept their counsel and agreed on July 18, 1883, which fell on a Saturday that year, not just a time when a lot of folks—there was a railroad in Norbiton now—would be enjoying their summer vacations but part of a weekend, too—timing was *every*thing—so that even those folks *not* on vacation would be in town to take advantage of the generous weekend discounts offered by Thicket House. They were quite lucky. The weather had been splendid for upwards of three weeks, no rain— they weren't farmers in Chapel County; the soil was too alkaline; no corn was ruined, no soybeans or tomatoes or greens—the temperatures hot but bearable, and the wall filled with holiday makers along its great, winding wooden length. Pelgas and the others were ready. The wall was a tinderbox. When Louis Paul and the other domestics, after first preparing the most strategic struts, pilings, and braces with oil, finally ignited it, it went off like a firework. Two hundred-and-fourteen tourists and holiday makers either burned or fell to their deaths on the thorns and briars, the burning brambles and bushes, incinerated and drowned in the lake of blazing liquors of the primed, fermenting fruits forty feet below them.

By law, there were no laws in this corner of the state. There was no conspiracy. There was no arson. There was no murder. There were not even any courts, and the jail, unused for years, was only another curiosity on the tour. As honorary as Maurdon Legurney's titles, as emptily symbolic as the badge the sheriff still wore. So they *had* to lynch them.

Who knew if, in defense of what they'd done—the domestics were all dead; they had no defense—the claim of the citizens of Norbiton and Chapel County, that The Thicket had merely been "salted," was true? That they'd dug up the graves of white men and Negroes already legitimately dead and slowly, careful as puppeteers, lowered their bones into The Thicket? There could be no lawsuits so nothing was ever proven. And, at the time, the records were simply unavailable to the hordes of yellow journalists who descended on Norbiton to investigate what had happened. Indeed, they didn't even know if there *were* records.

For the record, there were records.

Here is a partial list of slaves encouraged to believe they could escape into The Thicket:

The Emmas Woodhouse and Bovary. The Harrys Morgan, Bailey, Angstrom, and Lime. Tom Jones. John Jarndyce. Phil Esterhaus. Dick Diver. V. K. Ratliff. Dorothea Brooke. Flem Snopes. Becky Sharp. A Titus and a Hamlet. A Cricket and a White. C3PO. A Dobbin. Someone else, whether male or female has never been ascertained, known as J.R. A Tulkinghorn. A person named Gatsby, initial J. Henrietta Stackpole. Elizabeth Bennet, Hester Prynne, Arthur Dimmesdale. A Babbitt, a Toots, a slave girl named Leia. A group of blacks probably from the Caribbean. Julien Sorel. Swann, Casaubon, Vautrin, an old man known only as Goriot, and all the members of the Guermantes family. Hazel Motes, Angel Clare, Hyacinth Robinson. Uncle Toby.

I've not told you yet about that Director of Admissions named Louis Paul Pelgas, and my hour is just about up. You will be thinking, of course, that he is descended from the Louis Paul Pelgas who led his fellow domestics to torch the wall. And probably have surmised that because he studied American History at the University of Minnesota and did his doctoral dissertation on the terrible incidents of the commonwealth turned state, that he accepted the Directorship of Admissions in order to exclude whites and turn Clifton College into what, under his tenure, would probably have become an all-black school. But you would be wrong. This particular Louis Paul Pelgas is white and no relation. Coincidence. Nothing but coincidence. Because of his name and the associations it has for the people of Norbiton, you might suppose he takes a lot of ribbing. He doesn't. The fact of the matter is, he's not all that interested in administration. He's looking for another post, has sent out several dozen letters, half a hundred curricula vitae. No takers so far, though he's promised his wife he'll keep trying. Well it's the job market. The job market stinks. It's a lousy time for historians. And he hasn't published.

Gee, I haven't told you that much about names at all, have I? Unless detail functions, as perhaps it does, as a kind of noun, and a menu of proper names as a sort of register of fact. What I suppose I've been talking about is connection. Connection, invention, and all the enumerate, lovely links, synapses, and nexuses of fiction.

Oom boom!

Esmiss Esmoor!

Only connect!

Thank you, drive carefully, and goodnight.

THE FIRST AMENDMENT AS AN ART FORM

Anyone here still believe in the sweet as-we-know-its? Presume, I mean, upon the steady-state across-the-boards? Play in the unified fields, strum, that is, the broad base?

Here's what *I* think—

That democracy does harmony in, that faction and the partisan are relatively new political developments, that Genesis had it about right and And-then-there-was-light precedes And-then-there-was-spectrum and the fine distinctions. I except courtiers and discount attendants, hangers-on, entourage, and all the houses and roses of the Shakespeare wars, and even understand that Guelphs and Ghibellines may have been this kind of *ur* Democrat, this sort of *echt* Republican—— bloodline's oldest money and the known forks of the chosen.

Because who in old times ever held anything so uncalled for as an opinion? (Maybe the Persians, maybe the Ming, maybe cloudy dynasties of the ancient French, primal régimes of the German and the ruined lost tribes of Poland.) Or, getting bread, achieving soup, conquering cloth, had even just (granting They'd let them, given They'd grant it, letting them give it) that first seed cent toward a whole two cents worth of attitude?

Because history, history *really*, was, still is, the agenda of activists. The rest of us, you, me, the rest of us, are mere fans of a world view and use the news like theater—— episodes, chapters in some Sabbath soul serial. (Which is why Sunday papers are thicker than daily ones, why "Meet the Press," "Face the Nation," and "This Week" are shown only on weekends.) Let George do it? *Let* him? Try stopping him! Still, even if we don't have the gift for effecting change, we have the solace of criticism, and those who ain't shy may freely speak. (It's impossible to *talk* to other people). And wasn't the first thing I called for after my quadruple bypass surgery—not knowing I hadn't actually made a sound, unaware of the tubes in my throat, the heart/lung apparatus I licked like deep candy, the full complement of all those strings of the medical (the endotracheal tube, the naso-gastric one, the IV feeder and A-line in my wrist, the penile and Schwann-Ganz catheters) that pulled my life, that loaned me breath and handled my suctions, my autonomics and bodily functions on automatic pilot, virtually as in vitro as any test-tube babe, the first thing, when I came to in the intensive-care cubicle which, through the French farce that is illness, I misapprehended as my room, the *first* thing, after the formalities—the Welcome Back kiss from my wife and kids—my portable radio?

Why wouldn't they listen, damn it? It was on the nightstand when they took me down that morning. (I say down, it might have been up, it was certainly away. I hadn't realized the operation had already happened, didn't know I was already well.) Or my son approach when I held up my hand for him to hold? (More contretemps, more hitch and thwart and mazy skimble-skamble: my wrists, unbeknownst, were tied to the bedrails.)

Don't get the wrong idea. This isn't like that. This isn't any eye-witness account. This isn't harrowing. This isn't some mortality affidavit. One man's struggles with the cancer and poison ivy. I bring in the catheters, the tubes, and invasives for an instance, to shed light, to show the lengths. It's the strictly beknownst that's of interest here. I'd become caught up in the hospital, catching up on my call-in shows like a shut-in on soaps. This public-opinion rooter. (Though I myself never called one. ——Well, once. A few years ago. *Erev* Mother's Day.

The host wanted to hear from the oldest mom in the audience. Women in their seventies called, crones in their eighties, pie chefs, grandmas of dozens. I called. "I'll be one hundred twenty-four my next birthday, Mr. Baker," I said in any man's normal voice. "Oh?" "A hundred twenty-four, yes sir." "My," Baker said. "Oh yes," I said, "one hundred twenty-four years young in September." "Imagine," Bob Baker said, "blowing out a hundred twenty-four candles." "A hundred twenty-five, Mr. Baker," I said. "Oh?" Baker said. "Sure," I said, "one to grow on." And went on, before I lost my nerve, to tell him how it was a sad time for me, Mother's Day, the children being dead and all.) My baser instincts up, you see, a tropism for the notions of foes, a thing in the heart for the aversions of others, to hear them spelled out, sounded, feeding on all the virulence of the anti, the country's contempts and hatreds—for minorities and welfare artists, or, in the politician's famous phrase, "A Black, a Jew, a woman, and a cripple," like the staples of poisonous food groups. Adrenalinized—"Die, fuck," I shout at the radio—by all mean-spirited outlandishness, as though a man's opinions were his character. (And could never understand the *absence* of opinion, the Don't Knows on polls, who had, once I saw— or on the radio heard—which way the wind blew, an opinion on *everything* and for whom a neglected stand and tenet were not so much signals of an incompetence of argument as the collapse of the knee jerks, a failure of actual gait. Because ain't polls what we *do*, even when our responses aren't specifically solicited? Because ain't such spectator/sideliner stuff, even though most issues enjoy only this brief, short growing season, like certain melons, say, the only national game in town in a free country?)

So no wonder I reached (metaphorically reached, reached metaphorically) for my radio.

Once I had this peer vision, the notion, when I was a kid, that everybody had just about what everyone else had. For a long time I was an only child. Brothers and sisters were exotic to me. Hell—we were a Butternut household—Silvercup *bread* was exotic to me. (Unfamiliar breakfast cereal, soap not Lifebuoy, soap not Lux, everything not a Pontiac, anything but Philco, everyone unrelated by marriage or blood. Because brand names are maybe the beginning of politics, the insinuation, or, rather, the plunked down of the familiar and accustomed into one's world, some lifelong seduction of one's turf, the beginning of taste, and security, too, merchandise known early enough, like an imprinting in nature. Because all we ever wanted is not just to know where we stand but to stand there forever, locked into safety like a mouth around a pacifier. Doesn't, to this day, my colleague's mother call from New York before she makes a visit, to discover what treats she may bring, whether there's rye bread, whether there's lox?) But, hey, I was a kid. And had the kid's farm-boy hick imagination. Kids are peasants and can't hold in their heads the simplest things. Their souls go ooh and ahh, I mean, run off with new information like thieves hauling the silver, making ado over the tall buildings and fixating on the dinosaurs. Because all we ever really learn is awe; dread, I mean, and wonder, what keeps us put and freeze-frames—Rosebud! Rosebud!—the inclination of our hearts. Give us, say the Jesuits, a kid, and he's ours forever. No big deal.

So my radio's found (a G.E. in the $15 to $20 range, about the size of a pack of the 100-mm cigarettes that put me here, low-tech despite its carry-cord, its jack for where the earphone goes, its AM/FM capabilities; low-tech despite its capacity to focus sound waves or decode electricity), and I'm flat on my back (who, resting, ordinarily takes to his side like a swimmer loafing, in the browse mode, say, some Sunday driver of a guy copping the sights, or a fellow on lunch break sidesaddle on benches, your day-game gent, your afternoon-movie one—— and how did such a laid-back chap ever get into this position anyway?), and maybe my wrists were still strapped to the bed rails, I don't remember, maybe I even had to ask the nurse to tune it for me. (Why not? I don't put it past me. Because maybe what makes me such a terrific patient is my no-holds-barred willingness to ring for the nurses, to turn my bodily functions over to them, let them in on my every anxiety—— ill health's poor sport.) So my radio's found and I'm flat on my back, afraid even to think about turning over (all those wires and leads, the signals they send of my heart's blow-by-blows—*why, I'd become a sort of radio myself!*—and there's good old Bob Baker giving out call letters and phone numbers and welcoming me back to a telephone call-in show he hosts—"Give us a honk," he says, "on the old kazoo"—and the thought occurs, Why, I really *am* cured, I really *am*, soothed by his tenor's sweet voice, musical, accentless, but

which I think of anyway as a noise in the key of brogue. You wouldn't—
though the program is called "The Party Line"—hear this kind of
show in Russia.

Because the nature of good dialogue is confrontational, some Friday-
night-fight-nite ring to things, or no, better, quotes from the weigh-
in, a suggestion of the dangerous, the barely contained, a hint of
hidden, menacing agenda, a whiff of lunacy, of the fine line between
grudge and show business. Hemingway's killers, for example, their
tough talk in the lunchroom in Summit when Al asks George what
people do there nights and Al's friend says, "They eat the dinner. They
all come here and eat the big dinner." Just that scant increment of
restraint like the harsh moderations of Geneva Conventions, courtesy
and civilization reduced to the blindfold they give you, the final cigarette, what's on the menu at the last supper, whether they deliver
your mail. The grudging proprieties I mean, what really goes on in
the parts of speech. (And once, at high table in a college at Cambridge,
the guest of a visiting, adjunct American pal, myself and my wife—
so Americans; possibly, in this bird's eye, Colonists already twice removed, maybe, counting our adjunct friend, even thrice—offered
brandy after dinner in the Senior Common Room and this perfectly
Edwardian Englishman asshole extending fruits on a tray, things I
didn't recognize—a fair distance from Butternut, let *alone* Silvercup—
and, pausing, I nervously chose the grapes, knowing it wasn't positively
de rigueur to peel and cut them, that I could probably pick them off
their stems and get away with it, and the Master said, "Oh good, we
were all a bit nervous of the persimmon," and I didn't know why, or
even quite how, only that I'd been roughed up, told off, taken down
a peg, killed with his kindness.) The measured, careful, Mexican
banditry—for its softly spoken ominosity, the big unseen sticks it carries—a language of toughs and bullies I'd love to know how to speak
myself.

Because it ain't the found art, the occasional "anti-Arctic" you hear
that gets you. It ain't malaprops, bad grammar, or other, merely way-
ward spoonerisms of the head. "Anti-Arctic" is only a mistake. There's
no intent to injure. (And when, at the beginning of the school year,
a TA in grad school, I, with other TAs, thirty or forty of us perhaps,
working two to a desk in this, well, academic boiler room in Lincoln
Hall, reading the themes of incoming freshmen, to wheat and chaff
them, magisterial as Customs agents or guards at Ellis Island, say, to

size them up—fun with the greenhorns—and "place" them in the freshman rhetoric course we deemed—at thousands of themes at thirty or forty readers two to a desk—commensurate with their skills, and we came across something particularly infelicitous and shared it, or, as the day wore on, and we grew less particular, and called out, "Hey, hey listen, hey you've got to hear this one!" shouting all the innocent double- and triple-entendres, all the solecisms of all flawed—fun with the greenhorns—language, screaming even misspellings finally, bidding up our offended sensibilities, our pretend outrage—fun with the greenhorns—hectic, antic, and frenzied as actual traders on some Bourse of Usage, I lost my taste for faux pas, for an entirely accidental *trayf* linguistics—even, I think, for jokes; I don't enjoy jokes, their stand-in, small-talk essence, the soft conversational purposes they serve—as if it were impossible to talk to other people.) Just this momentary clumsiness and lapse, of no more significance, finally, than a jarred glass. What's wanted is *character*, consistency of vision, inspired Pavlovian pattern, conditioned or not, natured or nurtured. What's wanted, I mean, are the hermetic, locked-in obsessives of art.

During the last days of the 1987 National League pennant race, St. Louis had to beat Montreal to stay in contention, and Virginia McCarthy, another host on "The Party Line," remarked to a caller that it wasn't fair that foreign countries be allowed to play major-league baseball—— and the caller agreed. Beautiful, I remember thinking, typical. Because doesn't someone have to be there to mediate and pass judgment? What was ever the point of preaching to the converted, and who enjoyed Mrs. McCarthy's remark more, me or the caller? Because all her caller got from it was reassurance, and, on that famous scale from One to Ten, reassurance always comes lower than judgment and disapproval. (Which is why it's more fun to read letters to the editor in the *Daily News* than letters to the editor in the *Times*—— for distance, for insular scorn, for all the beaming solace of critical discount and the goose it gives to pride. *This is where I want to be*, I think when I hear them, the hosts on "The Party Line," the folks who call in, talking history, current events, Bitburg to Bork, Ollie to the bombing of Philadelphia, *this is where I want to be, right here, provided and snug beneath the blankets of distance while the world outside threatens like rough weather, war, and its rumors like rain on the roof.*)

And can't wait till the next disaster. Not the earthquakes. Not the floods and not the fires. Not even the serial killings or grand heists and pestilentials. (There's no call on the call-ins for these. Everyone is at peace with fury.) But the scandals. Because it's the world that makes the best gossip, and only a madman would take sides in a hurricane. (Catastrophe has interest only if it's man-made.) So it ain't, as I say, mere spoonerism that serves my purposes, any of the accidental "anti-Arctics" of found art, however foolish. (Though foolishness, ignorance, and stupidity, if habitual, are at least along the approaches to the approaches, somewhere in the foothills of character and personality.)

You hardly hear of it anymore, but a year or so ago a good deal was made in the papers about something called "shock radio." St. Louis, where I live, doesn't do shock radio. It's more a New York, Miami, Los Angeles, Chicago sort of thing, blood-sport programming for your anything-goes towns, but I've heard it and it ain't much. The formula is perfectly obvious. It is, quite simply, to be outrageous. Outrageous, say, as a professional wrestler is outrageous, or some caged dunk-me artist above five feet of canned water on a narrow plank on a boardwalk. Outrageous for money, I mean, so a little pathetic even at its nastiest, as Joe McCarthy was a little pathetic because no one could really *believe* that crap, all that top-of-the-voice, sky-is-falling *geschrei*, all that trained pitchman's get-'em-while-they're-hot, get-'em-while-they're-hot-here.

Once I tuned in. It's nothing, just show business. They don't mean it, they're only fooling.

Howard Stern was ridiculing a man about his weight, not even a man who'd called in, just some fellow New Yorker he'd read about in the papers. The man weighed, as I recall, over 1,000 pounds. There may have been a question about his eligibility for welfare. And I seem to remember something about blankets, that the fellow didn't have enough blankets. It wasn't, the blanket part, metabolic or anything, that once your body weight hits four figures something physiological takes over and you require extra covers. He didn't, I think, have enough covers to begin with. Maybe it had something to do with the Welfare. Who knows? I live in St. Louis where much of your goings-on are blacked out. But, anyway, there was Stern, making fat jokes, carrying on, when an astonishing thing happened.

Richard Simmons, the TV aerobicizologist, called in. He knew something about the case, he said, and was quite angry with Stern.

He tried to get him to apologize, at least to quit it, knock it off. They seemed, Stern and the aerobicizologist, to know each other and called each other by their first names—though it may have been a show-biz thing, the first-name basis like a professional courtesy—even when Simmons was at his angriest and most scolding, even when there was this catch in his throat and you knew that something had genuinely touched him, moved him on behalf of fatties and the glandular everywhere to call in, to have this face-off, celebrity to celebrity, man to man.

And lost control, or lost control as celebrities lose control, a vague, persistent notion like a nagging question that it was part of the show, a vaguer notion that it wasn't.

Because I don't know if Simmons was really crying. Just as I don't know if Stern was really embarrassed.

Though that was the best part of it, wasn't it, better than the stupid fat jokes, better than Howard Stern's professionally willful, deliberate bad taste, better than Simmons's heroics?

But we're close to the bone here, theatrically, artistically, maybe even humanly in situ. Because it's that inch of art that makes the difference, art, like baseball, being a game of inches. Because the subject is art, and art, first of all, is a noise, a testing, stretching, then a busting of the decorums and proprieties, child's play—literally—in some cautious, juridical, Cinderella's slipper, try-it-for-size sense. The full stop I-dare-yous. Seeing just how far one is prepared to go, I mean.

It's the nagging question that nagged me then and nags me still.

When I was a kid, maybe seven, maybe eight, Sonny, our downstairs neighbor, Gert's husband, took me to White City to watch the wrestling. Maybe we went twice, traveling on the cars, Chicago's mattered trolleys with their tight, lanyard-weave yellow-straw seats and ridged wood floors, complicated, busy as a bootheel. I had never seen professional wrestling and, of course, it wouldn't have been then what it is now. There would have been no elaborate capes and costumes or glitzy special effects, no prop hairdos or, in those relatively ethnic-neutral days, bewildering stereotypical styles. What I chiefly recall about the White City fights was that the bad guy, in extremis at the tide's turning, when the referee finally caught on to his villain's behavior and scoundrel's ways and even the good guy, slow to anger, who until this minute, perhaps alerted by the crowd, had not seemed to understand what was happening, never mind that somebody in that ring was kicking the shit out of him, pulling his hair, gouging his eyes, choking the very breath from his body, was starting to suspect that it was an imperfect world, always—*I mean always*—reverted to type (well, *reverted*, I mean you can't very well *revert* to type, can you, when you've been living up to your ears in it all along?) and, craven, showed his coward's colors like the woven yellow straw on the cars, threw himself on the good guy's mercy, offered his hand, mimed new beginnings, mimed *phooey* on my old ways, oathing remorse, change of heart, rebirth itself, on invisible Bibles, body Englishing self-abasement so down at heels and abject it made no difference that the abaser was insincere or the good guy taken in. (Who, human, could afford *not* to be taken in by such voluntarily complete disgrace, or what would become of mercy or the benefit of the doubt? What, I mean, would happen to possibility, to salvation?)

Was it, I asked, part of the show?

Sonny, inculcating in me that the suspension of disbelief, like Christmas propaganda (Santa, Mrs. Claus, the elves and helpers, even the North Pole like some powdery mise-en-scène), is the necessary beginning of mystery, shrugged.

Or the circus. Where it's part of the show constantly to raise the question, whatever the intrusion, whether it's part of the show, where it's part of the show to invade the fourth wall, to mix worlds, world and art intermingling like elements of un-water, un-oil. The drunk in street clothes in the audience who rushes into the ring before anyone can stop him and climbs up the high wire. The volunteer who may or may not be what she seems. Even the near-fatal misstep, even the last-minute recovery. Even, since it's part of the show to make what is dangerous seem even more dangerous than it already is, the ringmaster's plea for absolute silence during this next trick and, when you think you can practically hear a pin drop, the flyer shakes off the signal anyway and looks to the ringmaster to see whether he can or cannot control this crowd, God damn it, and he tries again, the ringmaster, taking a cue from the performer himself (whose life it is anyway) and, stern now, no more Mr. Nice Guy, masterly, a masterful ringmaster, once again requests, no, *demands* absolute quiet, silencing even the drumroll and shouting backstage to the animal trainers to see if he can get them to get their beasts to hold it down, to quit that rumbling, someone's trying to do a triple out here.

Because the circus, dealing as much in imminence (the possibility of fuckup) as it does in awe, requires, like shock radio, a sort of verisimilitude, some you-are-here, street-scene quality to the quality of life, by the side of the road when the accident happens and blood gets spilled. Because all naïve forms—professional wrestling, circus, radio call-in shows, the pantomime—are dependent upon the *engagement* of witness. I can't prove it—*prove it?* Hey, ain't I the guy who entered Bob Baker's Mother's Day Sweepstakes?—but I'm pretty sure the percentage of people who ever actually call one of those shows, who aren't just there to listen, is smaller, oh, *much* smaller, than the percentage of people who act in movies compared to those who pay money to see them. More, I mean, witness the world than have any practical use for it. *(Who makes a fist? Who takes a stand? Who learns to fly? To ski, to go sailing? Who gives up a throne for love? Who has a throne? Whose ship comes in? Who has a ship?)*

Just to witness. Not even to bear it. Only to *be* there, this voyeur of the dictions, just one on whom impressions are made, just another privileged, please-stand-by artist, a piece of the public, a part of the great grandstand for whom all the grandstanding gets done, one share of all civilized, tellurian creaturehood. My *God*, I might well have thought in that hospital, not distracted understand, anything but, the cheap portable recovered whose absence had so exercised and damn near killed me all over again in my first confused hours as a surgically salvaged dead guy (and that had been the first miracle, I thought, remembering my father's RCA portable, in '40, '41, which you turned on by pressing the catch and lifting its lid like some shoebox of sound), the First Amendment is surely our national art form.

Choosing from the formats fanned out on my dial like paint on a palette—— country, classical, easy listening, big band, top 40, golden oldies, adult contemporary, all news, all talk, all sports, all Praise God and Die. What a country we are! Tragedy, comedy, history, pastoral, pastoral-comical, historical-pastoral, tragical-historical, tragical-comical-historical-pastoral. But it's true, this abundance is true. This overkill is true, this surfeit and riot and profligate plenty are true. Right on the money our luxurious redundancy and gorged, *de trop* profusion. (Now there's even shock TV. There are nude talk shows on cable. Because nothing's sacred, not even talk shows, and history is only your get-an-inch, take-a-mile arrangements, progress some leaps-and-bounds smash 'n' grab, roiling and arbitrary as the tectonics of smoke, and—you heard it here first, recall—there could in the offing be—

shock ballet, shock opera, shock world-team tennis, why not. As already there's shock news—— the *Enquirer*, the *Sun*.) All naked, suck-thumb comfortable now, all snug, supine coze and satisfied stand-pat, sit-pretty contentment and pleased ease. Safe in the intensive care, serene in the hospital corners. Because "all talk" is my format, character my poison. Character, I get off on character, character and opinion, and they're slogging away on "The Party Line," going at it hot and heavy, to-ing and fro-ing, having it out. These people astonish me. They have opinions on everything. They take all the papers. They never miss a national news show on TV, a controversial miniseries. They listen to all the call-in shows on all the stations, see all the *Donahue's*, all the *Oprah Winfrey's*. I think they must be recovering heart patients themselves, the intensively cared for, and suddenly I understand that the world is much smaller than it is, shrunk to the size of a changing neighborhood, a backyard, so small, finally, you probably can't find it on maps anymore. But persistent in its instincts, some rage to keep talking, never to change the subject or to have it changed, and that what I'm hearing is not so much some continuing national debate as a neighborless gossip, racism only something to do over the coffee klatsch and the reactionary just a way of making friends in a pluralistic society. Maybe it ain't even the real thing, the true gen mean spirit and 24-karat narrow mind here at all, but merely mindless chatter, making conversation, small talk, only all coal-hauled, censorious bicker and find-fault's scandalized, scolding tut-tut, its venemous niggling carp and recriminative tongue lash—just loneliness batting the breeze while the laundry hangs drying and the bread bakes.

Sure, I think, that's probably it. It probably is. Even the best of formats has its reasons. And if it's something of a letdown to realize that what I've been identifying as character is only, well, this scheduled, prearranged rage, fixed as a fight, this nostalgic black hole, this absence populated, *seeded* with ogres of the political, with stand-ins and straw men and stalking horses, with mere beards for the demonic, with all fond, pining idleness's inept transference and fuzzy displacements.

Here, three plus years into my post-op, my lazy valetudinary set as a spell of good weather, is what they were saying to each other just the day before yesterday.

It was the dawning of the Age of Aquarius, a day or so into the Moscow Summit conference—— Nuclear Spring. Reagan had thrown his picnic for the dissidents, all ears, Santa Claus and Our Lady, too, to the juggled grievances, promising nothing but touching the bases of agenda, never mind that the Russians had already begun to pull out of Afghanistan, or that just about everybody, even Reagan, could see that the cold war wasn't going anywhere, that, like the Vietnam War, like the one in Afghanistan that the Russians were pulling out of, it had bogged down. Could see that history had too much on its plate already— AIDS, the Middle East, the Central Americas, all the world's flashpoint economies, all its nasty, insoluble nationalisms. Could see it had had it, the world, had had enough. It don't *need* any cold war, it don't *need* any arms race. *It ain't*—O frabjous day!— *gonna study no cold war no more!*

Glasnost glasnost glasnost.

I settled back.

Virginia McCarthy has a slightly nasal voice and speaks with this thin, just melodious, whine. When, for example, she gives out one of the station's telephone numbers, she always sings the "5," raising it a stave above the numbers beside it—4 ⁵ 1—like a note on sheet music. It is almost visible, and it clenches my teeth.

She was telling her caller, who had told her that, say what you will, it's just bad manners for a president to go into another fellow's country and keep harping on what's wrong with it, that she thought much too much was being made of the summit conference anyway. She thanked him for calling. Then she took a call from a man who agreed with the first caller. He was, this caller said, no bleeding-heart liberal. Why, he wondered, would Reagan bother with a bunch of refuseniks? We certainly didn't want any of them in this country, did we?

Mrs. McCarthy, both of whose wings are right, is rarely confrontational, though she usually speaks her mind. She's always polite, but you know where she stands. On the issue of Reagan's behavior in Russia, however, though she defended him, it was pretty clear that she was bothered by the mixed signals. She said she hoped he wouldn't give away the store. Her callers were starting to come down rather heavily on Gorbachev's side, and I was beginning to lose interest.

We've never met. I've no idea what she looks like. The only things I know about her are her public opinions. But something was happening to both of us. Our zeal was going off was what.

Now caller after caller seemed to take issue with her. Not violently, not even very exceptional their tentative exceptions, only, their mood, a little more reasonable than usual, only a little more let's-wait-and-see, let's-hold-our-horses. Only a pinch of the benefit-of-the-doubt in the brew like a seasoning, a dash of hopefulness, a splash of sanity. And this woman who speaks her mind suddenly seemed just a little uncertain about where she stood. And I'm thinking for her now, with her.

It's the entropy, we're thinking. It's dragon loss, demon deprival. It's all monstrosity, we're thinking, suddenly endangered as a rain forest. And what if it *is* over, we're thinking, what if it really *is?* What will happen to the call-in shows, all our partisan opinion operas, all our patriotic countersong? This is almost embarrassing, we're thinking.

Because I *love* talk shows, I *love* my quick-draw angers and resentments, would defend to the death no one's right to say anything so much as my own right to hear it said. Who has this voyeur ear, this hold-your-coat heart, who needs, if only because it satisfies a sense of the dramatic which, if not deranged, may be, at bottom, a kind of sin—— the sin of *casus belli*, say, of provocation, the sin of human interest, of fuss blunder, some melodramatic turpitude, agent-provocateur error, the rabble-rouser heinities, gadfly sin, flat-out archetype lust!

And begin to fear, even as I go, even as I lob these soft *culpas* at my head, that somewhere, in some tiny corner of the scheme of things, there's this toy hubris of the Grand Antinomies and that I, too, am a part of the show.

THE MUSES
ARE
HEAD

AND JESUS, I'M THINKING AT THE TIME, THIS SNOB OF GEOGRAPHY, this longitude-latitude fop, it can't have been but three weeks ago I was living in a villa on Lake Como, taking the gelato, the customized pastas; servants were cutting my meat. And tucking in, too, feasting on the blood-oranges architecture folded into the terraced hillsides organic as agriculture, the lake's thin gray porridge and lumpy Chinese mists. Well maybe, I'm thinking at the time, in spite of Missouri is my hometown, distance is only a different time zone of the head. Because I recognize nothing here, all jet-lagged out in the van, two or so hours southwest of St. Louis on I-44, deep—I see by the recurring billboards that keep on coming, popping up at us like an infinite loop of highway in some redneck video game—in the walnut-bowl belt, in roadside zoo land, cavern and cave country. Among fireworks stands. Live bait mines. And there's a sense, God bite my high-hat tongue, of something so un-gun-controlled out there we may have fallen, may my swank wither and drop off, among a race of Minutemen. There's billboards for the Passion Play, for Silver Dollar City, for rides on the Wet Willies.

This ain't any America of franchise and one size fits all; this is a time warp. Some live-by-the-tourist, die-by-the-tourist figment of the imaginary bygones and halcyons, of fiddles and corncobs and jugs. We are, I mean, deep, real deep, in a hanger-on economy, in some landscape of the novelties, and I ask Ross Winter, founder and artistic director of the Mid America Dance Company (MADCO), the man who leads our troupe of modern dancers bound for Springfield, Missouri, where we're performing Friday and Saturday evening, what folks do hereabouts when they're not minding the bait stores and walnut-bowl factories.

"Don't know," he said. "Perhaps they groom each other for ticks." It's improbably close to what I've been thinking myself, for we seem to be traversing tracts of the summer pests and poisons, a vast American steppe of allergens and contact toxins, of wicked itch banes in the woods and high grasses.

The van, something in a fourteen- or fifteen-passenger Ford, has been rented for the four days it will be required. A second vehicle, also rented, containing the company's props, wardrobe trunk, special equipment (some of which is also rented), and rolls of the vinyl theatrical flooring it has just acquired and that will have to be paid for by matching grants, had set out earlier, is probably already in Springfield, setting up.

The dancers, I think, are used to me by now. (We go back.) We are practically colleagues, these toned, flexible, almost jointless young men and women in their twenties and the crippled-up fifty-eight-year-old man who has to negotiate the high step up into the van by means of a high step up onto a milk case, a breathtaking piece of choreography in its own right, let me tell you. They call me by my first name, something that normally squeaks against my blackboard like chalk—I am, by ordinary, when not playing *la strada*, a teacher—but that, here, in these circumstances, oddly I do not mind at all, and even find flattering, though I must say it's a little difficult to keep *their* names straight, wait for others to say them first, only gradually constructing a private mnemonics. Liz is the married one. Her husband, James, is part of the tech crew and has gone out with David in the other van. Raeleen is the one with the close-cropped hair. Ellen is the tall one, so Darla must be the one with the reddish hair and the expressive face you associate with clown-white makeup and one dark apostrophe standing for a tear. The men are a bit easier. Paul is driving,

Michael is reading the Stephen King. Jeffrey, unseen in the van's last row, is apparently sleeping.

No one calls me by my first name now or says much of anything, really. Indeed, they seem a bit torpid for a group normally so casual with gravity. Not like last time when they stretched out on the long ride to Winfield, Kansas, by improvising themselves into various riffs of position, a kind of jazz yoga. Not like last time when they passed the time in the moving vehicle playing board games without a board and counting cows and doing license-plate poker. When they made up ideas for dances. Even me. "You pass out these dinky cardboard glasses," I said. "You give a pair to everyone in the audience. There's this green lollipop cellophane over one eye, this red over the other."

"So?"

"So you tell them if they put on the glasses they can see the dance in three-D."

"Right," Paul said, "then we chuck spears at them."

Not like the last time when I smelled, I swear it, the lightly scorched odor of composition-rubber gym shoe in the van's closed air and browsed the curious sampler of upscale magazines, *Interview* and *Elle* and *M*, that the company favors, and dipped at will into proffered community snacks, introduced for the first time to the delicious sodium nitrites and scrumptious carcinogens of beef jerky, on whose long, tough leather I chewed with pleasure for half an hour, for if I am crippled up and need assistance to get into a van, I have the jaws of a grown man. Nature gives with the right hand, takes with the left.

Now we don't stop for gas, so forget beef jerky. Forget dinner, too. Not like last time. (Place in Kansas? No fast-food joint or truck stop or theme restaurant but the genuine article, the kind of place you see on the network news when Tom Brokaw breaks bread with vox pop— a farmer, a banker, the John Deere man. And there are plaques for Rotary, Jaycees. And Angie—the company's high school apprentice— asked what the Optimist Club was, and Liz told her it was a support group for people who are too happy.)

Hi-diddle-de-dee, the actor's life for me!

Only it isn't the boards I want to trod, it's the Road. Having been born with this J. B. Priestley sense of good companionship, some troupe notion of traveled kinship, a true believer—my pop was a traveling salesman—in lobby encounters, this vet of the shifting, shared geography, this heart's perpetual reunionist, you see, this sucker for chums, this long-standing-enough guy on that pavement in Paris who eventually runs into everyone he's ever known—— this, this auld acquaintance. Because it ain't really friendship I'm talking about, it's *Miller time!* And even today I imagine all sports announcers, men covering not only different teams but different games even, know each other, and are always bumping into one another in the best hotels in the different towns—though it's always Cincinnati—and going off together to the good restaurants to catch up, to do the divvied shop talk of their lives, speaking in a jargon so closed it's almost ethnic of the great patsies and fall guys—did you see *Broadway Danny Rose?* like that—doing the anecdotal schmooze and war stories, all high life's tallest tales.

Still, not like last time. Because we really do go back. Well, a couple and a half years anyway.

Ross Winter was born in Australia. He studied at the University of New South Wales and, though he took modern-dance classes while he was a student, he ultimately went for an architect. Emigrating in 1959, he was with a film company in Portugal for a year, moved to London and set up in the design and architecture trade. He choreographed dances for the London and Edinburgh festivals, married, started a family, came to America and moved to St. Louis, and in the early seventies went to work for the Wetterau Corporation, a wholesale-food-distribution company, where he was head of the design department. While at Wetterau he founded, in 1976, the Mid America Dance Company, a sidebar to his life. Then, in 1984, the company closed down Winter's department, and it was suddenly a compulsory hi-diddle-de-dee on him. Missouri, Illinois, Kansas, Nebraska, Oklahoma, Arkansas, Texas—— this is the venue of their modern dance.

Winter looks, in profile, rather like some King George on currency and, like other educated Australians, talks a sort of soft-edged English Prim, the vaguely indeterminate accent of someone raised in a mother tongue but an alien in the land where he speaks it. It's an agreeable, even amiable, sound, but you can't imagine anyone ever shouting in it and so it seems, well, vulnerable, the patient calm of a forced, stoic courtesy. (*Aw geez, come off it. What are we talking about here? Some great Greek patsy fall guy? A few not-like-last-times and we're into the tragics? As Georgie Jessel said about his chauffeur forced to stand outside the limo and wait for him in the rain, "Nobody told him to go into his profession.*") At fifty-two, Winter is slightly egg-shaped. "The irony about dancing," he says, "is that as a dancer gets better his body only gets worse." In any event he hung up the taps years ago, though he still performs in "The Madcracker," his parody of *The Nutcracker* and the company's most popular dance.

MADCO doesn't do badly. That is, it's a wash. The company takes in and disburses about $150,000 a year. Between $35,000 and $40,000, or about 28 percent of its income, comes from grants; touring brings in another 34 percent; fixed-fee performances in St. Louis, 8 percent; box-office sales, 14 percent; educational performances in schools, 11 percent; fund-raising, 3 percent; with a miscellaneous 2 percent coming in from classes and such. Salaries for the dancers range from $115 to $210 per week. Liz, who's been with MADCO eight years, gets $210 (for a thirty- to thirty-five-week season), but the mean salary for the dancers is $150. Ross allows himself $330 a week. David Kruger, the tech man and company manager, books the tours and works on commission.

I come into it in 1986, about.

Ross wanted to choreograph a dance to prose and asked me to write a story that I could read downstage left while the dancers carry on behind me. When "Notes Toward a Eulogy for Joan Cohen" is performed on Saturday night in Springfield, it will be the fourth time, not counting rehearsals, we will have worked together. It's a long piece, about forty-five minutes, and although, owing to my location onstage, I've never seen all of it, the bits I have seen—in MADCO's rehearsal studio—have always seemed to me rather sexy. Well, all dance is about screwing, finally, even the barn dance, even the waltz, but we're talking leotards and leg warmers here, we're talking spandex and muscle. We're also talking, in the instance of "Joan Cohen," about a rabbi who officiates at the funeral of a woman with whom he's been carrying on an adulterous affair—talking porno movies in a Philadelphia hotel room, talking blow-job discussions. We are a distance from *Swan Lake.* And did I mention that Springfield is the world headquarters of the Assemblies of God? Not so much the people who gave you Jimmy Swaggart as the folks who took him away.

When we danced the dance in St. Louis those other three times there seemed to be a lot of enthusiasm for my cane, applause all around the minute they saw it when I limped in from the wings to take my

seat behind the table where I do my stuff—all my plucky Look, Ma,
I'm Dancin's and show-my-flags. Well, I'm known in St. Louis, a
known cripple. When I stumble on in Springfield Saturday night
and they *don't* applaud I will think, this is some tough audience!
Well, I'm spoiled. (And why, incidentally, do top-hat, white-tie-
and-tail types like Tommy Tune and Fred Astaire use canes in *their*
acts?)

If the collective mood isn't like last time, maybe it's because these are
the final performances of the season; and for Liz, who is married now
and who, whither thou/thither me, will be leaving the company and
moving to Arizona with James in a week or so, it's a last tango in
Springfield altogether. And because Darla, she of the reddish hair and
supple face, has been in severe pain for eight months now and has
either torn ligaments in her hip or a ruptured disk in her back, maybe
both, which isn't great for the leg extension and presents difficulty for
her turnout, and has given her more downtime than a computer; and
even if the company *is* family, unlike real families it's forced to function, is burdened always—unlike me with my merely hail-fellow,
good-time-Charley, Miller-time intentions, all my visions of those
sugarplums in a weightless world—and if that's the case, what alternative did she have except to ask Ross if he had a minute and then
offer her resignation?

Only I don't know all this yet. I'm still sitting innocent next to the
Stephen King–reading Mike, a few rows up from invisible Jeff, apparently sleeping. Passing with Ross the time of the day and, deep in
my heart, wondering what the place will be like where we're going to
stay.

Well, not much. It doesn't have a restaurant, it doesn't even have
a coffee shop, let alone a lobby where one can transact old times with
the other announcers. It's a hot day in the summer of the great drought,
and though there's an air conditioner in my room, it doesn't work.
Oh, it has the *sound* of air-conditioning down, but no B.T.U.s. And
there are bugs squished against the walls. But hi-diddle-de-dee anyway,
because isn't this how it's supposed to be? To all intents, ain't it a kind
of vaudeville we're doing, riding the tour van like a time machine, all
symbolic trains, rails and clickety-clack like a montage in movies,
name, pop, and elevation wig-wagging above the stations like the
accepted synecdoche for distance itself? Ain't it? We're paying our

dues, man. Look, Ma, I'm playing Springfield! Ain't I? Ain't we? We're *taking* this show on the road! Ross, me, and the mean-average twenty-five-year-olds, those hundred-fifty-buck dancers. Hell, if we had any sense we'd go *all* the way, split the motel altogether, maybe look for a boardinghouse maybe, some place with just the one telephone next to the landlady's apartment in the front hallway, or something *really* fleabag, a hotel with old bus-station chairs and ripped-up green plastic cushions in the lobby. And that's *one* muse. The Muse of Myth, of How It Was. There were hobos in the earth in those days, a race of fry cooks, of broke-mouthed old fellows, closed-jaw, and all wide, ear-to-ear, turned-in lip like Popeye the Sailor. And you know what? If you permit me to get ahead of myself, you know what? There still are. I saw them.

Friday, breakfast morning of show time, a bunch of us were sitting around Orville & Betty's Café—SERVING DOWNTOWN SPRINGFIELD FOR OVER EIGHT YEARS—doing the large o.j., French toast, sausage, and coffee, $3.25, when this bo came up. His hair was perfectly black but he was toothless. He was wearing a T-shirt, his exposed arms so covered with tattoos he looked abstract, as closely decorated with geometry as a mosque. He needed a light for his cigarette. Liz, or maybe Jeffrey, lit his cigarette, and he asked if anyone happened to know the time. It was ten-thirty, and Liz filled him in. "Thank you. Is that A.M. or P.M.?" "A.M.," said Liz, "it's ten-thirty in the morning." "You want to buy a floor lamp for two dollars?" There it was, in the corner, this classic floor lamp with this classic lamp shade, this classic wire, this classic plug. (And for my money, in my book, right there's another muse—— the Muse of the Bizarre Confrontation. The muses are singing today, I'm thinking. How it was is how it is, and I should get out more.) Liz didn't live in Springfield, she'd have no way to get it home. "I can understand that," he said reasonably. "I'm not from here myself. You can have it for a dollar." Betty, at the cash register, beside a wall mounted with a half-dozen stuffed heroic silver bass, is watching closely. Liz just plain doesn't want the damn thing. "Take it off my hands," pleads the tattooed man. Who is difficult to look at, on whom time, booze, and circumstance have worked their magic and whose colors are running, who, like some ancient, benighted schoolboy, cannot seem to stay within his own lines. "Take it off my hands, take it for nothing." Betty shoos him, but before he goes he asks the time again, and once more needs to know if that's A.M. or P.M. (Later, Ross

will mention he's seen him in the street, that he didn't have the floor
lamp with him so must have gotten his price, better than his price.
There were two bucks in his hands, and he was counting them out
like some crazed miser, turning them over and over. "A dollar, and
a dollar, and a dollar, and another dollar . . .")

There are several agendas.

Even if five of the eleven of us showed up for breakfast today, it
isn't often we're in the same place at the same time. Michael likes to
stay in the room when he's not working, though when he's with us
I've noticed he's a superb mimic, a parrot of the zeitgeist. Of the male
dancers, he is the most solidly built, the most powerful, though it's
Paul, I think, who is probably the best athlete. It's surprising to see
him at the motel pool. Dancing must be a sort of ultimate acting. In
a bathing suit he's almost scrawny. He *is* scrawny, yet when he swims
there's no wasted motion, no energy loss. A few strokes take him the
length of the pool. The women are similarly deceptive. Except for
Ellen they're all relatively short, yet on stage they appear tall. In one
of the dances Liz moves across the stage, apparently without effort,
with Paul on her back. (*What's going on? Are you funny, are you in
one of the high-risk categories?* No, of course not. *Of course not?
Michael's powerfully built, Paul's the best athlete, Liz plays horsey
with him? Of course not?* Well, it's the fashions. *The fashions.* The
way their clothes fit, all right? *Are you caught up yet?* The way their
clothes fit, I tell you. My clothes never fit me like that. *You're fifty-
eight years old.* Don't make excuses for me, they *never* fit. *Whiner,
you're in mourning for a wardrobe?* Yes, sure, why not? Only not for
a wardrobe, just that accident in the genetics that skewed my architecture and made me silly in caps, jeans, in Jockey and boxer shorts
either, in all the extraordinary accessories of the rakish, windblown
young down to the beaches in boaters and scarves. The only equality
is the equality of sexual style, the Me Tarzan's, You Jane's, all the
level playing fields of dalliance. You bet your ass I'm in a high-risk
category, the highest. I'm not cute! *The grass is always greener, eh?*
Always. *All right, get on with it.*)

So there are different agendas. Raeleen is at the theater with Ross,
holding up costumes so David and James—who wears clip-on suspenders with a length of Mickey Mouses attached to trousers so baggy
(fashion) he could be that Dutch kid who saved Holland—can preset

the proper cues on the lighting board. Darla and Ellen are sunning themselves. Michael relates the plot of his Stephen King, and Jeffrey retrieves tossed dimes before they sink to the bottom of the pool. I chaise lounge alongside. Paul is dressing. There's a technical rehearsal at one.

"Step leap step skip," Liz drill-sergeants in theory class in Richardson Auditorium the afternoon of the performance at Southwestern College in Winfield, Kansas. "Swing and up, left two three. Over right, two three up," she calls out, commanding mantras of the dance, square-dance calls.

"Oof."

"Shit."

"Find your center, you're not finding your center."

Ellen pushes up on her push-up sleeves. Angie, the apprentice, fixes the off-the-shoulder sweatshirt on her shoulders. Everyone wears leg warmers, even the men, who appear oddly old in them, as if their circulation were impaired. Liz, a cappella, continues to snap her fingers, never surrendering the beat while the troupe in its artfully ripped sweatshirts (fashion! *fashion!*) hunts its lost center. Difficult, I imagine, to find in the near dark they're working in, all the three-ring din of the crew's preparations—— they're putting together a jungle-gym forest for the set of "Lemurs," they're testing the fog machine, adjusting sound levels for the romantic, boozy music of "Silver" while a stagehand kneels in the dark and blows up props, two dozen silver cushions. "Are you the curtain puller?" Ross asks a student. "When you're closing you can always be a little faster than when you're open-ing," he says to him. "He's a quick study," he tells David as the curtains come smoothly together.

"Two, that's warm." David addresses a person or persons unknown in the booth. He speaks, like an air-traffic controller, into a microphone cantilevered across his mouth like a prosthesis, some orthodontics of sound. "Two and a half, that's even warmer. Two and a quarter. Okay, that's good."

Liz crickets away, the dancers swarm.

They are theoried, beliefed, suffused with us/them, farmer/rancher, mountain/shore antipathies and yin/yangs. Well, they have nothing against ballet dancers *personally* . . .

Ballet dancers are bun heads.
   "   "   " robots.
   "   "   " toy soldiers.

As ruled and rigid as ice skaters doing all the compulsories and mandatories of their frozen art. Ballet a by-the-numbers game, *tableau vivant*, not classic so much as stiff, dead to the arts as Latin is to language. Modern dance is to ballet what jazz is to golden oldies. (Though how much is terror I can't say. Much would have to be, no? It stands to reason, doesn't it? Life up on pointe? Or down in plié? Lowered in painful rice-paddy mother-squat? Because all dance really *is* about screwing. Even ballet.)

When we get to the motel Ross hands envelopes to each of us. They are pay envelopes. Because I think the check for my fee will be in it, I am embarrassed to open mine in front of them. I open it in the room. It isn't my fee. It's my per diem—a lump-sum $45. This is Thursday, we will be leaving Sunday. It will have to last me. (But I come back with money to spare. I could have lived a week and a half in Springfield.)

When I finally see it, the Landers Theatre gives me the hi-diddle-de-dees altogether. It's the real thing. A classically legitimate legitimate theater. A theater like the theaters there used to be a broken heart for every light on Broadway for.

Once, years ago, in Rome, dubbing a film into English (I was Sextus, son of Pompey) and asked "What hour is it?" I was supposed to answer, "It is a quarter past the hour of the second watch." I delivered the line not only without credibility or good evidence that I could even tell time, but without any clear understanding (me, Sextus, a grown co-conspirator) that it was the time I was being asked to tell. I worked almost the entire morning before being fired. The point isn't that I was fired. It's that once, years ago, in Rome, *I* dubbed a movie. Wait, I take it back. The point is also that once, in Rome years ago, I was fired. Legitimate legitimate theater.

And the Landers is it. Built in 1909, it has two balconies. Its seats are plush, ornate. Great fierce gilded masks—almost gelded masks, not asexual, but not Comedy, not Tragedy, only dramatic—with bulbs sitting on their tongues line the sides of the theater and the bottom of each balcony, perched like gargoyles on Architecture. The second balcony isn't used now, but, in its day, a full house would have been about a thousand people.

This is it, all right. By *God*, it is!

There's a kid, maybe he's eighteen, who volunteers his time as a stagehand at the Landers. He says his ambition is to own a place like this someday. Not an actor, mind, but an impresario. I don't know why this should move me but it does, as I am moved by the theater, as I am moved by the dancers, as one is always moved by odd, off-center hope, by people hanging in there and the persistence of the obsolete. (*You, crybaby! You're so moved, why didn't you buy the bum's floor lamp? Why didn't you take it off his hands for two dollars?* That's something else. *Something else. Ri-ight.* Well it is. *Sure.* All right, smartguy, I've reason to believe it may have been an ill-gotten floor lamp. *Oh, an ill-*gotten *floor lamp!* I was *too* moved, I was *too!* Sometimes you're moved, sometimes you're only embarrassed. *This is a postmodern thing, right?* I could ask the same of you.) Because there's something in the blood, I think, eager to hold the other guy's coat, to present his card, to serve as second. That admires a blacksmith in the late 1980s but wouldn't necessarily care to be one. (*Didn't you used to be Charles Kuralt?*)

In the event, I am delighted to be at the Landers, thrilled in fact. And I can say *exactly* what it was like. It was like turning sixteen and getting your driver's license, receiving, I mean, the high privilege of doing what *real* people do. Because the guy is right, the grass *is* greener, and I wish I had Ross Winter's guts, or his dancers' bodies, or Ross Winter's guts *in* his dancers' bodies. Having it all on the low mean average. Not to fuss. Because *I* don't know how they do it. Hi-diddle-de-dee or no hi-diddle-de-dee, it can't be much of a picnic to have to live in America the Third World life.

To live it on a lark, of course, is a different story. Though it's odd, I'm thinking at the time, that I don't much care for backstage, that I find it oppressive, in fact. (David Kruger says the Landers's "stagehouse"—the term for the dressing rooms and work areas, everything not properly the auditorium—is badly in need of attention.) Indeed, the stagehouse is itself a sort of Third World, as cluttered and underdeveloped as a *favela*. Everywhere are cables, ladders, light trees, sets, wardrobe racks, sound equipment, props and gels and Styrofoam cups, all the detritus of fast-food lunch, all theatrical schmutz, all dramatical squalor.

But mine ain't the only game in town. The company will perform two different programs in Springfield—"Pretty Fooles and Peasantries," "Silver," "Hard Day," "Tango Freeze," "Continents," and "Lemurs" Friday; "Flashpoint," "Canon Studies," "Hidden Walls of Time," and "Joan Cohen" Saturday—and they're doing the techs, not run-throughs exactly so much as a fitful electronic blocking on the new stage, vetting the audio. The dancers, for all their flexibility, are hostage to equipment. If movies are, as they say, a director's medium, then movies are the exception, for all the other performing arts belong to the technicians.

Indeed, watching the rehearsals, one is reminded of the book on movie stars, all the rap about the downside of glamour. The cliché must be true about the poor dears bored in their trailers. It's like the army, or being on time for your doctor appointments, like hurry-up-and-wait enterprises everywhere. These folks are disciplined but, not like me out of harm's way on my chair on the stage—— where the easel once stood that identified an act in old vaudeville days. First, I can't make out Ross and David's soft conferences, David's mumbled relays to James in the booth. I don't even understand Ross's minimalist comments to his dancers, his remote-control ways, the data they seem to store about stages everywhere in their collective show-biz unconscious, a stage's invisible cuts and primes and vectors, all its unmarked markings paced off in their heads meticulously as the universal weights and measures of duelists' strides. Ross waves them over or calls them in. He moves them about like a manager adjusting his fielders.

It's *very* technical.

And, that night, it's the technical side that blows, the equipment that fails.

I'm seated beneath the overhang of the first balcony near the back of the house, in a good seat on a side aisle. I want to get a feel for the demographics. Which are sparsish, a scant sparsish of demographics. Better than a handful, oh *way* better, but hardly the "pretty good house tonight" that the house manager promised, driven, I think, by hi-diddle-de-dees of his own, as if—Kansas, Springfield, St. Louis: I'm an old hand by now—the body counts and reassurances were intended to dish the same calming hush-hush politics as government handouts in a war zone, say. Only kindly meant, servicing, stroking some perceived need for the old there-theres, palpable in performers as an open wound. Except I'm only crippled up, not blind. There are, oh, perhaps 150 summery souls in the demographics tonight. In a theater built to hold 1,000. Of these the vast majority are women. Plus, of course, a bun-head contingent of little girls and their younger brothers. A smattering (maybe) of the underwriters, patrons, benefactors, contributors, and sponsors of Springfield Ballet listed in the program. Most in frocks, the comfortable, neutral, down-home dowdy of people who have nothing to prove.

And they are appreciative, generous. On our side, they laugh in the right places, applaud with enthusiasm. Though they are so thinly spread out, I doubt if the dancers receive their message. I've noticed an audience's sound is tricky to hear onstage, as though acoustics were a one-way street, or the stage a transmitter, the house a receiver. Though the observation must be tempered. The dancers have told me they frequently speak to each other on stage, not pepper talk but flashing the clipped, distant early warning of contingency, guiding each other through the lifts and all the double- and triple-time of their close-order drill arrangements. Close to them as I am when we do "Joan Cohen," I've never heard them. So that's another thing—dead spots like the lead opaques of Superman's vision, all the willed limits of transmission, all reined-in, shut-lipped, back-of-the-throat pronouncements. For Performers' Ears Only's like the cleric's promptings and inaudibles to the bride and groom at a wedding.

But something's up—or down—with the sound system. MADCO's tapes are incompatible with the Landers's sound equipment. There'd been trouble at the technical, some missing-nail thing in the tape deck in a for-want-of-a-nail sequence, temporarily papered over by a run out to Radio Shack by somebody in one of the crews. (The Landers has a crew of its own.) Tonight, when the curtain rises and the lights come on, the bouncy, lusty music for "Pretty Fooles and Peasantries" is neither bouncy nor lusty. Indeed, it is scarcely heard. Certainly the dancers, who must take their cues and rhythm from it, have trouble hearing it. (What happened was this: The papered-over part tears. David, backstage, stage-managing, sends an SOS. James leaves his post at the light board and rushes to the second balcony, where their guy is running the sound equipment. James punches up the sound levels, amplifies the amplification. It's like Scotty giving the *Enterprise* warp speed by rubbing two sticks together. Afterward their guys will

say our guys had improperly plugged something or other into something
or other. It's a their guys/our guys thing, an honest-to-God territorial
dispute.)

After the intermission the sound is back where it should be, but it's
too late. The dancers are in a foul mood, David and James furious,
Ross depressed. Personally I don't see what's so terrible, and argue so.
They were pretty good despite, I tell them after the show. But there'll
be no hanging out tonight. Again.

I am dressed in my suit of lights—— my Brooks Brothers Golden
Fleece and special-ordered pants. And, give or take a row, pretty much
in the same seat I'd occupied the previous night. I'm not nervous so
much (though I'm nervous) as apprehensive, and not so much apprehensive as a wee gone with guilt. More than a wee. Why am I here?
I don't have Ross's mission. The Regional Arts Commission, Arts and
Education Council of Greater St. Louis, and Missouri and Illinois
arts councils don't fund *me* to build an audience for modern dance.
Build an audience? If I had my way, I'd disassemble what's here.

Though it's hardly SRO, or even the mythic "pretty good house"
of our comforter's reports and special pleading, it's up from last night.
Maybe 250. Many are little girls, even more than on Friday. More
homemakers, too. I'm thinking of what I heard two ladies say to each
other after MADCO's performance in Winfield: "Pretty neat, wasn't
it?" "Oh, I thought it was *real* good." This far south in Kansas, I
remember thinking, people sound as if they're from Oklahoma. It
could be, this grammar, this music, this language of placed persons,
the true, sweet, inflected neighborlies of Prairie itself.

Because I know what's coming after intermission.

Me. Yours truly's coming, the larky, city-slicker Jew with his love
rabbi and his love rabbi's blow-job conversations and his love rabbi's
death jive. Right here in walnut-bowl country, deep in the cavern
counties, hard by Orville & Betty's two-buck ham 'n' egg breakfasts.
In Passion Play territory. Only it's not like it sounds. I swear it isn't.
I'm *not* afraid of them. I'm not. I just don't want to upset anyone's
apple cart or ruffle the feathers. I would leave everyone's dander down
where I found it. I've no desire to build an audience, even my own.

Only it goes without a hitch. Technical *or* spiritual. The applause
is even more generous than last night. There are curtain calls. I get
roses.

• • •

It's Ross, ringing me in my room, can he come over.

He sits in one of those light, polypropylene, contoured shell chairs, universal as coat hangers. He's drinking a generic 1.75-liter bourbon with ginger ale. I'm dressed, sprawled on the bedspread. He drinks, I think, recalling "affairs," like a Jew.

"I thought show people," I tell him, "were supposed to be sentimental, ceremonial. Well, those awards shows, those Oscars and Tonys, that Lifetime Achievement crap. Well those curtain calls, well those roses." We're really talking about Darla, who drove off after the performance with her parents and boyfriend and scarcely a word to anyone. "I'd expected a scene, *counted* on a scene. At least toasts, at least hugs and handshakes and the we'll-meet-agains people taking their leave owe each other out of respect for endings, rites of passage. My turnout ain't any better than Darla's."

"Well," says Ross, "maybe not everyone can throw herself on the mercy of the court with your abandon."

Ross is in a mood. Not a *bad* mood. Actually he's rather pleased with how things turned out. Especially after last night's performance. He blames the dancers. "They should have gone to their battle stations."

We're gossiping, getting down. I have to be careful what I ask him. He won't duck a question. He tells me what he makes, he gives the reasons he broke up with his wife.

"Do you ever think of leaving St. Louis?"

"I think of changing my life. I don't mind about the money. You can decorate an apartment quite nicely with what people throw away. I would have taken that floor lamp. I didn't because it was ugly. Some street people have no taste at all."

And ah, I'm thinking, ah, the young 'uns out on the town, me and Ross waiting up for them, bandying our eleventh-hour truck-farm confessions and plans, talking all the high and dry, buddy-stranded locutions of lull.

"Well," Ross said, "I don't socialize with them anyway. They're my tribal family, I'm their elder. It's nothing personal. I guess Liz was teacher's pet. If I had one. By dint of long tenure, her right-hand-man manners. *Droit de* right-handedness."

"I have to laugh," I say. "You know what they said at the reception? 'Springfield needed to hear that.' *Jesus!* Want some gum? I chew lots of gum since I quit smoking."

"I don't chew gum. In Australia, during my formative gum-chewing years, it was rationed. Now it's too frustrating. I feel I should be able to break it down and eat it."

"I understand. I really do."

If the place had room service I'd have sent out long ago. There's nothing to nosh but gum, but we're all over the board. We could be in Cincinnati, I'm thinking.

"Liz used to be a mouse," Ross says. "She used to dance with her body screaming 'Don't look.' And it hasn't quite clicked with Ellen yet that she's there solely for the pleasure of the audience. She's too shy with her talents. She has to learn to throw them out into the house. An audience wants to be flashed."

Paul's too intense, Ross says. He's very smart but too intense. In a mood, Ross doodles his dancers. Of the women, Raeleen's the strongest. Jeff has the best stretch and turnout, the most extension. Michael is a teddy bear and could be a wonderful dancer. He watches too much TV.

"Too much TV?"

"Turnout, extension, strength, and stretch are important. Mind is a dancer's most important instrument."

Liz, James, Jeffrey, and David are at the door.

"Come in," I say, flattered, "come in. Come in."

"Is Ross around?"

"Come in."

Jeffrey, subdued, is already anxious to leave. After Friday's performance he went for a walk. He'd been thinking about his career. He didn't get back to the motel until 2:00 A.M. He was pretty tired, he said. He thought he'd better get going.

Ross is using my bathroom. Liz says, "He has to know."

"Tonight? Come on," David says, "tonight was terrific. Don't bother him tonight."

"He should know. I don't care, he should. David, James, I'm going to tell him."

"Jeffrey should tell him."

"He just told *us.*" When Ross comes back Liz says, "Ross, that Saturday Jeffrey missed rehearsal? When he said he'd made plans? He was in Chicago auditioning with Shirley Mordine's company."

Ross didn't say anything for a while. I know that's what they all say, that they don't say anything for a while. Or that they blanch, go white as the unimpeachable testimony of Darla's clown-white pain, but that's what happened. Maybe there's a muse of the autonomic physiologicals for bad news, or when you've been let down, badly disappointed, some Muse of the Involuntary Facials, and a muse working, too, when he recovers, finally speaks. The Muse of At a Loss, Vamp 'til Ready.

"If he'd asked I'd have let him. I would. It's helpful for a young dancer to audition, to get someone else's opinion of what he does wrong. I'd have let him."

"Did he get the job?" I ask.

"He says he has a good feeling," Liz says.

"You know Jeffrey," David says, "he has a good feeling if the ketchup on his hamburger isn't green."

"I'm dissolving the company."

"Ross, you're upset." Liz is stroking his arm, giving out comfort like first aid.

"Darla's gone. Liz is moving with James to Arizona. Now Jeffrey? I'm dissolving MADCO. It's my company, I can do what I please."

"And put the others out of work?"

"Sleep on it, Ross," James advises. "You're upset. Don't make rash decisions when you're upset."

"I'm a grown man. I'll make rash decisions when I please. More than just wedding bells are breaking up that old gang of mine," he tells him. "I'll tell them tomorrow."

But he doesn't. The Muse of Second Thoughts.

When Ross sent Jeffrey's check he thanked him for his patience but told him he was not being asked back for next season due to his lack of professionalism and commitment to the company. The women have been replaced, but until he can find a replacement for Jeffrey, they'll be dancing with two men, not three; six dancers, not seven. They book programs in advance. "Continents" may have to be dropped from the repertoire, though Paul thinks that with a quick costume change either he or Michael ought to be able to double up on one of the parts. "Hidden Walls of Time" and "Pretty Fooles and Peasantries" are definitely out, as is, of course, "Notes Toward a Eulogy for Joan Cohen."

The Irony Muse that plucks my gig and leaves this crippled-up old soul hi-diddle-de-deeless. Until, at least, Life breathes on my life again, the all-embracing Muse of Lark and Unexpected Compensations.

AN AMERICAN
IN
CALIFORNIA

I

To pass carte blanche into the heart of the clichés, that's the proposal, power dining, power this and power that, spooning like meat from a melon the key to all mythologies, translating California to my foreign tongue. It's my idea to see the high points, in the footsteps of tourists following, in the shade of the points of interest, by all myth's scenic overviews, in California's busy surf, all the PR of a tanned and chosen people; to the Proposition State come, the invented land. I'm this pilgrim from the folks, this now voyager, who would tour fantasy itself—sit where the deals are made, next year's history now; smell the stars close up; do tea with Ann Getty; come to see the fashions like wonders of the world—who will go home not empty-handed or bro-kenhearted but with his notions tampered.

I'm, as I say, the consultant, this self-proclaimed geography guru, volunteering to explain California like some miracle rabbi the meaning of life in a joke. My agenda shining on me, bringing it in from the deep Midwest, middle America in general, St. Louis in particular, coughing it up out of the Central Standard Time zone, dealing in mean-average meanings—— in *all* the central standards; in the middle of the road; rock solid; steeped in clichés—the changes of seasons, the traditional values—as in a kind of tea. And more power to me because I am damaged—this is not incidental—this like holy cripple, this heart-bypassed, foot-braced, chip-toothed, balding old gent, morning-breath'd all hours of the day and night, a lowardly mobile, body-imaged chap whose opinions are all the more precious to him because if suffering teaches you anything, it teaches you to take yourself seri-ously. And what I'm seriously thinking, I allow to Andy—the writer from the magazine come to pick me up—is that the cool, canned voice giving crowd-control over the LAX P.A. is precisely that of a nurse in a hospital calling out in the most pleasant, neutral tones for all the docs in the world to come running, make a note, Andy. Of-ficious, I'm officious. Because I make allowances and give myself leeway and professional courtesies like a golfer playing through. Make a note, make a *note!* Because the meter is running and I'm developing a theory—— that the state is laid-back because that's only fitting in a place where the sun is the state bird. Though in the strictest sense, of course—ain't it some electronics musician in Oakland who's working on a kinder, gentler siren to stick on fire engines, ambulances, and police cars for emergencies?—it could be laid-back because it's com-mitted to some principle of not spooking the horses. On the other hand, I confide to Andy—I've lots of theories, up to my toneless old ass in them—it may not be laid-back at all, finally. All those cars in all that traffic could indicate how the Puritan ethic lives on out here in the high-tech mode, that folks are so righteous and *un*laid-back, there's probably room in their lives only for drive time, office time, and quality time with the kids (which might explain—you think?—the presence of so many expensive, upscale automobiles I see out the window, how if Californians spend so much time in and money on their cars, well, it's not for the show of it at all, probably, not prestige so much as creature comfort, the holistics of horsepower, really, the leather-option package a sort of prosthesis, more essential to health, finally, than to grooming). Oh, sure, I revise, it's to stay fresh for the office, fresh for the day, fresh for the return trip to the family. Why, come to think, California must be the quality-time capital of the world—— the dads out-daddying and moms out-mommying, leading

the nation, beating the band, spotting the rest of the country a one-
to three-hour time differential and sending it messages anyway of all
the what-will-be's. Hey, Andrew?

Search me.

Rife with theories, a theory-*shtupped* middle-American cripple——
that the palm tree is the basic building block of the California style,
that it *is* the California style inasmuch as Western Civilization is
essentially a *wooden* civilization, and that palms are not wood but some
goofy subspecies (if not a different genre altogether), and where wood
doesn't obtain, *fuel* doesn't obtain, carpentry and architecture, all the
familiar, conventional as-we-know-thems, throwing up in lieu thereof
some sprawled geometry, low on the horizon and various as signature,
loose as anarchy. That palm trees—consider their bearded, soily
crowns, their long, long leaves—are only this sort of exposed, visible
root system, essentially comic, topsy-turvying nature and encouraging,
for culture, the bright, colorful calypso equivalents, authorizing (where
nothing seems authorized, properly zoned) calypso-facto, some suitless, coatless, tieless world, oddly, in the matter of dress code at least,
a *child's* world, this, well, un-Europe. (Think of California's brick-
lessness and stonelessness, its stilted beach houses like a kind of car
park for architectural Hovercraft.)

So many theories. Because everyone *thinks* about California. It's
almost a subject, like abortion or the deficit. (Once, years back, I was
offered a job at UC Santa Barbara and came out for the summer to
see what it would feel like. I turned the job down, finally, because I
didn't know what I would do for conversation, the only talk, even
decent talk, being about California itself, who was a native—sabras,
I think they're called—and when the rest of us came over. It could
almost have been shop talk.) It would be my subject here.

Only—I told you it wasn't incidental—I'm disabled, and, after
sizing up the bathroom situation and thinking over the long, restless
night about what has to be the California innkeepers' image of their
fit and fettled clientele, after worrying all the tub's footholds and hand-
holds, and contemplating, serious as a mountain climber, the alternative routes and faces of his ordeal, or a jeweler where best to strike
a diamond, I fell out of the shower. Tumbling the towels, tearing the
rack that held them out of the wall, flailing, absurd, my pale Missouri
body falling from grace—only no one falls from grace so much as
from its absence—recovering, almost calm, observant and objective

as someone in a near-death experience, shooting a palm to the top of the toilet tank to break my fall, to save my life.

David Milch, the TV-mogul horse player, would tell me later that my thirst, desiccative, monumental as drought, meant I was "diuressing," only a sort of dangerous stress— that I mustn't worry, and to keep my nitroglycerin dry. It could be. His father before him was a doc. Mine, before me, was a patient. *Something* was going on. Here, at the end of the road to Manifest Destiny, I'd become a sort of dust bowl, as if I'd swallowed an Okie, say.

I'm on the phone to Judy Zwicker, my chairman's wife, a sabra returned to L.A. on a visit, filling her in, panicked handouts from my front, the casualty figures, this witness to dark acts, unable to organize, to shade, stipulating my condition in pure diuressed Cottonmouth like a language even its speaker doesn't understand; and fixing assignments, what she should do—should the queered gown of my clumsied muscle come down to it—with my body. In a rage now of indiscriminate explanation, half dressed, here a shoe, there a shirt, pocket paraphernalia—wallet and handkerchief, room key, change, and gum, useful numbers and addresses—scattered about (because I've forgotten my cripple's own credo— that you never do anything twice), dragging her willy-nilly into my life and laying dark charges like some guy eliciting promises on a deathbed. Because sabra or no, Judy's in town from Missouri, too. She's seen the seasons operate, watched leaves drop off actual wooden trees. She is, here in L.A., my connection to earth, a talisman from reality and the middle distances. Desperately, I'm trying to explain about the upper reaches of my tuxedo shirt.

In crisis and farce, everything happens at once. My mogul, Milch, whom I've arranged to meet for breakfast, is at the door. ("Think when I'm out there," I'd airily told management from my lower ZIP code, "I'd like to sit in on a power breakfast, fly-on-the-wall sort of thing. Oh, and I've another idea for the piece. I go into this boutique on Rodeo Drive, pick something out, anything, doesn't make any difference. A tie, a shirt, whatever. I ask what it costs. Guy says, 'That tie, gouache on Canadian silk, will run you $245.' I make a counteroffer of eleven bucks. He throws me out. I say, 'It's a waste of time trying to bargain with these people, the natives won't dicker.' If he comes down, I tell the reader not to pay the asking price, you can do better." Only no one wants me at their power breakfast, of course. This one, fly-on-the-wall sort of thing, I've had to arrange on my own.)

Dave Milch and I go back. I knew him when.

Except for his mogul-in-Hollywood's big, oversize clothes, his wide, vaguely Dutch-boy pants, he looks about the same. Clearly he's easy as ever. David is this Look-Ma-I'm-an-Egalitarian kind of guy, the sort of fellow who makes a point of not closing the door when he does number one, drilling his pee into the toilet bowl like a laser. A forceful hugger of men. You know the type. Anyway *I* do. Built as I am, shaped to condescension, practically asking for it in every gee-whizzed-out fiber of my being. This pardoned, made-allowance-for, governor-reprieved clemency monger catching all the waves of mercy like a surfer. That's *how* we go back, I expect. Because, like most poor relations, I'm a good listener. You could eat my awe off me. And here I am, small in the doorway, rocked in his arms. He couldn't have asked for better. When I saw him fourteen years before at Yale, I wasn't even limping yet, the M.S. still only up into my posture, slanting me forward as if I were trying to stand in place before a stiff wind. Now he takes in the cane, the brace, my orthopedic shoes. I fill him in on all my humpty-dumpties, as I'd filled Judy in when it was her turn in my confessional. He checks out the bathroom, my unrigged tile.

"Shmuck," he says, "there's no grab bars in there. What were you trying to do, shower above your station? You need a different room. I'll make the arrangements."

Now my memory is, I'd *made* the arrangements, but in the event I let David make them again, make them better. He'd see the guy at the front desk, he said, lay a few bucks on him, get me the grab bars I deserved. (*Hotel lessons*, in the time I was an American in California, everyone was to give me hotel lessons. Taxicab, waiter-and-wheelchair lessons, all the tipping clarifications, the Higher Honoraria. Two weeks later, B.K., the editor who helped me with my curbside check-in at the San Francisco airport the day I left, handed me, for reasons that are still unclear, I don't know, a ten-spot, six or seven dollars more in loose bills. Earlier I had given her five dollars, I think to tip someone or other when she checked me out of the hotel. Perhaps this is what you get for your *finif* upon the waters out here. In any event, I handed the money, the sixteen or seventeen bucks, over to the ancient Asian skycaptress who pushed me in my chair to the gate. B.K., possibly because she didn't see me giving money away, excused herself and ran after her and, how do you say, what was my surprise, when I saw her stuff still more loose bills into the old lady's wrinkled palm. *"Don't you know,"* I demanded, *"that the going rate for cripples in airports these days is three dollars? Tops?"* These, I believe, were our only harsh words during my ten days in the Gratuity State.)

Over breakfast, Milch fills me in on life in the fast lane. "Shmuck," he tells me, "I'm married to a beautiful lady, I have a beautiful kid, I own a string of twenty horses." He explains claiming races, he explains how the TV writer's place in the Hollywood hierarchy is greater than the screenwriter's, he explains about the Golan brothers, he explains, three months before the fact, why Milken, the junk-bond king, will be arrested. I don't understand anything he's talking about, nothing, not claiming races, not anything. He will take me, he says, to Santa Anita, what do I have on for the day after tomorrow. Gee, I can't, I tell him, the day after tomorrow's "The Newlywed Game." (Another theory—— that if California is to be understood, it must be understood through its game shows, that that's where the *echt* California types live, on the game shows. Milch has no idea what I'm talking about.)

He picks up the check in the restaurant, leaves the tip for the waitress, tips the bellman who has transferred my clothes and effects (because I'm still diuressing; because I still think I'm going to die), and even runs back to the room I'd abandoned for a few California theory notes I'd left on the nightstand. Earlier I'd explained why I'm so worried. It's what I'd been trying to tell Judy when David showed up. Joan prebuttons my shirts before I put them on. She buttons the cuffs, everything except the collar button and the button beneath that one so I may slip the shirt on over my head in the morning, as you'd slip on a T-shirt, as you'd pull on a sweater. Except for the top stud, except for the collar button, Joan had fixed my studs for the Reagan dinner before I even left St. Louis, loading them into the tuxedo shirt like bullets in a cartridge belt. It stymies me still, how these are to be managed, even, though it isn't the kind you tie yourself, the bow tie that has to be fastened about my neck. Who will help me with this? (It's a kind, though for me it hasn't quite come to this yet, of incontinence really, this being crippled, a second infancy, such dependence. One must respect one's parameters, learn, like some athlete of the odd, the daredevil, say, who must work out to a fraction of the inch the clearance of his stunt, the customized turf of one's limitations. It's very brave of me being an American in California, or would be if I weren't so terrified.)

I didn't ask him. It could be grandstanding. Self's old hat trick, but

Milch volunteers to send one of his production assistants over to the hotel to work my shirt for me that evening. Or earlier. Right now, if it will make me any easier. I'm in a suite. She could stay in the living room, or outside, posted in the hall, downstairs in the lobby.

"My," I say, "a production assistant. What a production."

Milch, his hand on one of the suite's three phones, affable and easy in California's balmy gravity as a body comfortable in water, is waiting to dial.

"You call it."

"Well," I tell him, grateful, bamboozled, but not entirely comfortable to be one of his strays, "I do *need* help with the shirt."

And that was the morning of the second day. The afternoon of the second day, I'm in a taxi on the way to lunch. It won't be the last time I notice that cab drivers here seem nervous about their bearings and destinations. Maybe it's the lack of good public transportation, that there aren't enough buses to follow, or the absence, once one leaves the beaten paths, of landmarks, but a hack in the Los Angeles area—and this might be a clue, that L.A. is an area, not a place: that there's plenty of there there, just not enough here—seems to want the passenger drawn into his thinking, as if, by offering options, by making him a co-conspirator, he's preparing a kind of deniability, some break-bread sharing of responsibility for getting the both of them lost. But I didn't tell him to go into his profession. I'm a stranger here myself, still worried about what tomorrow's shower may bring, still diuressing for that matter, and contemplating, Milch or no Milch, that final stud, all the ways there must be to live and die in L.A. I no longer care to hear the driver's anxious opera about where such a restaurant at such an address on Santa Monica Boulevard could be. *My God,* I'm thinking, *I'm only an American in California, and even* I've *heard of Santa Monica Boulevard.* Anyway, I'm a little ticked they've chosen—the editors from the magazine—a venue so far from my hotel. Because I'm suspicious by nature, not so much tight as this strict accountant of my outlay in life, generous enough with my own, more than, to a fault in fact, a soft touch, mushy in fact, and with others willing, even anxious (lest, God forbid, someone have a bad opinion of me, think me cheap—or what would that largesse in the San Francisco airport be all about?) to pay my fair share, but a stickler; not so much tight as *up*tight—and this isn't incidental, either—worrying the tip, the receipt, desperate to keep expenses down because I'm wondering if I should quit, resign, pack it in, tell them hello, how are ya, glad to meetcha, and turn around and catch the first cab out, back to the hotel, then back to the airport, then back to America. I'm of two minds. Then, before I know it, the cab pulls to the curb, and Andy, who doesn't even ask for a receipt, is pushing a twenty-dollar bill through the window and into the driver's hands.

Then, because I'm gone mad now, certifiably insane, furious inside my unquenchable thirst, out of my element, or no, probably in it, actually, as at home in my rage as if it were a levee, some salon I host, inside the restaurant, which looks like a hangar, I tell them how it stands with me, or tell B.K., rather, my contact in the Production Assistant State, though I haven't met her until this minute, and am still resigning as we are shown to a table.

"My blood," I tell her, "is on your hands."

The others, embarrassed, examine their menus, while someone, maybe Bob, maybe Andy, recommends the chicken sandwich.

"Sure," I say, "I'll have that. The chicken sandwich. It better be good."

"It was written up."

And somehow it's decided that after lunch B.K. will call Joan, that they'll bring in Joan, that Joan will come thousands of miles to guide me in and out of bathtubs and the story will be saved, though both of us know that if Joan comes it's to lift the blood curse from B.K.'s mitts, and only *I* know that she won't come, that Joan didn't tell me to go into my profession, just as I didn't tell the cabbie to go into his. And this is what happens, too. And I, of the two minds, of at *least* two minds, *always* of at least two minds, because every choice cuts off every other choice and the only real choice is both to have Joan come and bring me safely through California's difficult showers and toilet arrangements and to keep her down in St. Louis and hold my options open because here I ain't been in California quite twenty-four hours yet and I've already got a production assistant to do a wish on my collar button for me.

So I'm calming down, and B.K., mistress of ceremonies here, and a veteran, I suspect (because she has this tendency to speak glowingly of everyone, assuming, like the more fortunate everywhere, that, by and large, everyone now living, assuming you could only find a table big enough to accommodate them, would make companionable guests at a dinner party, and because, too, no one's called "B.K." unless she's born with a silver service for eighty-two in her mouth), of far more complicated arrangements than any I could ever possibly provoke, is going over the itinerary, scratching out a scheduled two or three days in Santa Barbara and extending my stay in Los Angeles, revoking (sizing me up or, more probably, down) an outing to a Lakers game with Bob, and penciling in, Jesus, I don't know, bedrest. We still have no official word on whether Shelby Coffey III, the new editor of the *Los Angeles Times*, will be escorting me to the Reagans' Welcome Home do at the Beverly Hilton that night, but if not Shelby Coffey, Andy. In any event, it's the beginning, as I'm passed off from hand to hand, of my bucket-brigade life.

It looks, I swear to you, like a giant bar mitzvah! A bar mitzvah with secret service, G-men in tuxes. A bar mitzvah with movie stars passing through metal detectors. (Andy wants to know how Mr. T. will ever make it through that thing. It's a good question, but this is a hotel in Los Angeles, Bobby Kennedy country, and somehow—I spot a *federale*, circumspectly hiding his gun hand under his tuxedo jacket, half a foot or so down the back of his pants—I've never so forcefully been made to feel the lack of due process before.)

A bar mitzvah—but I don't know, I don't get out much anymore— with all the latest wrinkles. (I speak of the long haul, of the march of affluence. Once it was enough, like jacks and oranges in a Christmas stocking, rubber balls, packages of chewing gum, if you gave the guests coffee, if you let them eat cake. Then—this is history, you could look it up—things got elaborate. Menus became more impressive, invitations. There was a place, right there on the R.S.V.P. you sent back in the mail, where you could mark off your choice, fish or fowl, and you thought, *This is it, these are the last days*; we have come, that is, deep into the moving parts of modern times, what will they think of next.) This is such an affair—— what they thought of next, *all* the latest wrinkles.

There's the press in the lobby, clusters of celebrity, white, under the media's lights, as platinum. Everywhere I look there are minicams. (I'm willing to bet some are government issue, only History locking the barn door, getting its bearings.) When one focuses in on me— everybody plays, no losers here, a prize in every box—I am cool, cooler than the stars, cooler than Heston, cooler than Ed McMahon. *My* version. To stand up straight, to try to draw myself within at least

five or six inches of my former six feet. To scrape all expression from
my face, like an art restorer removing pigeon shit from statues. But
it's an effort. At the champagne reception, I have to sit down or die.
Andy organizes a chair and sets it next to a row of only four or five
other chairs in the entire room. For other old-timers, looks like, folks
like me, up past their bedtimes. I plop down next to this robust old
bird. He extends a hand.

"Hal Roach," he says, "Ninety-seven."

"Stanley Elkin," I tell him, "Fifty-eight."

Two immense screens flank the front of the Beverly Hilton's big
ballroom. There are gifts at each place setting, medallions of the
Reagans, bronzed bas-reliefs, peculiarly flattering or unflattering, aging
them or taking years off, changing in accord with the angle at which
you hold them, like the little holograph on a Visa card.

Already I've grown accustomed to my gifted, chipped-in-for luxury,
miffed that our table (at $25,000 per), a charity table, miles below the
salt, almost closer to the kitchen than the ballroom, is so oblique to
the action. Though, oddly, so uppity I've become, it's exactly the table
I'd have put me at if I were in charge of the seating arrangements.
Whoever is has perfect social pitch. (At our table is a woman who was
on the organizing committee for Ronald Reagan's first Inaugural Ball,
her husband, an undersecretary of the Treasury in the days of Donald
Regan; a couple from Santa Barbara. When we introduce ourselves,
the lady from Santa Barbara stunningly inquires, "Do you teach at
Washington University?" "Why yes," I reply, all smiles. "Then you
must know Howard Nemerov," she says. "He was my professor at
Bennington." "Uh-huh." "Darling," she tells her husband, "this is
Stanley Elkin. He teaches at the same university as Howard Nemerov."
"You're kidding." Something like this will happen to me often out
here. But the real point is this sort of flat-out, bungled *schmeikling*.
In Berkeley, at the Saul Zaentz studio, a young man, a writer/director
getting his first film ready for a screening for distributors in Utah, has
hired the hall so technicians may do the complicated transference of
sound from 16mm to 35mm. When he hears my name, and that I'm
from *California* magazine, he's all over me. I have witnesses. "You're
him? You're Stanley Elkin?" "Why, yes," I modest. "Gee," he says,
"do you know what a pleasure this is for me? Have you any *idea?* Do
you know who this *is?*" he asks his producer. Handshakes all 'round,
then back to the tedious process of looping. Fun's fun, and Emily,

my *schlepper* in northern California, and I watch for a while without much understanding what's going on, but we *do* have another appointment. I convey this to the young man, who's downright disappointed to hear it. But resigned. "Say," he says when I get up, "before you go, can you tell me the names of some of the books you've written?") Only if we're to see the entertainment—Sinatra's down on the program for some songs—we shall have to watch it—I can just see the band if I put my head in my plate and look past the Republicans when they lean into one another to catch something they've missed in the din—on the huge screens. It's a huge screen I'm watching— people are still filing in—when it starts to register images of big shots I've seen in the lobby. Shelley Duvall, Mary Martin, Zsa Zsa, Merv Griffin, the Collins girls (Jackie and Joan), Betsy Bloomingdale, Charles Bronson, Cesar Romero, Gary Coleman. Where are they now? Nowhere near *my* table! (I'm like someone bumped up to first class in an airplane. How you gonna keep 'em down in coach after they've seen Paree?) The table behind ours, which *is* next to the kitchen, the Inaugural Ball lady informs, is occupied by Secret Service.

"Really?"

"Well, sure," she says. "To block the exits if, *you* know."

"Look," Andy nudges. "Up there on the screen."

It's me, big as life, bigger, eight-foot-nine, -ten; cool as I could have hoped, cooler, a dignified gimp in a tux, so devoid of expression my face is absolutely cruel, me, the sweetheart of Sigma Chi. And it's on my image, held up there so long it could be the fix is in, like, oh, the surprise birthday cake you've had baked for your kid and served up in the restaurant and the waiters all sing "Happy Birthday," that the screens finally go to black, the lights come down, and a color guard brings the flag by. They Hail to the Chief, who I'm sure is saluting, or would be sure if I could actually see him.

This will give you some idea. It's the first sentence from the "Certificate of Authenticity" in the jewelry box with our medallions:

"They came like the fresh breath of a California wind at a time our nation needed them most."

It's the rhetoric of myth, the rhetoric of epic. It's the language of coming attraction. It's the copy in block, three-dimensional lettering, on a poster in a glass case outside a movie.

The buzz in the room is that Sinatra has canceled, that he sulks in Palm Springs. He's mad, the buzz is, at the president, or the Republican Party, possibly at the republic itself. The rumors are received, digested, grudgingly accepted by the tribe, but it's too bad. I'm just a guest here, it ain't my place, but seeing Sinatra in his native element would have been a feather in this American in California's cap. (Finally, it turns out, more things won't happen to me in California than will. Danielle Steel won't give a party in San Francisco, and I won't be invited to it; Ann Getty won't be having me over; George Lucas won't come through in time with an invitation to Skywalker Ranch. I will, on my own hook, skip a wine tasting at Yosemite. There's to be a gala in honor of renaming Fred Hayman's of Giorgio's store, the debut of his new fragrance. The boys and girls from Chasen's, La Scala, Jimmy's, the Bistro and the Bistro Garden, Spago, and the Grill are down on the invitation as "Dinner Present[ers]." It's not to my taste. I will decline. Likewise, I won't be signing up at the Center for the Investigation & Training of Intuition's seminar on Enneagram Studies.) So I sit back to enjoy the show on those humongous screens.

It *is* a show. I do enjoy it, some of it. Merv Griffin's anecdote about the first time he was invited to the White House. How can anyone, I'm trying to figure, the owner of this very hotel, and something, I hear, of a billionaire, still pack such boyish, open-eyed astonishment and prodigious, drawn-breath wonder, all those magical pinch-me's-I'm dreaming's? Except for Don Rickles's predictable, if remarkably fitting, routine (because suddenly it ain't the International Ballroom of the Beverly Hilton anymore; it's not even this century; we're all of us at, oh, court, say, in Shakespearean tragedy, and Reagan isn't just the president, he's the *king*, and Rickles isn't a comic, he's his court jester, and it's very scary, really, and I'm wondering if perhaps there shouldn't be a Constitutional amendment somewhere about the separation of State and Show Biz— no more commercially sponsored Bob Hope Christmas specials from the decks of aircraft carriers, no more Army and Navy troubadours; more bread, fewer circuses), it's a good show, I'm enjoying myself, but the thought recurs even during the program's most fantastic, dazzling moment.

Because Sinatra's a no-show—nursing a severe cold, protecting his voice for a long projected tour, and saddened, according to Merv Griffin, insult-to-injurywise, because he can't be with us tonight— Mary Martin is run in as a last-minute substitute. Well, all right, I'd never seen Miss Martin, and one legend in its own time is about as good as another. Mary Martin does her stuff, then talks Nancy Reagan up from the president's table to join her. I'm certain it's spontaneous, but who knows from show people? It seems they'd worked together in the 1946 Broadway musical *Lute Song*, and Mary convinces Nancy— it's all right to use first names if you're a citizen in a public-domain sort of country like ours—to join her in singing "Mountain High, Valley Low." Well, the highs ain't as high, and the lows ain't quite as low, and Nancy can't quite remember all the words, but, like good sports everywhere—my *God*, how we're suckers for a good sport!— they bring down the house. They bring down *my* house, too. Until I remember Mr. Rickles and the blurring of State and Show Biz. *Christ*, I'm thinking, *probably they* do *put their pants on one leg at a time! And these are folks we trust with the bomb?* And I think to myself, then amaze to Andy, how the United States has surely got to be the most remarkable country in the whole damn world, that you couldn't imagine it, that you could never make it up, that you'd almost have to live in it to believe it!

When it comes down to doing my haggle on Rodeo Drive, I don't have the guts, of course. Michelle drives around the block a couple of times, even pulls up along one or two of the shops. We discuss what sort of thing I can say I'm looking for, but, as I'd told management, it doesn't make any difference, a rag, a bone, a hank of hair. I don't have the stomach to play the fool anyway. So we go on.

Michelle has me today. Michelle does the restaurant column for the magazine, reviews restaurants in the valley for the *Times*. Frankly, I don't understand that kind of writing. Me, I'm a gossip. I love a lowdown, insider-trader information. And though people sometimes deign to gossip with me, they don't like to violate the other guy's confidence. This drives me nuts. Because it takes the juices out, freeze-dries the scuttlebutt and the tittle-tattle, and always raises to a level of pure theory and platonic proposal what might have been more interesting with names and dates. Gossip with some people is just, well, *scholarship*. My friends know my secrets. I have their opinions. With me it's always personal. The personal is what it *ought* to come down to, a way of dealing with relationship, as if it were— well, as if it were death, reminiscence and eulogy just a polite way of talking about people behind their backs. Which is why, I try to explain, I won't read a restaurant review unless I've not only been to the same restaurant as the reviewer but practically ordered the same meal.

But I see I'm going to get along fine with Michelle. Like me, she'll talk about herself. And she's a gutsy driver. We're touring Los Angeles by car. We drive by the Reagans's home on Saint Cloud Road in Bel-Air to study their fence—you can't see much of the house—all their electronic bristle and doodad, while a vaguely generic utility truck I recognize from stake-out movies studies us, and—who knows?—maybe transcribes what we're saying even as we say it.

We see more of the sights. Château Marmont, where John Belushi went up in smoke. The freeways where, I'm told, rush hour can sometimes go on for an eight-hour day and Californians, to-ing and fro-ing, play out their slot-car lives. Me and the restaurant reviewer dine where the chef is John Sweeney, who killed John Gregory Dunne's niece, Dominique, and got three years for his trouble. (A chef pal of Michelle's, who never murdered anyone, wonders why his career's on hold and he's still just a caterer.)

Weatherwise, sunwise, it ain't much of a day. Indeed, it's almost blustery, some late-fall day back home again in Indiana, say, the kind of day that, if I were actually resident here instead of merely this Marco Polo sort of American in California, I'd find excuses for, a way to write off, like someone parsing his tax deductions. Michelle (a sabra herself, who still lives, I take it, in the same neighborhood in Pasadena where she grew up) has seen Rose Bowl parades, all southern California's higher meteorology, known that perfectly climateless condition where there's no real difference between outdoors and in, and doesn't even mention it, let alone try to apologize for it.

Melrose, touted as the new place to shop, is a little disappointing. I want to see bizarre, outlandish fashions, outrageous prices, stuff no one in their right minds. . . . But Ecru, the one place we actually stop, seems almost reasonable to me, its clothes and prices of a piece with clothes and prices I remember back in the States.

And maybe it's the American weather, the gray average of this ordinary day, but *all* California seems strangely familiar today. Of course it's *always* familiar, but always before familiar in some déjà vu sense, like prepared nerves, old synapses like track laid down in the nervous system. This is different, and much stranger, I think. Different, I mean, in the sense that this isn't any message California has consciously sent. I've a feeling I'm being let in on something, that there's something quite extraordinary about the ordinary out here. This evening I will watch local television news and see officials in overcoats.

When they pronounce into microphones, I will see their breaths. (And no one is in the streets! Michelle points it out, but I've noticed this before. They're not in the streets, they can't *all* be in their cars; and from the look of the houses, they don't even seem to be at home. Perhaps they're like frogmen in the navy, or submariners, say, sent off to decompression chambers for bends avoidance; maybe *that's* where they hang out, in mysterious closets and pockets and bottlenecks, all the hidden arrondissements of space.) Some of the buildings in downtown Los Angeles are equally familiar and look as if they may have been made from actual rock rather than petroleum byproduct, steel, concrete, or glass. City Hall, for example, like some twenties' *Brigadoon*. Union Station, the Ambassador Hotel, the shadow, it could be, of L.A.'s old Art Deco days with its shoulder-padded, fedoraed, double-breasted Art Deco men and women. Echo Park is as east as I get to East Los Angeles and the gangs. But I see Little Tokyo. I see Chinatown. I see boat people and understand that what's going on here is sure to change the country at least as much as it was changed during the great waves of immigration of the last century, the first couple of decades of this one. Then, before swinging across Mulholland Drive in fog, low clouds, and rain, we do a pit stop at Philippe's, this sawdust-on-the-floor, working-class restaurant, and eat the same French-dip roast-beef sandwich served up, I swear it, on the same bread as in a place—Garavelli's—I used to go in St. Louis. It's pure, sweet, Proustian madeleine, this roast beef, this bread. This day. This weather. This chill. No wonder I'm feeling nostalgic. (And, too, sawdust is a wood product, don't forget.)

On a day so absolutely sharp and clear it might almost be off an engraving, Ed (from the magazine) calls to tell me he has the loan of Sharon's BMW, that it would be a swell day to go to the beach.

He means drive by the beach, of course. He means swing by the hotel and pick me up. He means, without saying as much, no heavy lifting, only what the mind and eyes and heart can take away with one. Well, I'm game, a game-legged old guy trapped in this trick body like someone strapped to a myth. Even before even. Like most. Come down damaged with the cat-got-your-tongue, with whatever, not modest, probably not even shy, just maybe only somebody for whom courage was always pretty much a nonstarter. Ladywise, I'm speaking. Who never had the courage not only of his convictions but of his secret tastes. Who doesn't have them now. As harmless as a dirty old man as ever I'd been as a young one. Because California's supposed to be the capital of this sort of thing, it's honeypot Mecca, I've my eye out for high-impact aerobicizers, champs, surf queens, blondes from Ipanema, girls who do their bodies the way, in my day, they worried over their nails—tan, pumped-up types who know holds to break your holds and can do the fireman's carry.

But it's the same story. Nobody's home in Los Angeles. They're not in the streets, they're not in the sea, they're not on the sand. Venice, except for the builders and rehabbers, seems deserted, Muscle Beach abandoned. Still, as it happens, it's never too late to be impressed. You'd be surprised with all, in the right mood, you can take in, even from a sickbed, or from a passenger seat either, how sheer damn breathless beauty can leave you, breaking your hold and doing fireman's carries of its own, lifting you above your expectations. Like this lovely city with its toy canals. Anyone can call anything anything, of course. Easy enough to come up with names like Appian Way or the Via Dolorosa, and there's certainly plenty of contrivance with the place names here, but even Eden had a naming day, that old heroic festival of roll call and nomenclature. There's a sweetness, however corny, to the local monikers, a touch of the poet, must have been, in those old developers and founders.

We're driving back to meet Andy for "The Newlywed Game," and, though it's chilly, the light is impeccable. I am this planetarium of focus. In the distance I can see bright foundation lumber for a new house spread-eagled across half a mountainside, an incredible necklace of wood. Would it have been so terrible if I could have changed my life?

Movie lots, television sound stages, have tighter security procedures than most airlines. It isn't a metal detector you have to get past, it's a guest list.

Andy, who used to be a writer for *TV Guide*, does the song and the dance. While I hang back, feigning indifference, throwing my attentions like some ventriloquist of the elsewhere, Andy Mr. Elkin's me up and down the Sunset Gower Studios to the producers and crew. We make a team, Andy and I. Good cop, lazy cop. (Because, although it seemed like a good idea at the time, I have absolutely no idea why I'm here. Because there's nothing I want from these people. Because they're just doing their job, and I haven't a clue what mine even is.

Literally, I have nothing to ask them. Well, maybe one thing: what Chuck Barris—whom I've admired for years and who, in my opinion, should have first earned and then retired the Nobel Prize for Television long ago, for his exquisite feel for our nation's great voyeur heart, not only for just how much it can take but for exactly how much it needs, for our vampirical cravings, as if vulgarity were one of prime time's vital blood sugars, and who, long before there was ever a Geraldo, ever a Sally or a Phil or a Morton, *invented* reality programming, and who for my money is smarter than they, better, and certainly, God knows, a lot more fun, who may have been blessed from birth, with, I don't know, this—— what, Sweeps Week vision?—is really like.) Besides, it's cold in this place. The only heat is that generated by the show's announcer and warm-up guy, an old smoothie in a black turtleneck who works the largely high school crowd like some professional summer-camp demagogue, a pep-rally, emcee, say, the host of the campfire and marshmallows. What he needs from us, he keeps saying, is noise and energy. (During the show, Andy, a better sport than I'll ever be, applauds, yuks it up, observes the house rules, and, I'm thinking, acquits himself with considerable grace and class.) Meanwhile, the warm-up man moves through the audience with his mike, asking personal, devastating questions. I'm dangerously close, in the first row, and hope he will not sing to me. He sees me, of course, but this old smoothie is a smooth old smoothie, and I see I had nothing to worry about.

Just before the show, he introduces Paul Rodriguez, the star of "The Newlywed Game." Paul Rodriguez? What happened to Bob Eubanks? I'd expected Bob Eubanks. My God, I'd practically grown up on Bob Eubanks. Paul Rodriguez, it's explained, is Bob Eubanks's replacement. I can't understand it. I can't understand why they would want to replace Bob Eubanks. Bob Eubanks was a charter member of Chuck Barris's roundtable. And always—I don't know why, maybe it had to do with the set's comic-strip style—vaguely reminded me of a youthful, humorous Dick Tracy. (It's a syndicated show, it slips in and out of time slots, on and off channels. Once, two or three years ago, when I'd lost track of it, when I hadn't seen it for a couple of years, I suddenly came upon it again, Bob Eubanks seemed old to me, as if something awful had happened to his expression, his incredible, unflappable takes. Then I got used to him all over again, and it was as if he'd never been away. This new guy, Rodriguez, is a kid, younger than the newlyweds. How's a kid going to fill the shoes of someone like Eubanks?) Maybe, Andy offers, Eubanks is tired of newlyweds.

Sometimes I don't know how I feel about things. Or if I feel what I say I feel. That stuff about my becoming this planetarium of focus? I think that's how it was, but I don't know, I could have been faking it. I fake things. I pretend, for example, to a lot more gratitude than I usually feel. I make out I'm this really swell guy, humble for a cripple, when in actuality I get a lot less mileage out of my disease than I believe I deserve. So there's lots of phony good cheer and approval in me.

You're just going to have to believe this. You're just going to have to take this next one on faith.

When the show comes on, the set for "The Newlywed Game," the set is *beautiful!* It takes my breath away, the set. You'd never be able to see it on television. I looked at it on the monitor and right away could tell how flattened out it all was, not only how details were all merged but also how even the colors looked as rancid as the colors on baseball cards.

But that set, well, that set was something else.

Well, it was the neon, of course, the gorgeous sticks of colored gases like so many wands of fluorescent Crayolas, or the shining, luscious waters of a swimming pool. That set, that set. If only the furniture were nicer or the place a little warmer, I think I could have lived there.

Do I know my *echt* Californians or do I know my *echt* Californians?

All six contestants on the show that day are Californians. (According to Bruce Starin, producer of the "Newlywed" and "Dating Game" shows, 98 percent of the contestants on these shows are California residents. It's only a hunch, and maybe not as true as it used to be, but it's my impression—I think it's everyone's—that the site of most television shows *is* California. Mork and Mindy lived in Boulder, Colorado, of course, and the yuppies on "thirtysomething" are supposed to live somewhere in Philadelphia, but "Dallas" or no "Dallas" and "Hawaii Five-O" or no "Hawaii Five-O," one somehow has the feeling that the floating locale of all American dramatic life is a sort of platonic California.) They're like the structure of a racial joke. (There's this Indian couple, this white couple, and this black couple. . . .) I have my choice of which to interview in the green room afterwards and, making racials of my own, immediately choose the white couple. (So as not to skew my perceptions of what an *echt*

Californian is, I qualm. And something like this is true, I suppose, but only a *little* true. It's because I don't want to make waves. It's because there's even less I want to ask the white couple than the black or Indian couple.)

"I'm from Huntington Beach, California."

"I'm from northern California. Palo Alto. Stanford Hospital area. And I went to high school in San Diego, and I went to college from San Diego to USC."

"And that's where you guys met, huh?"

"That's right. She was a song girl, and I was on the football team."

"Say your names."

"Erin Johnson."

"Matt Johnson."

"How'd you get on this show?"

"I got a phone call at home. I believe they got our number from a bridal expo at the Disneyland Hotel. I wrote my name and phone number on a bunch of little slips to win prizes, and they called me and asked if I was interested, and actually my mom got the message, and I called them back and said, 'Sure, why not? Give it a try.' "

"You had no reluctance to come on the show?"

"The only thing I was worried about was, I had to take a couple of hours off work, *twice*, to come up here. If we had had to come probably any more times to try out, we probably would have said 'Oh, forget it, it's just not worth it.' "

I'd always assumed people came on these shows for larks, for, well, the tapes, to build up, in effect, their home movies, their memories, planning ahead like folks thinking into their annuities, planting seeds of the When-I-Get-Too-Old-to-Dream's. When I asked if they were disappointed they hadn't won, they said that they'd have been a lot more disappointed if the prize had been a major appliance. (It was a trip to the Poconos. Matt had been around the block; he'd played Penn State, he'd seen the Poconos.)

They understood they were supposed to give each other a going over. *Echt* Californians understand about show business and are in it, it seems, for the major appliances.

Erin, a legal secretary in Orange County, likes "the suburban Orange County life-style." Matt, who has played in both the Rose Bowl and the Hula Bowl, tried for a defensive back in the pros for a year or so before he was released. Already he's had arthroscopic surgery on his weakened knees. He has this faith in networking and believes people he met at USC will be there for him when he launches his political career. They call Costa Mesa home and live in "a typical Aztec-style apartment complex. All the usual amenities— weight room, Jacuzzi, club house with big-screen TV." Ideally Matt would want to live in wilderness conditions in some house overlooking a lake in Oregon. Erin doesn't agree. It's not her sort of life-style. Each of these young people keeps saying "life-style," but what did I expect? *Echt* Californians know about "life-style," too. (And why not, for goodness's sake? Because California is as much about Happiness as about anything else— Happiness, Fulfillment, Good Weather; the almost Constitutional givens, all warrants and the guarantees of being like doctor's orders, necessary food groups, or the Recommended Daily Allowances. But no mere *pursuit* of happiness, finally, so much as a mission of absolute search and destroy!) They invented it, after all, and stand in precisely the same relation to life-style as Chuck Barris does to vulgarity and the conspiratorial, participatory heart. *I only wish*, I keep thinking, *I'd had the togs and garment bags these kids do when I was their age.* I only wish, I mean, I'd known about show business and the *really* major appliances.

"The only time I don't work," Milch says, "is at the racetrack. What you find is that you're working at such an accelerated pace, you relax the same way. You've got to bet $10,000 a race, or $20,000 a race. Or if you start betting $10,000, at the end of the day you're betting $40,000. There's the same acceleration of expectation, and that's horseshit. You can only do that for so long before you lose respect for other forms of reality."

He lists California's racetracks for me, their circuits and seasons like stations of the cross.

"My horses are stabled at whatever track is running at the time, the horses of mine actually running. The horses that are crippled are out on the farm being rehabilitated."

We're at the barns, low green sheds like contiguous houses on Monopoly properties.

"These guys are all undocumented aliens. Periodically the Immigration Service comes in and sweeps, and then the next day nobody's got guys to lead horses around. Those are the outriders leading the horses over for the third race. The first race has been run, the horses for the second race are already being saddled." He leans into his big car for the telephone. "I'm going to dial and find out the results of the first race. I've got a service which gives the call of the race. And the horse that we want to hear is Sovereign Appeal.

" 'That's Sovereign Appeal looking for racing room, *looking* for racing room.' . . . Ah, we fucked the dog. My fucking horse didn't even get third."

Among Milch's extensive holdings are several bushel baskets of carrots. In the barns he gives me some, which I then feed to Marvin's Policy and Jet Charlie. Feeding the horseys is a sort of kiddie privilege. Why, though he's at least fifteen years younger than I am, do I let him treat me as if he were my father? It's all those carrots, all that explanation. This Milch, I think, is interested in a strictly monogrammed lore and legend. No truth, I suppose he supposes, like a home truth.

He tells me there are about fifteen hundred horses at Santa Anita, a horse population like a small town. Initially, at least, I'm delighted to be here. I mean it's interesting. Some guy's set up a shoe-shine stand just off the track's mucky environs, probably the best location for a shoe-shine stand I've ever seen, a perfect example of economic synergy. The dominating maleness of the crowd is interesting. The racetrack's specialized, zoned geography is. The outriders are interesting, the jockeys like some manly, human nubbins, their vaguely toreador presence. From the grandstand, Santa Anita itself looks like a giant, living game board, this open-air palace of fun and hope. There are flowers planted about the premises bright as racing silks. Even— money's at stake here, so much it's almost theatrical—how long a time it takes to change scenes is interesting. The bookies, laying off bets, tuned in to the world on upscale portable phones in their expensive carrying cases. All of it's interesting. Like that first jolt of green vision that floods your senses when you step into a stadium and catch, full-force, the bright, spectacular apparency of a night game. But it wears and tears finally, such interest, and has no compounding. Milch, that good daddy, has tipped the wheelchair *schlepper* twenty-five bucks to bring me to the box. He offers hot dogs and cocoas and presses explanations. I feel like some Sunshine-funded kid out on the town for all of an afternoon. But this turf is his turf, he doesn't let me forget. Everything is explained, everything.

"I bet so much money that if I put it into the machines where the odds are figured, it'd distort the price. It'd ruin my odds. What personal

bookmakers do is book the bet themselves. They lay it off with organizations elsewhere, and those organizations book the bets themselves.
Pari-mutuel just means 'among ourselves.' Betting amongst ourselves.
That's what it means in French. All that the people here do is, the
track takes twenty cents out of the dollar and then. . .You're spilling
it on yourself."

It's not Milch's fault, but I'm rapidly going into a sort of fugue state.
No wonder I'm spilling my cocoa. Perhaps there are things wrong with
me beyond even the things that are wrong with me. I can't deny that
for all his sealed, airtight obsession, David is a better host than I am a
guest. Though the way Milch goes at it, being a host is obsessive, too.

"The most interesting thing today so far is what hasn't happened.
Which is, I've got a very strong tip on a horse in the sixth race. I'm
out about five grand, but if this horse hasn't been tipped around the
track, that means instead of his odds being 5 to 1, which is what he'd
be if he were tipped, maybe his odds will be 20 to 1. We bet three or
four or five or ten thousand bucks the difference between 5 to 1 and
20 to 1 is very significant. So it's interesting that so far it seems like
the horse has not gotten around."

Milch is away from the box as much as he's in it. I'm given responsibilities, little-kid chores to occupy myself. I mind people's binoculars, I hold their programs and racing forms, I watch their seats for them.

Milch is a kind of folk hero here. Everyone's glad to see him, and,
since I'm with him, they're glad to see me, too.

During races on which he hasn't bet, he cheers for his friends' horses.
"Come on, go faster, go faster! For Richie, for Richie! He didn't make
it. Richie got beat."

"Who's Richie?"

"That guy. You should know. Richie was here. He got beat. He
didn't win."

After the race, this guy shows up, so happy he can hardly contain
himself.

"I hit the nine!"

"I didn't think you were alive with the nine," Milch says. "Good
for you, good for you."

"Three, six, nine."

"So what you get?"

"Fifty-two hundred."

"*Good* for you!"

"He held on, didn't he?"

"Oh yeah."

"I went and bet everything like you said. You know, I put the two."

"Yeah, you gotta save."

"So I saved."

"That's called 'dutching out.' "

" 'Dutching out' that's called? I dutched it out, baby. I put everything in my pocket."

"Good."

"Boy, I needed it too, lemme tell you."

"Hey, Rich," someone says, "can I borrow forty-eight hundred?"

"Ha ha ha ha ha ha."

"Good boy."

"I'm gonna go to the class," Richie says. "I'm gonna learn how to read the numbers. Yeah, I'm gonna go do it."

"The 'numbers' he's talking about," Milch explains, "is a system that is really changing the way people bet. It's a way of evaluating performance that neutralizes the racing form. Every horse's previous race is reduced to a single number, and then they analyze the pattern of the numbers. The argument is that when a horse runs the best race of its life, when people would typically bet the horse, in fact that's a time to bet *against* the horse because they feel a horse has a characteristic channel of performance, and once it goes outside the channel and exceeds itself, it typically will exhaust itself by that effort and run badly next time instead of running well, so what the system does is tend to exclude favorites. The guy who perfected the idea is an old Marxist-Leninist who gave it all up and went into this thing. The way he gives the numbers is by the distance the horse runs out from the rail, so that if a horse is running in the eight path, he'll get a much lower number. Well, it's self-evident. The horse is running a larger circumference, and so if he finishes even with a horse that's run on the inside, that horse has run farther, and so he *should* get a better number. So it's a way of discounting apparent performance."

New Wave Marxist-Leninist odds makers. Richie's going to take the course. The New Wave State.

"A bookmaker will tell you," Milch tells me, "out here nobody gets killed for owing money. That's why bookmakers have trouble out here. One of the guys I introduced you to, he says, 'Back home in our game, there's an expression—— that clubs is trumps,' meaning if it comes to it, somebody gets hit over the head and he pays the money. Out here, if anybody uses violence they get arrested. So ultimately, it's only a matter of honor. On the other hand, it's so affluent that if even three out of ten people pay off, the bookmaker still winds up with the biggest house. Another thing is, there's such an absence of tradition, such a pastlessness, you never know where people live, you never know where to find them, they move so much. With me, I've had it happen the other way. Bookmakers go belly up. I've busted three bookmakers out. You've just got to wait and hope they get well."

He points out a kid teaching himself to call races. He questions him closely, advises him, invites him out to the viewing room at the studio, where the kid can watch himself, maybe pick up on some of the things he's doing wrong. Together they chat about the man who calls the races at Santa Anita, Trevor Denman, a South African Milch regards as the best caller in the business. "What makes Trevor good is, he can tell when a horse is past it, when he's expended himself. He can see the boy move his hands when the boy is asking, or if he's asking too soon. And if he's got a double handful like that, that means he hasn't asked him yet, so if the horse is doing well and he hasn't asked him, you know the horse is likely to perform well. And then when the boy moves, when he asks him, if the horse responds, then you call the horse as optimistic in terms of his chances. But if the boy asks him and the horse *doesn't* respond, even if the horse is in front, you know he's done. So you'll hear the guy call, 'There's so-and-so on the lead but not doing enough,' or 'So-and-so is on the lead and finding more.' He's extraordinary. *Extraordinary.*"

"So how come I didn't hear him?"

"Because you don't pay attention."

I do to the tall tales, to the one about the 117-pound jockey whose weight is really 160 but is kept down by the killing fasts to which he subjects himself, all the ways he's learned to absorb nourishment without actually taking in food— through its smells, the different noises it makes in fire. Milch and the kid scaring each other over accidents they've seen, bones busted as lessons jockeys teach one another. There are nice bits of jargon. Apprentice jockeys, for example, are often given a weight advantage, and an asterisk goes down by their name in the program. When the asterisk is dropped, the jockey is said to have "lost his bug."

It's racetrack theory I can't take, the horsey universals Milch swears by.

"The thing about the track," he says, "is it's a completely exfoliated ecology. There are real artists out here. There are certain trainers who are *extraordinary* in the way they understand how to deal with a horse, and there are a million different variables about how to change a horse's performance, from equipment, to feed, to shoeing, the kind of bit that they use, what they do with them in the morning, and the guys that are good are amazing, just amazing. The other part of being a trainer is the science of dealing with the owners, and the psychology that's involved there is amazing. I mean talk about hustlers, not just hustlers, human nature, understanding. There's a fully developed vocabulary for the way you deal with an owner at different moments of the experience. Like when you say, 'Cool out.' That's a racetrack expression. You know that an owner, when his horse has run badly, is going to be angry and sweaty, and the trainer has to find a way to give him the cool-out story, but if the owner knows he's being handled he'll get pissed off, so the trainer has got to seem to be talking about something else. 'It looked like he was giving us everything he—— I wonder if the boy asked him too soon.' So now the owner's got something to blame besides the defect in the horse. The trainer tells him, 'Geez, I think we had some bad luck. I mean, it looked like he was just getting ready to move at the half-mile post, and the hole shut.' You give him something to blame. What you're trying to do is rekindle hope, as opposed to saying the horse is too fucking slow.

"Then you get trainers who get sick of that, of having to handle owners, and yearn for the owner who's got all the money in the world and doesn't give a shit, and doesn't need a big story every time, so then you get big society trainers. It's a whole spectrum."

It is *not* a whole spectrum. It's not even a fraction of a spectrum. Tops, it's an itty-bitty piece of what isn't even a primary color.

Here's what happened:

The rough formula is that at a distance of a mile, five pounds is supposed to be worth about a length. All else being equal, a horse carrying five pounds less than his competitor should beat him by a length.

Here's what happened:

Milch's very strong tip on the horse in the sixth race—I put $50 down on it to win, but David doesn't even give me its name until practically post time, this despite the fact that I'd need the wheelchair and the wheelchair guy both if I were going to tip it around the track— is that it has been turning in good times even though it's been carrying thirty-five extra pounds during its morning workouts. Seven lengths, according to the rough formula.

Here's what happened:

The horse goes off at 9 to 1. Milch bets $50,000 on the horse to win.

Here's what happened:

It's difficult for me even to see the horse, let alone read its numbers, let alone pick out the colors of its racing silks. So I'm listening for Trevor to call the horse. I'm paying attention, and listening for Trev to call Milch's horse. (Not *my* horse, understand, Milch's! Not my merely 50-buck nag, but Milch's full-fledged, $50,000 *horse!*) Then he does, he says its name, and I *explode* into cheering, urging, encouragement, whatever the word is for the will thrown into gear like that, whatever the telekinetic forces are for this sort of simple, engaged, innocent-bystander energy.

"Come on. Come on. Come on," I yell. "Come on, come on, come *on*. Cmon, cmon!" I scream. "*Cmoncmoncmon!*" I act out.

Here's what happened:

I clap Milch on the back and excitedly, crazily, mistakenly, congratulate him. "You won!" I yell. "You won, you *won!*"

"What the hell do *you* know about it? You lost fifty bucks, I lost fifty thousand."

It's just a momentary flash of anger. He recovers immediately, is once again good father to this little orphan-outing'd, Sunshine-funded boy. In the car on the way back, we're polite to each other but have little to say. So I'm thinking about all those palm trees, California's bearded botany, and the locations I've scouted—"The Newlywed Game," Reagan's bar mitzvah at the Beverly Hilton, Los Angeles's empty streets. I'm thinking of the production assistant Milch offered to have stand by on twenty-four-hour call in the lobby of the Bel Age Hotel to adjust my cummerbund or fix my studs should the need arise. Then, out of the blue, Milch says to me, "You know, Stanley, California isn't really any different from anyplace else."

II

The San Francisco bay area, I'm thinking on the plane, is the experimental mother-lode matrix, the SiliconValley of the New Age. I'm about to enter this duty-free zone of the olly-olly-oxen-free anarchies, the source of all the bold, outrageous, five-and-plus-year plans of the neo-chic, a Jerusalem newer than Blake's, with a claim to the highest territorials—— northern California as the West Pole. But first—

The flight from LAX to Oakland is a straight shot, but the airline loses my bags. It loses my Lanoxin. It loses my Valium and dipyrimadole. It loses my Procardia. (This is the establishing shot. I'm flat on my back at ground level, and God and the world are taking potshots. It might not be any safer here than back in L.A.) I let B.K. and her husband, Charlie, handle it. I let them deal with the lady in the missing-luggage department, play Pick the Shape of Your Suitcase from the chart the airline has worked up from untold thousands of valises it's lost over the years. I don't know why, but these charts depress me, remind me of those silhouettes of enemy aircraft air-raid wardens study during the wars. I suppose it's the futility of the exercise, how I can't conceive why being able to recognize what just bombed the shit out of you, or picking out the give-or-take, more-or-less, sort-of-a-profile the airline offers of what used to be your suitcase (almost), could ever do anyone any good. It's just more mug shots, is what I think.

So I sit this one out on the edge of the baggage carousel, taking my ease, saving my strength. Because it ain't but 9:30 or so in the morning, and I can already see this is going to be some day.

And it is.

Charlie drives us to the St. Francis Hotel to register. I'm impressed. Lots of hustle-bustle in the lobby. Very downtown sort of place. I can almost cotton to spending a few days here. Naked. Tuxless. Suitless. Shirtless and pantsless and shortsless. But Lanoxinless? And without all the other chemical whatnot that keeps me alive, that winds my watch and eases my blood past its tight squeezes and narrow situations, threads it through all the eyes in all the needles of its obloquy? What a piece of work is a man! I'm here to tell ya.

So Charlie takes my Gold Card to the hotel pharmacy with the 800 number to test the waters, see is it true I'm caught short without my prescriptions they'll get me fresh ones? Anywhere in the world; it could be Mindanao, it could be Argentina, it could be California. I feel all the spurious defiance of David Horowitz challenging a commercial.

Meanwhile, I've seen the bathroom, and—shades of the Fall!—it's without grab bars, sans the shower orthotics. I'm sorry, but once burned, twice shy. Plus, the room ain't made up yet. (Because I'm this *fastidious* cripple who'd never stretch out on the other guy's sheets, this suspicious fastidious cripple who's lost his bags, who gave, in a sense, at the office and honestly believes—listen; we're talking *honestly* believes; faith, the heart's sour, grounded orthodoxy—he ought to be exempt from ever having to give anything ever again ever, who has this license to take and to *kvetch* and maybe even to kill and who thinks, for all that the airline vows otherwise, he'll never see his bags alive again!) It's a large room; but unmade, crowded with twisted sheets, with blankets kicked to the foot of the beds, with an extra cot and strewn newspapers, with opened cans of nuts and mixes, with flattened club soda, packets of potato chips, empty pony bottles of booze, and even the absolutely meaningless telephone numbers and code words one scribbles to oneself on hotel notepads with hotel ballpoints, drenched, I mean, in all the anonymous detritus of invisible, hungover lives, seems oddly cramped, close-quartered, no place even to sit (so that one perches on some cleared-path edge of things), never mind stretch out.

So I've seen the bathroom, and there's a call in to housekeeping, the engineers.

Charlie comes back with the prescriptions, enough for four days. And here's housekeeping, too. We're feeling so good as things start to fall into place that B.K. goes to the minibar and pulls out stuff to nosh—juices, crackers, and cheeses.

But man don't live by no bread alone. He don't live by even the illusion of kemptness. Or *I* don't. Though neatness—I was toilet trained by nine months, but I bet you knew that—counts. Yeah, and cleanliness is *too* next to godliness, or maybe I wouldn't be so skittish about that shower. But when the engineer comes with the handicap bench, it, with its grips, is more like a gymnast's horse than a proper transfer bench. If I could swing my legs up over its big concatenatory handles, I wouldn't need any cripple-friendly shower prosthetics in the first damn place. Fully clothed (well, not *fully* clothed; I don't have my tux or my suit or any of the rest of my hijacked apparel), and in my shoes, and with an assistant manager and the engineer and Charlie and B.K. to witness and, should the need arise, help out in an emergency, I demonstrate my high-wire act. I can get in, all right, but out's out of the question.

The assistant manager, summoned by B.K. (in whom I've somehow awakened an outraged, born-again advocate of gimp toilet rights), a sympathetic, fatherly man in his early fifties, vaguely Oriental-looking and dignified as a scholar, seems interested in a just solution to my case. Clearly something has occurred to him, but it's a long shot, and he's reluctant to say.

"What?" I ask.

Doubtfully, he mentions a number to the engineer. As soon as I hear it, I know it's some *experimental* room, or haunted perhaps, but just the ticket. I'm invited to take a look at it.

Oddly, it looks as if it's being aired out. The furniture, pulled in, is at queer angles to the walls. Stripped, the bed looks like something in a summer house after a year's vacancy. It's a trade-off, maybe a third the size of the room I'd be giving up, but it has a stall shower. Unfortunately, there's this two-foot step to get into it, sharp, dangerous-looking tracks upright as knives on which the shower door slides, and, as the faucet and fixtures and shower head would be *behind* me as I got out of the stall—I do another dress rehearsal for my captive, not uninterested, audience, who suggest possible gravitational compromises, slick finesses, all the jujitsu bathing leverages—there'd be nothing to grab on to. "I'm sorry," I tell the assistant manager, "but as you see . . ."

He understands, he assures, and I believe he does. Back in the original room, he speculates about alternative configurations. If they put a grab bar here, if they drove a handle into the side of the wall outside the tub there . . . Would that help? That would be perfect, I tell him. Is it feasible? he asks the engineer. It might *take* a few hours . . . Would a few hours make that much difference to me? *Heck* no, a few hours, *heck* no, absolutely not. Well, he'd have to speak to his boss, of course . . . Of course. "Well, then," he says.

"It's just too bad," I say, "there was that huge step to get into that shower stall. If I could just have *stepped* into it. If there'd just been a drain at the bottom of the stall . . ."

"Yes," the assistant manager says, "like the one in my house."

"You have one like that in your house?"

"My son," he says, "is a quadriplegic."

"Oh, Jesus," I tell him. "Oh, Christ," I say.

Then the two of us are practically sobbing at each other, all lumps-in-the-throat and mutually moved, and it's good he has to leave to make the arrangements because I can't even talk to the guy, I'm so ashamed. It's not as if I were a *real* cripple. I'm a goddamn disgrace to the handicapped, is what. B.K. wonders if he's handing me a line, and it would be better all 'round if he were, but boy, I hope she's wrong. I just hope to hell his son can't move a muscle, that even his hair is paralyzed when they try to move a comb through it. Because I'm a sucker for a moment, is why.

Tracy and Emily, from the magazine's San Francisco office, have joined us. We're supposed to go to lunch, but my bags still haven't come, and I want to be here when they work on the room. We do room service instead. I order exquisitely, if I do say so. As if I had no appetite, or just exactly the sort of appetite a classy, exquisite-raised gent like me ought to have, this food-doesn't-matter soul drill I do for company once in a while if I'm not very hungry. Oh, perhaps a sandwich, maybe a small salad, a glass of iced tea. Emily, this tough, young, streetwise waif—who lets you know it, demonstrates it, I mean, who drives, for a waif, a big, improbable station wagon, who parks it and leaves it for hours in front of hotels without so much as a by-your-leave to a doorman or cop—orders heartily. (It's Emily, low girl on the magazine's totem pole, who brought up the idea of my doing something for *California* in the first place, and who, I take it, contacted me before she ever said anything about it to her bosses. Emily and I go back, too. I met her when she was a graduate student in Ohio and she asked me to do a piece for the Bowling Green literary magazine and I declined. Then, after graduation, she wrote me when she worked for *Arrival*, a short-lived, San Francisco–based magazine too counterculture for someone like me, still trying, even at fifty-eight, for an upward mobility he can call his own.) Emily's an enthusiast, a kind of throwback, at once this believer and skeptic, who seems to require demons, cultural straw beings, not personally paranoid—anything but, considerate, kind, generous, helpful—so much as suspicious on behalf of others, on behalf of mankind, perhaps, some feisty patriot of the other guy's country. She reminds me of someone from the sixties. This attractive, old-fashioned girl on the cutting edge. (Emily believes an important new genre is the adult comic book. Emily, Emily is a pistol.) Tracy *looks* Californian, smart, capable, and centered as some sitcom shrewdie with the best lines. Of the three of us—there's been a changing of the guard; B.K. and Charlie have left—I'd guess only Tracy orders precisely what she wants off the room-service menu, not like me, who's showing off, and not like Emily, who may be thinking about the doggie bag.

Against all odds, my bags arrive.

Then, late in the afternoon, the assistant manager comes back. He's all remorse and apology, but his boss has told him that changing the bathroom around isn't a good idea. They can't guarantee the new equipment they'd have to punch into the tile will support me. They don't want me to fall. I'm welcome to stay, of course, but meanwhile they've contacted the Hilton, a newer hotel where the tubs all have grab bars and there's a ramp in the guts of the building so guests can drive right up to their floor. He makes it sound like some Big Rock Candy Mountain for the disabled. In addition to picking up the tab for my first night's stay at the Hilton, the St. Francis will be happy to absorb all the charges I've managed to put on the magazine's account in the seven or eight hours I've been in possession of the room— all B.K.'s and Tracy's calls, the juices and crackers and cheeses from the minibar, our three lunches. In addition, he tells me, they'll throw a stretch limo into the bargain to take me there. I'll need help registering, I inform. Perhaps the ladies? he suggests. Sure, they agree. But what about afterwards? I lay on. The driver, he says, will be instructed to wait, he instructs.

When we get there, Emily, seeing no point in my having to tip the guy, lifts my two big suitcases and carries them up to the room herself. Tracy, wisely, doesn't lift a finger.

Though I hate to think it's so, some people, by dint of sheer geography, may lead luckier lives than other people. A pal, Herb Bogart, interviewing for a job at San Francisco State years ago and asked why he wanted to leave the University of Illinois campus at Champaign-Urbana, told his prospective employer, "Because when I look out the window it's too beautiful and I can't get my work done." Well. The Bay Area really *is* beautiful. World-class views. One day, crossing the bridge back from the Marin headlands (where I'd seen surfers in wet suits, where I'd seen Sausalito like a hip Italian hill town, where I'd seen an Army post, abandoned and sad against the Bay and hills as if it had recently been conquered, overrun, left to stand in the weather like a wooden ruin) to San Francisco with Tracy, the full force of this gorgeous city hits me in the eyesight like a blow. It doesn't seem fair that one can see all this and get his work done, too. A silly twist of fate, of geology, some perverse variation on the there-but-for-the-grace-of-God's; an accident, I mean, to be a San Franciscan rather than a Hoosier. Tie goes to the guy with the view. Nothing as important as life should be wasted. And it strikes me that California is a choice one makes, a blow one strikes for hope. (Oh, St. Louis, where I'm from, is a choice, too, but not in the way California is. Unless a job's waiting, or he has other, very specific, reasons, no one ever wakes up one day and says, I must move to Missouri. No one chooses to find happiness in Maryland. And California, whether it delivers or not, is *about* happiness, as America, whether it delivers or not, is about freedom.)

One morning, Emily, Matt (another *California* staffer), and I drive out to Berkeley. We cruise by the Krishna Copy Center, the Cheese Board and Juice Bar collectives, People's Park. Up and down the Atlantic Citiness of this western campus town we go, and I have an impression of having come in the off season—the university is on break—to this odd zone of the not historical, exactly, so much as the *nostalgical*. I learn there's talk of making a Palestinian refugee camp on the West Bank Berkeley's sister city, and this strikes me as fitting in a community so fixed on itself as a place on the cutting edge of conscience. Social fiddling has lent it the air of a one-industry town, some Las Vegas of the ideological, almost, at least between terms, blowsy, fat with assumption. In a way I can't explain, it seems to me like a sort of graduate-student theme park—— of the young, by the young, and for the young. I'm not uncomfortable here, quite the reverse, actually. I feel larky. For all my grampsy, gruntled ways, I have a sense of tolerance, safe passage, letters of transit in my pocket, the ease of one with all the bona fides of his blemishes working for him. Berkeley, I sense, is a big support-group town. I can just imagine the different hot lines in its telephone directory.

We drop by Peet's Coffee & Tea, not, as its name and campus-town locale might suggest (and what I expect), a coffeehouse in any eighteenth-century, Dr. Johnson sense of the term, but a kind of Häagen-Dazs of coffee. Except for a bench outside the store and an even smaller one inside, there's no place to sit. The newspapers, astonishingly various—I count fourteen—and dispensed from vending machines rather than fixed to wooden wands, round out a sense one has of Peet's' penny-arcade aura, some coffee shooting gallery, say. With its stock of gleaming, stainless-steel coffee machines, cups, boxes of filters, and all the rest of its assorted cappuccino paraphernalia, it might almost be a coffee hardware store. Matt, who went to school in Berkeley, recognizes regulars, as I, who didn't, almost do myself. I mean, they *all* seem like regulars, people hanging out. These people, strolling up and down examining the beans, looking over the different teas displayed in shallow glass cases like ant farms, wired on caffeine, on coffee so strong it smells, not unpleasantly, like a kind of rancid bacon, are mostly lanky guys with a sort of folksinger look in their eyes.

The magazine folks told me that if I'm going to Berkeley, I mustn't miss the Center for Independent Living, a service organization for the disabled—— another support group in the Support Group State. I go where I'm told. I do what they tell me. So I drop in. Rakish, leaning on my cane, I present myself. Boldly, larky in Berkeley, I tell the lady at the desk I'm there for a fitting.

I couldn't have picked him out of a lineup; he'd have fooled me on "To Tell the Truth." I don't know what I was expecting, but the fellow who showed up in my hotel room that afternoon didn't look like any Will Hearst *I* would have imagined, or even, for that matter, like any scion, give or take a few mil, up or down, in or out, here or there, at all. (I'm from St. Louis, I've seen Joe Pulitzer, *fils*.) Though I recognized the type, God knows. Was, once upon a time, the type myself. He was dressed like a grad student. Or no, not a grad student, like someone with his Ph.D. already stuffed and mounted on the wall and working his first university teaching job—— slacks, tweed sport coat, and tie loosened at the throat. I could imagine him in the sixties, JFK's sixties, mine, the sixties of grace and Frisbee, of lunch taken on the quad in shirtsleeves. (Not *his* sixties, surely—I put him as a man in his mid-thirties—or his cousin's, though Patty's sixties were actually seventies, a matter of spilled time.) I saw him, that is, anachronistically, or maybe that's the only way the rich ever look, athletic and easy as people sockless in loafers.

It was my idea that he come to the room, though I wanted Tracy, who already knew him, there as a buffer, to ward off the mean spirits of my tied tongue. (This, this is chronic, congenital. I can't speak to the gifted or the very rich. Possibly I'm not comfortable with the lucky. It's not my best trait, but let him without sin, etc.)

I'd been given a choice—— to sit in on an *Examiner* editorial meeting or tool around the city with Hearst in his limo. I picked door number three. I wanted to feed him lunch out of my minibar. And though he consented to come up to the room and even to look at the room-service menu, he seemed antsy, anxious. There was, he said, this terrific Japanese place, Nikko. I don't do your Pacific Rim foods, am not experimental, and have, well, these like racist taste buds, but it was getting pretty clear, finally, that if I needed Tracy as a buffer between myself and Will Hearst, Will Hearst needed Tracy and an entire restaurant between himself and me. And not just antsy, he was like an actual kid let out of actual school once he'd left that room; Hearst leading the way down the hall, disappearing around a corner, waiting for us farther on, bouncing up and down on the balls of his feet like a jogger waiting on a stoplight. (Because if I'm not comfortable with them—the rich, the gifted, the lucky—possibly it's because we don't speak the same language; not English, maybe not even money or talent or good fortune, so much as the fried fish of one's sheer otherness.) We have nothing to say to each other. He agreeably answers all my questions, dumb as they are, boring as they are. (What influence has television had, do you think, on the newspaper business? In what direction do you want to take the *Examiner?*) He knocks them out of the ballpark, my questions. (I should have asked if he ever had a paper route; I should have asked about his cousin, what the Symbionese Liberation Army was really like.)

At the restaurant, he tells Tracy about a trip he's just taken—Tracy and Will are journalist buddies; Jon, Tracy's husband, writes a daily column for the *Chronicle,* the *Examiner's* rival, so, in a way, they're family—ninety miles cross-country skiing over a spine of Sierras. And when Tracy mentions that she and Jon have been snorkeling off Indonesia's Banda Islands, Hearst perks up for the first time all day. For all his graciousness, this is the only time he's genuinely interested. (This, I get the feeling, is the *real* direction he wants to take the paper.) Till now he's not shown that much interest in even the Japanese food. He asks the questions: Which airlines does one take? How long is the flight? What else can one do there? Well, Tracy tells him, there are these Dutch ruins. Dutch ruins, oh, Jesus! How he can't wait to go! *I* can taste it.

But this is supposed to be journalism going on here. I pull him back into the interview.

It turns out he's this booster. He wants to see downtown San Francisco even more developed than it already is. When Tracy indicates surprise, he tells her it's "provincial" for people to carry on about progress. Tracy says parking is already a tremendous problem in the city and wonders what he would do to accommodate even more cars. Well, Will Hearst suggests, they can always take taxis.

Then the check comes and I perk up. Who couldn't have cared less about TV's influence on the press, or whither the *San Francisco Examiner*, or even Patty Hearst and the Symbionese Liberation Army, I do! Because I sure ain't going to pay for all that raw fish, and neither, I see, is Will Hearst. Not that this is an awkward moment or anything. It isn't, not in the least. Tracy picks up the check. She puts it on her credit card. Now this, this, I'm thinking, *this* is interesting! I know it's business. I do, I really do. I know he didn't have to agree to see me, but it's interesting, almost as interesting as me giving him lunch out of the minibar would have been, and later I'm disappointed when B.K. tells me I'm not being fair, that he'd offered to take all of us out, that she'd had to insist this one was on the magazine. Didn't I tell you I'm a sucker for a moment? Don't you know I'd go to almost any length to set one up?

Jon shows me the "WELL," a kind of party line for people with PCs. An acronym for Whole Earth 'lectronic Link, a service with maybe 3,000 subscribers and possibly 100 "conferences," or subjects—Psychology, Sexuality, Macintosh, Writers, News, Politics, Words—anything, really, someone introduces and can get someone else to talk about, the WELL, it seems to me, is exactly like an electronic séance, subscriber calling to subscriber, soul to soul, in some mutual SOS of interest.

Jon enters his password and is into the WELL quick as Alice tumbled down the rabbit hole. He checks his "mail," messages left for him under his personal rubric, not the same as his password, which is known but to him and Electricity. He has mail, or, rather, a reply to something he'd said when he'd logged off. "As a matter of fact," writes *cee*, "I was just reading about the proposed Erotica Conference. Oh, baby!"

"There's a question," Jon explains, "about whether or not Erotica should remain in the Sex Conference or should be in its own conference, and so there are people discussing this issue."

Oh, baby!

It occurs that the WELL is just about the most California thing I've seen yet—I know subscribers can live anywhere; it's only my hunch that they don't—more California than the real estate channel I watched

in Los Angeles, even than the two-dollar-an-hour parking meters they
were talking about in Beverly Hills.

I take in an AA meeting like a matinee. I'm touched by these people,
these cheerers and encouragers, these mutual urgers, stirred by the
energy of their engaged sympathies. Because it's hard, what they're
trying to do, their concern a little like the shouted telekinetics of my
day at the races, all those Come on, come on, come *on's* of pure
rooting interest. Only I was rooting for just one horse, and these folks
want them *all* to win. And nervous as someone in the other guy's
church. Because I don't know the forks, and a little embarrassed, too,
by all this goodwill, under the cumulative weight of all that love.

Hey, my part is small, not even a walk-on. Not even a spear carrier.
I have a line, but it's the same line all the other guests at the meeting
have. (I'm not even sure "guest" is the correct term.) Plus, I almost
blow it. (I almost *really* blow it. What I almost say is, "My name is
Stanley, and I have multiple sclerosis.") I get my name right, all right,
but mumble the explanation—I still can't remember it—for whatever
it is I think I'm doing there. Nevertheless, the force of their choric,
antiphonal "Hi, Stanley!" so takes me back that I'm certain anything
I might have said would have been greeted with the same goofy acceptance and understanding. I smile back at them. As if "Hi, Stanley!"
collectively executed is just about the nicest thing everyone ever said
to me. These people can't, in their lives, be as kind as they seem, but
together, oh, boy, together they're as focused and effective as a SWAT
team. There really ought to be a way to take your pep rally with you.

Two nights before I leave, Ellen, my wife's niece, joins Matt, Emily,
and me for room-service chicken. It's my idea to bring the three
together to tell me their life stories. I figure the bunch for latter-day
pioneers—— not gold miners so much as life miners, panning northern
California for their fates. People enjoy talking about themselves, and
it's in the interest of science. I don't see the harm, I don't see a problem.

Ellen, from Indiana, and someone I'd always somehow thought of
as my maiden niece, tells about the four years she worked in textile
design in New York, about the time she went off to India with a
medical student the rest of us thought she was going to marry, about
joining him in Canada when he went there for his internship, their
breakup a few years later when he moved to Pittsburgh. She applied

for Canadian immigration papers and stayed in Vancouver, waitressing in a Mexican restaurant, moonlighting in the artist trade. Then, in 1984, in Europe, she fell in love with a Dane. He invited her to Copenhagen. She sold her Canadian all and went to Denmark with two duffel bags and her portfolio. "This major relationship in my life lasted sixty days," she says, "maybe ninety." She moved to San Francisco when married friends invited her to stay with them in their apartment.

"You people!" uncles Stosh. (Because I mean it. Most trips us tourists take are largely photo opportunities, the documentation of our lives posed next to beauty, standing against history, climbing eccentricity, rappelling down quirk—— portrayed, I mean, in contiguity with monuments of victory or loss. But it's wearing, finally, doing the acrobatic Blarney Stone contortions, figuring the angles at Stonehenge that will snuff out the other tourists and leave the kid, or even just positioning oneself in chummy proximity beside the lifesize cardboard presidents and pasteboard kings. But then California is chiefly an idea. What's the f-stop for ideas? You must look out for your listening ops, too.)

"Then my friend Diane met a guy in New York. We'd gone to New York. It was the most depressing month of my life. I didn't want to go East, she wanted to go. Christmas 1985, I sat alone in an apartment eating an Entenmann's cake and a bag of potato chips. I don't *do* stuff like that. I just saw gloom and doom. Even after we came back. It was a combination of not having any money and not really wanting to *be* in California."

Her friend married the man she'd met in New York, and Ellen moved in with her hairdresser.

"Straight?" aunts Stanley.

"I learned more about femininity from the hairdresser than I ever knew in my life. This guy had nicer lingerie than I did."

She stayed with him four months. The flat was unheated, not very attractive, but the hairdresser, my niece says, was a gem. He gave Ellen his bedroom and slept in the living room on the couch. When he was drunk, he threw things out the window. Ellen would excuse herself, go into the hairdresser's surrendered bedroom, and close the hairdresser's surrendered door.

My maiden niece's new boyfriend is a black singer ten years younger than she is.

She found work in an art gallery. Other things started to go her way. She began to sell some of her work. She'd been meeting people in the Networking State and was given a show at the Diva Hotel.

"This was my first one-person show. September 14, 1987. A monumental day in my life. Big opening, festive, lots of people. I sold seven or eight pieces. No, *more*. I got a commission for three pieces. I quit the gallery in November, thinking, I'm on my way. Commissions, all this neat stuff happening, I needed time to paint. So—*bummer*. In June I couldn't pay my rent. Couldn't pay it, didn't have it."

She asked for her job back.

Through the gallery she met a woman with whom she's starting a product-design business.

"We're getting our business license. Maybe happiness has as much to do with giving up some of your dreams as with having them come true. I mean, I did this to myself. I didn't *have* to suffer, but I ended up doing it anyway. I don't have to do that anymore. My mom's known about Jules almost the entire time, and this Thanksgiving I told my brothers and their wives. I said, 'I want you to know this is who I've been going out with, and I've been going out with him for two-and-a-half years.' I don't know what I expected, but it was no big deal."

Matt grew up in New Jersey, majored in poly sci, then worked two years in Washington for the Department of Energy writing legal decisions in the Office of Hearings and Appeals. He hated it, but it was an easy job and the first time he had any money. Then he decided to go to graduate school. He moved to Massachusetts when he was accepted by Tufts's graduate English program. This was 1984. He was dumped by the woman he lived with, and a few weeks later he got hepatitis and had to miss most of the spring term. He was very low. The following year he took only two classes and applied to other schools— Harvard, Berkeley, Rutgers, Brown. He got into all of them except Harvard.

"So I was trying to decide. I went to look at New Brunswick. It was a very depressing visit. I got on this train to go back, and the train hit a woman and killed her. It sort of sealed the day for me. For both of us. I'd go to Berkeley.

"The only problem was money. Berkeley is a huge department and accepts lots of students but gives out very little money. So it was a question of whether I could *afford* to come."

He took out $9,500 in loans, got a grant that eliminated in-state tuition, and was forgiven out-of-state tuition for one semester. After paying for one semester and his student fees, plus servicing fees for the loans, he had about $6,000 to live on. "Then, second semester, I was a grader and made $1,200, just enough so I could feel okay about the decision to come."

Emily's story, in a sort of Texas drawl, seems odd for somebody from West Orange, New Jersey, though fitting enough, I suppose, for one who's lived her life like someone in a ballad. Emily's farmed, window-washed, gardened, painted houses. She's waited tables, been an editor. In high school she was a competitive classical pianist, a competitive ice skater. She's belted in karate. She was grounded her junior year in high school. Once, she says, she was a stowaway. She's lived in London, she's lived in Kenya, she's summered in Spain.

After graduating from St. Lawrence University, she enrolled in Bowling Green State University's writing program because once she'd run off to Ohio with a sailor and thought it an exotic state. After taking her degree, she stayed in Bowling Green because she'd become in-volved with Darryl, a young man with dreadlocks and a ska band. The restaurant she worked in gave you two free drinks when you got off your shift. Emily's was the morning shift. In the two-and-a-half months she was there, she never got a paycheck. Then, cold turkey, she quit waitressing. She helped manage Darryl's band but didn't want to go with it to Cincinnati. She applied to join the Peace Corps but, when that fell through, came to San Francisco. Two of her friends were there, and Emily, like Ellen, came out to live with them. She got to San Francisco in August, about a week before the beginning of the fall term. She would teach. She called on all the colleges in the Bay Area, showing up at Berkeley the day after classes started. The woman at the desk turned to the others in the office and said, "Hey, I've got this girl here from Iowa or something, and she thinks she's going to get a job teaching freshman comp." She got a job selling puppets. Darryl and the band came to California and settled in Santa Barbara. For a while Darryl and Emily took turns commuting. Then they broke up. What she'd really like, she says, would be to go to Thailand and teach in a Cambodian refugee camp.

So I'm wrong. Passports are in it, immigration papers. What they did was kick around the country, the world, using geography up like fre-quent fliers, and at least a little of their moxie, a lot of their patience.

Not gold mining, not life mining, not panning for fate. And home is neither where you hang your heart nor where your hat is. Home is wherever the cookie crumbles, random as chaos, beyond any trajectory you'd ever have guessed. People like Emily, like my niece, live in California like Foreign Legionnaires. Matt came because the college of his choice gave him financial aid. He chose it, really, as one might shop for a house or look for a neighborhood—— with all the picky proximities in play, the major centralities, some cautious, good-sense feel about schools and transport, access to churches, to culture and water. They trekked the long continental plank. Above water, they wait on time, on chance, on what happens next.

Me, I was born in New York, I grew up in Chicago, I live in St. Louis. Most people live inside certain fixed lines laid out like the inviolable markings of a tennis court or baseball diamond. It isn't any failure of bravery, some less-existential way of doing business, how one conducts the world. In my case, what happens next has already happened. I thought I was a picaro, I am only a tourist. Which is plenty hard work and doesn't always leave you with enough energy to buy into the other fellow's passion. It ain't just the rate of exchange that gets you, the strange food and queer customs. It's that you're breathing the other guy's views, his geology and architecture. Yes, and his real estate, his wholesale and retail, all the difficult, altered metrics of value, what you give to a bellman, what you leave for the maid—— whether and if. Every vacation has its perils, does some significant damage, and the cliché has it just exactly backwards that tells you that X is a swell place to visit, but you wouldn't want to live there. For me, what happens next has already happened.

It may even be that Milch is right, that California isn't much different from anyplace else, or that I am beyond Happiness, Serenity, Euphoria, the conventional building blocks of California quietude, quiddity, the vexless verities where nature lies down with life-style; or that California is not so much a place as an invention, a kind of aspiration, really, what imagination does to opportunity in a decent climate to make a benign and goofy nationalism.

But anyway, I'm on this airplane, a California dreamer thinking about the WELL, thinking about those two-buck-an-hour parking meters, and suddenly I understand why I unloaded all that money on the lady in the airport when she pushed me in the chair to my gate. For the same reason *any* tourist dumps his spare francs, or dinars, or pesetas, before he boards his plane and goes back home.

AT THE
ACADEMY
AWARDS

AT THE ACADEMY AWARDS, THE ENTRANCE TO THE SHRINE CIVIC
Auditorium is flanked by four giant Oscars quite, or so it seems to
me, like sullen, art deco Nazis. Set maybe a hundred feet back from
these, two temporary grandstands have been constructed for three thousand or so fans—day-of-the-locust types, extras, all the tribal, repre-
sentative legions who come to these things, drawn, it could almost be,
by the limousines themselves, gleaming cream-colored packages of
celebrity.

*Maybe because Galati never returned my calls or that I couldn't get
into Swifty Lazar's private party at Spago for a few hundred of his
friends. Or, first things first, putting, as it were, the horse before the
cart, because* off my turf (those few or so blocks of Washington University campus and the several more of proximal neighborhood where
I've lived almost thirty years now like something deposited in the fossil
record) *I am essentially cloutless, this pushing-sixty geriatric babe, out
of my element, in over my head.* I wait while Joan assembles the
wheelchair stashed in the trunk of the cab before I even try to get out.

But that's the point of these exercises, yes? The upstairs/downstairs, city mouse/country mouse, liaisons— all the slicker/rube relationships. Why, it's practically science fiction, journalism is, or this *kind* of journalism anyway, the refractive we-go-there or they-come-here displacements. Reactive chemistry just one more bankable myth, or, no, not one more, almost the only game in town, at the core, I bet, of half the plots in all the pix I've come in person all this way from Heartland to Coastland to watch being honored. More, probably. Isn't *The Accidental Tourist* about an educated, affectless, upper-middle-class writer who becomes involved with a spunky, blue-collarish, Jean Arthur type who keeps a kennel and trains his dog? And doesn't *Dangerous Liaisons* have the experienced mix it up with the innocent? *Working Girl* transforms a girl from Staten Island into a kind of Cinderella when her scheming, upper-class boss injures herself in a skiing accident. And *Rain Man*, the ultimate rube/slicker story, is a tale of two brothers, one your sweet, helpless idiot savant, the other your callous, high-flying car salesman. (With the exception of *Mississippi Burning*, I'd seen all the candidates for Best Picture 1988. Do I have a life or what?)

All the movies are some variation of *The Prince and the Pauper*; drama, that is, through collided worlds. But plot is *about* mixing it up. Not *this*, then *that* so much as characters caught out, embarrassed, in a dream. This is fiction's essence anyway, the thematics of opposites. Cops and robbers, cowboys and Indians, are nothing if not versions of the class struggle.

And all stories are travelogues, finally, or why would I have said what I did about journalism? Us Marco Polos are wide of eye, bumpkins, rubes and rustics, hicks and insulars. We travel by turnip truck (as Joan and I, minding the pennies, made the trip west on a carrier almost, it made so many stops, like a streetcar). Something surreal in the heart, something slapstick in the head, all the binary opposition of rigged polarity.

So, hardly your customary correspondent. More your plant, more your little old hand-wringer. There, in the clear California sunshine, beyond the California velvet roping off the red California carpet, below the 3,000-plus plebes in the charity-built grandstands, your reporter taking the air in black tie and wheelchair, basking at ground level— get this picture—among the milling celebs, bucking in the bowels for celeb himself, nonchalant, see, his face absent expression, unless indifference, carefully composed as the neutral poker puss of a high-stakes gambler, is the giveaway, my mean, squeezed mien, I mean. I give them nothing, *nothing*. My gimlet glare, my crabbed judgmentals, the studied, Prussian composure of some old-timey studio head. (I *ought* to be in pictures!) Projecting both to the cheap seats and to the stars themselves, all those famous, by-bone-structure-fated lives ambling the red carpet, outgoing and chipper in the still photography as brides and grooms. Because it *is* like a wedding, and they move past the press, straining toward them with tape recorders and microphones, as if along a receiving line.

Here is Roy Rogers. Here is Dale Evans. Old Roy packs a six-shooter on his spangled pants. Miss Dale is beaming and looking demure in her late seventies as if, despite her stylized cowlady duds, no woman was ever libbed.

Here is Dorothy Lamour, so much resembling my mother, I feel, my face breaking ranks, like waving.

Here is Karl Malden, here's Vincent Price.

Here are Cyd Charisse and Tony Martin. Here's Alice Faye. Here are the Bridges, Lloyd, Jeff, and what's-his-name. Here's Jimmy Stewart in his pink old age.

Most of them—this is peculiar—I *don't* recognize. (Michelle Pfeiffer, River Phoenix, Melanie Griffith, people whose movies you wait till they come out in video.) It's just these that the fans in the bleachers, sending some distant early warning of celebrity, alert us to. They actually go "ooh," they actually go "ah," making this raw, rough purr of awe.

And it really *is* like a wedding, it really is. We're looking at—what?—a dozen million dollars' worth of duds here. Some of the younger guys wear postmodern tuxedos. Blair Underwood, a lawyer for the home firm on "L.A. Law," has dark sequins hanging down the arms of his tuxedo jacket like a kind of glazed hair. Several fellows wear black running shoes with their tuxedos—— formal Reeboks, dress Nikes. I see, no shit, a leather tuxedo. And there's another man in a tux with a long rabbinical coat over it. And another whose bow tie spills over his shirtfront like a growth.

Security is trying to hustle the ticket holders—our comps, in the thirty-third or thirty-fourth row, cost $150 each; that's the incredibly inflated figure that's printed right on them in what I can only conceive of as Weimar Republic numerals; the ones to the Board of Governors

Ball afterward claim to be worth $450 apiece—into the Shrine Au-
ditorium, but I don't want to go in just yet, and the wheelchair, like
some flying carpet for gimps, provides a sort of cover. A woman in a
black floor-length skirt and dark, sheerish blouse, her outfit vaguely
reminiscent of a circus performer's, the dog- or bird-trainer's snagged,
stitched fishnet, say, and who carries a walkie-talkie, gives me permission to stay outside awhile longer to watch the movie stars arrive.
(There's Tom Hanks, there's Olivia Newton-John, there's Michael
Caine.)

Gradually I feel the features of my great stone face subside, erode
in the presence of all this fame, my ego not put down but beside the
point. If I could see my reflection now I would probably look windblown, punchy as the Sphinx. Someone in the bleacher seats waves
a sign that says JOHN 3:16, but it ain't *really* any day of the locust
here. The crowd's much too mellow, befitting the time zone and
circumstances. Though perhaps a bit barmy. The things people say!
There's John Cleese. Someone shouts out at him, "Good luck tonight,
good luck. Thank you for all the comedy you've brought us over the
years. Thank you, sir!"

And still they keep coming, a parade of the physically elect, the
incredibly handsome, the fabulously beautiful. It suddenly seems astonishing to me that presences like these could play *just* human beings.
It seems, I don't know, a sort of reverse hubris. (There's Jeff Goldblum.
There's Gregory Hines.) They better watch themselves, is what I think.
They better cool it, this weird dressing down they do for a living like,
oh, grown-ups squeezing into the getups of children. They better look
what they're doing or they could freeze like that.

There's Kevin Kline.

*Maybe because I didn't say anything to Roger Ebert when I spotted
him standing with the other reporters. Maybe because I didn't identify
myself and remind him that we were both of us scheduled to speak in
two weeks at a memorial service for a mutual friend.*

To say I feel betrayed would be overstating it. But I do feel had. A
little. A little I do. It takes a while, maybe through the first half hour
of the Awards show, but pretty soon I realize that no one is here who
doesn't have to be. The two hundred or so nominees in the twenty-
three categories. The fifty-some-odd presenters—there's Candice Ber-

gen, there's Sean Connery, there's Kim Novak—the hundred singers
and dancers—there's Tina Omeza, there's Regan Patno, there's Carla
Earle—and all the not-to-be-numbered members serving on the eleven
Academy committees. Then, when spouses and friends are thrown in,
well, there you are, you've accounted for a least a couple of thousand
people. I can't account for the rest of the folks in the hall— people
vaguely associated with the industry, I suppose, or society types, perhaps, who come every year but who almost certainly no one from my
part of town would recognize. I would think many of us occupy proffered seats, as, in a different season, we might be the guests of corporate
season ticket holders at a ball game or concert.

It's the same in my business, the same in yours. Most folks have
edge, some little piece of the action, first refusal, or the privilege of
wholesale, the travel agent's unlimited mileage, the congressman's
frank or salesman's discount, this one's backstage access, that one's
dibs on the float's leftover roses, the meat that would only spoil otherwise.

What I mean is, there's no such thing as the gratuitously high-
profiled here. We're an audience of cliques and special interests. The
real players are home, watching on TV, or with Swifty at Spago. Joan
and I are tucked a bit to the right and toward the back in a section
two or three steps above orchestra level; in the thirty-third or thirty-
fourth row, as I say, just under the overhang of the balcony in what
is probably a forty-row auditorium.

Why I'm steamed, to the extent I am, is that I've watched these
ceremonies on television for years. Always I'd come away not star-
struck but filled with some prize-in-every-box sense of a homogenized,
evenly distributed fame. Now, in my immediate area, except for a few
stars straggling into the hall and walking past our discrete little
acreage—there's Max von Sydow—to take their seats by the 5:30 P.M.
deadline, I recognize only myself and my wife.

Clearly, the star-spangled demographics are off this evening. Even
money they always were. And suddenly I understand something, that
all the splash and flourish of all those advertised lives I'd seen on all
those Oscar shows had been nothing but camera angles, a sort of trick
photography, doctored like Chinese news. And why not? Pros put this
stuff together. There are tricks to every trade— maybe there are actual
filters that take out bystanders like a kind of sunscreen. Or maybe Fame
is only the fine-tuning of some driving, evolutionary will, natural

selection doing its flakked and flashy thing. You think Zapruder shot his film by accident? He aimed that camera at that gunned-down president. Like Oswald himself, he was only following his heart, some abiding tropism that turned him toward history, that turns us all toward what seems important. If nothing's going on, you pass, you fold, you excuse yourself and get a sandwich.

So if this is the gala, where *is* everybody? is what I'm saying.

What can I tell you about an Oscar ceremony you don't already know? You've watched them for years, too. Taking in our pageants like our bonbons, the secret sinfuls—— the Miss Universe, the Miss America, the Miss Teenage America, the Miss *Mrs.* America. The Tonys and Emmys and Grammys. The People's Choice, the Golden Globes, the Country Musics, the Clios and Peabodys. All those endeavors awards, all these little faits accomplis. Do *I* have to tell you?

This is how far we've come. This is the ascent of man, awards only the persistence of a presumed justice, the shortest distance between thumbs-up and thumbs-down; lions, Christians, and the development of the jury system. The Academy Desserts. Because it isn't competition or truth at the core of entertainment; it's judgment, it's criticism. It's having a say. It's having a say and getting to change it from year to year. Even the World Series starts up again the following year. As if we *demanded* qualitative distinctions, a world with heroics, champions.

My first celebrity, the worst thing I ever did, and some observations:

In 1955, about three or four weeks into basic training, we were doing bayonet drill. This was in a field in the Colorado Rockies. As I recall it now, and it's very fuzzy, we were either two lines of recruits lined up across from each other or a long, continuous line facing practice dummies, some stuffed, canvas enemy. It could even be that nothing was across from us, that we were only going through the motions, doing what wouldn't then have been called imaging, thrusting our bayonets, fixed to our M-1s, in some choreography of vacant engagement, the sergeant in charge of our charge calling out half a catechism: "*What's the spirit of the bayonet?*" To our lunging, choric response: "*To kill!*" Shouting "*To kill!*" but thinking "chicken shit." Then something happened I'll never forget. Suddenly there was this officer on horseback, a one- or two-star general. I'm no more equestrian than soldier. I don't know the gaits. I can't tell the moment a walk becomes a trot, a trot a canter, a canter a gallop. What this was was none of those anyway. It may not even have been motion so much as some practiced, show-the-flag horse/man ballet, the mixed and ambled military leisurelies of mince and prance and strutting in place. I remember his long gleaming boots; I think he had a sidearm. If he'd broken into iambic pentameter or rallied us with speeches out of Shakespearean history plays, recited the chain of command, King to St. George, St. George to God, or tried to rouse us with the For-God-and-Country's, I couldn't have been more surprised. No— stunned! I'd never seen a general before. Mostly sergeants dealt with us, corporals, NCOs whose power came out of the barrel of their mouths, the sheer threatening noises they made. This man, if he even was a man, on that horse, if it even was a horse, was dead solid Power itself. He could have owned the field, the mountains. He could have *been* the field, the mountains, and if he wasn't my first celebrity, he was— to use Faulkner's word—my first avatar. The upshot was that I suddenly understood the spirit of the bayonet clear as crystal.

And here's the worst thing I ever did:

In the spring of 1975, I was a visiting professor at Yale living in a third-floor apartment at Timothy Dwight College. Timothy Dwight has in its endowment the Chubb Fellowships, grants that bring visiting politicians in for three-day visits. The semester I was there, Jimmy Carter, John Lindsay, Maynard Jackson, and Hubert Humphrey were all Chubb Fellows.

On the morning of the day of the worst thing I ever did I was coming downstairs with my laundry just as Hubert Humphrey was stepping out of the Chubb apartment. His hostess, Shelley Fishkin, saw me and introduced us. Humphrey and I shook hands and went about our business. That evening there were to be three functions in the senator's honor, a cocktail party at the master's house for everyone, a dinner to which I wasn't invited, and, later, a party at the Fishkins to which I was. Two out of three ain't bad and I hold no grudges. When I showed up at the cocktail party, Humphrey spotted me, broke away from his group, and said, "*Saaay*, I didn't know you were *that* Stanley Elkin!"

Now, unless the senator was confusing me with the historian Stanley Elkins, I don't believe he thought I was any kind of Stanley Elkin at all. What probably happened was that after our brief introduction

Shelley must have identified the guy with the laundry basket as the visiting writer. In any event, I was being patronized. I knew it and it annoyed me. In the two-hour interval between the dinner I hadn't been invited to and the party I had, I'd had some drinks and arrived at the party a little late. The Whiffenpoofs were serenading the senator. They finished and left. Immediately, everyone in the room crowded around Humphrey and started asking him questions, about the up-coming conventions, about foreign affairs, whatever was on the agenda that spring. Really, it was more like a press conference than a party. And that's when I made my move.

"Excuse me, Senator," I said.

"*Yes?*"

"Could you get me a Coca-Cola?"

"You want me to get you a Coca-Cola?"

People were paying more attention than they had even to the Whif-fenpoofs, baa baa baa.

"If you would, please. There's a whole tub of them behind you. Right there. Over against the wall."

I know it sounds dramatic, but Humphrey was watching me closely. Christ, everyone was. "All right," he said finally, and handed me a can.

"That's the way you hand somebody a Coca-Cola?" I reproached him.

"What," he said. It wasn't a question.

"Well, it's just that there's that little tin whoosie on top. I might cut myself. I better not try opening that. No sir," I told him, and gave the Coke back. Very deftly he did something deliberately to disable it.

"Gosh," said Hubert Humphrey, "I can't do it either," and put the useless can back in my hand. He'd won, the happy warrior, and by now he probably had all too clear an idea about the kind of Stanley Elkin I really was.

Or the time we lived in Virginia, maybe a hundred miles from Washington, and every so often we'd go up for a weekend, poke around the museums, do a monument or agency, maybe take in a congres-sional hearing, then come in at six o'clock and eat the big seafood. The thing of it is, Washington has always depressed me. I have the feeling, as I have in Paris or anywhere glamorous, I'm not only a tourist but a stranger, that big things are happening, important shifts, large goings-on in the social and cultural tectonics, the great, carved intentions of the world, but not to me. For all that the guides insist it's my White House, I know better. I know it's worth my ass to sit down in one off-limits chair or touch, unauthorized, one lousy velvet rope. I had a sense, wherever I happened to be in those days, that the good stuff was going on elsewhere. Georgetown was where the action was, the Virginia hunt country, and this knowledge broke my heart.

There's a shop in Los Angeles on Melrose where the used clothes of movie stars are sold to the public. The appeal of an autograph, I think, is the homeopathic magic it contains, the voodoo I-touched-you's—and not *just* the voodoo I-touched-you's, however farfetched or removed (the hand that shook the hand that shook the hand), but the voodoo you-touched-*me's*, too. Ain't it feasible, I mean, that the inventory in that Melrose shop and the rags, bones, and hanks of hair of the saints and martyrs should have, at least from the consumer's point of view, something in common— that religious feelings, the love of God even, may only be a higher type of star-struck awe and agape, what there was before TV and the talkies? We do some of our best business in the atmosphere of angels. Be still, oh, be still, my bobby-soxer heart!

It's hard, at the Academy Awards, to distinguish between those stars I saw outside, in the flesh, and those I see on the stage. Joan has the same difficulty. A couple of months later, watching a video of the ceremonies, both of us will be unable to remember having seen particular parts of the show. We sat through all but the last ten minutes or so—missing Best Performance by an Actress, missing Best Picture, to beat the crowds, to put dibs on the rest rooms—but neither of us remembers having seen Cher, or Richard Dreyfuss, or Carrie Fisher. Jane Fonda has dropped through our short-term memory, Merv Griffin. Angelica Huston and Donald Sutherland are out of the loop. Indeed, both of us have more vivid memories of the acceptance speeches of people we'd never heard of, achievers in art direction, achievers in sound, than we have of the coy presenter banter of the household names. Television and movies at once create and obliterate fame. I recall what Dustin Hoffman said in his acceptance speech because he said it clumsily, because, unless he was acting, there was this unscripted slippage into the human register.

• • •

It's easy to knock these ceremonies, of course, which, on television at least, and even in person, seem an invitation to archaeologists, some artifacts from the Zircon Age. It's easy to knock these ceremonies because here at the Academy Awards, where glitz hands off to glitz and it's this Mardi Gras of diamonds larger than rhinestones, structure surrenders to motion, to din, to appearance as arbitrary and frantic as a chase scene. Ironically, at the Academy Awards, all sense of the theatrical gives way neither to wit nor spectacle but to stunt— how many presenters, like so many clowns, can be crammed into the Volkswagen. (And I'm failing the form here, am insufficiently a stand-in for the little guy. The slicker/rube is inoperable. There is no awe, only humiliation, stripped privilege like a scuttled form, and I've slipped genres, my piece at one remove—*I blame Galati, I blame S. Lazar, I blame Roger Ebert, I blame Molly, my daughter, who at approximately the same time her father is being denied access to the Action is taking the Middle East by storm, is dining with the Rabins at their home in Jerusalem through the good offices of a connected friend*—from the freshman's classic theme about why he can't write one.) The show—and I had almost said "services"—reminds one of summer camp, of tacked-on, interminable verses, stanzas of pointless, round-robin story told first by A and kept up by B, by C and D and E and all, that do not so much advance the plot as simply continue it.

The president of the Academy of Motion Picture Arts and Sciences introduces Tom Selleck, who brings on Melanie Griffith and Don Johnson, who banter reflexively, list the nominees for Best Supporting Actress (always, somehow, all nominees and the films for which they've been nominated will be announced in the vaguely runway accents and unnatural singsong of a fashion show, almost, it would seem, in Don Pardo's descriptive RV and Turtle-Waxian tropes), open the envelope, and give Geena Davis an Oscar. Miss Davis thanks Anne Tyler, Ruth Myers, Larry Kasdan, Ray London, Bill Hurt, and Jeff Goldblum. And we go to commercial like a seventh-inning stretch.

Rhymeless and reasonless, this is how the evening happens. It's the show again. A Voice, like the disembodied sound of some Las Vegan casino god, introduces Jane Fonda, who talks about Best Pictures and presents a film clip. (With its film clips, all of which are identical to those I'd already seen on Carson and other American hype outlets, the Academy Awards may be the quintessential TV show.) In keeping with the evening's surrealism, the dead-solid arbitrary of its *auf zu-lachen* will, Ms. Fonda brings out Jimmy Stewart and Kim Novak, who give the awards for achievement in sound-effects editing.

Until gradually I'm proved wrong and the true structure of the ceremonies (neither car chase nor stunt, motion nor din, how many presenters on the head of a pin, nor even long summer's endless ninety-nine bottles of beer on the wall or its row, row, row your boats around the campfire) finally begins to emerge. Why, it's a *board game* is what it is! Certainly! Of course! Drama and suspense, action and irony, the Oscars according to Parker Brothers! The Academy Awards designed for the long, lazy laid-back of a rainy day. All the culs-de-sac, skipped turns, jumped spaces, bonuses (a Special Achievement Award to Richard Williams for animation direction of *Who Framed Roger Rabbit*; an honorary Academy Award to the National Film Board of Canada), and even its graduated values (Achievement in Art Direction is less important than Best Actor exactly as Baltic Avenue is less valuable than Park Place) suggest all the drawn-out, delayed gratification and jittery interruption of the final winner-takes-all, Best Picture, like the kid holding the most houses, hotels, and cash.

At the Academy Awards, you can't get there from here. It's a de-Ezekielized world of detached and scattered bones. The Voice produces Walter Matthau, Walter Matthau produces Bob Hope and Lucille Ball. At the Academy Awards, it's a pointless, incomplete vaudeville. Bob Hope and Lucille Ball present nineteen "Oscar Winners of Tomorrow" in an endless every-man-for-himself song and dance about ambition and narcissism philosophically distilled from A *Chorus Line* without the benefit of that show's melody, passion, talent, or wit. At the Academy Awards, it's a drawn-out, almost fastidious, customary kowtow. It's the obligatory standing ovation. You could put money down on who's going to get one, but who'd be sucker enough to take your bet? Bob Hope and Lucille Ball get one. Out of almost Chinese respect, only it's not so much ancestor worship as a gift for survival, for longevity, and, really, in a business where it ain't any Oscar winners of tomorrow who take the cake or stop the show, not even for talent so much as for the legendary, inoffensively bankable. We *love* Lucy. We're nuts about Hope. We eat up their routine. *They* eat up their routine.

HOPE: What a night! I haven't seen so many gorgeous girls since I spent Father's Day with Steve Garvey. (*Lucy laughs heartily.*) But I've got the *most* gorgeous girl right by my side— Lucille Ball, right *there!*

LUCY: Thank you. It really is wonderful to be here, and a particular thrill especially with you, Bob. It's a very secure feeling being up here with a man who's been on the Oscar show twenty-six times.

HOPE: That's true.

LUCY: And never won.

HOPE: You had to mention it, huh?

LUCY: Well . . .

HOPE: It's not that I haven't begged. I've been on my knees more than Jimmy Swaggart. Anyway, a lot of people are wondering what Lucy and I are doing up here together. You know, we made four pictures together.

LUCY: Yeah, talk about dangerous liaisons.

HOPE: Even though we haven't been working in a while, we still keep in touch with everything. In fact, today the Ayatollah Khomeini called me and asked who wrote *Ishtar*.

LUCY: And I heard they've offered you a role in the picture about Dan Quayle's visit to the White House.

HOPE: Yeah, *The Accidental Tourist.* Actually, I was called back to Washington to paper-train the puppies.

LUCY: Aww.

HOPE: You know Millie, the White House dog, had three puppies. Actually she had five, but the Senate rejected two.

LUCY: Bob, can we stop now? . . .

HOPE: Yeah. (*in his but-seriously-folks voice*) You're about to see nineteen of the hottest young actors and actresses in pictures. These are the people who will be winning Oscars way into the next century.

LUCY: (*In a but-seriously-folks voice of her own*): That's right. You've already seen them act in hit movies, but tonight you're going to see them sing and dance.

Because there's always the "but-seriously-folks" voice. Because there's always the silly double entendre of show business's mixed signals, its Trust Me idiomatics like some dead language. (Because I never heard of these "Oscar Winners of Tomorrow" and neither have you.) Because it *is* a sort of archaeology here, because in a real way, here, at the Academy Awards, we're on site, in the very future's very digs, at Routine's locale, perhaps the single place in all geography at the one moment in all time when so many could understand without recourse to footnotes the merely momentarily humorous argot of the Proper Noun, self-referential, egocentric. The "Father's Day with Steve Garvey," "Jimmy Swaggart," "dangerous liaisons," and "Ayatollah Khomeini/*Ishtar*" lines (Salman Rushdie understood): the incredibly labored setup and syntax of Bob Hope's playing the lead in a movie about Dan Quayle's visit to the White House and calling the film *The Accidental Tourist*; the joke about the Senate rejecting two of Millie's puppies, are already like relics, like stuff pressed into geology.

And these anger me too— his banter, these "jokes." From my resentment pool, deep as some sea trench, rises a personal bile. It's the second time I've felt had, and this time "betrayed" *wouldn't* be overstating it. It ain't the papered house now but something on actual behalf of actual art. It's stupidity that has me down, Bob Hope's simplistic, condescending view of history and of ourselves, me. Because I take it personally, the good-natured contempt, the artificial scorn, the false assumption like a wink up in your face like a slap, or the car salesman's nudge like an elbow to your rib that we're all pals here, that we're in it together. Well— we ain't.

(Physically, it's been a hell of a year for me. In February my multiple sclerosis started to multiply. In March I got my wheelchair. In late June I went into the hospital for a course of Solumedrol and Cytoxin in the hope that those drugs would strengthen me, or at least freeze my disease at its current level, but before they were even started I had a strange experience. I was trying to tell Joan I had a terrible headache, but all I could say was "I have this awful haircut." I knew what I said was wrong and understood everything Joan and the nurse were trying to tell me. I thought I was having a stroke. "I think," I told them, "I'm having an Australian crawl." I was taken for Doppler exams, for angiograms to the head, and it was discovered that only 2 percent of my right carotid artery was open. The left carotid artery had shut down completely. I was given an endarterectomy on the right side of my throat. They cleaned my plugs and points, but I suffered a mild heart attack from the anesthesia. This is the House that Jack built. After a time, they said, when I was strong enough, they said, I would need a heart angiogram to check out the damage. I would have, they said, depending on what the pictures showed, three options: I could be "managed medically"; I might be a candidate for an angioplasty—they send tiny balloons up your arteries and Roto-Rooter the schmutz from your system, all that old lox and cream cheese, all that ancient butter and eggs, all that red meat and smoke—or, they said, I would have to have open-heart surgery, a second heart bypass. "Out of the question," I told them. "Never again." But there is more to the quality of life than the quality of life, and when the angiogram showed I would either have to have the bypass or die, I chickened out and chose to live.)

Because there *is* more to the quality of life than the quality of life. Because one would to the woods no more with flibbertigibbets. Because camp is not enough, nor hype, nor kitsch, nor glamour, nor glitz, nor all pop culture's various altitudes, low to high like some kid's practice scales. Because *vita's* too *brevis* and *ars* ain't *longa* enough by a country mile. And because here, at the Academy Awards, it isn't good enough finally to fabricate quality and celebration like some currency minted by hoopla, ads taken out in the trades—the clang and bang and claque of cash. And because it's a masque here, finally, some deal with the graced and favored, power in league with bone structure, haute couture, physiques as mannered and looked after as French gardens— Youth and Beauty like some topiary architecture of the only platonically human. (And it may just be something this side of sin in the actor's art, a stooping to conquer, a feeling I cannot shake all evening that pacts have been signed, the stronger pledges taken, temporal *quids* for immortal *quos*.) *Of course, if Galati had only returned my calls to the Four Seasons it might all have been different: Galati, up for an award himself for his screenplay for* The Accidental Tourist; *Galati, whom I'd put into pictures, the single person in all the world—save one's children—whose life I'd changed, whose name in those brief old days when I could have been a contender, Charlie. I had at once volunteered when asked if I could think of anyone who could do the adaptation of a book I'd written and on which this teensy little option had been taken out like an inexpensive hit. Who might have gotten us*

a place, tourists at the Tourist *table, supping with Geena Davis,
with Jeff Goldblum, with Lawrence Kasdan, with Charles Okun
and Michael Grillo, producers, with Bill Hurt if I really got lucky
and my theory proved wrong about no one coming to these do's
unless something was in it for him. Perhaps then the grapes would
not have been so sour. —— Or not. Maybe it was the time zone,
hours behind my own, psychological months even, the overlapping
seasons of my humiliations between hospital and Hollywood, the
bleak occasion of my below-stairs perspectives, the gut-hard feelings
between my mortality and their own blessed lives like gifts from the
Genes Fairies.*

(I forgive Galati. I even understand him. He's up for an award,
there's lots on his mind; there are probably studio flowers in his suite,
baskets of fruit, congratulatory telegrams all over the place. It's a simple
question of who needs the aggravation, hospitality to some guy you're
into for your career, a pain in the ass on unfamiliar turf. It's Swifty
L., who doesn't even know me, I'll never forgive.)

Though we get to go to a couple of parties anyway. (And, later, I even
have an opportunity to speak to Larry Kasdan personally. Joan is calling
for a cab from a bank of phones at the Shrine. I'm right behind her,
maybe five feet away, in my wheelchair. At the next phone over there's
this important-looking young man, and I hear him say something like
"Tell him Larry Kasdan. Yeah, thanks." When he hangs up I say,
"Excuse me, sir, but are you Mr. Kasdan?" I don't think he sees me
in the chair because he's looking around to see where the voice is
coming from. Then he glances down and spots me. "Yes," he says.
"Aren't you with Frank Galati?" I ask, syntactically putting, as it were,
the accent on the wrong syllable. "He was at my table all evening,"
he tells me, annoyed, and stalks off.)

The Shrine Exposition Hall looks like a soundstage. It's been made
over for the Board of Governors Ball, but it could be a set for an
immense wedding party or the most expensive prom in human history.
Or, indeed, the venue for almost any formal "affair," from bar mitzvah
to state dinner. There's a kind of carpeting, there are ice sculptures,
a tiny dance floor around a round raised platform for the band. Everywhere, as decoration, there are battalions of those muscular art deco
Oscars like some futuristic fascist coinage. Our table, in the two-

hundreds like a dangerously elevated blood pressure, in deep steerage, is maybe a block-and-a-half from the entrance as the wheelchair rolls. I pray there isn't a fire.

I cast my eyes around the huge hall for a celeb but come up empty. Of course, we are, in terms of the seating, somewhere in space, about, if this were the universe, where *Voyager 2* might start to give out. It's all, as far as the eye can see, limbo hereabouts. At our table there seem to be a bunch of folks down from Sacramento— politicians, their spouses. There are no place cards. No effort is made at introductions. The cat has got this reporter's tongue. Joan breaks the disinterested ice, and it turns out there *is* a celebrity at the table. It's Willie Brown's, the influential California Democrat's, daughter. She's there on a date. The presence of the others at the $450-per-person sit-down dinner is, and remains, completely puzzling. I wonder aloud if *anyone* in this immense room has actually put out cash money to be here and have again the sense that we're all beneficiaries of some huge, pointless charity, a sort of Sunshine Fund for the already tan. No one responds to my observations, but it could be the din. We're on a sound stage indeed. I find I can talk (save Joan's grace) only to the woman on my right, a political spouse (I think) and, in her own right, a travel agent. We spend the evening, or she does, discussing frequent-flier miles, letting me in on the almost Hermes Trismegistean arcana— tricks of the trade, arrangements, how to crack the system, all the secret alchemicals of turning paper credit into distance and upgrades. You must never cash your miles in for a free flight, you buy your tickets at the discount. I don't think I understand a word she says, but I recognize passion when I hear it. She's flown farther than the Secretary of State, she tells me proudly. Sitting there in my tux, I'm too ashamed to admit that we beat the system by coming out here on this flying trolley car that keeps stopping to pick up passengers along the way and gives you a transfer in Phoenix, Arizona.

She is giving me the headache. To break her concentration, I study the menu to get some idea of what I've been eating. This is what 450 ghost bucks will get you these days:

POACHED SALMON AND ARUGULA ROULADE
With yellow and green french beans
and sliced mango on baby spring greens
with creamy honey-lime vinaigrette

BREADS
Homemade corn sticks,
whole wheat walnut rolls, and
garlic-herb knots with sweet butter rosettes

CHICKEN BREAST GRILLED OVER ALDERWOOD
Pommes soufflées in potato baskets
Grilled zucchini, baby white eggplant,
fresh baby corn

And that, Dear Diary, is all there was to it. Absolutely nothing else happened to us that night at the Governors Ball.

"You really think we should go to the party?" asks Joan.

"I'm on assignment," I tell her, "I'm duty bound."

"I'm a good sport, do you know that?"

"You *are* a good sport," I admit, which is just about when she goes off to break the dollar to get the change to call the cab to take us to the El Rescate 2nd Annual Academy Awards Benefit at Vertigo in downtown L.A. It's supposed to be one of the "alternative parties" the younger, more serious movie people are said to favor these days.

The $150-per-head admission at the door, like the $1,200 we've already cost our phantom benefactors for the privilege of going to the Academy Awards and watching the big TV show in person and, later, eating the garlic-herb knots and baby white eggplant—all that bread and veggies to the Stars—has been mysteriously waived. I don't get to identify myself—as per instructions—to Patrick Lippert in "Joe sent me," speakeasy inflections, or even flash the tickets Nanci Ryder (whom I don't know and have never seen and only spoken to on the telephone twice, on which she calls me Stanley—*me, Stanley*, a crippled-up old man who in just over three months is doomed to have his throat cut and his chest cracked open for the second time in four years; *Stanley*, not Your Mortalityship or Your Woundship or even Mr. Elkin—*Stanley*, as if, as if, well, as if I were one of them, the larky freewheeling, high rolling of Earth) has sent over by special messenger to our hotel in Korea town. Indeed, it's as if they've been waiting for us, keeping an eye out. As soon as Joan starts to assemble the wheelchair, two young men, too polite to be anything but bouncers, come to assist us. They take us through a special entrance and into the room.

Into an astonishing scene, one that I, Stanley, bad health's good sport, would never have expected ever to have witnessed. Not only too old but out of an altogether different, whatchamacallit, ethos, a different conation and even phylum maybe—— my faint, poor pale human to their strident, unselfconscious, powerful, but entirely alien, life force.

Black tie, according to the invitation, is optional, but that ain't it, that I'm the only man in the club in a tux, probably, for that matter, the only one in a jacket, or even in pants not artfully, sexually ripped into designer-torn, teasing jigsaw, fig-leaf puzzle patterns, or, as far as that goes, a buttoned shirt. They look vaguely like Oscars themselves, these guys. The women, oddly enough, are more formally dressed, many in gowns slightly reminiscent of hoop skirts. A girl near my wheelchair has to lean forward and flip up the back of her dress each time she sits down. Somehow she reminds me of a cartoon hen settling herself onto a Sunday-funnies egg. And that ain't it either.

What it is.

There used to be scenes in movies. Cut to an all-but-deserted night-club. It's (metaphorically) quarter to three, there's no one in the place, Joe, except you and me. Most of the chairs have already been turned upside down on their tables. Only one couple, oblivious, obviously in love, is still dancing, gliding in the dim, romantically lighted room along the floor to some bluesy, dreamy tune in reeds, soft sax, muted brass, a tinkling piano in the next apartment. Waiters, impatient to go home, fidget, glance balefully at their watches, each other, sigh, toss "What can you do? They're in love. No one told me to go into my profession" occupational-hazard-type shrugs.

Now forget about the time (it's barely midnight) and the waiters (cocktail waitresses do the heavy lifting here) and the one lone couple (Vertigo isn't crowded, but there can't be more than eight or ten people dancing.) Throw out the dreamy tune, the reeds and sax and muted brass. Forget the tinkling piano in the next apartment. You couldn't hear it with a radio telescope. Turn off the lowered, romantic lights. In their place substitute strobes popping and flashing like a bright barrage of incoming. On the club's small stage a heavy-metal band (of an element *so* heavy, *so* dense and base that whatever metal it represents has yet to be measured or even identified—— black hole, perhaps) issues sounds so loud they would be heard by posts. Every instrument is electrically amplified, even the drums. For the second time that night I pray there isn't a fire.

The El Rescate 2nd Annual Academy Awards Benefit is a war zone.

A cocktail waitress shouts would we like a drink from the cash bar. A hundred and fifty bucks apiece at the door and it's a cash bar.

El Rescate was set up to assist a half million Central American refugees in the Los Angeles area with a variety of social services. It seems to me to be charity with a somehow coastal spin, though what is most striking is the pure surrealism of the event, the insufficiency of dancers in the big room, the hyperbolic music. Everywhere there are TV sets running videos of real war zones, their soundtracks silent against the explosive din and bang of the band. Earlier, of course, the sets had been tuned to the Awards, but we weren't here earlier and it isn't easy to imagine the scene. One thinks of sports—— the World Series, Super Bowls, important away games, home games blacked out in their own cities, of all the taverns in all the towns with their enthusiastic, youthful clientele, whooping it up, making "We're number one, we're number one!" with their fingers, crowding about the reporter, mugging for the TV cameras, the CBS local news at ten. It's impossible to imagine any of these people up for that sort of thing. For all their energy, the come-on of their driving, up-front dress, they seem detached to me, cynical. Like royals, they give off a faint stink of imperial airs. They're young, but somehow they seem as if they never had a youth. But what do I know, a guy redlined years ago by the underwriters? Probably it's just more sour grapes, the prejudiced *pensées* of an embittered ex-contender manqué.

(And there's the match-up right there, the carefully arranged marriage of my stipulate, *shadchen* journalism, not rube/slicker at all, but alive/dead—your reporter all gee-whizzed out in the wheelchair.)

At any rate, this ain't, for us, where the action is anyway and, like pols or priests at a party, we do maybe twenty-five minutes, then metaphorically walk back to the hotel in the metaphorical rain.

Joan's gone back to the room and left me in the lobby to wait for Steve to join us for breakfast. He's a few minutes late, but I know he'll be here soon, is on his way, is even now parking his car. Meanwhile I take my ease in one of the hotel's deep, comfortable chairs. It's a cold comfort, but one of the things I've learned since losing my ability to get around is, well, patience isn't it exactly, but a sort of passive curiosity, a compensatory faculty like the sharpened acuity of hearing in the blind, say, their increased tactility. Anyway, I'm peculiarly suited to my disease, content, up to a point, as a baby, absorbed by motes in the light, distracted by the parts of his toy mobile riding the currents of the air. This is the close attention I pay to the world now, my cripple's nosy scrutiny. I watch people checking out, their clear plastic garment bags holding evening gowns, tuxedos, and although I recognize no one, I figure them, like me, for stringers, singers, boys in the band, on the fringes, that is, of last night's ceremonies. I hear them double-checking, questioning the desk regarding their bills, the patient, difficult Oriental accents of the clerks. Many of the guests are Korean. These chat up the clerks carelessly, cheerfully, *paisans* in this foreign hotel. Then I notice something strange, startling even, comic, even moving.

Across from me is a well-dressed married couple. They are Korean, probably in their forties. Arranged at their feet are bags from significant shops and stores, their logos, chic, flagrant as modern times. They have been on a shopping spree, and this is somehow oddly touching to me. Then I see that they're joined by a young man in his late teens. He has shopping bags, too. He's in blue jeans, wears a light sweater. He laughs and puts his arm familiarly around the man's shoulder. He hugs the woman. Only the kid is white, American. I can't quite make out what they're saying, or even the language they say it in. Why, he's adopted, I think. *They've gone and adopted an American kid!* And I'm stirred by the improbable ecumenicism of the world, the odd, turned-tables of things, and feel suddenly hopeful, better than I have since I've been here.

But then the boy shakes hands with the two Koreans, waves so long, and leaves the hotel just as Steve comes into it.

Steve Zwicker is the outgoing chairman of our English Department at Washington University. I like him because he's sane, a decent man bereft of neurosis and shtick. Unless you count, as I don't, his fear of, or maybe just his distaste for, flying. (A native Californian, he makes his frequent trips home on an Amtrak sleeper.) I'm fond of the Zwickers. During my sabbatical year in London, we rented our house to them. They didn't break anything. Steve and I agree about books, movies, have mostly the same opinions of our mutual friends. I go to all his kids' bar mitzvahs. He visits me in all my hospitals. He's an immaculate man, wry, sharp as good grapefruit. But chiefly, chiefly his sanity, his even-keel heart, which has less to do with any level, steady-as-she-goes fixity of purpose or unflappability of temperament than with his pitch-pipe instincts, some almost musical correctness of the emotions. Indeed, he has the benevolent, intelligent look of a musician in a symphony orchestra.

He's glad to see me. I'm glad to see him. And I have a familiar dividend of well-being, this jolt of bonding I feel whenever I'm with a friend I know from one place in another place essentially foreign to me. Though we share the turf here. It's my hotel, it's his hometown.

Then Joan steps out of the elevator, and we all go in to breakfast.

I'm not in my wheelchair, have elected to go the distance to the restaurant on my cane—— and on Joan's arm. He's never seen me in my wheelchair. None of my friends has. My new, exacerbating disabilities are not out of the closet yet, but I'm stumbling badly, have to move along the wall for stability, leverage, playing the percentages with gravity, my waning strength. I notice Steve noticing. But once we're shown to our booth and seated, we're all equals again.

He asks how it went at the Awards, but I haven't sorted it all out yet and I can only tell him that for all the backstage and gossip I got out of it, we could have stayed home and watched on TV. And I tell him about Galati, and Swifty Lazar—— all my fish that got away.

Then we order. We order melons and berries, plates of lox, bagels, baskets of bread. Joan will have half a grapefruit, a poached egg, whole-wheat toast. Coffee, we stipulate, is to be brought later. I love breakfast. I always have. In my book, it's the only meal—— the long, luxurious leisurelies, at once normal and as ceremonial as high tea.

We talk. We talk about Molly's junior year abroad at Wadham College, Oxford University, my daughter the boater, how she earned her oar, her invitations to country houses on weekends, her trips between terms to Italy for the paintings, to Austria for the slopes. She's between terms now. Hilary's term ended in March and we went to see her. We tell how she talked the manager at Durrants Hotel into upgrading our accommodations. We talk about our week in Paris together, her pals in the discos, from Oxford, Madison, Sarah Lawrence. As we speak, she's still in Israel with her connected friend. They'll be going on to Greece before they return to Oxford for Trinity term. Hilary term, Trinity. We discuss the morality of envying one's children.

Breakfast begins coming. The melon is swell, the berries and grape-fruit. The lox, piled higher than corned beef in a sandwich in a deli, is more than we bargained for but not more than we can handle, its sheer weight incremental to our appetites. We try out different rolls, share pony pots of jam.

And talk easily, as comfortable with each other as the closed circle of movie stars at the Academy Awards. Wickedly, we discuss colleagues. I tease Steve about his money. He needles me about the long airplane ride ahead of us.

"TWA must have dozens of nonstops to St. Louis. Change carriers. Why lay over in Phoenix so long? Why do you have to stop in Houston? *Houston.* Isn't Houston on the Gulf of Mexico?"

"The magazine isn't paying for it. I am."

"That's not a good argument. I'm unimpressed."

"It's a difference of about $700."

"Suppose there's weather? In terms of time, you'd almost be better off with Amtrak."

In July, Steve will no longer be chairman of the English Department. Wayne Fields will replace him. Steve was our first Jewish chairman, and when I see him in the halls I'll no longer have the opportunity to greet him as I used to do. "Good morning, Reb Chairman," or "Good evening, Reb Chairman." But we've finished our coffee. The breakfast, which has lasted longer than our dinner at the Governors Ball, and has been, for Joan, for me, much more fun, is just about over. I sign the check. "We have a plane to catch, Reb Chairman," I tell him, and rise carefully. Clumsily, I walk back into the lobby. I shake hands with my friend and say I'll see him back in St. Louis.

While Joan returns to the room to collect the wheelchair and arrange with a bellman about our bags, I prop myself against the cashier's counter and see to the bill.

By the time she comes down with the chair, I'm more than ready to sit in it. The bellman takes our bags and Joan pushes me toward the hotel's driveway, where we wait for the cab that will take us to the airport where we'll go to the gate to catch the plane that will bring us back to the town where we live in a house that stands on a street not far from the world that Jack built.

THE REST
OF THE
NOVEL

FOR CONVEYING IDEAS, NOVELS ARE AMONG THE LEAST FUNCTIONAL and most decorative of the blunt instruments. (Could this be a universal truth, some starry, operative mathematical principle? Most stars are decorative too, of course, their function merely to peg the universe in place like studs in upholstery, servicing the elegancies, strumming its physics like a man with a blue guitar, fleshing all the centripetals and centrifugals, stringing the planets like beads, some beautiful pump of placement, arranging night, moving the planetary furniture, and fixing the astronomical data, but less useful, finally, in the sense that a handful more here or a dollop less there could make as much of a never mind as corks or rhythm, less useful, finally, than mail or ice cream.) And if, a few times in a way, novels like Richard Henry Dana's *Two Years Before the Mast* or Beecher Stowe's *Uncle Tom's Cabin* or Steinbeck's *Grapes of Wrath* come along to legislate, or raise a consciousness or two, or rouse a rabble, to make, I mean, what history or the papers call a difference, why that's decorative, too, I think, a lip service the system, touching the bases like a superstitious braille, pays art— like, oh, the claims made a few years back for the "We

Are the World" folks when it was really the Catholic Relief Services already on site during the Ethopian famine that did the heavy lifting.

Well it's not the novelist's fault. Not that they don't deserve some of the blame, leaking encouragement like someone paying out line to fish, some of your have-cake-and-eat-its like a little miracle of the loaves. And there are still a few big mouths who stake claims for the ameliorative shamanism of—hark! this is interesting: not the book so much as the writer—the practice of fiction—— the loyal, Nutso Art Jerk Groupie, like some devoted cultist, the last Deadhead, say, worrying like holy beads the shoelace on his wrist he thinks is a bracelet making confrontation with an Elvis Presley impersonator.

Isn't it pretty to think so, though? To take oneself as seriously as one's readers sometimes do? To believe, if only briefly, and if only by the light off the gloss of the brittlest mood swing, in the justice or even the palpability of one's cause, to Don Quixote principle, any principle, and raise to the level of purpose what in the final analysis is only what given egos, fashionably or not, fashion or no, frozen in mere season's hipped au courantness, perceive as beauty.

Because aesthetics is the only subject matter, because style is, and all calls are judgment calls. Because ideas are even scarcer than those fabled two or three stripped plots, those fabled three or four basic jokes, art a fugue ideal finally, the hen's-teeth variations, genre revolving around itself, the spin-off, like a few chips of colored glass in a kaleidoscope.

Because ain't, when you come right down, the rest of the novel like the rest of the novel, as all detective stories are like all other detective stories, dick-fic a piece of the mother-lode main? Not just who done it but how it's done, how it's *always* done, the who-done-it as orthodox and ritualized as positions in ballet in which, like the do-re-me's, all music has its source, from Natchez to Mobile, from Memphis to St. Joe. Almost as if a detective's relentless, endless questions along the stations of his investigation, the forced march of his focused, inquisitive rhetoric, were the natural music of the world, or as if such men were tone deaf to intrusion, to all the hectoring socratics of their quest. And the hell this plays with character, all the battering-rammed intent of obsession, the armored callus of the soul, the boring tyrannicals of personality. To say nothing at all of the other played-upon players in the game, their passified, invaded lives and suspect, squirmed evasions. *Form*, I mean, *creates cliché*. It horses stereotype. Think of Mr. Falk's

Columbo and you have almost encyclopedically the finite limits of
the genre—— only his rumpled raincoat and his smarmy awe and
merely partially put-on turnip-truck airs and naïves, only the feigned
clutter of his personal human laundry, only that final question delivered at the door and springing, it would seem, from the goldened-over
grove of his slapped and mythic forehead a studied idosyncratics all
he has for character, *shtick* in lieu of life and charm and will, tic in
lieu of depth, as if Hercule and Holmes and Dalgleish and Marple
were really, give or take an eccentricity, ultimately the same invul-
nerable party, their very invulnerability almost a product not so much
of their slick sleuthfulness as of their authority, the fascist bent of their
being, and their recyclability as characters, their cloned and clannish
serial essence, not even the motives of the criminals changing—love-
greed or cash-greed—only always the victims and cases, sometimes
the weapons. In it, amateurs or not, professionally, which is to say
objectively, which is to say marginally, indifferent and blind as Justice
herself, with no more rooting interest in who did what to whom than,
ideally, the jury impaneled to determine the guilt or innocence of the
party arrested. In it professionally. So standing outside the loop of the
novel itself. Which is, of course, no place for any *proper* protagonist
to stand at all. Their invulnerability protected, too, not just by the
almost apostolic authority of their badged office but crazily, by, well,
profit motive, so that sometimes even after their authors age and sicken
and die, their characters live on, doomed like ghosts to sequel their
lives, their impersonate lives assuranced, too, by the genre in which
they ask their bruising, devastating questions, questions that, in real
life, would earn, at least for the amateurs and busybodies, the private
eyes and mercenaries, blows, bullets, all the wrenching, gut-kicked
pile-on of a cornered rage; even the Mike Hammers, Sam Spades
(colored into character by first-person rhetoric), and laconic dirtied
Harrys a sort of race of stunt men finally, their asses covered by camera
angle, so that for all the knocks they take to the head, for all their
stand-in saviorhood, they are guaranteed survivability, too, as though
the life/death arrangements of their furious, spurious danger were only
a kind of faked sportsmanship, like taking fish with a net, say, or
shooting game from out the window of an airplane.

Because the rest of the novel is like the rest of the novel. The bottled
myths and all the archetypes and by-the-numbers forms, fixed as
kitchen-dutied molds, shaped as sealed, airtight paradigms, all the

directed, incremental givens of a genre like the marked trails, posted milliaries and pointers of a trapped geography. Like the unvarying inevitables of the We-go-theres or They-come-heres of our refractive, strictly social, science fiction. Because the rest of the novel really *is* like the rest of the novel. Not just the high noonery of endgame ballet in the showdown of a Western fiction or the jaunty round of cumulative recruitment in a book for children, the abuilding ragtag of their con-joined—tin man or not, scarecrow or not, wimpywuss lion or not—kiddy crusades with their always stepped-up, accelerating degree-of-difficulty of the problem at hand, exactly as if, exposed, writ small, the basic dynamic of fiction was a sort of compounding stress level (it is, it is), some taut, tauter, tautest, uptaut crescendo of din and skirmish growing and exploding like a bolero from the lull of apparent quies-cence to the ripsnorting reality of a disturbed perturbation that lurks just fractions of fractions beneath the papered-over calm of surface, as if (it is, it *is*) fiction's other dynamic was strictly religious— all dif-ficulty (all, I mean, plot) cautionary, purposeful pain (because the *Book of Job* is the only book), God testing men's waters, as if this is the day the Lord has made in order to break your bones, in order to cheat you and mug you and play you for a fool and leave you for dead bleeding in the street (or why are the table stakes of dramatic prose such high ones, why are antes elevated above the systolics and diastolics of merely ordinary and routine, acceptably parametered risk? or why wouldn't fiction be pure success story, fused, conflated victories, not *even* victories, givens, givens of being, man in his picnic-lunch, wicker-basket condition, in his reaping one of a tenfold incoming of cast, rewarded bread, pleased men in the high-flying, bust-button peacock mode of their svelte and gifted grace, the character of characters un-tested, untried, untrialed, taken for granted, and given, along with the proceeds of the broken bank and everything else, the benefit of the doubt?), validating their hearts like a parking voucher stamped at the dentist's, hearing the song they sing for their supper, as though men's only real mode were the snap-quiz and tasked one? As if, further, we must learn at the beginning—it's still storybooks we're talking about here—what we will certainly know at the end— that there ain't no free lunch in story, that it comes charged with challenges to a pro-tagonist's grace and honor and heroism and the laying of one's ass on the line, qualities decorative and ornamental as the pretties on a Christ-mas tree.

Because McLuhan was right, and not only is the medium the message, the genre is, too. Clear as crystal, right as rain, plain as the nose. That showdown on that Western street beneath the windows of the town's only hotel, hard by its single livery stable, across the street from its major saloon, next to its sole drygoods store, near its newspaper, its telegrapher's shack, its jail and bank and assay office, the stop for its stage, within, I mean, spiritual spitting distance, holy public earshot, of that tumbleweed agora where the final agon happens, the wooden mall in the wooden town where fated push comes to inevitable shove, no mere convention of the Western, or of the *mere* Western, or even of literature itself, but the rules it must play by, no just obligatory nod in expectation's direction but, orthodox as the preliminary bow of Sumos, say, primary in story as red and blue and yellow are in spectrum— mythic in some bespoke, locked-in sense of the term, a ritual of chemistry, of physics, of some highest math. Just as, to face each other in that final showdown, you do not send boys—unless they are designated, apostolic boys—to do a man's work but must send to the confrontation only the major antagonists themselves— the Good Guy from Heaven, the Shyster from Hell. Almost—it's a law, solid as gravity, certain as celestial navigation; you can set your watch by its movements, its rigorous quartz and atomic timing—as if you can tell how much is *left* to tell in a story by who's still alive— fiction as chess piece; the loyal opposition and villain's higher henchmen versus the hero's faceless allies on up through his intimates and trusted sidekicks. *No mere sidekick, however skilled or brave, has ever shot it out with the major bad guy and lived to tell the tale.* Because there'd be no tale to tell, you see, because a tale is about its principals or it's about nothing. Fiction isn't always a class act, but it's always about class, its cast, like every classed society, fixed and ranked as playing cards, prissy with privilege, prerogative; fettered by precept and precedent, all those inside-the-lines moves prescribed as the knight's broken waltz on a chessboard, the pawn's slow snail's pace or the swift rush of the bishop's blindsiding diagonals, the queen's graceful free-form and king's hobbled freedom, each player fixed on its marked-star mark. Story in its essence nothing more than role being faithful to its nature, following some programmed itinerary toward redemption.

So of *course* the novel is religious. Even the romance, even nurse novels. With their watertight, ark-worthy hand-in-hands and two-by-twos. With their mutual soul-lotto like discovered treasure, their plighted troths and holy I-love-you's. Because if marriages are made in heaven like VCRs in Japan, where do you think novels are made? Why, in heaven, too, of course, or why would anyone have had to make up the term *anti-hero* for some character who does not fit the template or cut the compulsory figures of all those literarily fit, virtuous, gorgeous, ball-in-their-court, take-charge boys and girls of conventional story—— all those timeless, reliable doers and thinkers and carpenters of the plumb and the true—— all those righteous Republicans and fiscal moralists of the world's literature? Because all books *are* the *Book of Job*, high moral tests and tasks set in fairy tales, encoded as clues from the sibyls, all their tricky, forked-tongue talk, land-mined and unforgiving as golf greens, as steeplechase and game board and obstacle course. It's a winner-take-all world, fiction is, and if you lose it's because of your tragic flaw, as in any other blame-the-victim teleology. Story is just just desserts is all. I told you—— religious, man in the crucible like jack in the box.

All right, there are exceptions. Don't call me on this because I could never bring myself actually to read the stuff, but it's my guess that a lot of Eastern European literature, this sort of magic *sur*realism, a fiction forced so far underground it takes on the look of the chaos of middle earth itself, was an exception. I use my tenses advisedly. What with perestroika, the winds of change and blown smoke of political alteration, Polish, East German, Bulgaric, and otherwheres, such crypto-soliptic tales will turn round soon enough, if they haven't already, and climb up from and out of their almost geological layers of allegory and emblematic symbolicals and into the tried and possibly truer, if still tainted, air breathed by the rest of us, and we shall have once again Eastern European romances, bedtime stories, Westerns— there's a thought—— the East European Western—science fiction, the perestroika'd detective story, glasnosted nurse novels. And there shall be no exceptions, all fiction about the oppressor's velvet, Mexican-bandit charm and anxiety's obligatory peptic toxins, or husbands mistaking their wives for their dinners, the house pet leasing new quarters for its master, metamorphosed back into recognizable shape like the acceptably pinched crown of a hat or the properly punched pocket of a baseball mitt.

Because the reasonable and recognizable *is* where it's finally at, and the rest of the novel *is* like the rest of the novel. There are genres to spare, genres to stock all the remainder bins—"has bins," they're called—that ever were. Pornography riding a ribbon of critical theory, obeying, like all books always, the felt—I mean felt in terms of the known, of natural order, some uninstructed sense of right rhythm, of what goes where, and when; I mean felt in terms of what feels right— laws of the literary—— that what begins sedately and quietly enough with, say, a couple holding hands will climax in some spectacle of outrageous sky's-the-limit orgy of almost Busby Berkeley proportion, as choreographed as battle, as all Barnum'd and Bailey'd three-ring'd, combination lust, as if progression and complication were basic tropes—they are, they are—of the novel—— art as a sort of intimate geometry, tricky as the lacy tracery of a snowflake. Even the softer excitements—— prize fight, floor show, for example. For who would think to put on the preliminaries *after* the main event, or have Sinatra open for the lounge act? For evolution is the very *type* of fiction and Man comes on only after the worms and chickens, and man's imagination and genius only after man's elbows and toenails. It is, the novel, *like* evolution, a process, a progress. You don't get to the Emerald City until you can say "I don't think we're in Kansas anymore," and you don't get to go back to Kansas until you've been to Oz. A force of nature blows you sky high, and magic—three times you click the heels of your ruby slippers together and three times you recite "There's no place like home, there's no place like home"—sets you gently back down where both you and the novel began. (Story in its essence nothing more than role being faithful to its nature, I said. The reasonable and recognizable being where it's at, I went on. Yes, and didn't Dorothy have those slippers with her all along? Aren't they just standard ordinary issue to anyone from under the rainbow? So that the furniture you use up in a fiction is only the furniture you're furnished. Nothing up your sleeve unless you put it there in the first place?)

But surely the rest of the novel is more than the sum of its genres and subgenres? Well, it is and it isn't.

From time to time, when I was seven or eight years old, I had a chance to stay home from school and live the high life, this on the evidence of a slightly elevated temperature, the merit of a marginally swollen gland. It was a sort of willed, maybe even willful, hypochondria that did no real harm and drew no real blood but just sufficiently rasped my throat or, in certain acrobatic positions, ached my head to keep me, if not exactly honest, then at least within the fudged and fuzzy range of a judgment-call credibility, my mom's hung jury, tie-to-the-house, that would not, back in those old polio-fraught days, take on either the risk or responsibility of sending an only child out into the first- or second-grade world when a day or two in quarters might provide if not the cure then perhaps the prevention (a limited, voluntary quarantine back then being a kind of quasi, self-imposed exile, part stylite, part masque-of-the-red-death). In any event, there I would be, still in my pj's and all cozed out in the apartment by the grace of having pled my iffy fifthy. All dressed down and nowhere to go and, all comic books read and all radio serials heard, nothing to do.

Except, of course, there were always the dining room chairs. Because there would come a time, often in the late afternoon or the early postprandial, during that part of the day at any rate when my fraction of a degree of fever had broken—"the crisis," I believe, was the official medical term we used in those days—and the idea of school, while still not attractive, had, on the scale of things to which I refer, abated upward— at least recesswise, at least assemblywise. (I've always been a sucker for a good assembly, or even not such a good one, and enjoyed them even on those occasions when they were called by the principal— there was no public address then, no Big Sister, whose voice boomed out at you, like a pilot's on an airplane, from the very walls—for the purpose of reaming out at one time in one place an entire grammar school for the infraction of some rule—certain hooligans didn't obey the patrol boys; those among us raised in barns had chewed gum in class; there was talking in the halls.) This was a time of day conducive to the development of bedsores, to ennui, to, I mean, getting the hell out of bed to begin one's recuperation, to start the blood up again, to play, I mean, with all the toys of one's stuffed and blunted imagination, to have kick in, I mean, without ever having to leave home, some out-of-doors, out-of-body experience. To seek, I mean, after all the hard work of filling the minutes, quarter hours, and hours of that wasted, drowsy day, some crisper, more brisk sense of life.

So I'm at my dining room table, under it, examining the latchwork there, the minimal, limited machinery whose pulled levers permitted the insertion of additional leaves to accommodate company and special occasion, or heighten those lazy Wednesday and Tuesday afternoons of which I speak. This dining room table, this reddish runway, this wooden playground, this long, manipulate mahogany toy. And I'm under it, lost in its carved, ball-and-claw stump forest, supine on the queer, colored grasses of the fantastic, alien landscape of the dark Oriental like a mechanic beneath a car, all the juices of possibility running now, loose, amok even, alerted by some programmed tropism for snug adventure. When I come out it's to arrange, rearrange, the dining room chairs, not just, in our small and, at least in Chicago, practically relationless family, the three for ordinary meals, but pulling away from the walls, too, and from beside our breakfront, the additional unused (at least for dinner parties or anything more specially occasioned than a poker game) five.

Lining them up into an eight-seated spaceship or, alternating the configuration, into a comet like a comma, riding my frozen, bunched celestials, yippee-yiyo-kaiyay, like The Cowboy from Furthest North. Did I say there were broom handles poking through the fret of the back of the lead chair? There were broom handles poking through the fret of the back of the lead chair. These were the spaceship's controls, the comet's accelerator lever, the joystick for its brakes. Or did I tell you that blankets hung along the positioned chairbacks like a sort of space laundry, or lined the seats like flying carpet? Did I mention the neatly folded blanket in the commander's cabin at the front of the comet? The bars of soap I dropped on enemy planets? My flashlight and extra batteries? The toolbox for emergency repairs? The purred, back-of-the-throat noises of warp speed, the whishes and whooshes of intergalactic steering? The folded Illinois road map by which I negotiated the universe? My just cause? The cookies and milk, raisins and oranges stashed away in the sky furniture?

Because if ever there was an essential trope or basic dynamic of fiction, this is surely it. And if the rest of the novel is like the rest of the novel, its truly essential trope and basic dynamic is *certainly* this—action and respite, tension and release. All rat-a-tat-tat, take-this-you-guys, one minute, all cookies and milk the next. *Story*, I mean, life and death followed by remission, by all contented suck-thumb abeyance, gravity defied, the dining room chairs made up into high-contingency machines that don't skimp on the cookies and milk. (*Or why are there candy counters in movie theaters? Or why do we watch TV and plays in the dark?*) Story finally—consider the exhalated endings of novels, their sense, happy or otherwise, of frozen ever-afterness— something to go to sleep by— death's mood music.

So what *will* the rest of the novel be like in the next century? Blunt instruments don't change their shape. It will be, the detective stories and romances and sci-fi and adventure yarns and all the novel's subgenres, like it has been in this one, like it was since it began. As conditions change it will fine-tune itself, for the novel, in order to escape being dated, has always, in a race it's doomed to lose, been forced to run with the world. (Consider, for example, John Le Carré tinkering his themes in *The Russia House* because the cold war has ended. That book is a novel in a petri dish, a specimen of spy fiction in transition.) But history is dated, too, of course. As is the world. As are fashions and customs and belief systems. As is myth and the various versions of God, and if any received wisdom was ever closer to a lie it's that *plus ça change, plus c'est la même chose.* Things often change, but nothing, I think, nothing *ever*, remains the same. Each generation, even, I should think, each individual, if he would live on comfortable terms with his times, is forced to play catch-up. To keep learning, if only about what's been discarded. Which is why, finally, the only *proper* study of Story is not Man but men, and the novel's only legitimate genre is the unparametered masterpiece. I mean, I mean, that all the other stuff I've been talking about, the detective's Q-and-A rhetoric, the showdown, and all the subgenres I haven't even mentioned—— the war novel, the political novel, the ghost story, novels that take readers backstage to dramatize processes they've never seen, and all the infinite rung and wrung-out changes of novels that are about ideas or specifically about anything at all except themselves, are *only* novels. They do not breathe, they will not live. They are mere topics, they are only opportunities. They aim to please. What I'm talking about is harder. It is always the hard history of singular human beings, and, until it's written, you'll not see anything like it.

PIECES
OF
SOAP

THIS WOULD HAVE BEEN AFTER THE MS WAS FIRST DIAGNOSED but before the chair glide was put in, before, in fact, anything very important was wrong with me at all. Before the wheelchair, before the walker. Probably before the canes even. Though I may already have owned a cane. Using it larkily, boulevardierly, like Fred Astaire, say, like a prop for my disease.

Ourselves, a visiting professor, and the Lebowitzes in the living room conjoined. For drinks and dip and conversation assembled. And I forget now how it came up, though you have my word it was naturally. No one, I mean, set anyone else up. So it must have been naturally, in the sense, I mean, that anything coming out of left field like that is natural, thrown in compulsively—— from the hip, on the mind, off the chest. Naturally. Organically. The visiting professor had made this, well, confession. Or maybe not this confession at all so much as this shy, tentative admission, sly, something between a pretended amusement at a harmless foible and the genuinely expeditionary—— a little like someone fishing for a compliment.

I didn't need Joan's or the Lebowitzes' encouraging glance. What, for an opening like this? Your one-chance-in-a-million opportunity? I was out of my chair and on my feet like a shot. (So it would have to have been back in the mists of time, back in the golden age of my arms and legs, of my skin and balance.) I grabbed the professor's elbow and motioned for him to follow. "Come," I called over my shoulder, taking the stairs two and maybe three at a time. "Are you coming? Good," I said. "Come up, come up." I remember I was already laughing. (Because I knew what I was going to say. Because your chance-in-a-lifetime, one-in-a-million-opportunities don't come up every blue moon or cold day in hell, so maybe without even knowing it, you have reflexively, already prepared, primed and polished, not staircase wit but its opposite, as down pat as a comic's practiced squelch, except that mine was not even rehearsed but something all condition-ripened second nature, like ouch! or yippee! Natural. Organic.) And now he was in the upstairs hall with me. I directed his attention this way and that. "What," I said, "*you* steal soaps from hotels? *You* do?" I directed his attention to the bathroom. "You think so? *You* do?" And even had a reply ready, what I hope I would have said in his place. This was not staircase wit either. "No," I hope I would have said, and offered up the punch line from the old joke, "but the guy that sells *me* salt, can *he* sell salt!" Though come to think of it the professor's was close enough in its way, even though what happened was that all expression drained from his face, he closed his mouth, and narrowly shook his head a few times. It wasn't a punch line. It was better. It was pure submission signal.

Because I have, in basket and hamper, in all summertime's lanyard-laced, twiggy, wickery woodwork like a woven porch or patio furniture, stashed in its indoors-outdoors texture like supple, vaguely rain forest, vaguely jungly splinter (vine, picnic's processed straw like a coniferous soup or an evergreen vegetable, all the indeterminate tropicals and periodics of the American breezeway elementals—Adirondackian, Poconosaic, Ramapoaon—spread over good green loaves of lawn, all that luxuriant matter of the undeciduous year), five or six thousand bars of soap.

The thousand-bar point spread is not insignificant. There are men so rich they cannot reckon their true wealth and must wait on probate for even a ballpark figure. I do not really know the extent of my soap collection.

But this ain't about souvenir. It isn't even about memento. Proust isn't in it, or near it— or wasn't. And if I'm no connoisseur of soap, then neither am I soap's bag man. *His* assorted flotsam and jetsam, his cardboard dreck, is for the rainy day— provisional, pointed and purposeful as annuity. It is, I mean, contingent— plan abiding time, tool waiting on emergency. Not like my own two or three hundred pounds of wrapped motel, hotel, airline, railway, and steamer soaps and others, too, some of which I have and some of which I have seen only (from the stately homes of England, royal weddings, the sealed tombs of pharoahs, from all impressive, high-ticket places— the soaps of San Marino like an intimate postage, the Great Wall, soaps of the poles and trade winds) in imagination— equatorial soaps, space soaps, soaps of the jet streams and ocean currents. The stamped soaps of Heaven. The branded soaps of Hell.

I write, you see, more from the grave robber's viewpoint than the collector's, more from some spiritual homeopathy than either. Soap's little miniatures passed out like Halloween candy, soap as superstition, soap as sod and soap as relic. As a piece of my private public record.

Oh, it's complicated. Here, I think, is how it happened.

My father was a traveling salesman. On his rounds two and three weeks, three and four weeks at a time. Bringing back in the dop kit, like little picture postcards, the house Palmolives and Luxes, their Camays and Lifebuoys. From the Radisson in Minneapolis. From the Milwaukee Pfister. From Grand Rapids and Greencastle, Indiana. What Fargo looked like, what Rapid City did, Des Moines, Cedar Rapids. Views of Springfield, Illinois, and Joplin, Missouri, two and three bars high in the medicine chest. My pop's soap strictly for use, for blow, not show. Knee-deep in ethics, tutored in the waste-not/want-nots of his sensible prairie territory and ecologicals, my old man never stole a soap he didn't intend to bathe with. Glimpses of motor courts in Nebraska a bar's sidebar, never the point. For whom a mile held neither nostalgia nor beauty nor even simple interest, who kept score in a different currency altogether and who would have worried about me if he'd caught me pouring over, like some kid miser, the architecturals of the various hotels, counting the stories, its "fireproof" rooms, the skyline of individual blocks, studying the little cars out front, squinnying the tiny, to-scale, guest populations entering, exiting, the revolving doors on the wrappers. It was quite like examining the drawings on money, or the golden graphics on a package of Camel cigarettes, trademark's mysterious etchings. Some tropism in me for logo itself. With all the makings but without the knowledge of a stamp collector. This accidental tourist altogether. Who put no stock in baseball cards and had no hobbies. (Though, briefly, when I was seven, I actually *did* have a stamp collection, a hand-me-down from a college-bound distant cousin who put away childish things and gave not just into my charge but granted me in absolute freehold and fee simple forever her stamp books and catalogues and little waxy envelopes. All of which for a promised but reneged, undelivered quarter from a closer cousin, I tore up, burned, destroyed.) Not even, not yet, the simple hobby of soap.

Which came later. I was thirty-seven, already heart-attacked, and maybe three years older than my father would have been when I started those long, comfortable, belly-flop occasions on the living-room rug with the soaps in fuzzy, dreamy, contemplative, surrogate travel and exploration, one part speculate, investigative scholarship, geography lessons read right off wrappers, and four parts play like a dry martini. Something of a traveling man myself now. Once in a while. Occasionally. Whenever I was invited to read from the *oeuvre* to three or four dozen drummed-up students and faculty for a token honorarium and expenses plus all the motel soaps I could steal. And which, at least at first, I grabbed as pure reminder, some "our song" thing like an elbow to the memory box, sentimental as an ashtray or a matchbook cover or a bid from the prom. Dealing in manageable numbers. Spread out, three and four of a kind, on the sills and shelves of my bathroom like a lay in rummy.

But no connoisseur or soap snob, believing from the beginning in the thoroughgoing democracy of soap, even in its almost generical Ivories of placeless gigs, the unmarked bills of lodge and motor court, of all inexpensive, locally owned unfranchised inn, in, as it were, the plain-brown-wrapper soap of all off-ramp, off-strip, difficult-access and service roads, places you pay a deposit for the room key and another to unlock the telephone, where the coffee you brew beside the sink comes in little paper packets with nondairy creamer, wide paper cones you place in plastic holders a couple of shades lighter than Grey Poupon mustard, a wooden swizzle stick, and a packet of sugar hardened by humidity. (Because nothing that goes into the scrapbook is alien to me.) Already dealing in quantity rather than quality—though I didn't know yet that the one pushed to the extreme ultimately becomes the other—and was perhaps inspired beyond the parameters of memento, old times, and simple occasion, by the valueless ordinariality of the brand-name soaps in those unaffiliated chainless, disenfranchised motor hotels, to a benign smash-and-grab, or maybe even to actual outright thievery. Who would never think of swiping a towel or making off with so much as a wire coat hanger, but who, and even at first, was this conscienceless soap yegg and soap poacher, this footpad of handsoap, something exponential in the blood that made me this, well, brigand of the bath, this simple soapsy-sud fetishist, this collector-plunderer/hunter-gatherer of special soap booty, grabbing up my pieces of soap like pieces of eight, handfuls of discrete, magic, anal greed, filling my pockets, *shtupping* all my clothing like a contestant let loose in a supermarket. In any of those first minutes in a hotel or an airplane (early on in my career I developed the habits and techniques of some-one very dedicated or very crazy) locking myself like someone caught short, seized up with diarrhea, into the lavs of aircraft while we were still attached to the *chupah* or jetway or whatever it is they call that thing that connects the airplane to the terminal, the "Return to Cabin" already flashing its red emergency while I pull handfuls of handsoap from the little metal dispensers like someone scraping change from the coin return of a pay telephone, or like a Vegas mechanic dealing cards from a "shoe," working fast in the close quarters, even breaking if I have the time into long, plastic-sealed sleeves of the stuff, a knowl-edge of the eensy mop-and-broom closet arrangements in the tiny compartment, stuffing pants pockets, shirt, the inside pockets of sport coats I might not have even purchased had they not been deep enough to accommodate my special soap needs, ripping off between a dozen and fifteen bars at a time on my great plane-robbery raids, something not ungentlemanly about my m.o. withal; never, that is, taking the last few bars, leaving like a gent cat burglar's calling card these signature soaps, any self-respecting thug's Whoosis was here.

And actual method in my m.o., too. *I* shower, *I* bathe. I use the TWAs as keepers and to trade up, too. The first thing I do at a destination, after hanging my clothes, after emptying my pockets and hiding the airline soaps, along with all the soaps I can find in the room—you clear them off the bathroom sink, you open the curtains and look in the dish in the tub, you look in the medicine chest behind the mirror—in some hidden pocket of my garment bag, is call House-keeping and ask them to please send some soap up to the room please

as there wasn't any when I got here and I'm tired from my travels and
I'd like to take a shower, please. When they arrive I throw them in
with the dozen or so already in the garment bag, unwrap a TWA
which, small as it is, I will use for the duration of my stay, or until
it's only a sliver of a sliver or maybe even only one single lousy dried-
up sud before I break out another. Each day adding Housekeeping's
fresh soaps to the now considerable pile growing like a sort of culture
in the luggage—it has *become* the luggage—as yeast grows, as yogurt
begins, from those primal foundling seed soaps.

But how the punks do it I'll *never* know. Not Mister Bigs, not major
sluggers from the S&Ls, not even the wiseguys, stickup people or
smugglers bluffing past customs. Because felony I understand, breaking
and entering, all the large motor movements of assault and battery.
But mine are furtive kid-in-the-cookie-jar ways, clumsy I am as an
amateur card tricker, even in the locked privacy of those airborne
privies, work under the gun, high-pressured as shoplifting, my heads-
up, look-both-ways heart skipping beats as I did the dirty on soap. It's
a wonder I don't sweat through the paper wrappers, that I don't give
myself away in a trail of lather. So it's hard to imagine now how I
ever used to pause at maids' carts in the hall, picking over the soaps
like someone shopping fresh fruit. Because I never really had the nerve
to go for a soap rustler. Not cut out for a life of crime, lacking the
sinner's ballsy bearing, not even born with a thing for soap. Never
anything like rage in my soap lust, never anything like lust in it—
nothing personal. (So detached from my needs, I'd as soon send my
wife and kids, friends and acquaintances, even people I don't care for
very much, out on soap forays as go on them myself.)

It isn't a hobby. It isn't even a collection. If anything at all, it's an
accumulation. And no sense on my part of anything hanging over the
accumulation of even an accidental art. It has never occurred to me
that so many soaps in one place may have something of the monumental about them— a vernacular accretion like the Watts Towers
or the canes and crutches of Lourdes. Just, for me, this open-ended,
piecemeal, laying on of an unsystematic taxonomy, at once as all-
inclusive and indiscriminate (I have few rules for accumulating soap:
They must be in their original wrappers, they must be taken; once a
dear friend, stopping over in Indianapolis, purchased some miniature
theme soaps for me— classic Indy 500 racing cars decaled on clear
cellophane; out of love for my friend I buried them somewhere in the

accumulation, in it but not of it) as Kinsey's gall wasps, or all generic paleontologic fossil. Just *exactly* that unexamined. *More.* The soaps unarranged, not even sized, unalphabetical, *undisplayed*—— not set out like equipment in a tool box, fishing tackle, spanners, and drill bits. Indeed, the hardest thing to explain to my friends, all those enlisted agents spreading across the country on my behalf, over the globe fetching from the four corners—from Europe, from Alaska and Rio and Sydney and Bombay, sometimes in a kind of origami wrapped, in very jewel boxes mounted, my four- and five-star luxury soaps, my specimen soaps lying down in the hopper with, if I had them, the interesting rough industrials of jail and penitentiary, of high gulag and minimum-security prison, and distributed all assimilate by chronology and gravity in those big elemental picnic hampers through the halls and rooms of my house—is just this: where they actually *are*, how something so carefully and thoughtfully gathered up and retained, not in the least eleventh-houred or last-minute-remembered, schlepped from those four far corners, from Natchez to Mobile, from Memphis to St. Joe, not even checked through with the steamer trunk and matched Hartmann leathers, for God's sake, but hand-carried for God's sake, and got up in a pretty paper package like macadamia nuts, sourdough, or Italian cookies, from those four far corners fetched, Alsace-Lorraine to University City, Missouri, door-to-door in purse or one of those little canvas money belts travelers affect rather like external sexual organs, so specially, *specifically* cared for (and I don't know whether they mean me or the damn soap), and not only not an after-thought but sometimes—I've actually heard this—the hotel chosen, picked, for the soap it might yield; so what do I *mean* I don't know where their particular soap is? that I not only can't locate it in a specific basket but have no idea in which room the basket that contains it might be? All I can do is tell them what I've already told them—— that it really is the thought that counts.

"The *thought?*"

"Well, the physical soap, too, of course, but I'm really more interested in the weight of my collection."

"Simple quantity."

Which is a tough one. Because it's misleading, and only partially true. A single three-hundred-pound soap would mean nothing to me. Or a soap the size of a sofa. Quantity and quality, too, I suppose. The tiny airline soaps for ballast, for purposes, as I've explained, of trading up, sure, but for their cumulative heft, too, like, like, as it were, small change, like rolls of pennies, say, rolls of dimes. Because I see now there *is* something fiscal, at least something vaguely denominational about this accumulation of mine, something safed, vaulted, deposit-boxed, and counting-housed. Denominational, too, in the papers that protect them. Not necessarily, I mean, in the often embossed, bas-relief aura of the punched dimensionality of those vaguely origami'd wrappers, so much as in a sense of graduated value in the embellished, ornamental strokes of the adorned lettering on the seals and crests of the various hotels like the signatures on banknotes or stock certificates, this faint heraldry of wreathed logo, uptown as an address written on a canopy. (Or even—value, denomination—in soap's inflected hues, its declensions of ivories, creams, and beiges. Up the palette of its peachy, ultimate pastels to something like gold itself, like colors re-fined, rarified, extrapolated from precious stones and metals.)

Because I see this now, too. The value of the collection, my ac-cumulation, its very *meaning* is treasure! Pieces of eight indeed. (Once, transferring my soaps into smaller containers from an immense am-phora, at one time high and wide as a ten-year-old child but buckling now from the weight of the bars, I could see the various layers devolved by gravity into some sandy sediment of soap, its settled, powdery mol-ecules like an inverted geology, the topsy-turvy bedrock of my soapy ingots, shifted as treasure sunk in the seas.) It is treasure, it *is*, the world's strangest coin collection, something truly miserly in the pockets of my soul, perhaps. (And there was this one time, not when I first started out but back in the days when I didn't have so many, when I wasn't pulling down more than seventy-five to one hundred soaps a year, say, and it wasn't an accumulation yet and still manageable enough to exhibit, which I did, in various small baskets and shallow platters of soaps, in the bathroom itself, like one of those display cases in the natural-history museums where they trouble to place the stuffed bird not only in a mock-up of the nest on the branch of the very tree in which it would most likely pitch its tent, but to get the rest of the habitat right, too, the flora and fauna, the color of light in those latitudes, so that was my way of it, too, choosing as natural habitat for my soaps *their* natural habitat— the toilet, on top of the tank where I could appreciate them whenever I peed, and just that Tuesday I'd broken out a brand-new shallow basket for some brand-new bars of soap from an expensive ski lodge

in Sun Valley a pathologist pal of mine had brought back for me from
one of those getaway-with-the-rich-and-famous conferences scientists
send themselves on to talk about curing us, and now it was Wednesday,
the day the lady came to clean our house and that afternoon while I
was appreciating the Sun Valley soaps I noticed that something was
terribly wrong—— that three bars were missing—you know how it is
with the obsessed, we have these Dewey decimal hearts; a place for
everything, and everything in its place—and it was perfectly clear to
me what happened—— *the butler did it!*, and I was furious, I felt
violated—you're not going to understand this, you're going to take it
the wrong way—as a rape victim, and I yelled for Joan. "What, what
is it? Why are you screaming?" "Fire her!" "What? Why?" "Fire her,
she took my soap!" "I can't fire her, I like her." "*Fire her, fire her!*"
"Will you shut up? She'll hear you. So she took a couple of bars of
soap. So what? You have so *many*. How do you even know she took
them?" "Because everyone else in the house knows the soap rules——
that they're never to be used. That basket's brand new, I just put it
out last night." "She's honest, she's an honest woman. I won't fire
her for taking a bar of hotel soap. And aren't you forgetting something?"
"What?" "My God, that's how *you* got them!" There was a certain
raw logic in this, and I told Joan that if she explained to the woman
how important my soaps are to me and made her promise never to try
anything like that again, she could keep her job. "No," Joan said, "I'd
feel ridiculous explaining how important your soaps are to you." So
we worked something out. We agreed that if she never touched my
soaps she could have a raise. And that, though neither Joan nor I
demanded the return of the embezzled Sun Valleys and the accumulation will forever, like some surrendered, irrecoverable loss leader,
be a couple of bars shy of what it could have been, is exactly what
happened.)

But now it's not only after the MS was first diagnosed, but after the
canes were prescribed, the walker and wheelchair, after the bath bench,
the raised commode, the custom footbrace and special shoes, after the
stair glide; after the slow slipping of my balance, my giving way, it
sometimes seems, to the very air, eddies of inclination in the room
unfelt by others, after the special courses of prednisone which are a
little less effective each time I take them, after the new symptoms, my
fatigue during the day, my lengthening insomnia at night, the slow
capsize of the long habits of my body, after the piecemeal diminution

of my strength, since I have forgotten not only how to swim but even how to float, since I can barely stand upright in water even with the assistance of the woman who comes to exercise me three times a week.

And I have actually had thoughts of who I will, who I *can*, leave it to—— my joke collection, my toy treasure, my thousands of bars of pack-rat soaps.

Recently, only this past April as a matter of fact, Joan and I went to a conference in Italy on the novel in the next century. I'd had, as I notice I've had for perhaps two years now, second thoughts. Separation anxiety not only about leaving my city, my country, but my *area*, the second floor and, more specifically, the bedroom and office where I most comfortably spend my time. So I'd had second thoughts, third, about undertaking such an extensive journey, even to speak on such a silly, improbable topic. (The novel in the next century indeed! Just that past week I'd been to the doctor. It was all I could do, and with assistance at that, just to get up on the examining table. In his office afterwards he was describing to me some of the promising research on multiple sclerosis, that they would certainly have a cure for it within ten years. "Ten years?" I said. "In ten years you can fuck multiple sclerosis.")

I'm not a particularly brave man and, most certainly, not in the least a reticent one. I publicly whine, I mean. I don't keep myself to myself, which is where, in all probability, I probably belong.

So I was up to third thoughts about leaving my area. Three planes. The difficulty of maneuvering my walker down the planes' narrow aisles to the toilets. The alternative difficulty of, walkerless, swinging my way along the seat tops, like some ruined and grounded Tarzan. The three planes. The extensive journey. From St. Louis to Kennedy. From Kennedy to Rome, where we'd have a twelve-hour layover. From Rome across Italy to Ancona on the Adriatic. From Ancona by car to Macerata, better than an hour away.

In the end it wasn't Joan who talked me into going. She was no more eager, I think, for that long trip than I was, and had been having second and third thoughts of her own. It was me. Surely the soaps I'd have coming to me had something to do with it. (The three planes, the Rome hotel where we'd lay over for much of the afternoon, wherever it was they'd be putting us up in Macerata, wherever we ended up after the three-day conference was over. A trip to Europe, a trip to Europe could be worth 100, 150 soaps to me.) In the end I brought back something like fourteen. So if the soaps had something to do with it, it couldn't have been much. It ain't over, they tell us, until the fat lady sings. But one *is* the fat lady, and if I ain't heard nothing yet, it may be because of that same old superstitious anal greed, *shtupping* as much life as I can into what I still have for a body as once, under the gun, I'd stuffed the deep inside pockets of my sport coats. Working fast now too, *higher* pressured than shoplifting, "Return to Cabin" flashing redder than ever, redder than hell. But hey, *all* events have their degree of difficulty.

I still steal soap. I get out less often than I used to to do it, and, increasingly, the accumulation builds more by contribution than by my own efforts, but that was never the point of the exercise anyway. And something else has happened. I have begun to use the soaps, a different one every day. (What was I saving them for, a rainy day?)

Searching out scent like a lost chord. Because we're a long time dead and I mean, in my queer, reduced circumstances, to lather and unguent myself, poking about, stirring the pungencies, the macho savories and aromatics, the dim remembered love musks and the neutered, bracing scent of sweat. Perhaps as bought-into an illusion—we are what we smell, the sweet smell of success—as an ad for an aftershave, loading my skin with the odor of health, the higher cleanliness, whatever God-proximate order and arrangement flesh is heir to, seeking this soft and easy low-end high, the reflexive, passive passions, mechanical, available, and automatic as contagion or a contact rash, my body in quickest fix subsumed, transmuted, transubstantiated in some coated hotel heraldrics of smell, a few minutes of four- and five-star stink, all the expensive, windy pomanders. Which too soon blow over, evaporate, are gone, compromised by one's laundry, by breakfast, the morning paper, by almost anything (but which live longest in the mustache and the grasping hairs of my chinny chin chin) and, like a kind of Midas manqué, gilding the lilies, covering everything I touch, at least for a while, in lively, lovely, twenty-one-karat shadows.

PART TWO

A PREFACE TO
THE SIXTIES
(But I Am
Getting Ahead
of Myself.)

I WAS IN THE ARMY AND MY WIFE HAD A BIRTHDAY COMING UP. WE lived off-post, a mile or so north of Petersburg, Virginia. Not only off-post, but off-highway, too, literally alongside U.S. 1. In a defunct motel. We hadn't much money of course—I was a private, or perhaps a private first class—and although Joan worked, whatever cash we had, that was left over, that didn't go into rent or food or Brasso for my buttons, went into Richmond restaurants—seventeen miles north—into champagne cocktails in the John Marshall Hotel. To give us—me—the illusion that there was no United States Army and that even if there was I wasn't in it, that we didn't live in an old tourist cabin—you know the type, buildings like the mysterious structures put up along railroad sidings, red tarry shingles you can strike matches on, yet vaguely classic, the classic house, like a kid's drawing of one—to comfort us with style, which is the only way some people can be comforted. And I had saved five dollars, the gift of the Magi, but rather than buy something that she would have to return—I'm no good at sizes and this is astonishing to me, for I hang pictures with a surveyor's instinct, I mean I center them, have the professional's eye for margins, a natural bent for whatever it is that is the geometer's equivalent of perfect pitch (I'm a hangman, it's a gift)—I told Joan what I had to spend and asked her what she wanted. "What I want," she said, "what I want is the five dollars."

The incident gave me the idea for a story I wrote called "Fifty Dollars"—the official rate of exchange between art and life is exactly ten to one—about the five thousandth customer to enter a supermarket the week it opens. My character is given a prize of fifty dollars and is urged to spend it in the new multimillion-dollar shopping center of which the supermarket is a part. Her financial situation, like ours, involved a getting and spending that always, helplessly, came out even, a double-entry life. The fifty dollars put her ahead of the game and though she tries—in the story I take her shopping—she cannot bring herself to give them up. They become "her fate, and she needed them, all together, all at once, until she didn't need a fate any more." It wasn't a good story, but it should have been.

Or the time, later, we were going away the next morning and Joan asked if I had canceled the paper and stopped the milk, and I had the idea for a short story called "The Guest," about a middle-class couple anxious to start their vacation who suddenly realize on the Sunday morning they're to leave that they have *not* stopped the paper and suspended the milk. Almost as they're closing the door behind them, Bertie, a professional deadbeat they knew in the old days, shows up to ask if he can sleep over for a couple of nights. The husband, seeing Bertie as an opportunity to make the apartment "look lived in, to keep off the thieves," invites him to use their home while they're gone. He even gives Bertie spending money. Bertie, who hasn't led a normal existence in years, accepts the invitation and goes on a spree of exploration of the square world represented by the apartment that ultimately destroys it.

Another day, apropos of absolutely nothing at all, I found myself wondering what would happen if a person, not unlike myself, decided to see exactly what he was worth and undertook to convert everything he owned back into cash. His clothes, his appliances, his geegaws and coat hangers, back into cash. He surrenders his phone and gets back the twenty-five-dollar deposit; he sells his furniture, his sheets, and his pillowcases. He converts his policies. He dumps his car, pulls his savings out of the bank, and sells his postage stamps back to the post office, everything must go. I called the story "I Look Out for Ed Wolfe," and what I'm talking about is the Muse. I'm praising the Muse. I want her to know what I think of her, that I believe she is real. You are. There's no Lady Luck and I question the Furies, but you, Muse, are a different story.

I believe, that is, in inspiration. (Genius, they say, is 90 percent perspiration and 10 percent inspiration. They're wrong. In the hottest climates even.) Inspiration is real. It's real as digestion. Indeed, it *is* digestion. Of a sort. It's the metabolism of decision, conclusion, the brain's bum's rush, its whooshed fell swoop. *Because stories come at once or not at all.* A student of mine, James Goldwasser, told me about a marvelous idea for a story he wanted to write. A reasonably high placed and relatively well educated man takes an I.Q. test one day—a new policy his firm has instituted for its employees. He gets the results and discovers that he's really rather stupid. It changes his life. Now here's what Goldwasser really said: In his version it's a freshman in college who finds out his test scores. (Writers usually work with protagonists a year or two younger than themselves; to arrive at a writer's age you add one to two years to a character's age. We call this Carbon 14.) The student, shocked by his classification, drops out of school but continues to live in his dorm and even to sign up for courses and buy the books for them. Had the Muse given *me* the story it would have been in the first terms I outlined. I'm trying to show that the Muse is always personal, the custom tailor of the goddesses.

Situation—what the Muse says—precedes style, precedes plot, precedes everything. (Though style, plot, and everything are implicit in situation.) The lawyer-narrator in Melville's "Bartleby the Scrivener" asks his law clerk to proofread a document the lawyer has prepared. The clerk replies "I would prefer not to," and everything that happens in the story happens as a consequence of his response. Indeed, everything that *can* happen in the story happens as a consequence of it. Though Bartleby doesn't refuse to do the lawyer's bidding until ten pages into the story, Melville *must* have begun with that. All the conditions of the story are prescribed, all the conditions that are not the story are proscribed. (Well, not *all* the conditions that are not the story. A writer must breathe. Best to forget Poe and his loose talk about "unity of impression." Although, admittedly, historically, that has been the direction of the short story, but only because Poe has been calling the shots for a hundred and twenty years, not because of the form itself. The form is blameless.) What the Muse gives us, then, is situation, possibility's hothouse, fate's, fiction's genetic structure. (It's an odd circumstance of aesthetics, however, that while short stories must have situations, novels frequently dispense with them. Perhaps this is because novels are about character and character is ubiquitous in human beings, while stories are about character in crisis—*acute* character.) If a situation is good it will have gravitational pull. Event falls. (We say, don't we, that such and such an event befell a character, or that things so fell out that this or that happened? This is the classic language of the tale. Idiom knows.) It is lowered from level to level like ships in locks.

I mean it when I attribute to the Muse what others attribute to imagination. The imagination is perhaps not so much a process of invention as it is of recognition. (Perhaps talent is simply the ability to recognize the virtues inherent in the situation the Muse has given us; perhaps, that is, it's a critical faculty at least as much as a creative one. Here's a point. What's wrong with the fellow who tells you at a party of a story he'd write if only he had the talent isn't his ignorance of technique or the limitations of his vocabulary so much as the poverty of his critical judgment. Invariably the situation he gives you is impossible, awful. It couldn't work had you or he all the "talent" in the world.) The major difference between situation and metaphor, for example, is that situation—not *plot:* Plot is to situation what battles are to history—is recognized, received in a Mt. Sinai sense, and metaphor invented, scientific trial and error, practice makes perfect. (Consider the *look* of a manuscript: What's changed, what gets into margins and goes between lines, what's penciled or penned or clipped to the page, are bits of metaphor, pieces of language, a palimpsest of image and vocabulary. Almost never elements of plot and *never* situation. Stories and novels are abandoned, perhaps, but they are never revised. Revision is committee, conference— play doctors looking at Broadway shows in Philadelphia from the back of the house, the leading lady's love song spliced from the second act and the hero's rival given jigs to dance. It is professionally editorial, intended to bring material into line with policy rather than aesthetics. The notion, for example, of "comic relief" is not the author's but the director's or editor's.)

Details, too, are recognized—pins with colored plastic heads like tiny lollipops in men's new shirts; the dusty collection cans for obscure charities on the tops of meat cases in delicatessens; drawers in kitchens stuffed with owner's manuals—as is, I think, scene—a Big Ten football coach circulating at a cocktail party for the parents of his players, apologizing that their sons have to play with colored boys—and even landscape. (We are talking of high art, high. We are talking of art to give you the nosebleed. Not of fiction of the fifties or sixties. The real fiction of the fifties or sixties you wouldn't care to read. I mean the fiction of statistical incidence. For a time all blurbs on novels, including one's own, came with an obligatory rubric rhetoric, a code fixed as Morse. Humor, for example, was "wild" at the same time that it was "deadly serious." There was something vaguely federal about it, like the warning on a pack of cigarettes. Hopefully the stories reprinted here are not stories of the sixties, though they were all written back in those days.) Situation and landscape and detail are either uninventable or they are grotesque, for truth may not be imagined. No one makes up the sky. Who invents California?

On the other hand, it seems to me that fiction moves by means of *two* elements, an almost pharmaceutical mix of the learned and the inspired. Writers depend upon a sort of vocabulary—learned—of preexistent alternatives. I mean the big traumatic givens of literature, mistaken identity, poverty, adultery, a special assignment or, more pertinently, love at first sight (Curley's "Love in the Winter"), bad news from the doctor (Tillie Olsen's "Tell Me a Riddle"), a widow trying to make a new life (Calisher's "The Scream on 57th Street"), a challenge (Albert Lebowitz's "The Day of Trials")—all things that have their source neither merely nor necessarily in "life" but in prior literature, large, dependable displacements that put the heat on the characters. By "inspired" one means not so much the unique as the spontaneously generated, things that have *no* counterparts in literature, the wonderful courtship in the men's lavatory in Alfred Chester's "In Praise of Vespasian," the hilarious "Bravo. Hey, Harry. Bravo," in Targan's "Harry Belten and the Mendelssohn Violin Concerto." The point is that in all first-rate fiction a delicate balance between these two very different sorts of plot elements is maintained. In bad fiction, where the action is all "learned," the result is melodrama; in bad fiction where the action is all "inspired," the result is chaos.

One thinks of directors scouting locations with those little hoosies hanging from their necks, lifting them to peer through or, crouching, making frames of their hands in a gesture like a piece of sign language. If one were a director one would shoot in subways with cameras hip-high in turnstiles, or in drugstores perhaps, what the convex mirror saw, or through the TV camera above the teller's cage, jerky as a battery toy. Oblique angle, off-center prospect, steep vision like a goat's purchase. For, finally, point of view *is* art—Barth's "Menelaiad," the narrator at the still center of the turning town in William Gass's "In the Heart of the Heart of the Country"—what the Muse, speaking always in the tongues of personality, tells *me*. It is fiction itself, in some special, synecdochic, part-for-the-whole sense, for all stories drive all other stories out as surely as all music drives out all other music, or all consciousness all other consciousness. The individual fiction *precludes* fiction (the very concept of this anthology is a paradox), precludes the world, precludes time (the apparent gift of fiction, its essential trait, the thing it has that no other form has, is tense, yet in great fiction it is always—philosophically—the present) and, watch it, even the reality of your own existence. I'm your uncle, I like you, come home and I'll take you to the ballgame and get you a hot dog. Listen. Don't read if you would retain a sense of your life. Or read for meaning, quibble with a story's issues and themes and ideas. Those are its least important aspects anyway, there only as technique, integument, art's artificial gum base. All writers have only one of two things to say. They say yes or they say no, or shades of yes or shades of no—— the binary substructure of vision. Stick to that, venture beyond and I promise you an envy like the toothache.

INTRODUCTION
TO *THE BEST*
AMERICAN SHORT
STORIES 1980

Most fellows, they put together a collection like this, they go all humble on you. Or they break out in qualification, they're all over themselves with conditions, strings, all the head's fine print, all the heart's crossed fingers. Or they're quibbled as an Oscar winner. (Do I fetch it myself or send the surrogate? Am I in Paris on a gig? Is it Tuesday, my night for the sweat bath, my day at the races? Or am I actually disruptive? What *is* the mode for eleventh-hour reservation, qualm, the brain's butterflies?)

Or they'll tell you how hard they worked to reach a decision. The pains they took, all invigilate, watchdog scrupulosity and fastidiousness. With pointers accusing the relief map, the sifted minefields, the sluiced ores. ("Here the mind went ginger. Here judgment went two rounds with will.")

Not me. I *have* no qualifications.

And my decisions were a breeze, easy as falling off a log.

Because these are, quite simply, the very best short stories published in American magazines in 1979, and they declared themselves to whatever sense I have of the wonderful as succinctly as so many logos.

Because we're talking about taste, the buds of judgment. And of *course* there's an accounting for taste. This is an attempt to account for mine.

Only the flat-out hero—I mean the medalist, the beribboned, the campaigner; I mean the champ, the Heisman winner, the MVP—is valued for his deeds. The rest of us are esteemed, or not, for our opinions, judgment calls, the soul's favorite tunes. Even men of the world wheel and deal in mood, the artifact of temperament. We tend to take people at their word, extend credence like credit, and lead an *ipse dixit* sort of life. (We cash their checks. The woman in the coffee shop accepts on faith that we are guests and rarely asks to see the room key. Tape recordings are inadmissible but an eyewitness will do you in. Some fuddled soul can't tell you three things that are wrong with this picture, but if she picks you out of the lineup you're done for. Any lawyer will tell you: One implication is worth two inferences. See? I made that last bit up, but you'd already cashed my check. For all you know I might not be registered in this hotel and may just have charged breakfast to some other guy's room.)

Walter Cronkite says that after yesterday's Florida primary Reagan is the frontrunner, and so, in fact, he seems to be. Republicans are steamed. The budget is unbalanced. Chase Manhattan's best customers can get better terms from a loan shark by the docks than they can from the prime. America is everywhere on the defensive. Afghanistan. Colombia. The Mideast. The hostages have been in Iran 130 days and the commission has come back without even seeing them. Mary, called "Mary," in her guerrilla's *chador*, is making monkeys out of us paper tigers. What this country needs, it is claimed, is a return to sound fiscal principles, to principle itself. A beefed-up military. A trimmed-down bureaucracy. A conservative Republican frontrunner. But what did Mr. Reagan ever actually *do* that was conservative? When he was governor of California? What did he actually *do?* The point is, I think, that conservatism is only another opinion, only, that is, a kind of taste, as liberalism is, or fascism too. And, like all taste, it proceeds from a view in equilibrium, the prerogative of an essential disengagement— a question of druthers, of all else being equal.

Taste is the luxury of abeyant claims and occurs, like Wordsworth's poetry, in a kind of tranquillity, a repose of soul, when the mind (or not even the mind), like a pointer on a Ouija board, lurches simplistic alternative. It is an ideal, the choice we make when we have no choice, what we might look like when no one is looking, what we might look like invisible.

Taste is, finally, a series of first impressions, lodestar aesthetics that last a lifetime. A man's character is his taste, and he is as much a victim of it as the pictures, foods, music, films, books, furnishings, and clothes he chooses are the subjects of his necessity. It, taste, may even be one of the famous drives, like sex or appetite. And it has always a quality of aspiration, its eye on the next step up forever. My mother-in-law would be incapable of furnishing a living room without slipcovers, and, for her, the development of clear plastic was a technological breakthrough, a hinge event in science, up there with washable mah-jongg tiles. Because we're talking, in my mother-in-law's case, about cleanliness, lifelong *shmutz*-dread, that first impression she must have taken as a little girl in Russia of actual biological *traif*, fear of the Gentile, some sense of caste deeper than a Hindu's, a notion, finally, of *order*. Which is all that taste ever is. (I, who, like you, feel I have perfect taste, am no better. It ain't the Gentile I fear, it's everybody, everything. The germs on pennies, people coughing, the shit on dogshit.) Not the niceties and not notions gleaned from study, education, the great books. (The idea of an educated taste is absurd. You might as well speak of educating your need for shelter.) Taste can't, I think, be heightened, sharpened. It comes with the territory, is fixed as birthmark. Indeed, it *is* birthmark, what the gypsy wishes for us in the crib, the customized, bespoke astrology of the self.

Here is a little of what the gypsy whispered to me:

Delicatessen and the midnight nosh. Lox, whitefish, sturgeon, rye. Scrambled eggs and onions, corn bread, butter. Cel-Ray tonic, Philadelphia cream cheese. Milk, chopped liver, corned beef, rolls. Cheesecake, coffee, coleslaw, fruit. (Because taste is also nostalgia, see? It's love, staying up late, some stroked sense of privilege. It's being where the adults are, boon and holiday and overhearing shoptalk. It's unearned and not to be counted on and never to be expected. It strikes like emergency, but emergency in reverse. Someone has free passes, somebody has samples. *It's sentimental.*) And to this day a freezer case in a deli stops my heart. Not just the speckled food, the flecked pastrami like a meat confetti, the bins of bagel and the sesame lint, but the little engine itself, like a Scotchtape dispenser, which pokes out your number, bespeaking order, crowds, prosperity.

The Brooklyn neighborhood where my mother's folks lived, the Bronx one where my dad's did. I was raised in Chicago, we moved from New York when I was three years old. When we went back east in the summer it was to a bungalow in New Jersey. Since the time I lived in those neighborhoods, I've spent maybe five months of my life in them. But taste is nostalgia, first impressions struck like a coin, and no *tabula* is ever not *rasa*, and we're all cases of arrested development with arrest records long as your life. So a sweet tooth for cities, for some hustle-bustle un-Nature, though I live in a house across from a park in a suburb sedate as Connecticut.

The first grown-up books I ever read were Marion Hargrove's *See Here, Private Hargrove!*, Elmer Rice's plays in Pocketbook—*Street Scene* is the one I recall best—Kaufman's and Hart's in Modern Library, and Whit Burnett's *This Is My Best*, quite possibly the finest anthology ever published. (Or quite possibly not, but only the first one I read.)

The films—we're getting on now; I'm no longer in the crib but am still impressionable; maybe I'm twenty; what the hell, it's *all* crib—of Robert Mitchum. (Since this is an attempt to clarify my taste, there, right there, may be the paradigm for it. I have no patience with detective stories but will line up around the block to watch Robert Mitchum play Philip Marlowe. Mitchum in a trench coat is what men *ought* to look like. There should be his rumpled statues in our parks.)

But, in truth, my taste has less to do with aromas and neighborhoods and Modern Library editions and the projected vision—that's just the sweet side of nature, my suckered ethnics recollected in tranquillity— than it does with that bungalow in Jersey, my dual sense of myself as a kid midwesterner come east in summer and a would-be New Yorker laid over in Chicago the rest of the year. (I can't help it if it's silly. All pasts are silly.) My pals in New Jersey were from New York. They lived, they said, in the city. Their fathers were sign painters for Schulte's Cigar Stores. They were cab drivers, elevator starters, or, orthodox Jews, they simplified their names and opened furniture stores in Boonton, New Jersey, miles from the *minyan*. They were cutters in the garment trade. They sold Ship 'n Shore blouses out of suitcases. And they seemed—and their kids, my pals, too—to me real, much realer than myself, than my father who made more money, who wore custom suits and traveled great distances in airplanes, who played gin for money he would not accept when he won but insisted on paying if he lost, who kept a room in a good Manhattan hotel the entire summer and came to camp—we called it "camp"—only on weekends. Who had orchestra seats he bought from the scalpers. Who picked up checks all around and took it badly when others didn't. Who was, at last, a snob with a heart of gold who had no patience with the dross tickers (my father had several heart attacks between his first one and the one that finally killed him seven years later in low season in the good hotel) he suspected in others. He was this geologist of the heart, my dad, no alchemist but the true fortyniner, a panner of other people's instincts, an assay artist. "Four flusher," he'd say of this one or that, and never make his case, withholding details. So I looked for myself, New Jersey this side show, midsummer night's dream. And came away wih my taste for worried men. (Mitchum a variation on a theme, bulk a signal of grace, like fat men dancing.)

What's wanted then, unless voice or invention override, is this quality of nice guys in trouble, troubled. (I didn't know this about myself, I wouldn't have suspected it from my own work, but then that's taste for you—— the left hand that doesn't know what the right hand is doing. It's an emotional no-man's-land of neutralized pressure, the head and heart weightless and the soul in free-fall, the will not so much sidetracked as simply not at issue, on holiday, gone fishing, if you will.) There is a distance between one's slumbrous, unsuspected tastes and one's expectations for oneself. It's the difference between saying "I know what I like" and "I know what I like to do." Something a little hypocritical at either end of things, the receiving and the working. Taste is circumstantial, there's something windfall and passive about it. It smacks of the high-summer hammock condition, and we take our pleasures stretched out, our hands behind our heads. (While there isn't a story in this collection I wouldn't have wanted to write, there are several I would have wanted to write differently. And would've wound up perhaps with stories I wouldn't necessarily have wanted to read.) This accounts for the allowances nearly all of us make, for our serious friend who devours mystery stories, for "Auld Lang Syne" and the Bert Parks fuss and the Super Bowl—— all those stock gems of pop culture like some rhinestoned Las Vegas of the gut, our Whitman's Sampler appetite. There is, that is, something peculiarly indulgent about our real tastes. Which is why our real tastes are so often, if we have any stake at all in the intellectual or artistic life, our best-kept secrets, right up there with our sexual fantasies and that yen for the salami sandwich at the gourmet dinner. Sometimes this becomes a guarded theme in some of our most demanding literature. All Aunt Rosa's demon lover, Thomas Sutpen, in *Absalom, Absalom!*, ever wanted was a son, to be a family man is all.—Rosebud, Rosebud!

What is wanted then is sadness. (We're talking literature, not life. We're talking Kenny Rogers's chipped and country voice, not music.) This, it seems to me, is the absolute, ideal humor for respectable men. Sadness, mind you, not grief. Or grief under control, made courteous, deferential, the keening and lamentation practically inaudible, indistinguishable but unextinguished in the generalized white noise of the world. A sadness like a mourner's button on an M.C.'s lapel. There for the weight, the sharp ballast it lends to tumult. Sadness like an intelligent conviction, like a badge of bearing— a short cut, you see, a short cut and a convenience. (So many of the characters in these stories are widowered—it's a man's world—so many are divorced.) Sadness like documents, the heart's papers, what these characters show us or what we find on them at borders to prove they're serious.

And if the sadness is suddenly mitigated, or even retracted, so much the better. If it is mitigated by some unscrupulous vision—I mean when the *deus* in the *deus ex machina* is actually God, or when the character, acting on his own, sublimely lets go, or when the sadness is not repudiated at all but actively embraced in some higher emotional game of razzle-dazzle performance and shellgame dexterity, so much the better yet. (If the story can only hang on till the ending . . .Endings tend to be wonderful . . .) Isn't reprieve literature's last act anyway? Isn't it some notion of acquittal or deliverance that off and on vouches for our condition and cosigns our lives? (It's precisely the off-and-on nature of our visions that *makes* them unscrupulous, but now we're talking life, not literature.)

Anyway, most of the stories in this collection (though not consciously picked for these qualities, which I discovered afterwards, and this introduction a sort of apologia for criteria I had not realized were even operating) aim, consciously or not, for just this sort of justification of the character's life. They conclude with an overview, however partial, and some suggestive illusion of the vision's continuing momentum. Perhaps it's a concession to realism that causes several of the writers to have their characters lie down, literally or figuratively, on deathbeds. (Bellow has a character in *The Adventures of Augie March* wonder,

How do you keep the feelings up? Well one way is to make the protagonist terminal, foreshortening the time he has to sustain them.) It's what Frederick Busch does in "Long Calls" and what Singer does in "The Safe Deposit" and what Gordon Weaver does in "Hog's Heart." But, in a way, it's what most of them do. There is usually something summary and terribly final about the concluding rhetoric— the ringing long-range long view of language. Consider this piece of business from the end of John Updike's story, "Gesturing":

The motion was eager, shy, exquisite, diffident, trusting: He saw all its meanings and knew that she would never stop gesturing within him, never; though a decree come between them, even death, her gestures would endure, cut into glass.

Or Donald Barthelme's "The Emerald," at the point where Moll's strange offspring asks its mother what happens next:

We resume the scrabble for existence, said Moll. We resume the scrabble for existence, in the sweet of the here and now.

Mavis Gallant's "The Remission":

Escorting lame Mrs. Massie to a sofa, Mr. Cranefield said they might as well look on the bright side. (He was still speaking about the second half of the 1950s.) Wilkinson, sitting down because he felt sick, and thinking the remark was intended for him, assured Mr. Cranefield, truthfully, that he had never looked anywhere else. It then happened that every person in the room, at the same moment, spoke and thought of something other than Alec. This lapse, this inattention, lasting no longer than was needed to say "No, thank you" or "Oh, really?" or "Yes, I see," was enough to create the dark gap marking the end of Alec's span. He ceased to be, and it made absolutely no difference after that whether or not he was forgotten.

The same author's wonderful "Speck's Idea":

Because this one I am keeping, Speck decided; this one will be signed: "By Sandor Speck." He smiled at the bright wet streets of Paris as he and Cruche, together, triumphantly crossed the Alps.

As Schiff, in Busch's "Long Calls," on the sidewalk lies dying:

> *Schiff heard himself snorting, half-naked on the sidewalk. He touched at his burns. The klaxons were close. Now he had to call his wife back, now, he had to. He had to tell her he knew what to do— save things, place long calls—in emergencies at least.*

Isaac Bashevis Singer concludes "The Safe Deposit":

> *Although he was aching, he felt a rest he had never known before— the sublime enjoyment of fearing nothing, having no wish, no worry, no resentment . . .*

And Gordon Weaver writes, "Dying, Hog looks into the glare of the sun, finds his death is not pain or sweetness but totality and transcendence." Hog goes "into such light as makes light and darkness one."

One or two more and I'll explain what I'm trying to mean.

Grace Paley's "Friends" ends when the narrator tells us, "He was right to call my attention to its suffering and danger. He was right to harass my responsible nature. But I was right to invent for my friends and our children a report on these private deaths and the condition of our lifelong attachments."

The old activists in John Sayles's story, "At the Anarchists' Convention," team up at one last barricade:

> *And when the manager returns with his two befuddled street cops to find us standing together, arms linked, the lame held up out of their wheelchairs, the deaf joining from memory as Bud Odum leads us in "We Shall Not Be Moved," my hand in Sophie's, sweaty-palmed at her touch like the old days, I look at him in his brown blazer and think* Brickman, *I think,* my God if Brickman was here we'd show this bastard the Wrath of the People!

Well maybe just two more.

Barry Targan's English professor in his story "The Rags of Time," having escaped with his tenure intact after a reckless fling with a beautiful undergraduate, calms down in his office:

> *When she was gone he sat quite still and let the first terror she had brought in with her subside. He let fade the jagged collage of*

public accusation and denial that had first sprung through him, the tumult of fear that he would lose . . .what? Everything? But what could that mean? No. The loss he had sustained would be a small one, something he would hardly notice in his life as it had been and would be lived hereafter. There would be no more chances.

At last he was empty.

And, finally, T. Gertler's "In Case of Survival":

Helpessness settled on Harold with the steam from reheated potatoes. He opened his eyes and breathed in homely odors. The kitchen offered itself to him: burners, counter, sink, dishwasher, refrigerator, table, chairs, all vibrating against yellow-and-white-and-silver-foil wallpaper. The salt and pepper shakers danced on the tile shelf above the sink. His wife, in a blue kimono, presented him with a bowl of chopped vegetables. He sighed. Questions of guilt and innocence fell away; he contemplated instead his endless and enduring helplessness. The knowledge of it soothed him as the kitchen dipped, shuddered, grew still.

(Some of the best stories are not exampled here, not because they don't fit my category but because they don't save their rhetoric, as some of those quoted do, till last.)

I've cited eleven stories. In three of them—Weaver's, Singer's, and Gertler's—visions quite literally occur. In Updike's ("He saw all its meanings . . ."), and in "Speck's Idea" ("He smiled at the bright wet streets of Paris as he and Cruche, together, triumphantly crossed the Alps"), and in Busch's ("Schiff heard himself snorting, half-naked on the sidewalk. He touched at his burns. . . . Now he had to call his wife. . . .He had to tell her how he knew what to do . . ."), and in Targan's (the character knows everything that will happen to him and everything that won't for all the rest of his life), something very like a vision takes over. In an eighth story, Mavis Gallant's "The Remission," the language of magic ("It then happened that every person in the room, at the same moment . . .") controls what the characters fail to think and say, liberating them from their connection to Alec for all time. In Sayles's piece, the narrator's emotion is running so high as he thinks of the dead Brickman that his age practically drops away from him and it is "like the old days." A tenth story, "The Emerald," is itself a vision.

In all instances (those quoted as well as those that have not even been mentioned) we are dealing, at the end, with a kind of rhetorical sacrament. We are dealing with solace, the *idea* of solace, art's and language's consolation prize. The notion that the character needs bucking up. And the writer begins to play for keeps, laying on a from-now-on syntax that suggests, and powerfully too, that the conditions that obtain will somehow manage to sustain themselves forever. It's something a bit beyond the conventional notion of epiphany, inasmuch as epiphany is usually some sudden, fellswoop blast of insight. This is epiphany that sticks to the ribs. "He saw all its meanings and knew that she would never stop gesturing within him, never": the emerald is told twice—just as the word *never* is repeated in Updike's sentence and *helplessness* in the passage from Gertler—that what is resumed is "the scrabble for existence." Alec, in magical language already quoted, quite suddenly ceases to be, chased by Mavis Gallant's incantation, and the characters are not only consoled for their loss but freed. "Because this one I am keeping," Speck thinks, "this one will be signed." (Again the repetition.) So, through repetition, magic, visions, inversion ("He let fade the jagged collage . . ."; "Dying, Hog looks . . ."; "Because this one I am keeping . . ."), or series ("This lapse, this inattention, lasting no longer than was needed to say 'No, thank you' or 'Oh, really?' or 'Yes, I see' "; "He was right to call my attention to its suffering and danger. He was right to harass my responsible nature. But I was right to . . ."; "The motion was eager, shy, exquisite, diffident, trusting . . .") the rhetoric lifts subtly away from the story, its attention no longer really focused on the character's problems so much as it is on a kind of conversion, on bottom lines from the heart. There is a solace in finality and a grace in resignation no matter what one is resigned to— death, helplessness, the end of chance, resignation itself. But life's tallest order is to keep the feelings up, to make two dollars' worth of euphoria go the distance. And life can't do that. So fiction does. And there, right there, is the real—I want to say "only"— morality of fiction.

Not much, is it? It's all there is.

Taste is a gift of condition. In my own instance it is for the disheveled, what the cat dragged in, the rumpled in spirit, the soiled of heart. It is for Lily and Peter in James Robison's story, "Home," and Delia, their thirteen-year-old daughter who doesn't listen to them; for Lucas, the mourning biology professor of Robert Henderson's "Into the Wind." For senile Dr. Cahn, with his crippled vocabulary, in Richard Stern's "Dr. Cahn's Visit"; for Luther Glick in David Evanier's "The One-Star Jew"; and for the married man in Curt Johnson's "Lemon Tree," who dates a room clerk in Cleveland. It is for Elizabeth Hardwick's Dr. Z in "The Faithful," always true to everyone in his fashion. And for Markowitz, everybody's mark in Norman Waksler's "Markowitz and the Gypsies," a story structured like a joke and written in the idiom of one. I can't help it, these are my people. I too wish this taste of mine were not so one-sided. I wish it were for Henry James types, impeccable at tea, whose crumpets don't crumb, nobles of the middle class who know their way around a foreign language and can parse the value of another human just by the way his pocket handkerchief is folded; but that, Officer Krupke, wasn't the hand I was dealt. So I take my taste—which is always lazy, which ever, like physical law, seeks least resistances—and convert it to a kind of affection, to rooter interest (and it isn't even, all of it anyway, self-pity; my own pocket handkerchief waves like a little trapezoid above the breast pocket of my Harris tweed), to some low-down snatch of the sentimental (or what would be sentimental if the writers weren't so skillful) till all losses are reconciled, till, that is, they're underwritten by their authors with the beautiful cool comfort of a language that makes it all better, the soiled history, the rotten luck. My job in all this, as I say, is simply to lie back and enjoy myself, my sympathy floating the surface of these lives like fat in soup, I know what the characters can't, what probably even the writers don't, believe—that it won't work, that it can't last, that inversion and magic and series and transcendence and saying something twice aren't enough, that in real life they would have to print a retraction. But I'm easy. I love my remote virtue. I'm moved by my morality. *I enjoy my heart.*

Yet some of the best stories in this collection don't do that.

Peter Taylor's long story, "The Old Forest," must surely be a masterpiece, but in a way it's almost sociology, and a sociology that isn't even operative anymore— the stiff, cold codes of a Memphis of the mind. Never mind, that's all art, you see, and has nothing to do with my taste or anyone else's either.

And if I read Leon Rooke's story, "Mama Tuddi Done Over," correctly, it's about a woman my sentimentality couldn't touch.

And, finally, two stories are included here because, quite simply, they are so beautifully written— Larry Heinemann's "The First Clean Fact" and William Gass's "The Old Folks."

Some note should, I suppose, be made of the fact that Mavis Gallant is represented by two stories in this collection. That also was a decision easily arrived at. What was tougher was the problem of whether to include a third, "The Burgundy Weekend." We decided not to because we—Shannon Ravenel and myself—figured it might be construed as showing off.

About Shannon Ravenel. Anyone who has been keeping up with this annual for the last couple of years must surely know by now that Shannon does all the work. She reads *everything*. Fifteen hundred stories for this year's collection alone. And that's at the inside. (The guest editor is only required to read 125 or so.) I know that I've seen everything I should have seen, that very little, if anything, has fallen through the cracks. One has pals. One is under obligations. One asks, "What about So-and-so?" One says, "I don't see Whoosis." "So-and-so was a disappointment this year," says Shannon. "Whoosis is in a slump." "Please show one," one says. "Sure, buddy, it's your funeral," Shannon says. And goes to her files. Which are exhaustive. And hauls out So-and-so, and hands one Whoosis. But she's right. She lives, breathes, and eats short stories, and I am privileged to have worked with her.

FOREWORD TO *ARTHUR SCHNITZLER, PLAYS AND STORIES*

IF I COULD COME BACK IT WOULD BE AS A PLAYWRIGHT. FOR THE amiability of the thing, for the backstage and greenroom nexus and the gag telegrams on opening night. For the parties and endless, hopeful toasts and generally companionable, even intimate, round-robin life. To be collegial and pally. To be thick as a thief and bussed by the showgirls. To be part, I mean, of a small idea.

But not for the art. Almost certainly not for the art. There is, I think, a natural constraint on playwrights, on drama, the form itself. For one, there is the constraint of time. The play—and movies and music, too—is essentially a social form, invented, maybe, as they tell you in the sophomore anthologies, to be performed on the back of the church truck, or in the amphitheater on the Greek high holidays, but that was social, too, of course, and we know in our hearts it's done today, as it may have been done then, for the night-out of the thing, for its dinner-and-a-show aspects and ramifications, its birthday and anniversary ones—our own high holidays, I mean—theater, or at least going to it, a moveable feast, the sense we have of occasion. And the playwright's commitment is as much to his audience as to any fancy

notion he has of any fancy notion. The buses stop running, the subways. The baby-sitter has to be back by midnight, and the eight-thirty
curtain is no accident, I think, but some cozy tie-in with the deli guys
and restaurateurs—been to Broadway? the West End?—possibly even
with the baby-sitters. There's this mutual understanding that the playwright will get you in and get you out in something under two-and-
a-half hours—Eugene O'Neill's long nights' journeys into days were
windbag exceptions; *Nicholas Nickleby* was—and this whole business
of time limitation opens the play up to its vulnerabilities. Indeed, it
becomes its vulnerabilities—a format for one idea, often enough drawn
out even at that, padded as togs about some kernel of Eskimo; knee-
deep in time as in mud. Or the constraint of structure—why who-
done-it's (but all plays are who-done-it's, *Oedipus* no less than *The
Mouse Trap*, *King Lear* no less than *Sleuth*) run years—when structure
(scenes, acts, the explosive lines that bring down curtains, the frozen
moments and dimmed lights that end an act) itself tends toward form,
almost genre, as Westerns are a genre, as science fiction is, and theater
entertaining in relation, like Westerns, like science fiction, to how it
rings the changes, how it presumes to do it this time, turning on itself,
on expectation, with a twist and resolution like some closing couplet
slamming a door in a sonnet. Or an excuse—this now, not then, other
playwrights, not Schnitzler—for "production values," how the thing
is "mounted," its hi-tech arrangements and willful media mixing—
how plays try to burst their bonds and become, well, movies. Or the
other excuse, not the well-made play so much as the well-acted one,
"a vehicle," voice and carriage a substitute for—well, *two* ideas.

But finally those two-and-a-half hours that constrict playwrights,
that hole-and-corner them into convention—theater is a smorgasbord
of convention; even musical comedy, which, when it works, is possibly
the most satisfying theatrical form there is, if only because of the
presence of singers and dancers with their immediate access to the
communal lyrical, musical theater's marvelous ability to dispense with
logic and go with little or no preparation for the jugular emotions,
even musical comedy has its clichés and conventions, here masked by
movement and melody, the distraction of pure and pointless energy—
to close them off from an exploration of character and situation and
story and even language—astonishingly, "language," high rhetoric, I
mean, finds no natural home in plays—the only proper considerations
of fiction, forcing them into a kind of "issue dependency," those

hundred six minutes that make a false virtue of economy and an ironclad, no-loopholes law of Chekhov's dictum that any gun hung on the wall in Act 1 must by and by be fired. Such "economy" is, of course, a sort of penny-wise, pound-foolishness, a mean and mingy, wasteful thrift. Because it clips the wings of possibility and seals, mint and airtight, what ought to remain open-ended. The theater, one cannot breathe there. (I'm thinking of plays like A Man for All Seasons; I'm thinking of plays like Amadeus, where all that's allowed is the argument, some shuttlecock notion of confrontation, the obsessive back-and-forths of accusation and denial.) And because, finally, in drama it is always the literal present tense. Even in flashbacks it is the present tense for, unlike the novel, plays do not have the gift of tense. In a novel or short story all half dozen tenses are available to the writer all together all at once, and not just within a single scene, or even paragraph, but, if he chooses, within a sentence, within a single clause from simple past through all the perfect future, a pluperfect perpetual calendar of handled time. Do that in a play and you have reminiscence, a set piece, a *speech*.

One goes to the theater then—or *I* do—as to a museum, as a conscious act of secular archaeology. And reads plays like Arthur Schnitzler's as one might read an old newspaper. For an amusing account of the types and times. For the nostalgia, that is. To find out about the shopgirls and young men (*Flirtations*); the married ladies and cuckold husbands, the poets and chippies, housemaids and actresses, enlisted men, noblemen, and whores (*La Ronde*); to find out about the professional people, the professors and doctors, the priests, the lawyers, the journalists, and political comers (*Professor Bernhardi*)—— to learn about Vienna at the turn of the century.

But for all that a roll call of Schnitzler's Vienna, with its immense cast of characters, suggests operetta, what he gives us finally is not operetta at all. His playboys and young officers depict nothing if not the dark side of the Chocolate Soldier, and his view, if not tragic—it isn't; it's streetwise and cynical—is at least afflicting. He writes about the wide flaws and crabbed comeuppances of silly people. In a way, his tragedy is venereal—you pays your money and you takes your chancres—brought on not by love but urge, not conviction but dumb, even reluctant, obstinacy, not individuals caught up in their beliefs but in their culture's practices, all of which make Schnitzler a sort of consummate playwright, for his scolds and pulpiteering are pitched at

a collective audience in the snug snuffbox, safe and social circumstances of theater, and feed off a fixed, governing idea—the dramatic
conceit—convention—of hypocrisy. Audiences are suckers for hypocrisy. They love all the easy discrepancies, all ducks-in-a-barrel
morality and potshotted shortcomings. They love, that is, to lick the
finger that points at them.

Although *Professor Bernhardi* is not included in this collection, it
is instructive to cast a glance at it. In *Professor Bernhardi* Schnitzler
is working the tradition of what can only be called "integrity drama."
The trick is to present a character in a tight situation and turn all the
screws, bring on all the big guns of circumstances. It's man-against-
the-lynch-mob theater, the theater of choices, of the protagonist in
Kiplingesque "If-ian" contingency, where a hero absorbs all the mean-
spirited low blows his enemies can dish out, takes all those rabbit
punches to his integrity, and remains a man, my son. These are crises
not so much of conscience as of punishment and, in *Professor Bernhardi,* had not Schnitzler meddled with his own premises, would reveal
a character so smitten with his martyrdom that the play might almost
have become a set-piece of heroically smug dimensions. What saves
it, I think—and what saves a great deal of Schnitzler—is the subtle
reversal that occurs at the end of the play, a reversal that suddenly
introduces a real, and far more interesting, possibility—that we have
been duped into philosophy, fooled into philosophy. Startlingly, we
are presented with the idea that Bernhardi may have been wrong. The
doctor, back from a two-month prison term to which he's been sentenced on trumped-up, antisemitically motivated charges that he'd
physically interfered with a priest come to grant absolution to a young
girl about to die in the septic aftermath of an illegal abortion—Bernhardi had intended to allow the girl to die in a state of narcotically
induced bliss, the sudden appearance of the priest, or so the questionable premise goes, needlessly forcing her down from her high to
die in despair—has an interview with Councillor Winkler, an admin-
istrator with the Ministry of Education. Bernhardi is loaded for self-
righteous bear.

BERNH: . . . all at once it seemed as though the broadest ethical
issues were at stake; responsibility and revelation, and finally the
question of free will—
WINKLER: Oh yes, you always end up with that if you dig down to

the root of things. But it's better to break off before you get so far, otherwise one fine day it may happen that you begin to understand everything and forgive everything. . . . Undoubtedly you were not born to be a reformer—

BERNH: Reformer—? My dear sir—

WINKLER: As little as I—We are not prepared, deep down, to follow up our principles to the final consequences—to stake our lives, if necessary, for our convictions. And therefore the best thing, in fact the only decent thing, is for men of our sort—to leave such matters alone—

BERNH: But—

WINKLER: No good results from meddling. What end would have been attained after all, my dear Professor, had you spared that poor creature a last shock on her deathbed? . . .

BERNH: . . . I simply did what I held to be right in one specific instance.

WINKLER: That is where you went wrong. If we always did only the right thing, or rather started off one day at breakfast time, without further reflection, to do only the right thing all day long, we should certainly land in jail before supper time.

BERNH: And shall I tell you something, Councillor? In my place you would have acted exactly as I did.

WINKLER: Possibly. Then I should have been—you'll forgive me, Professor—just such an ass as you—

Curtain

This is the curtain speech and opens the play's ends, as it were, permitting if not genuine ambiguity then at least a sort of theatrical counterpart—— textual double take.

Which—opening ends, fiddling dramatic form—Schnitzler, though I think his strong suit was fiction, may have had some real interest in. Despite the fact that his plays remain chiefly, well, charming and conventional, there is the feeling in Arthur Schnitzler's work that he was at odds with his countrymen, with the Vienna that may have been, at least for him and at least symbolically, almost as much the city-state as the Venice to which his worn out Casanova returns under the humiliating terms of his lifted exile, a sense of odd man out, of exclusion, a rift as deep as the sexual one between men and women that pervades his plays, that, indeed, is largely the subject of them. Yet his plays *are* conventional—*La Ronde* is certainly an exception, if only for its pas-de-deux arrangements—and it is an interesting exercise to count the convenient encounters between characters in the entrances and exits in a given play. They seem, in their dependable comings and goings, scheduled as trains. The second act of *Flirtations* is simply an example.

Christine is dressing to go out. Katharine enters. They talk. Christine's father, Weiring, enters. All three talk. Christine leaves. Katharine and Weiring talk. Mitzi, Christine's friend, enters. The three are talking (mostly about having to leave) when Christine enters. Weiring and Katharine leave together. Mitzi and Christine talk. Fritz, Christine's lover, enters. Mitzi leaves. Fritz and Christine have, for this act, at least, a longish talk. (A little about the picture on Christine's wall, "Parting and Return.") Theodore, Fritz's friend, enters. The two friends whisper together while Christine "busies herself at the window" (the stage direction) until she "is near them again" (another stage direction). The three talk together. Theodore and Fritz leave. Christine, "uneasy, remains standing, then goes to the door left ajar. She is subdued," calls Fritz. Fritz enters and holds her. He says "Farewell."

Six characters appear in this brief act; there are seven separate entrances; two characters leave individually, two others exit together. While important information is obviously exchanged, much of the dialogue—since Schnitzler, not even excluding the deliberate experimentation of *La Ronde*, is essentially a realistic, even a naturalistic, playwright—is necessarily small talk, the Hi's and How-are-ya's of ordinary life. (And much talk of weather and, since characters leave as well as come on board, there is leave*taking*, not only a Hello for each Goodbye but regards to the wife and all the polite conversation of primarily civilized people.)

What we're talking about here is plot by conversation, some Aristotle-grounded Law of the Off-Stage; life in the wings. (Here *La Ronde is* an exception, though, at least in reading the play, one gets an impression—all those asterisks where the good parts go—of staging by ellipses, of the partners going to the shadows to do their business.) Because what we're talking about finally is melodramatics, soap opera, the peculiar pulled punches of all distinctly social art forms.

And yet—And yet—And yet there is his fiction.

Schnitzler's use of stream-of-consciousness in *Lieutenant Gustl*, though certainly innovative, is, on the face of it, clumsy, his use of the "I" in his silly, blustering young officer's interior monologue unfortunate, probably impossible (rather like trying to sustain in even so short a piece of fiction as the short story the second person point-of-view).

> How much longer is this thing going to last? Let's see what time it is . . . perhaps I shouldn't look at my watch at a serious concert like this. But no one will see me. If anyone does, I'll know he's paying just as little attention as I am. In that case I certainly won't be embarrassed. . . . Only quarter to ten? . . . I feel as though I'd been here for hours. I'm just not used to going to concerts. . . . What's that they're playing? I'll have a look at the program. . . . Yes that's what it is: an oratorio. Thought it was a mass. That sort of thing belongs in church.

People do not think to themselves syntactically; they don't remind themselves—"That was funny a week ago when she was at the Gartenbeau Café with him, and I was sitting opposite Kopetzky; she kept winking at me"—of what they already know. The effect is not only unnatural, it is insane, as talking to oneself is supposed to be insane. Yet in Schnitzler's remarkable novella all sense of the innate falseness of the point-of-view drops almost immediately away, and it is as if the author had invented for this particular character in this particular situation a diction and tense and viewpoint entirely, and distinctively, and perfectly, his own, as if Schnitzler were taking the affidavit of Lieutenant Gustl's soul. Indeed, that seems to be precisely what he's doing, giving the reader privileged information to another man's character. The effect is extraordinary and very powerful, for Gustl, with his straight, humorless failure of perception and highfalutin' notions of himself, makes a terrible witness and becomes, before our eyes, a sort of witless, unforgivable Falstaff, unregenerate and unforgettable. That this is a consequence of the very clumsiness of the point-of-view in hand-glove relation with Gustl's measly character is almost certainly the case, granting the reader not only his inside information about Gustl (and advancing, incidentally, the difficult technique of the "unreliable narrator") but a kind of licensed omniscience, and not only creating, within the small compass of a brief book, a memorable character but turning his voice into what is possibly a unique trope in literature.

Schnitzler's Casanova, in *Casanova's Homecoming*, is an even greater achievement, if for no other reason than that he has a more interesting mind than Gustl and finds himself in a more interesting situation, Casanova's problems being "real," while Gustl's are only made up, self-inflicted, the product of a locked-in imagination engined by an unrelenting egoism. But there *are* other reasons.

The character of a great man, now aging, whose deeds are "by degrees passing into oblivion" is not an unfamiliar one. Movies have rendered him for years: broken-down sheriffs and old gunfighters, all the worn-out spies come in from the cold, all the drunk docs called to draw upon depleted skills in times of crisis, have become stock stick figures in the literature. What Schnitzler has going for him in *Casanova's Homecoming* is the conception of using a legendary character—though this isn't new either; Shaw had recycled Don Juan; Joyce Odysseus—with whom we're already familiar, so that neither the protagonist nor the other characters have constantly to remind us how the mighty are fallen. We know because he is in our heads. What he has going for him further is that Casanova *isn't* called upon in emergency and, further still, that his particular depleted skills are only personal, and that all Casanova wants is to have a last fling and go home. The "only personal" is, of course, the best and most difficult situation of all, not more valuable to literature than its great other half—going home, coming to terms, resignation and acceptance—not more valuable because, finally, they are the same.

If the cliché about novelists not making good playwrights is true, as I think it is in the case of Arthur Schnitzler, it isn't because talent lapses or undergoes some radical sea-change as the writer turns his attention from one form to the other but because of something in the nature of the forms themselves—that, broadly and vastly oversimplified, theater is public and political—an actor's lines are even *called* "speeches"—an occasion, while fiction, with its disregard for time—or at least length—and its concomitant gifts of extension and an almost holographic ability to project in the round, is essentially private and personal, an occasion, too, of sorts, but lonelier, no occasion at all, really. Which is why, if I *could* come back, it would be as a playwright.

A LA RECHERCHE
DU WHOOPEE
CUSHION

PAUL SMITH OWNS THAT MAIL-ORDER COMPANY WE REMEMBER, THE
Johnson Smith Company, candy-butcher of Joy Buzzers and Whoopee
Cushions to the world. There is nothing Phil Silvers about him, nothing top banana in the patter or handshake. If he hadn't been his father's
son he would probably be doing something else now. He is an inheritor
and has about him, even after all these years, the vague, shuffling
quality of the stand-in. When his brother, Arthur, retired in 1967—
what can one say?—*all this became his*. And he can hardly wait to
retire.

"Why?"

"Well, frankly, I have other interests."

"What?"

"Philosophy."

"Phi*lo*sophy?"

"To some extent I'm interested more or less in keeping up with
various things that are going on." To some extent he is blowing smoke.
He means it but would not be saying it if he hadn't been asked. "I
believe we're in an evolutionary culture. What interests me mostly is

what you might call positive motivations of people. In other words, inspirational, creative aspects, if you want to call it that, and since I'm science oriented, my feeling is it's learning more about the unknown."

"The occult?"

"No, not the occult. For me the most interesting thing about living is solving problems. When the dynamics of a business is gone—I don't rate my ideas about life or about business very highly—I feel compelled to read and to try to learn as much as I can."

"Who do you read? What philosophers?"

"Buber. Teilhard de Chardin. Proust. Proust isn't a philosopher, but I read him. Wodehouse is my favorite author. My eyes are—"

There is something wrong with his eyes. He blinks, rubs them. He carries two pairs of glasses and changes them frequently. Sometimes he wears neither pair, allows his eyes the air as one would walk barefoot. I like him.

"What will you do?" I know that he majored in math and physics at the University of Wisconsin. "Will you take up your physics again, your math?"

"It's all changed. I don't think I can even do calculus now." He pauses, brooding over his ruined calculus. "We'll travel. We'll travel a lot."

He looks a little like Dean Jagger, the actor of executives, and he wears the calm, off-dark, handsome clothes of the conservatively dressed. He speaks quietly, in Jagger's sprung rhythms, a flat, faintly archaic American at distinct odds with the copy he has written all these years for the Johnson Smith Catalog. Great Lakes English. For some reason even his description of what Johnson Smith sells—"hobby merchandise, unusual rings, self-improvement books, electrical and scientific kits, fortune-telling, magic, novelty jokes and tricks, practical gadgets, time-savers"—sounds anachronistic, the dead diction of his father's faded spiel. What is there about the terms "hobby merchandise," "unusual rings," and "novelty jokes and tricks" that sounds, well, imported, faintly road show?

Alfred Johnson Smith founded the Johnson Smith Company in Australia in 1905. Following some homeopathic instinct, he brought it to Chicago in 1914. Chicago was the headquarters of Sears, Roebuck, another mail-order house. He published his first catalog there and stayed on until he moved the business to Racine, Wisconsin, in 1923, and then to Detroit in the late thirties. Three years ago Paul Smith built a new office and warehouse in a small industrial park in Mt. Clemens, Michigan, so that everything could be on one floor. Always near the shore of one Great Lake or another, good, honest place, Green Bay Packer country, locatable on maps, and not just this P.O. Box or that Drawer Something Something of ordinary mail-order arrangement. Smith has a theory that a mail-order business should have hub-ness. Trust and patience—it can take weeks to receive what you've sent away for—diminish exponentially with distance. Johnson Smith has always drawn most of its business from Chicago, Milwaukee, Cleveland, Toledo, and Detroit— its freshwater-port nexus and the proximities of trust.

The items are a blur to him, he's seen so many, but he loves the catalog. A dozen exotic catalogs, opened and unopened, ride his desk like a convoy. Thousands, in love with their childhood, doing as adults that self-reflexive ancestor worship that is nostalgia, dote on their memories of the money they spent, the decisions made so carefully, the items chosen deliberately as first furniture. Smith loves the catalog and he can parse it like a scholar.

"Almost all Sears catalog illustrations were woodcuts. This was before photographs and halftones came in. I knew most of the fellas who made the woodcuts for us. We'd send the article to the woodcut maker and he'd reproduce it. You'd be surprised. It would have more detail than a photograph. Most of the great woodcuts came from Chicago. One fellow in Chicago and one in New York were the last fellas to do the woodcuts. I think they're still being made, but they're prohibitively expensive. They cost twenty-five to thirty dollars when we stopped having them made. The trend was toward photography and halftones. Now *this*, I think, is the perfect way to illustrate an item. You show the item and then you show what it does."

We are looking at #2753 in an old Johnson Smith Company catalog— the Rubber Coat Hanger. I think the man still in his coat and leaning forward on his cane is related to the man whose hat is falling. For one thing, their hats are alike, and they both have canes. They may have injured their legs on an earlier visit. I don't know who the fat man is.

I know *what* he is, however, Smith tells me.

"A lot of our practical jokes came from Germany. Before the war, our main source was Germany. The Rubber Coat Hanger is a German item. I would say all the items on this page are German."

"The Whoopee Cushion, was that a German item?"

"I would guess that the Germans had it. Whether they had it first I don't know."

Whether they had it first. One thinks of the Whoopee Cushion Race, of Whoopee Cushion Capabilities, Whoopee Cushion Gaps. Smith continues to point out page after page of German practical jokes. "There's an element," he says, "of sadism in almost any practical joke. A leveler. My way of bringing you down to my level, or at least pricking your bubble if you're too pompous. To an extent humor is retaliatory. A leveler. To my mind I guess I'm not a practical joker."

German. Germany. German. The funny little men whose rubber heads you pressed to make water squirt from their cigarettes— all Germans. All the fellows smiling benignly into trick kaleidoscopes that blackened their eyes as they ground their vision against the belly dancer. All the sneezers, their eyes squeezed tight as children's waiting to be shown a surprise, their faces distorted in the perfect way to illustrate an item, their mouths open in *"ah!"* and collapsed in *"chow!!"* And Germans too the scratchers, fingers mining their itches, prospectors of their own persons in a desperate pantomime of greed and relief. As German as the nose holders—four out of five in the illustration oddly left-handed—pinching their schnozzes like men fixing the crease in fedoras, their jaws like clamps and the line of their mouths in puey's down-angled disdain.

I read the copy— "We also have PERFUME BOMBS. These are identical with the ANARCHIST STINK BOMBS excepting that the odor from the Perfume Bombs is more agreeable than that from the Stink Bombs. Perfume Bombs can be sent by parcel post. Stink Bombs are not mailable and are shipped only by Express"— stare at the illustration, for despite the lockjaw, closed-for-the-duration position of their mouths, these men are speaking. Dialogue balloons from their heads as in any deodorized comic strip.

"WOW PU."

"-R-R."

"This way out. The street for mine."

"My. Oh my. What the——! smells so bad."

"SAY BOYS SOMEONE HAS A LIMBURGER HERE." (This remark unattributable, floating balloonless over all, the thrown voice, perhaps, of someone who has mastered the secrets of ventriloquism on another page.)

And from the sixth who walks among them. "That's an awful smell, boys." The speaker does not pinch his nostrils and he alone is smiling. I think he's the anarchist. Why doesn't he suffer? Has he been on the game so long? Has he realized that you can't make an omelet without breaking eggs? Does he *like* Limburger? Is the stink bomb an acquired taste? Whatever, there is a quality of "What's Wrong with This Picture?" throughout the Johnson Smith catalogs, particularly the older ones, as if the lacunae are planted, a necessary touch of the awry and askew to get you to look twice.

But all that was in the raw old days, times when Johnson Smith could call a spade a spade and worse. Since then the company has climbed down from true, gone soft on victims. Explosive matches and exploding cigars and auto scare bombs have given way to gift-wrapped pop boxes, and even the copy puts "explodes" in quotation marks. Illustrations make clear that all one is getting for one's $1.59 is a sort of modified jack-in-the-box. ("When the dynamics of a business is gone—") Nader's Raiders are abroad in the land, and ride childkind.

"Occasionally we'll get a letter from a parent who takes exception to an item. We've dropped itching powder and almost everything applied to the skin or taken internally. Five or six years ago the Food and Drug fellow came through. . . . There's been an increase in product-liability suits all over the country. Settlements are quite high. Until twenty years ago we didn't even carry product-liability insurance. Now our premiums compare to a doctor's. The company has become cautious. Our catalogs are submitted for inspection to the authorities. Fifteen or twenty years ago you could advertise indiscriminately. We subscribe to the Comic Code."

"The comic code?"

"Yes. Our advertising budget runs about one or two hundred thousand dollars a year. No, that's too high. Probably it's something under a hundred thousand. We do about a third of our advertising in hobby type books, *Popular Mechanics*, *Popular Science*, *Field and Stream*, and another third in miscellaneous places and, of course, comic books."

Oh, the *Comic* Code. I remember the Comic Code, the official-looking little cartoon seal like a stamp burning on a passport, remember the slick inside front cover of the comic book, the squeezed, tightly printed brick ads like a high wall of the classified, the windows with their smear of illustration, the reduced crosshatch of woodcut like spoiled fingerprint or an imposition of fur, all the faces—who knew they were German?—bearing their stigmata of muddy track like galosh-marked rugs in the hall. Recall—but one was babied, only-childed, holier than thou—the sense one had that there was something not just illicit but perhaps actually illegal about the devices offered there, like flying soiled flags or photographing money. Maybe it had to do with state lines, maybe that's how they could do it. There was, when I was a boy in the thirties, a teenager in the forties, a mystique about state lines.

State lines were, for a few miles on this side and a few more on that, free ports of a kind, where ordinary ordinance and day-to-day due process could be fudged—law's and territory's olly olly okshen free, an odd three-mile limit where fireworks were openly sold, liquor and cigarettes at reduced rates, where kids could drive cars and people could get married without waiting for blood tests, where you could bet on horses or buy lottery tickets and the pinball machines paid off in cash, where whorehouses thrived and gambling in roadhouses, where soiled flags were flown and money photographed. West Memphis, Arkansas, and West Yellowstone, Montana, and Covington, Kentucky, and Calumet City, Illinois, and Crown Point, Indiana—— American Ginzas. "Wide open," Father said, but somehow working both ways and watch out for the speed traps. Everything up front, Wisconsin pushing its cheeses at you as soon as you left Illinois, Georgia its pecans. So maybe that's how they worked it, because it was all through the mails and they couldn't see you were a kid.

"The biggest problem of the mail-order business is finding an unusual item that's economical to ship and will get there without being broken. Another problem is handwriting. Sometimes I have to try to interpret what's wanted."

We are examining the 1974 catalog, the sixtieth-anniversary edition. "It's only eighty pages.

"Our 1929 catalog was seven hundred sixty-eight pages. My father wrote virtually all the copy for that. I guess the last really hefty catalog we put out was in 1952. That was five hundred seventy-six pages. That catalog could be published for forty cents. We couldn't do that now."

As one goes through the 1974 edition, one notices certain things; it is changed yet unchanged. It's true that there is nowhere to be found among its sixteen hundred items—the 1929 edition must have had at least seven thousand—the "NIGGER MAKEUP WITHOUT BLACKING."

("Slipped on or off in a minute. No burnt cork or muss.") And I cannot find "THE JOLLY-NIGGER PUZZLE." ("The grinning nigger clings on to the brightly polished steel ball in his mouth. . . .") Or even "THE JEWISH NICKLE." ("A very clever pocket joke. Hand it to a friend, streetcar conductor, or a storekeeper and watch his face as he examines it." The illustration shows the pawnshop's odd testiculars on one side and on the obverse an anonymous, head-covered, pubic-bearded man with a great hooked nose.) But even in the current catalog there is #2870, a "BIG NOSE & GLASSES" set. The copy describes the nose as "realistically formed" and ambiguously advises the reader that he can "make fun of city slickers." City slickers? *City* slickers? Izzy, if the nose fits . . .

And if there is a tendency in the new Johnson Smith to pull punches—#2092 is a "JAW HARP" and #1171, "1001 INSULTS," contains a section called Transylvania Jokes and Slams: "Sign on a Transylvania Garbage Truck: WE CATER WEDDINGS"; "Did you hear about the Transylvania beauty contest? Nobody won"—there is a strong, if deliberately vague, crime-in-the-streets orientation to the inventory. Along with the traditional five-foot shelf of body-building pamphlets and the more faddish how-to Kung Fu stuff, there is the "Pocket Shriek Alarm—You can Almost Knock 'em down with Sound"; a "Wide Angle Door Peek—See without being seen. Gives full view. No need to open door"; there is #1306, DEFENSE TACTICS FOR LAW ENFORCEMENT ("Deal effectively with the most common assault situations without reliance on weapons. Covers the wide range of problems the policeman encounters on the job"). There are regulation police handcuffs, badges and badge cases, "official looking . . . realistic," the rubrics carefully imprecise: "Special Investigator," "Special Police," "Private Detective." The badge case is "perfect for use with all three badges" and comes with a "police identification card." And there are, if all else fails, weapons: an eight-inch "Zip Knife. Opens quickly and locks into position"; "Paratrooper" knives; knives for "emergencies"; ten-inch Bowie knives, designed by "Jim Bowie, great pioneer knife-fighter." (None of these may be sold in the Detroit area.) There are explosive pellets ("For use with slingshots") and shoulder holsters ("Conceal most any pistol under coat, shirt, jacket, etc. Similar holster often worn by special agents, commandos, detectives, etc. Takes most size handguns").

"I'll tell you the type of letter we get a lot of. It's kind of interesting.

We get letters from a fella who will say, 'Gee, will you send this catalog to my son? I remember ordering from you in the thirties and I had more fun. You got me into more trouble, but I want my son to have the experience, or to have the fun. They don't have the fun they used to.' "

Who *is* this man who floats above the levelers he flogs, this detached dealer who, trading in tricks, turns none? Who is he, this married-with-kids man—a son eleven, a daughter fifteen—this ecumenical Episcopalian who goes to church with his Catholic wife and drops in at the synagogue once in a while, who lives in Grosse Pointe Colonial and goes skiing in Colorado in the wintertime or down the man-made stuff in Michigan?

He writes copy, plants subliminal and liminal suggestions. I mention a friend who once ordered a microphone from his company that was supposed to let him broadcast his voice through the family radio, but who could never get it to work, who'd have had to have been an engineer just to attach it. "Yes. We get enthusiastic in describing the ads. I think the children's imaginations carry them a little further. But there used to be more embellishing of the article. Basically, in our business we sell an item in its original development form. The ballpoint pen when it first came out was a good mail-order seller, but if anyone remembers, I'd say fifty to seventy-five percent of them didn't work for any length of time. And that's the type of state in which we usually get an item, when it's in its semideveloped form because it's a novelty and everyone wants to buy it. Sometimes it does what's promised but usually it's a little bit overstated." He fingers the novelties at the Leipzig Trade Fairs, rummages the gadgets at the Chicago and New York ones (though not so much anymore, not so much, only occasionally now). Who *is* he? An American. A-merican, like some ingrained quality of the privative as in *a*moral or *a*political, *a*symmetric, and maybe that's what America means finally, to be in but not of, some condition of dizzying *a*ssimilation, the state lines all erased and the country clean as a whistle.

And isn't my catalog of the catalog misleading? Hasn't Johnson Smith always given equal time? On page 369 of the big 1929 catalog, the company published a full-page advertisement for a volume called *Morgan's Exposure of Free Masonry*. On the next two pages it lists twenty-six "Books for Masons." Some are neutral, three or four hostile, and the majority pro-Mason. On page 227 of the same catalog there is an ad for something called "The Alabama Coon Jigger," a mechanical black man standing on a platform of his own machinery. ("Perfect Time. Wonderful Agility. Marvelous Heel and Toe Work. You have only to wind up the very powerful spring mechanism, and the Coon will 'shake his legs' in the most amazing way.") But on page 372 there is a full-page ad for a book called *Ku Klux Klan Exposed*, the copy for which rages against the practices of the Klan, particularly in its treatment of Negroes.

Johnson Smith still has it both ways. Crime stoppers, and a course on locksmithing and key-making—— "How to pick locks . . . make master keys. . . . Many 'tricks of the trade.' " There is Houdini on escapes—**"Special emphasis on handcuff and jail escapes,"** bold-print Paul Smith's. A book on how to pick pockets without detection. "An invaluable guide to magicians," writes Smith in the copy. Marked cards and a two-headed coin. A cigarette maker. "Use any tobacco to suit your taste." (One is thinking now of Transylvania, of Transylvanian sausage and the Transylvania Corridor.) There is "phony money." ("With a bunch of these bills, it is easy for a person of limited means to appear prosperous by flashing a roll and peeling off a generous bill or two from the outside of the roll.") And electronic bugs. There is a secret money belt: "Wear under shirt. . . . Used in bandit country, smuggling. . . ."

"We're the biggest company in the world of this specialized type. Basically there's a limit to how big we can grow. First of all, our customers go into a phase where they're interested in practical jokes; and after a person has done a few, then he grows up and drifts away from these novelties. It's not a repeat business. The longevity of our customers is relatively short. So we have to keep getting the youngsters."

And "Life-Like Rubber Masks."

"The rubber masks have been used in holdups. As a matter of fact, that Brinks robbery in Boston—— the F.B.I. came and went through our letters for a year back and tried to locate . . . They took every order for rubber masks and checked it."

"Were they *your* rubber masks?"

"Oh no, but every once in a while I'll read where a gas station has been held up and the thieves were wearing rubber masks."

"Does that sort of thing happen often? I mean when your merchandise is used to . . . ?"

"I don't think so. Not often. Some boy will steal some money or he'll forge a check, and the police will go to his room and they'll find something that he's bought by mail, and they'll want to know if it was ordered from us, so we'll try to look up the order."

And if Johnson Smith sells marked cards, it sells marked men as well. Shoe lifts to make you taller, "bigger and stronger." Even "chest" hair: "Instant virility. If mother nature forgot you, simply press on this chest piece. So authentic that no one can tell the difference. On or off in seconds. Apply anywhere." The illustration depicts a three- or four-inch triangle of mat and, for my $1.95, it may be the most bizarre item in the catalog.

"Teenage boys are our biggest market. Very few girls seem interested in our items."

So. A-merican. Privative. Something neutral in things, in *things* themselves, something both-sides-against-the-middle. Something guns-don't-kill-people, people-kill-people, and cigarettes-don't-cause-cancer, people-smoking-cigarettes-cause-cancer. In the Johnson Smith Catalog, the Peace patch lies down with the Swastika, the Love band with the Skull ring. Something neutral in things, on the fence, the democracy of matter. Something in things, perhaps, that does away with the fence entirely. And still I'm unfair to the catalog. I haven't talked about the engines and motors, the optics, computers, the coins and the stamps, the cameras, recorders, sporting goods, planes, the watches and rockets, art supplies, banks. (Catch the rhythm? There is rhythm in chaos.)

We are in the warehouse. Blue-jeaned women come down the aisles, order slips in their hands, bearing shallow tin trays. Abstracted, they fill the orders. They might be shoppers, housewives in some A&P of the odd, or browsers, perhaps, in the stacks of a wide Borgesian library of merchandise. They reach into bins consecutively numbered in shipping-clerk Dewey decimal, little Jacqueline Horners of the extraordinary, and pluck out the cloacal geegaws, a Noisy Nose Blower here, there some brown and yellow plastic upchuck like melted peanut brittle or cold pizza. Deadpan—Johnson Smith's on Automation Road— one girl lifts out a rubbery coil of dog poop like a shit rattlesnake and places it in her tray.

"We accept Bank-Americard and Master Charge now. We fill two hundred fifty thousand orders a year, but I would say the average order doesn't run more than a dollar fifty or three dollars, so our sales are somewhere in the high six figures."

It is like strolling through some comic, transmogrified version of Victor Hugo's basement Paris, a sewery landscape of mucous membrane and intestine. Past the loaves of toilet paper— "Birthday Toilet Tissue" (*"The only gift everyone can—and has to—use.* Comic birthday wishes printed on each section. 'Relax and do a good job on your birthday!' "), and toilet paper printed in the form of money, and "Used Toilet Tissue" ("Oops! Looks like someone forgot to throw this roll away. You can bet nobody is going to be anxious to use it!"). Past the pay-toilet coin slots you attach to your bathroom door. Past the cigarette (spelled "cigaret" in the catalog) dispensers, the jackass that drives a cigarette at you out of his behind when you pull his ear, the elephant when you pull his tusk. (A-political.) Past life-size Peeping Tom torsos you put in the toilet bowl, and past the Whoopee Cushion ("When the victim unsuspectingly sits upon the cushion, it gives forth noises better imagined than described"), to the "Hilarous Talking Toilet" ("No more rest in your rest room! When victim sits down, 'someone down there' speaks out. Real surprise for party poopers!").

I ask Mr. Smith if I may listen to the talking toilet, and he finds a battery somewhere and rigs it quickly. He presses the white rubber bulb that triggers the mechanism.

"HEY! CAN'T YOU SEE I'M WORKING DOWN HERE?"

And the feeling reinforced as we pass the last bins of the cloacal— the "Disgusting Mess" (fake dog mess and vomit), the "Oops! Somebody Missed!" contour turd you fix to the lid of your toilet like a bracelet. As we pass "GLOP," pass "Funny Phony Bird Mess" (two smeared yolks on a palette of fried eggs). "The S.S. Adams Company does those. Now to my mind the S.S. Adams Company of Neptune, New Jersey, is the most famous joke company in America. Mr. Adams, he was the one who had the best line of good-quality jokes in the U.S. In fact, Mr. Adams invented and sold the Joy Buzzer, which I would think comes pretty close to being our all-time best seller and still is a good item. Now it's made in Japan but Mr. Adams held the patents on it."

And into another section— what? What can we call this? *Petit Guignol?* There are "Realistic Bloody Life-Sized Butchered" hands, realistic giant flies with "hairy legs, transparent wings," "real-looking fake blood . . . like the kind used in the movies, wrestling, roller derby, etc. Make cuts, bruises, gashes, scars. *Great way to get sympathy.*" There are plastic eyeballs that float in your drink ("weighted so pupil always looks up"), dummy nails and bandages, the bloody razor blade that "snaps on finger or toe."

"Shirley Temple used to be a customer in her heyday. Orson Bean, Johnny Carson, Rudy Vallee in the thirties. We had an order from the King of Nepal two or three months ago. It was for two or three hundred dollars. He sent two or three orders before that."

There is the amputated bloody finger and the magic finger chopper and a skull "molded directly from a real human skull." (Real. Real. You could reel from real.) And I'm thinking of the voice of the toilet again, of the niche all men must have if there can *be* a talking toilet. *Molded directly* from a real human skull! Who knew him, Horatio? Who was he? Some silent toilet star who couldn't make it when the jakes went talkie? Who? *Who?* And one sees in this warehouse of toy pain and joke shit that there *are* more things in heaven and earth than are dreamt of in anyone's philosophy.

"Our all-time most popular item is the midget Bible. It's the size of a postage stamp"—things in Johnson Smith's Gulliver world are often the world's largest or smallest; I had already seen the world's largest bow tie, its longest necktie—"and we print it ourselves. In volume sales it's our biggest seller— two hundred thousand a year. We used to print a hundred different books. I wrote some of them myself."

"What books have you written?"

"Let's see, what books have I written? I wrote a book, one book on dance steps. I wrote most of my books before the Second World War."

"Were you in the war?"

"No. I was at the University of Chicago during the war."

"Inventing the atom bomb?"

"No. Working on it. I understood the science and I knew what was happening, but I was in administration, in purchasing."

Of course, he had decoded the catalog. No question. By dint of his legacy, his inheritance, middle child of the middleman. Middleman himself, from the exploding cigar to the atomic bomb, a purveyor of practical jokes, harmless and ultimate, to all the world.

And there is one last thing, *item.* One is rounding off the Borges image of the warehouse library. (The catalog holds a fun-house mirror up to men's desirings and imaginings, the hope of the heart, writ small. Eschatological and scat—midget Bibles and counterfeit poop—the dream of power—the strongman's copper wristband—and treasure— metal detectors that may strike you rich in longshot's dirt landscape— all, all, everything, all, every last kick in the mind's cakewalk ward- robe.) Number 1929 in the new catalog is a reprint of the 768-page Johnson Smith catalog of 1929, #1169 a book on how mail-order fortunes are made. Paul Smith, who wants to retire, who has other interests, whose calculus is ruined, and whose eyes bother him, who feels compelled to learn as much as he can, who no longer goes to the trade fairs, and who never really cared much for practical jokes, wrote the copy himself. "Live," goes the last line, "like you've always wanted to live."

INTRODUCTION TO
EARLY ELKIN

I WAS NO PRODIGY. THE THREE PIECES IN THIS COLLECTION THAT are, in some early, fugitive sense, the real thing—"A Sound of Distant Thunder," "The Party," and "Fifty Dollars"—are not, I'm afraid, very good. Indeed, with the possible exception of "Fifty Dollars," they are no good at all. They are not, that is, promising. I hear no voices struggling to get out, no themes, here muted, that I would return to later on when I was better equipped to handle them, and, while I welcome the opportunity to have them published again, I don't think you can guess why. So I will tell you.

It's because, assuming you know anything at all about my work, they demonstrate some up-from-nothing quality about life that says a good word for human possibility. This is my book from the sidelines, pepper talk, my teacher-cum-coach's two cents worth of exemplum. I was, I mean, down there, and now—please, don't get me wrong; I'm not as full of myself as this sounds—I'm up here. Bill Bamberger is willing to put this stuff between covers. I sign fifty copies of the press run and—at least that's the assumption—a few dozen people will be willing to pay a small premium to have it in their libraries. I've arrived,

I mean. Me. Little me. Little *old* me. Who was no prodigy. Who was already twenty-seven years old when Baxter Hathaway, in what must have been a dry season, decided to permit "A Sound of Distant Thunder," the first story I ever published, to appear in *Epoch*. So, as I say, this, at least for me, is the point of the enterprise. Rally! Go, *team!* Take courage! Stand fast!

Because—I've read the stories, I've gone over the galleys—all I had, I see now, was resolve and patience. All I had was the desire to write. That isn't always enough, I know, but it's at least as much as talent.

Now, before we get down to cases, let me just say that in putting this book together there was never any real temptation to revise the stories, or tinker with them, or even to touch up obvious discrepancies. In "The Party," for example, Rose Harris, the grandmother's niece, is described as being almost as old as the grandmother. Indeed, for the grandson, Stephen, who makes a big deal out of it, the notion of one old woman calling another old woman "Aunt" seems to be one of life's major anomalies. Yet only a few paragraphs further on, Hymen, Rose Harris's husband, is said to be a student at C.C.N.Y. This, however, goes entirely unremarked. Maybe Hymen's her son. The story certainly doesn't make it clear, and I'm damned if *I* know. I've let it stand. As I have, too, even the idiosyncratic punctuation. Here's an exchange from "A Sound of Distant Thunder":

> "Listen, Ben; you'll be over for Friday night supper tonight?"
> ". . . Yes, well, look kid; I suppose the wife is expecting us?"

I was puzzled by the semicolons in those two sentences until I remembered that I wrote that story for Randall Jarrell's fiction-writing class at the University of Illinois in 1954. I was a TA at the time, and we were required to lower the grade of any paper that committed any of the ten basic mechanical errors. One of these, of course, was the incorrect use of the semicolon. Semicolons, I was taught to teach, were used to separate two independent clauses, and in my book "Listen, Ben" was one independent clause and "Yes, well, look kid" was another. And if I meant it that, at least for me, the point of this enterprise is to show my very humblest origins, then of course I have to admit these stories and all the bad things in them as grist and artifact for my little awful Elkin museum.

Another thing about this stuff is that for all the ersatz ethnicity of these early stories, they are, in a peculiar way, autobiographical. I tell my students to avoid their lives and invent their texts, but how, I wonder, did *I* get so smart? For years I was hung up on the blandest correspondence between art and reality. In "The Party," for example, the incident about the captain of the ferryboat and the episode about the Four Questions were plagarized from my own life. Similarly, my grandmother (a Feldman, like Stephen in two of the stories here) used to buy her fish from exactly the sort of fish kisser herein described. The reference to her glass cabinet and to Dubowski (my grandmother's maiden name) are also "real," as is the basic generative fact of the story—— the notion that Stephen, like myself, lived in Chicago but felt he came alive only when visiting his relations in New York. It seems strange to me that I can recall all this yet can't recall the slightest thing about the details of the composition of "The Party." (Though I remember *re*writing it. It was in an army hospital, down with the symptoms of something like mononucleosis, and Donald Fiene of *Views* wrote to say what no editor *ever* says, that he'd publish it if I made it a little longer.)

There are other similarities. My wife and I were subjected to a spiel very like the one Mr. Feldman gives Krueger in "A Sound of Distant Thunder." If "A Sound of Distant Thunder" has any redeeming social value at all—I mean reflexively—it must surely come in Feldman's sales pitch about his china. Crude as it is, it is, I think, the source for all the arias my characters often give themselves over to in my work. "That's a common fallacy. The biggest fallacy in the world that you can judge china by what is lighter"—exactly the words the salesman used on us—may be the two most important sentences I've ever written. (Even the situation in "Fifty Dollars" is, at least seminally, autobiographical. When I was in the army back in the mid-fifties I'd put together five dollars toward a birthday present for my wife. Because I'm a particularly unimaginative gift giver, I told Joan what I had to spend and asked her what she wanted. She said she wanted the five dollars.)

The stories collected here—"Fifty Dollars" was published in 1962 but was written in the fifties—are from and, in the case of the reading memoir, about, the fifties, those long-gone, almost ancient, days when I actually *was* early Elkin. "The Graduate Seminar," published in 1972, I include because, well, one, I like it, and, two, I think it feeds into what I hope has been my theme here—— some vaguely Newtonian notion of salvage and the conservation of energy.

John Leonard had asked me to write a retrospective review of Anthony Burgess's novels for the Sunday *Times Book Review*. The efficient cause was the publication, in 1971, of Burgess's novel *M/F*, and what I had to do was read all Burgess's novels. What I gave Leonard was everything—and much that's been dropped from what appears here— that Professor says about Mr. Burgess's book, and what Leonard gave me was his blessing and a $250 "kill fee." That spring, Mark Mirsky telephoned to ask if I had a story he could use in *Fiction*, his new magazine. As a matter of fact I didn't, but I told him sure. Knowing the minute I said it that what I'd do was simply recycle the Burgess review, put quotation marks around my remarks in that piece, which assumed, of course, not only a "Professor" but a class, which itself assumed students, classmates. Classmates suggested a field trip to me and a field trip a museum, kids misbehaving, acting up at the water fountain, everything that happens in "The Graduate Seminar." It came, as I say at the end of "Fifty Dollars," "all together all at once."

The rest, Elkin watchers, is history. But this is early Elkin and, alas, it's *all* history.

INTRODUCTION
TO *THE*
SIX-YEAR-OLD MAN

A GUY CALLED LONG-DISTANCE.

He was this producer, he said, and Columbia had given him some development money to get some original screenplays from writers who normally didn't write for the movies. Was I interested?

Was I!

Yeah, well, the guy said, he'd get back to me in a few days, see did I have any ideas.

Only much, much more charming. Here a compliment, there a pretty speech, a gallantry someplace else. Believe me, butter wouldn't melt. Trust me.

Then, before we spoke again, I happened to see the copy on the Anchor paperback edition of Donald Barthelme's story collection, *The Cabinet of Dr. Caligari*, where I misread the following words:

The narrator is 35 years old, 6 feet tall, with the logic and reasoning of an adult. He is in the 6th grade where Miss Mandible, his teacher, is frustrated in her desires to have an affair with him because, officially, he is a child!

"How funny! A six-year-old with a six-year-old's sensibilities who looks thirty-five." (This was my muse speaking, talking dyslectic tongues.)

So, when I read the story and saw that Barthelme's fellow was actually an adult, in sixth grade for reasons best known to himself and his school district, I realized I'd have something to say to the guy when he got back to me to see did I have any ideas.

Comedy, if it's to amount to anything, should be grounded in logic. Disruption, chaos, and misrule may come along afterwards, of course, but only if the foundation is sound. (This is why the Marx Brothers never worked for me, why the Three Stooges didn't, Abbott, Costello; why I found them merely silly when they were not flat-out deranged.) I wanted Paul, my six-year-old man, normal in all the important ways, in, I mean, the habits of the head. Probably the hardest thing for me was to work out the math. There had to be some ideal numerical symmetry to the given if I was to believe in the premise. This had to do with the problem of his weight. (Not his size, I could always finesse his size. Kids, after all, can twerp it out one year and shoot up the next.) Well, if he weighed 5 pounds at birth and doubled his weight each year that would put him at risk as a ten-pound two-year-old but might still not make him threatening enough to his dad, who ought to be able to take him as a 160-pound six-year-old. On the other hand, if he weighs in at 7 pounds his first year and goes 224 in his sixth, his very size would give him an entirely different set of problems. No, if you're going to be a six-year-old man you almost have to weigh 6 pounds your first year, 12 your second, 24 your third, 48 your fourth, 96 your fifth (normal until your fifth, you see, chubby, even glandular, but essentially normal), and 192 pounds when you're six years old. Because this is the point: at six years, at six feet, at 192, Paul is at the top of his form, at some perfect juncture and pitch of age and flesh. He is, I mean, at the peak, completely and entirely ripe, and thus in a position for his decay to amount to something. So that was the given. But what was the premise?

That—forget his size and weight—he's more six-year-old than six-year-old man, that he needs a baby-sitter, that his parents, if they're to come through this marriage intact, have to get out once in a while, that—remember his weight, remember his size—*they* need a baby-sitter! (Which is why, if you discount inflation, one of the funniest jokes in the script occurs early on, during the telephone conversation with the potential sitter, when Stu keeps urging his wife to tell the kid what they pay—$2.50 an hour. If I were writing the script today I'd probably make it $17.40 an hour and maybe throw in benefits—Blue Cross, a pension plan. Which points up, I think, one of the weaknesses in *The Six-Year-Old Man*—that it's dated. I wrote the screenplay in St. Louis during the fall of 1966, and its revision, the version printed here, in California—while I taught summer school at UC, Santa Barbara—in 1967. Too many of the jokes depend upon the style and aberrant behaviors of those days. Paul's encounter with the hippies is an example; Eleanor's sexual timidity is. Another weakness in the script, of course, is that it's way too long. I'd never written a screenplay, I thought I had to put in all the camera angles, tell the actors what the expression on their faces ought to be, how to speak the lines. But the major flaw in *The Six-Year-Old Man* is that often the farce is simply too much—I'm thinking particularly of the scene in the second "lovenest"—and has to be pulled back, toned down. Twenty years later I see that and am astonished at the mistakes I made, but what astonishes me even more is that so much of it works and how easy it would be to make it all work.) So the premise of the story is that Paul's never stayed by himself before, and when he's abandoned by his terrified baby-sitter he's so terrified on his own behalf he's willing to undertake his dreadful odyssey and go in the dark to look for his parents.

Makes sense to me.

Foundations the *mishegoss* in logic, I mean, so all else follows—disruption, chaos, misrule—as the night the day.

I worked on *The Six-Year-Old Man*, I recall, from a little after 9:00, when my class was over, until about 4:30 or 5:00 in the afternoon. Never before did time spent writing go by so quickly for me, never did I have more energy. That I was dieting at the time and wrote the movie on a prescription for amphetamines that ultimately put me in the hospital with what was probably a heart attack—they said diverticulitis and to cut my meat in tiny pieces and not to chew great boluses but I know what I know—may have had less to do with my diet pills than with the high excitement I felt at finally learning how to plot, for if *The Six-Year-Old Man* taught me anything, it taught me that— the close cause-and-effectness of fiction, its obligatory, mandatory logic, all its if-this-goes-here-then-that-goes-there's. (Farce is the best lesson in plotting there is.) And something else. Until I wrote this piece I had believed in a sort of Tom-and-Jerry principle of comedy—— that it may have no bad consequences, that no one dies in a joke, that the cat falls off that building and shatters into a million pieces in one loop, he's brand-spanking whole and new and sound again in the next. (As a matter of fact, after the guy got back to me to see did I have any ideas and I told him about the six-year-old man and he said alright it's a go and I wrote the first draft for him in which I actually killed Paul's parents off in an accident and he said no way! what, are you nuts? this is supposed to be a comedy, you think it's funny a kid suddenly comes up an orphan! not in America it's not, and you put those folks back together or you'll never work in this town again—only much, much more charming, here a compliment, there a pretty speech, a gallantry someplace else, elsewhere a trust me—I thought to myself, you know, the guy's right, and I merely crippled them for life in the revision—and let them find what they find when they get home.)

Because it certainly didn't make me rich and famous. Even if it was a long-distance call. The movie was never made. Columbia's development dough wasn't all that terrific anyway, nor the time I spent in the hospital in California. And when *Esquire* magazine ran a much shorter version of this—and in a radically different form—in its December 1968 issue, the guy wanted the money for it, and only Bob Brown, the fiction editor at the time, was able to talk the guy into letting me have it. After it came out I got a few calls, one from the actress, Stella Stevens, on Thanksgiving, when we were all just sitting down to dinner. She'd read it in *Esquire*, she said, and wanted to buy it from me. I told her I was sorry but it belonged to the guy. She even called a second time. The guy, I told her, I signed this contract, it's the guy's. (I saw a squib in a column one time, that Stella Stevens had a property called *The Six-Year-Old Man*.) And, later, ran into him, the guy, in New York, and he told me Hey thanks. Hey what for? Well Stella had called. The figure I remember is seventy-five thousand dollars; my wife recalls it was only sixty. But I'm the number magician in this family. Hell, ain't I the one figured out what that damn fool six-year-old kid weighed on his third birthday? But let's round it off, let's say it *was* sixty. Because if we say it was sixty thousand that narrows the "screwed gap" by a factor of fifteen thousand. I'm automatically fifteen thousand dollars ahead of where I'd be if Stella

Stevens had offered the guy seventy-five thousand for it. It must have been only an option she bought anyway. Because when the guy found out Bamberger Books was bringing it out in a limited edition he demanded my $250 advance. My God, this guy's Jackie Cooganizing me! I'm being Stephen Foster'd, Little Richarded!

And you want to know something? *The check's in the mail!*

INTRODUCTION TO *THE COFFEE ROOM*

I UNDERTOOK TO WRITE *THE COFFEE ROOM* ON COMMISSION FROM National Public Radio for their old "Earplay" series. They paid $2,000.00 per script and promised a first-rate production with important actors. (The actors, Edward Herrmann and Fred Gwynne, were in it—I have a tape—though there is no good evidence that the show was actually broadcast. KWMU-FM, the local NPR station in St. Louis, produced the play with myself in the role of Leon Mingus in November of 1985. There'd been such a delay between the time I wrote the script and its 1985 production that I had to raise all references to character's salaries in the play by thousands and thousands of dollars, thus confirming, at least to *my* satisfaction, my single economic theory—— that inflation is kinder to workers than management and unions combined.) They were looking, they said, for fiction writers who'd had no experience in working in either the theater or radio drama and hoped thereby, by getting people with few preconceptions, to reinvent the radio play. John Gardner had agreed to do a script. Donald Barthelme had.

It would have been during most of the summer and a piece of the fall of 1978 that I worked on the script, on my patio and poolside, by the remains of my breakfast—the scooped-out cantaloupe and yolked toast crusts and hardening dregs of sugared coffee. I remember this. Composing in a bathing suit in the serious sunshine. I remember smiling a lot and feeling outdoors like the sort of writer I never felt like *inside*. Feeling, I mean, pro as some sandaled, sockless, gold throat–chained guy in Hollywood. Ready to go for bagels. Ready to spring for lox.

The idea for the show came to me all together at once. I had been sitting in the real-life coffee room just off the main office of the Washington University English Department when one of my colleagues popped in and said something familiar (familiar in the sense that he'd said something like it before). Then another did. Then another. And it occurred to me that it is impossible for anyone—I don't exclude myself—to say anything that is "out of character" and that, at least in a way, it's what we're likely to say to each other—the anecdotes we tell, the complaints we complain—that constitutes character in the first place—that we speak, are compelled to speak, a sort of déjà vu lingo, repetitive and crazed.

It's not so much the theme of the play that interests me now— though I still believe in its essential truth, believe, like Mingus, that "frankly no one gets past the age of forty without going at least a little crazy. . . . We repeat ourselves like the tides"—as it is NPR's initial premise—— that by signing up writers with no expertise in dramaturgy we were likely to reinvent the wheel. I like my script, am still excited by a lot of the language, am still amused by many of the jokes, yet I see that the form of what I wrote was, and is, conventional. Indeed, it might almost serve as a sort of blueprint for modern theatrics. Since, oh, I don't know—O'Neill?—the traditional play—*Long Day's Journey into Night*, *Who's Afraid of Virginia Woolf?*, *That Championship Season*, etc.—has largely consisted of placing people in a room and letting them talk to each other, the conversation shifting from small talk to accusation to confession. Secrets are surrendered and given up as if theater were burlesque, a sort of noble verbal striptease. These are, I think, the old and ultimate tropes of drama, and though I know I said they're a fact of modern drama, it seems to me that they probably really go back to the Greeks.

I'm not even certain that that's such a bad thing, or a bad thing at all. It's the nature of the wheel to be circular, just as it may be the nature of theater—I mean stage shows, I mean radio plays, I mean movies, I mean operas—to be the high but natural occasion for all aria, spoken or sung, the snug platform of human speech and good talk.

FOREWORD TO
CRIERS AND KIBITZERS, KIBITZERS AND CRIERS

⬜ FOR REASONS NOT IN THE LEAST CLEAR TO ME, *CRIERS AND KIB-itzers, Kibitzers and Criers* has turned out to be my most enduring work, if, by "enduring," one refers not to a time scheme encompassing geological epochs or, for that matter, scarcely even calendrical ones, but to those few scant handfuls—twenty-four since it was first published by Random House in hardback in 1966—of years barely wide enough to gap a generation. Not counting downtime, when it was out-of-print, or the peculiar half-life when it was in that curious publisher's limbo known (but never entirely understood, at least by this foreworder) to the trade as "out-of-stock," it has been in print under sundry imprimaturs (Berkley Medallion, Plume, Warner Books, and, until I actually looked it up in *Books in Print* where I couldn't find it, I had thought Dutton's Obelisk editions, and, now, Thunder's Mouth Press), oh, say, eighteen or nineteen years. Set against the great timelines of history this ain't, of course, much, not in the same league with astronomy's skippy-stony'd light-years certainly, or even, for that matter, the same ball park as the solar system, but we're talking very fragile book years, mind, which are to life span approximately what dog years are to the birthdays of humans. At a ratio of seven-to-one (seven doggie years equaling forty-nine bookie years), that would make my criers and kibitzers, depending on how the actuaries count that half-life, either eight hundred eighty-two or nine hundred and eleven years old. A classic, antique as Methuselah— the test, as the saying goes, of time.

In addition—more new math—two of these stories, "Criers and Kibitzers, Kibitzers and Criers" and "The Guest," were adapted for and produced on the stage. "Criers" has been a radio play on the Canadian Broadcasting System—and one, "I Look Out for Ed Wolfe," was bought for the movies, though it never made the cut. ("Ed Wolfe," published in *Esquire* in 1962, was my first mass-market sale and put me, quite literally, on the map. Well, at least *Esquire*'s rigged 1963 chart about America's "Literary Establishment," where I found myself in shameless scarlet, short-listed among a small, arbitrary bundle of real writers—realer, in any event, than me—in what that magazine deemed to be "The Red Hot Center." [Just Rust Hills and Bob Brown kidding around.] It thrilled me then, it embarrasses me now. Had I had more sense it would have embarrassed me then, too. God knows it angered a lot of important critics who wrote letters to the editor, columns, even essays about it, a short-lived tempest in a tea bag not unlike the one old John Gardner provoked when he made his pronouncements about moral fiction. Not art for art's sake but hype for hype's. Like the PENs and Pulitzers, NBAs and National Book Critics Circle Awards, and all those other Masterpieces of the Minute that might not last the night.) "A Poetics for Bullies" was recorded on an LP by Jackson Beck, the radio actor and famous voice of Bluto in the Popeye cartoons, and somewhere loose in the world is a cassette tape of "The Guest" that I recorded for an outfit called The Printed Word. Oh, and eight of the nine stories in *C & K*—"Cousin Poor Lesley and the Lousy People" is the exception—have been anthologized, a few of them—the criers, guest, Ed Wolfe, and bully stories—several times— almost often. "Criers" and "Ed Wolfe" were in *The Best American Short Story* annuals back in the days when Martha Foley was Martha Foley. Indeed, for many years during the late sixties, the decade of the seventies, and into the eighties (it's starting to fall off), the stories have provided me and my family with a kind of widow's mite, a small annuity— "sky money," I like to call it. I regard myself as a serious writer, even a professional one, but deep in my heart I think of most of the money I receive from my writing as essentially unearned. This isn't, as you may suppose, a poetic wimp factor kicking in—I'm no art jerk—so much as the heart's quid pro quo, all ego's driving power trip, the rush, that is, many writers get out of their almost sybaritic wallow in the unfettered luxury of their indulged imaginations. (What, they'll pay for this? I may be a badass, but I'm an honorable badass.) Anyway, it, the money on the stories, all sources, never amounted to *that* much. I come cheap, after all. Maybe, top-of-the-head, all-told, thirty or thirty-five thousand dollars since 1966, my going rate for having passed the test of time. Nothing solid as a fortune, I admit, but tighter than loose change, something like the cumulative yield on a small CD, say.

What isn't clear to me, though, is why. Why this book, why these stories? Surely I've written better books. Surely I'm a better writer now than I was when I wrote these stories. (Five of them, including the title story, one of my favorites, were written when I was still back in graduate school, for Christ's sake, and only three, "The Guest," "A Poetics for Bullies," and "Perlmutter at the East Pole," were published after I'd published my first novel and before I'd written a second one.) So why? Why, really? I'd like to know.

One thing, certainly, is the accessibility of their style and (not behind that—indeed, quite the opposite—in absolute hand/glove relationship to the relative simplicity of the style) plain speaking's package deal with realism, time's honored literary arrangement between ease and veri-similitude. Here, for example, is Feldman, the butcher, returning to his store after a quick trip to the bank for change for his cash drawer. (In the story, had I been a better stylist in the realistic tradition, I would have used the word *silver*.)

> The street was quiet. It looks like a Sunday, he thought. There would be no one in the store. He saw his reflection in a window he passed and realized he had forgotten to take his apron off. It occurred to him that the apron somehow gave him the appearance of being very busy. An apron did that, he thought. Not a business suit so much. Unless there was a briefcase. A briefcase and an apron, they made you look busy. A uniform wouldn't. Soldiers didn't look busy, policemen didn't. A fireman did, but he had to have that big hat on. Schmo, a man your age walking in the street in an apron. He wondered if the vice-presidents at the bank had noticed his apron. He felt the heaviness again.

There's something comforting, almost soothing, about realism, and it's nothing to do with shocks of recognition—well it wouldn't do, would it, since shocks never console—or even with the familiarity that breeds content, so much as that the realistic world, in literature, at least, is one that, from a certain perspective, always makes sense, even its bum deals and tragedies, inasmuch as it plays—even showboats and grandstands—to our passion for reason. The realistic tradition presumes to deal, I mean, with cause and effect, with some deep need in readers—in all of us—for justice, the demand for the explicable reap/sow benefits (or punishments), the law of just desserts—— all God's and Nature's organic bookkeeping. And, since form fits and follows function, style is instructed not to make waves but merely to tag along, easy as pie, taking in everything that can be seen along the way but not much more and nothing at all of what isn't immediately available to the naked eye.

My point, then, is that the stories in *Criers and Kibitzers, Kibitzers and Criers* are right-bang smack-dab in the middle of realism. I may get things wrong or even silly—as I do in the improbable scene in "In the Alley" when my protagonist, top-heavy with incurable cancer, checks himself out of the hospital to wander the city and goes into a bar to die in an unfamiliar neighborhood, or, in red-hot-centered "I Look Out for Ed Wolfe" where, ending the story, as stories never should end, with a gesture, I have Ed throw his money away—but most of the stories have conventional, realistic sources. Only "On a Field, Rampant" and "A Poetics for Bullies" owe less to the syllogistic, rational world—though they're not experimental, none of my writing is; I don't care for experimental writing and, in my case at least, experimental writing would be if I did it in German or French—than they do to some conjured, imaginary one and, sure enough, only in those stories am I more preoccupied with language than I am with realism's calmer tropes. I offer the battle of the headlines from "On a Field, Rampant":

" 'DOCKER WOULD BE KING,' " a man said, reading an imaginary headline. "IMMIGRANT CARGO HANDLER SAYS HE'S RIGHTFUL MAJESTY!' "

" 'PRETENDER HAS MEDALLION WHICH TRACES LINEAGE TO ANCIENT DAYS OF KINGDOM.' "

" ' "AMAZING RESEMBLANCE TO DUKE" SAYS DUKE'S
OWN GATEMAN.' "
   " 'DOCKMAN DEFIES DUKE, DARES DUKE TO DUEL!' "
   " 'MAKE-BELIEVE MONARCH.' "
   " 'CARGO CON MAN CLAIMS KINGDOM!' "
   " 'KHARDOV CREATES KINGDOM FOR CARGO KING.' "
   " 'WHO IS KHARDOV?' "

And the abrasive, brassy up-frontness of the opening paragraph in "A
Poetics for Bullies":

> I'm Push the bully, and what I hate are new kids and sissies,
> dumb kids and smart, rich kids, poor kids, kids who wear glasses,
> talk funny, show off, patrol boys and wise guys and kids who pass
> pencils and water the plants—and cripples, *especially* cripples. I love
> nobody loved.

The point here is that a "higher" or more conscious—if not con-
scientious—style is not only less realistic than the sedate and almost
passive linears of the butcher's quiet street but much more aggressive
and confrontational. (Only consider the two operative words in the
titles of those two stories—*rampant*, with all its up-in-your-face fore-
pawardlies and dug-in hind-leggedness, and *bullies*—and you'll take
my meaning.) In fiction and style not formed by the shared communal
linkages between an author and the compacts, struck bargains, and
done deals of a reasonable, recognizable morality—my law of just
desserts—it's always the writer's service. Whatever spin, whatever "English" he puts on the ball is his. It's his call. He leads, you follow.
He leads, you play catch-up. (It's that wallow in the ego again, self's
flashy mud wrassle.) Obviously this makes for difficulties with which
most readers—don't kid yourself, me too—don't much care to spend
the time of day, let alone hang out with long enough to pass any tests
of time.
Who's afraid of the big bad wolf?
Damn near everyone.
Now I don't know how true this next part is, but a little true, I
should think. I'm trying to tell what turned me. Well, delight in
language as language certainly. (I'd swear to that part.) But something
less delightful, too. It was that nothing very bad had happened to me
yet. (I was a graduate student, protected, up to my ass in the ivy.) My

daddy's rich and my ma is good lookin'. Then my father died in 1958 and my mother couldn't take three steps without pain. Then a heart attack I could call my own when I was thirty-seven years old. Then this, then that. Most of it uncomfortable, all of it boring. I couldn't run, I couldn't jump. Because, as the old saying *should* go, as long as you've got your health you've got your naïveté. I lost the one, I lost the other, and maybe that's what led me toward revenge—— a writer's revenge, anyway; the revenge, I mean, of style.

One final word about the stories in this collection and I'm done. I'm particularly fond of at least four of them, "Perlmutter at the East Pole" for its main character and the curses he invents, "The Guest" for its situation and humor, "Criers and Kibitzers, Kibitzers and Criers" for its situation and humor, and the truth, I think, of its perceptions and characters, and "A Poetics for Bullies," for its humor and energy and style. I like the "Ed Wolfe" story a bit less but I like it—— for the imagery in the opening paragraph, for a lot of its dialogue, and for a reason no one could guess. Remember Polish jokes? I could be absolutely wrong about this, but I think I may have invented them in this story. It was published in the September 1962 issue of *Esquire*. In August of that year I went off to Europe to write my first novel. Up to that time I'd never heard a Polish joke, but when I returned to America in June 1963, they were all the rage. Everyone was telling them. A serendipity, of course, like penicillin or certain kinds of clear plastic, but *my* serendipity. What a claim to fame—— to have invented the Polish joke. But it proves my point, I think, the one about the distance to which a writer's ego will stoop to have, whatever the cost, to him, or to others, its own way.

MY FATHER'S
LIFE

ALL CHILDREN'S PARENTS ARE TOO COMPLICATED FOR THEM. CER-
tainly my father was too complicated for me. Love, like an obstacle,
gets in the way. We know them too early. Then they die.

What he left me—I was going on twenty-eight, he on fifty-five—
wasn't money so much as a pride in money, its powers of ratification,
its green nod, all its Checkpoint Charlie majestics and corroboratives,
all its gracious, sweet safe-conducts. The rich were all right in his
book, as they are in mine, as, finally, *he* is in mine. (What he left in
me broken, distorted, lapsed, the wear and tear of capital. To this day
I am too much in awe of them, the really moneyed, not jealous but
deferential, my tied tongue like the submission signal of some forest
animal.)

My father earned around $50,000 a year in the 1940s. (There's
nothing to astrology, its cusps and houses, its star swirl like thumbprint
or snowstorm, astral influence like the pull of a tide, but people have
their prime times, I think, their cycles, their seven-fat, seven-lean-
years menses and runs of luck. The forties were my father's decade.
He looked like a man of the forties. The shaped fedora and the fresh

haircut and the shined shoes. He was handsome, I mean. Like an actor in a diplomat's part, a star-crossed secretary of state, say. Phil *looked* romantic. The noblesse oblige of his smile and the faint melodrama of the poses he struck in mirrors. His soft silver hair, gray since his twenties; the dark, carefully trimmed mustache; the widow's peak; the long, patrician features; his good cheekbones like drawn swords. The vague rakishness of his face like a kind of wink.) He was a traveling salesman, a rhinestone merchant, purveyor of costume jewelry to the trade. He worked in the Chicago offices of the old Great Northern Building at State and Jackson for Coro, Inc., which, in its time, was the largest manufacturer of "junk" jewelry in the world, and his territory was, well, immense, most of the Midwest—— Wisconsin, Iowa, Minnesota, the Dakotas. Michigan but not Detroit, Illinois but not Chicago, Indiana but not Indianapolis, Missouri but not Kansas City or St. Louis. Some odd-lot, under-three-flags arrangement of compromised spoils he had with Coro's New York headquarters like the divvy of armies of occupation. It was big enough, at any rate, to keep him on the road two months out of three—though he often managed to get home weekends—and when one heart attack too many forced him to slow down in the fifties, he had to hire three men to cover the ground for him while he stayed in the Great Northern in Chicago and worked the phones.

Calling the buyers, calling them darling, calling them sweetheart, calling them dear. And how much was *schmooze* and how much traveling salesman's protocol and how much true romance I really can't say. Though some was. Some *must* have been, I think. He must have been irresistible to those Minnesota and Indiana ladies. Wisconsin farmers' daughters, the girls of the Dakotas, the Michigan peninsular. Though maybe not. He didn't frequent bars; would have looked, and felt, out of place in the rough taverns where farmers and fishermen and hunters traded the time of day and did the shoptalk of field and stream, the gauge of a shotgun shell, the test of a line. Would have hesitated to ask for rye, his drink and bread of choice. So not only can I not really say; I don't really know. He was no Willy Loman. I never asked him, "What happened in Philly, Philly?"

Nor would those farmers have understood his shoptalk—— the spring and fall seasons something different to them than they were to him. Nor understood his enthusiasm for costume jewelry, interesting to him as treasure chest, pieces of eight—— the paste pearl and glass gem, all the colored chips and beads of his trade, amorphous as platelets seen under a microscope, all the crystalline shards of the blood's streaming, what the kaleidoscope saw, the bright complicated jigsaw of the toy realities, random and patchwork as a quilt.

Proud of how much money he earned, proud of his wit, his Hester Street smarts.

The price of admission to the movies when my father was a kid was three cents, two for a nickel. He would range up and down the line calling, "I've got two cents; who's got three? I've got two; who's got three?"

Here are more traveling salesman stories.

When he first went on the road for Coro at the beginning of the Depression, my father worked out of New York City on a $35-a-week draw against commission, was given the clapboard and red-brick small towns of upstate New York for his territory. One day Mr. Rosenberger, the firm's president, called him into his office and told him that he was into the company for $200 or $300.

"I know," said my father.

"You know?"

"Sure," my father said. "This time next month it'll be another fifty dollars. In two months maybe another hundred more. In three more months it could be double what I owe you now. If I don't quit or you don't fire me, sooner or later I could bankrupt this company."

"Maybe I'd better fire you, then."

"Sure," my father said, "or give me a territory that isn't played out. Where the stores aren't all boarded up and the town's leading industry ain't torn shoelaces or selling apples by the bite."

It's the language of myth and risk and men sizing each other up. It's steely-eyed-appraisal talk, I-like-the-cut-of-your-jib speech, and maybe that's not the way it happened. But that was the way my father told it and it became The Story of How They Gave Him the Central Standard Time Zone—"I've got two; who's got three? I've got two; who's got three?"—of how he moved west and took up his manifest destiny in the Chicago office.

This was the thirties and the beginning of my father's itinerancy on the road—it's the American metaphor—to his luck. (Automobiles he used, berths, compartments on trains, and once, during the war, he rode back to Chicago from Minneapolis in a caboose, and was possibly one of the first salesmen to use airplanes regularly. There were, I recall, preferred-customer cards from airlines in his wallets, and recall the wallets, too, their fat leather smoothed to use, all his leathers, his luggage and dop kits.) Some golden age of the personal we shared through his stories, his actor's resonances, all those anecdotes of self-dramatizing exigency, of strut and shuffle and leap and roll. In those days it was his America.

Which he seemed to want to devour in long motor trips in the Oldsmobiles he drove on what wouldn't yet have been the interstates— to New York, to California and Florida, comparative shopping the window displays in the jewelry and department stores when we stopped for lunch, what the window trimmers were up to in Pittsburgh, in Denver and Atlanta, whether brooches or necklaces were on the mannequins' dresses. A luck defined by the good hotels we stopped at, by room service and gin rummy at a penny a point with pals—I remember those games, my father deliberately declining to cut the cards—trips to the track, the celebrities who stopped by the office—Durocher, Danny Kaye—cabanas rented poolside. And, down by the shore, an orchestra playing.

It was all about entertaining his customers.

It was all about plenty, I mean.

Ordering meats and groceries over the phone, buying in absurd bulk, and my mother's live-in help and the big, good-looking country girls to mind us, myself, my sister, Diane.

In a way, it was all about buying wholesale. Not for the economy but for the edge it gave you, the distance a knowledge of the markup puts between you and other people.

But, chiefly, something sporty about his dough—no one *ever* paid for his dinner; he picked up checks—something expansive and male, ostentatious as the sexually puffed throats of birds. Money performance, too.

We closed our apartment in the summers and went east, and one time—this would have been the forties, the last year of the war—I was staying over in Manhattan with my dad. (Though we had a place in Jersey, my father came out only on weekends and spent the rest of the week in one of the hotels around Herald Square near Coro's New York office—— the Pennsylvania, the McAlpin, the Vanderbilt.) And this particular morning he was running late and said we would grab a quick breakfast at the Automat.

I was following him in the cafeteria line and the girl behind the counter asked what he wanted.

"Scrambled eggs," he said. "And some bacon."

"Bacon is extra," she said.

I thought he was going to hit her. He slammed his tray down and started to yell, to call her names.

"Goddamn you!" he shouted. "You stupid ass! Did I *ask* if bacon was extra? Do I *look* as if I can't afford extra goddamn bacon? *Who in the hell do you think you are?*"

"Take it easy, mister," said someone behind us in line. "What do you want from her? She didn't mean anything."

"You shut up," my father warned him, "you shut up and mind your goddamn business!"

And the fellow did, terrified of the crazy man ahead of him in line. Then my father shoved some bills onto the counter and pulled me away.

I want to be careful here. What he did was terrible. He was something of a snob who didn't much care for what he would never have called "the element" but who may have thought like that, who had by heart in his head some personalized complex periodic table of the four-flusher fraudulent. (The element, yes, who traded in pseudo elements, in fractions and grosses of the manqué, the plated silver and the short karat.) But that woman had hit him where he lived, had touched some still-raw, up-from-Hester Street vulnerability he must have favored like a game leg. It was awful to see, but today I am sorrier for my father than I am for the woman. He *hated* four-flushers—it was the worst thing he could call you—and the thought that that woman behind the counter suspected something like that in him drove him, I think, temporarily insane. If they'd understood, no jury in the world would even have been permitted to convict him.

The other side of the coin is braver, his intact I've-got-two-who's-got-three instincts.

It was probably one of his milder heart attacks. He was to be discharged from the hospital that morning, and my mother drove down from the North Side to fetch him home.

"How are you feeling?" his doctor asked.

"Not bad. A little shaky. Pretty good."

"You'll have to take it easy for a few weeks."

"Sure."

"Even after you go back to work I don't think you should drive for a while."

"Hey," my father said, "I know the drill."

When my mother brought the car around from the hospital lot he asked for the keys.

"Phil," said my mother, "you heard what he said."

"Come on, Tootsie. Give me the keys."

"But you're not supp—"

"Tootsie," he said, "give me the damn car keys!"

The drive on the Outer Drive from the South to the North Side was practically a straight shot. There was this one stoplight, on Oak Street, in the few-hundred-north block. My father was a good driver but he looked at you when he spoke and was as much the raconteur in a moving automobile as in a living room. He could turn anything into an anecdote, and he delighted in the voices, in the gestures. He was telling my mother a story and waving his arm about.

"Phil," she screamed, "the light!"

"What? Oh," he said, "yeah."

He continued to tell his story while waiting for the long light to change on Oak Street. Oldsmobiles in neutral have a tendency to creep. The impact wasn't great but it infuriated the other driver. He came pouring out of his car like a dirge, like a requiem mass, a big, beefy six-footer. He pulled the car door open on the driver's side and started to curse my father, who simply reached his hand into the inside pocket of his suit coat and held it there around an imaginary gun. He interrupted the big man's angry obscenities.

"Get back in your car," my father told him quietly. "I'm counting to five. I'm not even bothering to count out loud."

The man held his arms up and backed off. Back in his car he ran the light. When it turned green again my father drove home.

When I was either seven or eight I bought my father a plaster-of-Paris reproduction of the Statue of Liberty. It was more than a foot high and there was a cigarette lighter in the torch. He took it out of the paper cone in which it had been wrapped like a rose and wanted to know where the hell I'd gotten such crap.

People, tender of the kiddy sensibilities, are appalled by his callousness and profess not to believe me when I tell them that I was grateful, at least after thinking it over. It was educational, a lesson in

taste. I buy neither souvenirs nor novelty items. No pillows with AT-
LANTIC CITY embroidered in satin have ever graced my sofas. No miniature outhouses are as frontlets between my eyes, nor is there anything
like them on the lintels of my house or on my gates.

And the first story I ever published was called "A Sound of Distant
Thunder" and it was about a man who owns a small jewelry store on
Roosevelt Road in Chicago. The neighborhood is changing, the store
failing. When it came out I gave my father a copy of the magazine
in which it appeared. He read the story while I was still in the room
and when he finished he put it down and asked what the hell was
wrong with me.

"Wrong with me?"

"Yeah," he said, "wrong with you. This guy has a little shop in a
lousy neighborhood. They're knocking his brains in. But a salesman
calls on him and he gives him an order for a gross of earrings. A gross!
Do you know what a gross *is?* It's a dozen dozen. That's a hundred
goddamned forty-four pairs of earrings. What are you, a fool? How's
he going to move that much merchandise in that location?"

But he was making less now. The salaries of the three men who
traveled for him came out of his own pocket.

A year ago my cousin Bert told me a story about my father's life that
I'd never heard. Often, when my father went to New York, he would
visit his sister Jean. One night when Bert came home from law school,
my father was in my aunt's apartment. She'd given him some supper
and he'd gone to the sofa to lie down. He was moaning and Jean asked
if he was uncomfortable, if there was anything she could do. (It was
the 1950s now, the decade of his heart attacks, four in seven years,
and he would wake up coughing in the middle of the night, hawking,
hacking, trying with those terrible percussives to bring up the poisons
from his flooded chest; it was the fifties now, the decade of his pain
and death.) "You work too hard, Phil. You'll kill yourself, working so
hard. Slow down; take it easy. So you make a little less money. Your
health is what matters."

My father said something she couldn't understand, and she leaned
down to understand him better. "What, Phil? What's that?"

"My health," he said scornfully, louder now, and Bert could hear
him, too. "Listen," he said, "if I have to live on ten thousand a year
like some ribbon clerk I don't *want* to live."

.   .   .

So, maybe, in the long run, it ain't more blessed to give than receive; maybe picking up checks all 'round is not only hazardous to your health but disastrous to your character. But maybe he knew that and picked up the checks anyway, who behind his glass-jaw sensibilities only wanted another shot at that line, to be on it again, the roles reversed this time, what he really wanted only to call, "*I've* got three! *I've* got three! Who's got two?"

MY
MIDDLE
AGE

His suits. My father's suits. The power of my father dressed. His suits. Their ample lapels, their double-breasted plenitude, their fabrics like a gabardine energy, their sharkskin suppleness, their silk like a spit-and-polish swank. Trousers, he said, were to be worn above the waist, two inches, say, above the belly button, though he never wore his there. His rode his hips like holsters and gave off not an illusion of bagginess but some natty, rakish, sporty quality of excess, bolts, cloth to burn. Full at the calves and shins, just spilling over his shoetops, fabric seemed to roll over him like water. He stood in clothing like a man swaggering in the sea. In middle age the power of my father dressed. What I invoke is the fierce force of middle-aged men, the fabulous primacy and efficacy of their prime-time, bumped-up lives. I want to be clear. I'm middle-aged too now. And in some ways—not all—I never had it so good. The terror is gone. Bogeymen don't scare me. I'm a bogeyman myself now and I know how we operate. With a smugness hard-fought-for, a carelessness and ease cultivated years. Like a game-show host for the immediate family.

Put the worst face on it. You're not reading this in an inflight magazine at 600 mph. You're not upperly mobile. Your neckties, if you own any, are not of the season. Nor your suits or your coats. Your rainwear leaks, your shoes lace, and the last time you had a chain round your neck dog tags dangled from it: a raised initial for your religion, another for your blood type. They had your number.

Put the worst face on it. You don't have an expense account or bother with the long form. You don't know what to give doormen; you don't know how to tip. When the tornado comes to town, the floods and the tremors, your home's overturned in the trailer park— there are broken eggs in the toilet bowl, coffee spilled on the bedsheets. Your daughter in Minnesota may have seen it on TV and you want to reassure her Mom's fine, yourself. But for a moment, just for a moment, you hesitate and wonder if you shouldn't wait for the cheap rates that come on at 5:00. (There's an hour time difference in Minnesota. Are they an hour ahead or an hour behind? If they're behind does the cheap rate apply? Does it have to be 5:00 in Minnesota to get the discount? Put the worst face on it. It doesn't matter, and it sure as hell does.—Geez, woman this ain't nobody's birthday. Come on, *call* the girl!)

The *worst* face, mind. No points for life savings, no points for a portfolio like a great hand in bridge. The worst face. No points for promotions, for kids in good colleges or a ship coming in.

You're this middle-aged failure with this middle-aged spirit, this balding, potbelly heart. Its pants turn down over its belt. Things have gone haywire. Scores, for example, standings. Teams are more important than they were when you were a kid. Now it actually hurts— why not? everything else does—when your ball club loses. This town ain't seen a winner—winner?—it ain't seen a *contender* since the last time the trailer overturned. Why couldn't you have been born lucky and grown up in Dallas, Philadelphia, some honeyed, moneyed California of the heart where athletes give 104 percent in the Oldtimer's Game? Once, just one lousy once before you die, you'd like to be there in the tavern when the televison crew comes, hold up a finger and scream, "We're Number One! We're Number One!" Because you're looking to root, you're settled in fanhood and the submerge-manship of community, and somebody better come along soon who can put it all together. How do you think it feels to have to go on national TV every year and mumble for all the world to see, "We're number five, we're number eight."

The worst face, which is tough, a judgment call finally, for the fact is there are limits to the negative imagination. The head never performs without a safety net, and bad news and pain are always surprises. We fantasize upwards.

But the worst face. For the sake of argument grant that, excepting bad health, things are as rotten as you care for them to be, that you're middle-aged and vicissitude-prone, a failure.

Now a better face. Failure or no—and this is the point—the chances are excellent that you never had it so good, either. You're earning more as a failure in your middle years than ever before. You're settled like an academic in tenure, your arrangements arranged, and it would take dynamite to blast you out of a rut that you came to think of years ago as a groove. If it's going too far to say that you're happy, surely it's not stretching a thing to declare that you're accustomed, used to it.

Because you can get used to anything, even your life.

Have you noticed the perversity of old people? How they insist on what appear to you to be small, pointless martyrdoms, how they almost invariably eschew comfort and small gains? This one attends a dentist who hasn't kept up; that one will not eat French food. Their habits are not loyalties, they are superstitions, some customized mumbo jumbo of accommodation, set in their ways as children, warding off risk by never taking one and putting their faith in the locks and dead-bolts of ritual and habituation.

Middle age is nothing like that. It puts its faith in the law of averages, which is what it still has in common with youth. What it has in common with old age, of course, is the beginning of an unpleasant consciousness of the body. Aches and pains like echoes in reverse, the mimic noises of the bones and flesh without any apparent stimulus. What it does not have in common with either is a certain privileged smugness, almost brave, almost heroic, status by dint of staying power.

If one stands on ceremonies they are one's own ceremonies.

For myself I am no longer vain of my appearance. If I'm flabby—flabby? I'm gross, I'm gross with grocery—I consider what it would cost me to alter my stats. Hard work, exercise, the bad breath of diets, a will power in the service of some will not my own, some sleek and glossy Overwill, what strangers might like to look at, playing some other guy's gig and force-feeding myself into youthful images so alien—

I'm no newcomer to middle age, if I live and nothing happens, I'll have had my fifty-first birthday in May—that I would probably feel comfortable only on Halloween. Your real dirty old man rarely looks his age. I'd as soon purchase a toupee or have my face lifted, my teeth capped, my shoes shined.

For years my wife cut my hair, then stopped. Now I go to a shop called The Happening. I am always the oldest man there by fifteen to twenty years. That includes the hair stylists, as barbers call themselves these days. I'll tell you the truth. Always, on the afternoons of these haircuts I find that I am depressed, out of sorts, vulnerable. The radio in The Happening is constantly tuned to a soft-rock FM station. Sirens and lorn love, all the torchy registers, all the two-bit griefs. Jane or Jan, girls in their late twenties—I can't remember the names of these girls who cut my hair—call me by my first name, like car salesmen or cops writing tickets. They mean well to pretend I'm still in the game. It's even sweet in a way. Certainly they don't suspect how patronizing it sounds, but almost compulsively I want to explain something to them—for never very far from my thin bravery is my fat cowardice; *it's mistaken identity I fear*—to apologize, to blurt out how I really need this haircut, honest, that the stuff gets in my eyes, tickles my neck. I hold my tongue, of course. When they ask how I want my hair cut I don't know what to tell them. What can I say? I'm balding. To me a haircut is a kind of affectation. I shall have to work on this. It's an imperfection in my middle-age stance, the real life that in real ways I've been working on for years.

Understand me. Swim laps, lay off the smokes, restrict your salt intake. If your motive is health, getting right with the underwriters, if you're sick and tired of sick and tired, I'm all for you. But good shape? At *our* age?

I made this holy silver-wedding-anniversary vow. If some lady in a strange town, really great-looking, really intelligent, nice and not a hooker, nice and not crazy, should ever come up to me at a party and say, "Hey look, I figure, a swell guy like you, you're a happily married man with this nifty family I wouldn't hurt for the world and I expect absolutely nothing in return, absolutely nothing, it's just that gross, middle-aged guys old enough to be my father turn me on. So what do you say, sailor, when it's over it's over, strictly goodbye-dear-and-amen, meanwhile everything my treat, what do you say, my place or yours?" Well, I'll be honest. I would almost certainly have to think about it. I'll be more than honest. It hasn't come up and I no longer expect that it will.

So, in my case, middle age is at least partly ascetic, in the sense that however okay it may now be deemed to be to come out of the closet—Paunch Power!—and however seemly and respectable it may yet become even to die, it is mostly a piecemeal withdrawal of expectation. It's too late to learn to ski with impunity. I shall never go into the wet suit or snorkle the seas. I shall never break the bank at Monte Carlo, and learning Chinese is out of the question. Neither do I expect to be asked to spy for my country, and I'll never solo. Nor will I handicap the ponies or get the knack of reading sheet music. I have almost given up hope of ever receiving a standing ovation.

But that's all small potatoes. Never my area of competence or concern. *Ski?* Even as a kid it hurt my hands to make snowballs and I'd catch cold pulling my sled. And what do I care about breaking the bank at Monte Carlo? I wouldn't know what to give the *croupier.*

They're strengths in disguise, could be, these holes in my training. They free up obsession and shut distraction off at the pass. All the things I won't do, or can't, focus my options, allow me to service only my necessities. They tunnel my hope and—— well, it's like this. As people get older they cease taking polls. More certain of their own, they're not so interested in other people's opinions. When fantasy flies out the window reality comes in at the door. He's not a bad fellow, Reality. Quite nice, really, when you get to know him. For every pipe dream he takes away he leaves an energy, some increment of measured confidence just as heady as the diffuse, winner-take-all vanities of the young. And you *do* grow negligent of appearances; you do better; you grow *weary* of them, of all the reflected stances. You take less offense in mirrors and, like sums done in the head, narcissism becomes an inside job.

Like most writers, I've always wanted a best seller. Nothing spectacular: eleven weeks, say, at number seven or eight on *The New York Times Book Review* best-seller list would do me, maybe ten minutes including breaks for commercials at the end of a major talk show, and David Levine to do my caricature. Perhaps an honorary degree from a minor major university. Modest, you see, bucking for average as these things go. (Indeed, as they go every day.) I'm working on a new novel now, perhaps the best, certainly the longest, I've ever written, but I doubt it will happen. I don't write it off—this is the world, everything happens—but I wouldn't bet on it. For now it's enough to do the work, to use my craft *for* my craft, and let the icing take care of itself. Leave me to Heaven, I say, and soak in my middle years as cynical and comfortable and unselfconscious as a man in his tub.

WHY I LIVE
WHERE I
LIVE

BECAUSE, TO ME, IT HAS ALWAYS LOOKED LIKE WHAT CITIES ARE supposed to look like. Like silhouette architecture in funny papers. Moon Mullins's downtown, Krazy Kat's, a warehouse style, a wholesale modality, the furrier's provenance, the jeweler's. Gilt lettering in upper-story windows. And brick from the golden age of brick. Brick so high it could be the dumping ground of brick, stacked as counter on a wondrous roll. And because grand juries seem as if they would meet here, returning true bills, parsing corruption: racketeers whose rackets are old-timey and flagrant and tinged with muscle—— teamster stuff, laundry trucks that don't leave the garage, taxis crippled, and tampered axles under the trucks that bring the milk, the bread, the paper. Vending-machine brutalities. Soft-drink killings.

And because I'm an American of the vaguely professional class, a tenured academic, the least mobile of men, and you live where they ask you in this business and get maybe two or three solid offers in a working lifetime, and because I've been luckier than most or less brave, perhaps, and have only received one—two if you count the feeler, pursued halfheartedly on both our parts, from the University of California in Santa Barbara thirteen years ago, and we tried it for a summer and didn't much like it, my wife because it made her nervous to go for bread at eighty miles an hour and me because, as I say, I'm not brave and didn't know if I'd like my friends.

Which is really why I live where I live.

I live in University City, Missouri, a block from the St. Louis city limits. (The city of St. Louis is self-contained as an island, exists in no county, is, in a way, a kind of territory, a sort of D.C., a sort of Canal Zone, gerrymandered as Yugoslavia, its limits fixed years ago, before the fact, staked out, one would guess, by a form of sortilege, a casting, say, of vacant lots, working farms and nineteen miles of the Mississippi River into the equation, the surveyor's sticks and levels and measures doing this tattoo of the possible, of the one-day-could-be, shaping a town like a stomach, stuffing it with ellipses, diagonals, the narrows of neighborhood.) University City is not so much a suburb as St. Louis's logical western addendum. There are over ninety incorporated municipalities surrounding St. Louis, closing it off like manifest destiny, filling it in like some jigsaw of the irrefutable. Mondrian's zones and squares like a budgeted geometry. And I live where I live because of the civilization here.

On the third Tuesday of every month there is a salon at the home of Eli and Lee Robins. The Insight Lady is there (I shall not blow her cover here but can tell you that she is a heroine of song and story, prose and poetry, and, like her husband—you couldn't drag her name from me—the older man and downtown lawyer Albert Lebowitz, a native) putting out her insights like hair or fingernail. Deans are there, chairmen of departments in street clothes. It's all very brilliant.

Eli's spread (both he and his wife are scientists, but the money is Texas) is smaller, I think, than the palace at Versailles but much grander than Madame Récamier's. And because, like me, he is a multiple sclerotic, much of the house is tricked out in the customized hardware of the handicapped, all the expensive gymcrackery of safety: stands of parallel bars like private roads, handles that bloom from the doorways like a steel ivy, cunning chair lifts like an indoor Aspen. Eli's electric cart, Eli's motor pool. We gather on these Third Tuesdays in the smaller of the two living rooms, the library really but with its phones hard by the furniture—I want to sit on the leather chair and call the couch—it could be some plush boiler-room operation. There are discrete files, the latest in dictating equipment, everything state-of-the-art, everything convenient; and for dark reasons I am at home in this house. (I'm crippled too.) And once a month, at the Robinses', I feel free to go public, to clumsy my coffee on the furniture, to crumb the carpet and ash my neighbors as myself. But chiefly to talk. At the top of my voice at the top of my form, vicious, a gossip, clever as a fag, with, to save me, only this: that I am never the hero of my anecdotes but always—I'm crippled too—the fall guy, whiner take all. (On New Year's Eve of 1963, before Eli's disease, before my own: Joan and I were invited to a party at the Robinses'. I had not really known about them, that they lived in a house as big as all outdoors. I had assumed what I assume about everyone I meet, that their backgrounds are the same as mine, that we drive the same cars, get the same mpg, earn the same salaries, and blue is our favorite color. That we're all each other's doppelgängers—how otherwise could we meet in this life?—that we all serve the same conditions, that we share the world like weather. The main party was going on in the larger of the living rooms, a room like a grand salon on an ocean liner, and though there might have been a hundred people in it, I swear to you it looked empty. We left just after midnight, and outside our third-floor walk-up Loop apartment building I kicked dents in the door of our '62 Chevrolet Biscayne. I ripped the ring off the steering wheel. I rent my clothes like an Orthodox. Why not? This was grief, this was grief too. It was years before we went back. When we owned our own home. When disease had collateralized us, when demyelination had doppelgänged us again.)

And this is the point, I think. I live where I live for the odd safety there really is in numbers. Are the crippled as comfortable in Santa Barbara? Could I aspire to Eli Robins's fail-safe gewgaws, his remote-control life, his disease's nifty setup like a model railroader's?

I have been keeping track now since the first Third Tuesday and have never seen the same hors d'oeuvre twice. And that's another thing about St. Louis, about University City. It is the hors d'oeuvre hub and honeypot of the world, its quiche capital. The deli is lousy and the entrées only middling—I mean its steaks and roasts, its chops and chickens—but there are knives, forks, spoons, and stars in its appetizers and something in its soups to float your heart. (It could be the water. Nowhere I have ever been is it softer. In the shower soap comes apart in your hands. It lathers like spindrift, froths and foams like the trick floors of discos. You're clean five to ten minutes sooner than you are in New York or California.)

There is, I think, an appetizer vision, the aperitif heart, something in the soul or character that bumps up hunger without the means or even desire to satisfy it, a teaser temperament—*forshpeiz* forsooth, foreplay forever. All I know is that I love that hour to hour-and-a-half before we go in to dinner (it's no longer Third Tuesday; we're at Martha Rudner's, at the Stangs', the Teitlebaums', the Gasses', the Pepes'), when the pâtés are passed, the barbecue chicken wings, the plates of pot stickers, the stinging dips and smarting cheeses, all that spicy consubstantiation, the lovely evening's high season of high seasoning, and the talk is general and the gazpacho melts in my mouth. And I live where I live, could be, because I am such a good guest, comfortable in other people's houses as a man in his club and under no obligation to bring wine, flowers, houseplants, the candy gifts and door-prize alms (empty-handed even in a hospital room), taking hospitality for granted as a Greek in an epic, never the first to leave though always the first to leave the dinner table, eschewing tea, coffee, the sugar-silted linen and the sedimental crumbs, no coffee klatcher but the Brandy-and-Soda Kid himself, cordial at cordials and drawn by a drawing room.

Inviting the others, ready to do business, calling "Come here, come here, the fire's still going. Bring your cups. Come where it's comfortable." And I live where I live because they come when I call them—well, what are friends for?—and know things I don't. And because I love to hear Julie Haddad, the Deep Throat of real estate, give the latest market quotation on a neighbor's house, or not *even* a neighbor's, a stranger's, someone the next town over, and Patty Pepe explain the complicated peerage of west-county Jews.

I don't mean gossip in the ordinary sense. There is little hanky-panky where I live. In the twenty years I've lived here only one of my friends has been divorced. No one seems to have affairs. Missouri lust is career-oriented, not sexual. It's one on oneself, not one on one. We want Nobel Prizes, things within Pulitzer's gift, National Book Awards, grants, honors, invitations, hosannas. We talk the ego's bottomless line. Or *I* do. And I live where I live because there are people who will listen to me speak Self like a challenge dance. Not boasting, understand, not look-Ma-no-hands but something involuntary, reflexive as perspiration, not loose lip, loose *tooth*, worrying away at this sweet-and-sour tooth I have in this city whose specialty is appetizer and whose shape on a map looks like a stomach. I sound awful but it's not what you think.

I haven't seen Bill Gass for a month, say. I bring him out. I draw him forth like a man doing card tricks. I work him close up as a Vegas mechanic, my sleight-of-mouth circumstances and the opening bid of my own poor itinerary in my juggler's distracted jabber. The same with Steve Teitelbaum, John Morris, Howard Nemerov, the same with everybody. (Not boasting, understand. *I* know where I've been. I need to know where *these* guys are.) All right, it *is* what you think; but win or lose, it clears my air.

And this occurs to me. The estimated population of the city of St. Louis on January 1, 1980, was 479,000, that of the greater metropolitan area, 2,410,628. I've lived here twenty years and have only two friends who work downtown. How many people living in Houston could say the same? Who in greater Omaha could? Who in Chicago? Boston? the Bronx? (Who, for that matter, in St. Louis?) When I moved here in 1960, the city's population was just over 750,000. Urban flight shapes my skyline. It cozies connection and snugs my skyscrapers. It's good, I mean, for the architecture and, the city emptied out, lends a scaled-down look to things. Downtown seems someplace foreign. Or no. *Not* foreign. An American city, but an American city like some Brechtian projection. St. Louis like the City of Mahagonny. And I live where I live because there's nothing beautiful to look at in the store windows. Because reality looms in them like a loss leader, furniture prole as low company or the circumstances of people on fixed incomes, the fashions dated as nurses' uniforms, a dry-goods sort of town, a hardware one. And I look. I do. Once or twice a month, at night, in the warmer weather, we cruise downtown's empty streets. We park, we window-shop.

Me, most of my friends, we don't dress well. We are barely presentable. And if we're out of the shower ten minutes quicker than New Yorkers, we're out of the bedroom fifteen. We are not laid back. Laid back is studied, sandaled, and lightly leathered, capped and cute. It goes with the hairdo. We don't have hairdo. I'm fifty years old and dress like someone on "Bowling for Dollars," like a guy driving cross-country. Third Tuesdays *and* downtown. The sweet-and-sour heart.

And I live where I live because I am comfortable, because the climate is equable, because the movies come on time but the theater is road show, second company, because the teams are dull but we get all the channels, because there can't be four restaurants in the city that require jackets and ties and there's a $25,000 ceiling on what city employees may earn and I make more than the mayor, the head of the zoo. Because I feel no need to take the paper. Because I feel no need.

And finally because nowhere I have been do so many other people seem to live so well. St. Louis, and University City too, is a city of sealed neighborhoods, gated as railroad crossing, of blocked-off streets and private places, chartered as nation, zoned as meteorological maps, the enclaves and culs-de-sac of stalled weather. Not fortress but sub-division America, everything convenient, stone's-throw as Liechten-stein. My subdivision, Parkview, is separated from Ames Place, the sudivision just west of it, by a walk called the Greenway (I could throw a ball into it, but it's almost a mile by car—— the closed-off streets, the wrought-iron gates that are opened on some complicated schedule I have never been able to learn), and, like so many other of the city's private neighborhoods, it is very beautiful. The houses are large. They are brick or stone, two stories or three, with slate roofs, red-tiled, green. Eighty percent of the homes were built between 1906 and 1915 in Gustav Stickley's Craftsman Style. No two are alike, but I have a sense of snowflake disparities, a fraternal-twin aesthetics.

One Third Tuesday a few months back I was telling the Insight Lady's husband that there was nothing I really wanted anymore, that I was just about consumered out. I have a videotape recorder, the TV camera that goes with it, a pool (Parkview looks like something out of *Meet Me in St. Louis*, but we're pooled now as Beverly Hills), quad, the middle-class works. It wasn't time yet to go into the electric golf cart; there was nothing I wanted. Well, maybe *one* thing, but . . . I described plaques I had seen on houses in London where authors had lived. A few weeks later Al brought over a replica of what I'd described. A dark lead slab with raised copper letters:

STANLEY ELKIN
1967–

He drilled holes into the brick for the screws and mounted it on my house.

I'm waiting for Joan. We're going to Bobby's Creole for the barbecue shrimp and then to a movie. I'm sitting on the top stair, next to the railing, at the foot of our walk. Across the street is a triangular park with its honey locusts and tall old pines and oaks. I look toward Pershing at the beautiful homes, seventy-five years old some of them, good as new, better. How lovely, I think. How fortunate we are. Up and down my street, Westgate, the houses make a long gentle convex. Three blocks off, beyond the northern gates, is Delmar Boulevard, a sort of student village, the shops recycled, periodically changed as marquee, head shops where kosher butchers once thrived, the Varsity theater with its 3-D festivals, the Tivoli, which changes its double bill nightly, health-food stores and bike shops, record stores, book, boutiques and the co-op grocery, the open-air market, a gallery, Bobby's Creole, where we're going. An odd nostalgia seems to hang over it all, a sawdust chic, grubby and moving. There's a store that sells old movie posters and Blueberry Hill, a pub where the serious darts players go. I lived off Delmar once, as I do now, when it was a ghetto for Orthodox Jews. But one sort of earnestness is not so different from another. Kids', old folks'. I've come a long way from St. Louis. Three or four blocks.

I live where I live. I have a plaque that says so. I wait for my wife and feel fine, within the gates, enjoying for as long as the tenure holds my tucked-in, deck-chair life.

WHERE
I READ
WHAT I
READ

Once I spent a year in bed reading.

I have never been able to read on a beach. I have never been able to read on a park bench.

An illiterate traveler, I do not understand why the airlines stock all those magazines. Indeed, the only printed matter I can concentrate on in the sky are commands, the "No Smoking" and "Fasten Seatbelt" signs, "Return to Cabin." "Occupied" and "Libre" on the lav doors like news from the front.

And nothing in waiting rooms, doctors' or dentists', the lawyer's, the barber's crushed leatherette, hairs stuck between the pages like bookmarks.

I cannot read in hospitals, I cannot read in cars. I can't even bring myself to read in libraries. The idea of a reading or browsing room is, for me, no idea at all.

We read, I've told my classes, to die, not entirely certain what I mean but sure it has something to do with being alone, shutting the world out, doing books like beads, a mantra, the flu. Some perfect, hermetic concentration sealed as canned goods or pharmaceuticals. It is, I think, not so much a way of forgetting ourselves as of engaging the totality of our attentions, as racing-car drivers or mountain climbers engage them, as surgeons and chess masters do. It's fine, precise, detailed work, the infinitely small motor managements of diamond cutters and safecrackers that we do in our heads. Ideally it is. Which is probably why we remember, even as we forget where we put our glasses and car keys, where we left our umbrella, if not the page number—if a book's any good we never read the page number—then what side, the left or the right, a particular passage appears on, even its generalized location, top, middle, bottom. It's why serious readers are as unlikely to forget an author's name or the title of his book read years before as they are the names of their friends. For much the same reasons— absorption, absolutely paid attention—I can tell you the name of every movie house where I saw any movie and, because I'm self-centered, not only the year but the season, too, when anything out of the way ever happened to me. I can't guess your age and weight but I can reel off my own cumulative, flickering stats, systolic and diastolic, shoe size and shirt collar, like some show-biz polymath of self, and recall not only the prevailing conditions, the weather I mean, but all the f-stop circumstances surrounding every book I've ever read. April in Paris, Autumn in New York, Moonlight in Vermont.

You remember this stuff yourself. It makes us real and stories our lives—— anecdoting in our anecdotage. What, you've amnesia? You don't recall where you were when Pearl Harbor was bombed, Kennedy killed, where you were standing for the heart attack?

I spent a year in bed, reading.

It was the '58/'59 academic year. In April 1959 I was to take the "prelims," the preliminary exams for my Ph.D. We called them prelims and, in a way, they were. I trained for them like some boxer in reverse. In bed, a month's worth of library books behind my heaped pillows in the headboard, Stanley Elkin's Five Foot Shelf, the perfect living arrangements for a graduate student. If a whaling vessel was Herman Melville's Harvard and his Yale, then a Sealy Posturepedic was my Stillman's Gym. Cookied and milked, sandwiched and Coked, I left the bed only for personal hygiene and to teach my MWF freshman rhetoric classes, and was back in it shortly after noon and, still snacked and still snug, remained there reading my books, getting up my centuries, my sixteenth and eighteenth, my two American, perfecting my timing, till, well, till it was time to go to bed. And weighed in a year later nine pounds heavier, overweight, Baugh, Brooke, Chew, Malone, and Sherburne my cut men, my trainers and seconds, in all the corners of my head, in perfect shape to go what I then thought was the distance.

It was a hell of a year. An idyll. I was twenty-eight, getting on toward twenty-nine. *Sic ibid op cit*, but it was swell. *I.e. e.g.*, it was! A shower, a change of sheets, and Fanny Burney *et al.* beside me in the wilderness!

A few years earlier—this would have been late summer, the middle of September 1955, I would have been twenty-five—I was in the army—this would have been the U.S. Army, I would have been in basic training and on bivouac in Fort Carson's Rocky Mountains.

I was, as I've said, twenty-five, already five to seven years older than most of the rest of my fellows, a two-year RA, which you could do in those days, on the seventeenth, eighteenth, and nineteenth of the month—you see? you see what total recall I have for my life, what attention I pay, my perfect pitch for the data and small beer of personal circumstances, my life like an open book, some limited edition, Reader, only I've read?—in strictly the best physical condition of my life—I would have been six feet tall, I would have dropped sixteen pounds from the 192 I was when I was inducted, I would have weighed 176 pounds—but still giving my comrades-in-arms those five to half dozen to seven years, still spotting them their youth, my own bookish, already middle-aged young manhood against their Detroit and even meaner streeted, late-prime-time kidhood, my own already declining, slug-a-bed sperm count against their blockbuster, highly motile, St. Vitus marathon dancing ones. (These were the mid-*fifties* high Rockies, recall. Colorado Springs seemed to me cowpoke, an army town. The Broadmoor Hotel was around then but, for my fatigue and khaki sensibilities, dislocated, anachronous, like some range Xanadu. I would have stared longingly at it from the bus.)

So there I was, shipshape, for me, but in heavy seas, force 10 winds (and the tops of the mountains indeed like waves, like the glaciers they'd been and some still were, displaced as stone like sinners in stories), worried about bivouac because the scuttlebutt had it how rough it all was, as years later I'd worry about those four centuries I was, as they put it in academe, responsible for, and as months later—this would have been December—I would arrange to have myself taken off orders to France only because I'd heard that you pulled two weeks of KP on the ship going over. In good shape but a nervous Nelly, I dreaded the nine-mile hike—this would have been on a Sunday— from the spot where they had to let you off the bus, where even a goddamn bus had to stop because it couldn't go another foot. Wow, I thought bookishly. Whew. Jeez.

Which was when the sergeant came by asking for volunteers to set out—up?—to bivouac in a truck on Saturday. We'd have to help set up camp for the fellows. We would get Sunday off while the rest of the guys were chinning themselves up and down the Rocky Mountains. That was about it. I volunteered and packed a paperback copy of Thomas Mann's novellas and short stories into my knapsack, saving it for my Sunday off.

Sergeant Turner—he didn't give his first name—was an eleven-and-a-half-foot black man who either wore customized, armor-plated fatigues or had Permapress flesh with razor sharp military creases down the front of his thighs and shins. He wore a dark pistol on his hip but otherwise was the most unencumbered looking man I'd ever seen. Like a swimmer, say, only dressed. His crisp breast pockets were not only empty, they seemed never to have been unbuttoned. It was in his truck that we drove to the bivouac area, never mind what it said on the side and never mind either how he found it or how the marching Sunday teenagers would find us. Maybe it hadn't been a bivouac area until Turner decided to park there. Maybe it hadn't even been America.

We set up a mess tent. He told us to blow up our air mattresses and set up our pup tents. He told us to hang around. And all *right*, we thought, when Turner went off forgetting to tell us what else to do. He said, "I'm going to get dinner." Maybe he knows a place, I thought. He came back, his pistol unfired, with three jackrabbits whose necks he had broken. (All of us thinking, What the hell, how bad can it *be*, maybe this is already it, maybe just eating Turner's home cooking is what they meant by setting up camp, maybe just *finding* this place is. Thinking, anyway how could just half a dozen men set up camp for a regiment? We ain't any developers, this is only 1955, there's barely even shopping centers yet.)

When it was almost dark he told us to dig a hole and bury the ammunition. He gave us its dimensions like God giving them to Noah. He may have even spoken in cubits.

All we had were our trenching tools, and we worked most of the night on it, till three or four in the morning, and it was quite a hole, a hole the size of a boy's bedroom, and all that kept us going was the thought of that Sunday off, Turner periodically reminding us of our reward. "All right," he said, before he went off to sleep at midnight, "you men already been through Saturday. You're on your own time now. The quickest you get done the quickest you get to enjoy the rest of your Sunday." When the tallest of us could stand in the hole without sticking up out of it, the hole was dug and we piled the cases of ammunition into it, covered it over with dirt, did our landscaping like responsible strip miners, and went off to pup tent.

I woke up at ten—this would have been A.M.—on perhaps the most beautiful day in the history of weather, the world at room temperature, the air so clear and fine one could see without glasses. I peed in the trees and washed in my helmet liner in water from a stream so crisp and sweet it might have been the headwaters of water itself, its source I mean, its sheer perfect wholesome, untrammeled, unsullied, thoroughbred, sanitate, unadulterate, immaculate taps.

I could smell bacon frying from the mess tent. There were eggs. There were toast and jellies and dining-car coffees.

After breakfast I got my air mattress and retrieved Thomas Mann from my knapsack. I wandered off a few hundred feet, out of sight of the mess and pup tents, and entered a thin pine forest, pine needles on a forest floor exactly like the one where the earth moved for Maria and Robert Jordan in *For Whom the Bell Tolls*—Professor Flanagan's course; this would have been March 1954—and settled the air mattress against a tree at precisely the angle where my helmet would make a comfortable pillow for my head.

It moved for me, too. I had picked a spot at the very edge of the trees, with a view of the passes and mountains beneath me wide as beauty. It moved for me, too. I could have been the only man in the world. It moved and moved.

I opened my book and began to read "Mario the Magician." It was, to then, the most wonderful story I'd ever read, the finest ever written. Or maybe it was the circumstances, maybe it was the day. Maybe it was the company. Didn't I tell you we read to die, to be alone, to shut the world out? (But there it was, you say. There the world was, all before me, Colorado spread out like God's best shot, all ripe Nature's good old summertime. All right, maybe I did look up, sure I did, I looked up to take it in, but I am not by nature an eater of jackrabbit, not by nature a mountain man, not by nature, finally, by nature at all, and if I looked up to take it in—look, I was *there* for the view— it was as much Mann's novella I was trying to absorb as the scene before me, trying to rhyme the novelist's world with the world's one. I was astounded by how beautifully men could write, stunned by how they could imagine worlds so much more beautiful, if not more com- fortable, than even this one, which, steeped with style, was so much more suitable, too, than even that laid-back graduate-student-cum- teaching-assistant bed with its crumbs and learning.) This was the happiest day of my life.

Which is when the scratching started, fellow civil engineers scur- rying about the brush and whispering, "The son of a bitch wants us back! He says we didn't cover it with a tarpaulin." "Did he dig the fucker up?" "No, man, he found the tarpaulin." And another voice, this one official, or at least charged and calling with some increment of delegated authority, you know whose. I knew whose.

"Any guys still back in there start hauling ass! Sergeant Turner wants that hole dug up!"

"It's Sunday, man. He give us Sunday off."

"Tell him about it."

Which is when I picked my book up in one hand, my air mattress in the other, stuffed my pot on my head, and started running, the air mattress held out stiffly behind me like a cavalry flag, in the one direction still available to me. Which was down.

Perhaps that day I invented hang-gliding, broken field, Rockies running, the encumbered downhill, downforest dash. I may have even invented the principle of civil-rights protests.

It wasn't fear that gave me grace, it wasn't even the senseless re- dundancy of digging up that goddamn Great Wall of Chinese Hole— Turner hadn't said a word about any tarpaulin—it wasn't even my outraged graduate scholar's sense of justice. It wasn't even gravity. It was simple invasion of privacy, a ruined read on the loveliest day in the world.

I didn't stop to catch my breath, I could have run all the way to Kansas.

I hadn't heard him call my name. I hadn't heard him at all. What it was, I think, were those engaged attentions, my Rocky Mountain High, my dual glimpse of what man could do, what glaciers and erosion, still hanging on from my reading about Mario, still hanging on from looking up, only diffused now, spilling over into the viscerals and atavistics, frozen in my tracks as one of Turner's jackrabbits. I turned, looked up.

"You're AWOL," he said in a normal voice three or four hundred feet above me, not even counting his own personal extra eleven-and-a-half feet. "You're A.W.O.L.," he spelled it out for me, "and stealing a U.S. government property air mattress."

I climbed Golgotha like a thief.

"Don't you want to dig?"

"No, Sergeant."

"All right," he said gently. "Those other boys be doing the digging. You read that book you reading. When they be done you can guard it till you be relieved."

This would have been just before one. They called me at two. (All they'd had to do was uncover the hole, spread the tarpaulin over the crates of ammo, and cover it up again. They'd have finished sooner but were a man short, they said.)

I was relieved at midnight.

(Nor was this the last time the army influenced my summer reading. The last time—this would have been August 1958—was a year after I'd been separated. I was in the Reserves. I'd been teaching summer school at the University of Illinois in Champaign-Urbana and couldn't make it to Camp McCoy, Wisconsin, for the two-week training session with the rest of the outfit. They cut special orders for me, but, when I reported to McCoy, nobody, in effect, was home. Only a skeleton crew was on duty, the RAs permanently assigned there and a handful of civilians. The next cycle wasn't due in for a week—they were coming, I think, from Kansas City—and they didn't know what to do with me. They gave me a pass for the mess hall and my choice of a dozen two-story empty barracks buildings in which to stay. I was instantly alert, thirty-five months after I'd last seen Turner all senses still go—because I had the Francis Steegmuller translation of *Madame Bovary* in my suitcase, see—only thinking not "go" exactly, but "leave! get out!" Where, I asked carefully, should I report?

(Report?

(In the morning. In the morning, *Sir!* What were my duties? What covered hole in what ground would I be marching round and round, ready and by this time willing to kill the first son of a bitch who might take it into his head sometime to throw up over it, lie down on it, or just pick a daisy off it.

(Duties?

(Thinking: This isn't any army, this is a nest of saboteurs, Reds probably or Canadian spies down from Lake Nipigon.

(But the fact of it was it was strictly don't call us, we'll call you, and I read all of *Madame Bovary* there, taking my time, stretching it out, moving from barracks to barracks and bed to bed to catch the light.)

On Labor Day weekend in 1953 I was asked by my summer employer, the Peacock Laundry and Dry Cleaners of North Clark Street, Chicago, Illinois, to accept as my last assignment for them the job of substitute watchman so that their real watchman could have the holiday off. I was to show up on Sunday evening and stay till they opened for business again the following Tuesday. They would give me twenty-five bucks, a half week's pay, and no trips to the vault, that chemical climate like the start of the world, where I had to hold my breath for minutes and shove fur coats into storage with my eyes closed.

I had been taking Harrison Hayford's Contemporary English, Irish, and American Lit. course at Northwestern University summer school, and though the course was over now, there was still one novel that I hadn't read—Joyce's *Ulysses*. I remember what Professor Hayford had told us; not to be intimidated by the book but just to allow that bold, black serpentine "S" that winds down from the top of its left-hand first page to "tately, plump" at its bottom, to wash over us. For weeks now I had been showering in that giant "S" but could not get past the third page. This was the book I took with me to the Peacock Cleaners.

I don't read sitting up and there was no place for a night watchman to lie down. In the back, though, were long tables, and I chose one of these, under a light like a fixture in a pool hall. There, in the dry cleaners, I took my last shower under the "S" and, pillowed on wet wash, began to read. I read for thirty-eight hours and finished the book and the course twenty minutes before the store opened up.

It wasn't until afterward, after I left the store, that I smelled the smells, tasted them, the naphthas and benzines, the agents and solvents, Clark Street and Dublin suddenly all mixed together, coating my mouth like sore throat, swabbing my throat like pus, stinging my eyes like chemical warfare. I had a headache that would last days, an olfactory hyperesthesia that would actually return full blown when I visited Dublin sixteen years later. Hey, I was like Bloom in Nighttown, like Proust in the cookie jar, the disparate impressions of laundry and literature like things bonded in genes.

These have been, I see now, a few from the fifties. Strange—to me strange—occasions from a decade when I read more books than I'd ever read in my life, when, as a student and soldier, I was more intellectually engaged than I'd ever been before or since. More intellectually engaged, sadly, than I will ever be again. I began to teach and write in the sixties, have been at it since, and while I still read of course, I no longer catch up. Merely—at best—keep up. Which, as anyone knows, is not the same thing.

I would hope that some day someone will read one of my books with just a particle of that sense of occasion that I brought to Flaubert and to Mann and to all the rest. I haven't said it here, am almost ashamed to own up, but once I opened books slowly, stately, plump imaginary orchestras going off in my head, like overtures, like music behind the opening credits in films, humming the title page, whistling the copyright, turning myself into producer and pit band, usher and audience, reclined, positioned as a dreamer, who could read in a barracks but not on a bench.

They were wondrous times, I think, and begin to understand my watchman circumstances, and all the things that happened back in those days and those nights when I was never bored.

A KINSEY
REPORT

NOTHING HUMAN WAS ALIEN TO HIM. ON THE OTHER HAND, nothing alien was alien to him. And he looked, in his brush cut, bow tie and baggy suits savvy as a high school coach in a small town, like a man with liquor on his breath. Though he didn't drink. Only to impress what he persisted in calling the "lower levels," only to put them at their ease, only for science, for the sake of the "sample." As, already in his late forties, he took instruction in cigarette smoking for the same reasons, as he altered his diction to suit the circumstances, all over you with argot or expertise, depending. But a little compromised, as out of synch as a white man's slam-dunk or the razzle-dazzle chorea of a brother's salute—— all hip handshake's fancy footwork. Patronizing, our patron saint of sex, obsessed, finally, as a scientist in Hawthorne—— Chillingworth, Rappacini's daughter's old man.

Yet, bother his methods, or sample either, that less than scientific, catch-as-catch-can collection of the impositioned, came back with the news—— our sexual Founder. And this morning, on Donahue, Christians with books. Flogging biblical liberty on national TV, scriptural passion, positions, oral stuff, God's blessings on the marriage bed, on all the humpty kinky dumpty hymeneal frictions, His go-for-it opinions. Because it wasn't always as it is today, singles' bars uninvented, consenting adults, the Pill. Sexual dark age, lust's hairy palms. When one sat home nights or paid for it in bad neighborhoods. (Me, for example. An old boy from the old school. Driven to the whores. Sure. In 1948, on Labor Day, Sluggo drove Butch—not their real names, but they know who they are—and me in Sluggo's uncle's Olds the fifty odd miles from Chicago to Kankakee to nurse three beers, and not a whole courage between us, in the tavern across from the Illinois Central tracks until the bartender himself pressed the buzzer and sent us through the secret door. Surprised, once one became used to the railroad men in their bed ticking overalls, that there were actually whores in whorehouses, girls in open shifts, casual as the loitering switchmen, firemen and engineers, the girls old, most of them, as our mothers and politely hustling sex like a box of candy, a bowl of fruit, as if, as if—— as if there *were* no bad neighborhoods. So surprised and relieved and a little moved, too, by the gentle daguerreotype civilities there, the railroaders browsing newspapers, magazines. It could have been a barber shop.) When sex was a big deal and Petty's and Vargas's slim art deco girls food for thoughts.

Queen Victoria dead forty-seven years when Alfred Charles Kinsey published *Sexual Behavior in the Human Male* in 1948, fifty-two years and still spinning when *Sexual Behavior in the Human Female* came out in 1953, and though the real effects wouldn't be felt for years he'd raised the shades and opened the closets, he'd cleared the cobwebs and aired the attics. He dusted, did windows, and it was the greatest, noisiest spring cleaning sexuality ever had. But it's a Columbus notion finally, for-want-of-a-nail reasoning, the idea that a single man alters history. Rome wasn't built in a day and Kinsey never got anybody laid. History happens piecemeal, in add-ons, in incremental software integers and suffixions and adjunctives. By frill and circumstance and fringe benefit. It's this all-the-trimmings life we live, our starter-set condition, the world continually trading up. (Because only bad men change the world single-handed.) Yet if there'd never been a Kinsey I'd never have seen Jacqueline Bisset's breasts, Jane Fonda's, Julie Andrews's, for God's sake. If there'd never been a Kinsey there'd have been no personals in the classified columns of *The New York Review of Books*. MWM would never have found SWM, and most of us would have gone to our graves believing only models or showgirls were these lovely flowers of meat under their clothes. (Because what he did, what he did *really*, once we took it all in—and it's still hard to take in—was to democratize flesh, return us to innocence by showing us guilt—Freud did the same but didn't have the numbers—transporting us back to the Garden itself perhaps, hitting us where we lived and breathed, our mutualized lust like a kind of cloud cover and parting our scandalous needs like a Red Sea.)

And if Kinsey himself seems to have been uninterested in sex except as a subject that could be measured (*his* subject, as Communism was Joe McCarthy's, just that jealous; he even repudiated Freud, was out of sorts with Krafft-Ebing), it was only because he was a taxonomist, a measurer, a sexual census taker, trained as a biologist at Bowdoin and at Harvard's Bussey Institution where he began to collect the American Cynipidae—the gall wasp—a parasite whose larvae lived and fed in a bruised oak tissue it irritated into being rather like a pearl growing an oyster, taking twenty-eight different measurements, a collection to which he devoted almost twenty-five years of his life and which ran to over four million specimens before it was finally donated to the American Museum of Natural History after his death. But more sociologist than scientist and, finally, more evangel than either. (Because maybe it's different for people with data, maybe the data permits, even obliges, them to fight back, maybe you question their data you question their honor. Maybe it wasn't thin skin or self-righteousness that made him impatient with critics, that deflected his science and lent him the aspect of someone besieged or gave him this ancient mariner mentality. It was almost like outrage, like someone trying to clear his name. He was certainly good enough at it, a real sweet talker. A friend of mine, Dr. Lee Robins, Professor of Sociology in Psychiatry at Washington University, heard him at a roundtable dinner at the annual meeting of the American Psychiatric Association in 1954. The subject was "Psychiatric Implications of Surveys on Sexual Behavior" and the famed psychiatrist, Karl Menninger, was one of the speakers. Hell, they were *all* famed psychiatrists: Kinsey's report had infuriated them; they questioned the reliability of a sample in which 75 percent of the 5,940 women represented had attended college and only 3 percent hadn't gone beyond grade school; they wanted to know, as Lionel Trilling and Margaret Mead and Reinhold Niebuhr did, where love had gone, and Kinsey told them. Lee remembers his speech—Kinsey never prepared a talk, he didn't even refer to notes—as a sermon, a barnburner, Kinsey, the avenging evangel, the John Brown of sexuality.) The studies that would become Kinsey's famous reports actually began as a noncredit, interdisciplinary marriage course offered by Indiana University in the late 1930s. (This was the age of Emily Post, of etiquette columns in the daily papers, of marriage manuals and all the soft instructions.) Asked by the university to coordinate the course and by the students to counsel them, he found that no formal statistical studies of human sexual activity existed, and he began to take data—histories—from the students themselves, to conduct extensive interviews about what people actually did, to themselves and each other, and gradually to codify his questions. Ultimately, each history would include between 350 and 521 items in face-to-face interviews and would take anywhere from an hour and a half to three hours to administer, longer if necessary. His goal, never achieved, was to collect the sexual histories of 100,000 people. When he died in 1956 there were 18,000 such histories in his files, 8,000 of which he had personally taken.

Which makes him a kind of intellectual Casanova, a scientific Don Juan, whatever the boozy, set-'em-up-Joe, torchsong and touchsing-song equivalencies are for the ear's voyeurism, all the scandals of the heart and head, all the gossip of the imagination. Because this wasn't even psychiatry, you see. It wasn't, that is, passive. Kinsey came on like a prosecuting attorney. Not did you, but *when* did you; not have you but how *often* have you—— all the D.A.'s bad cop/bad cop ploys and insinuations. That he got these people to talk at all—this was 1938, this was 1939, this was 1940 and all the 1940s; this was when men wore hats and women looked like telephone operators, their flower styles and print arrangements like those dumb sexual displays in nature, the bandings and colorful clutter on birds, say, who do not even know that what they are wearing is instinct and evolution, *that* innocent, *that* naïve, up to their thighs in silk stocking, sitting on underwear, a buried treasure of corset and garterbelt, all the comfy, invisible bondages of flesh, their curly hair submissively tucked under in pageboys like a sort of wimple—was largely a matter of flourishing his 76 trombones science like the metallic glint of a flashed badge, using science, always *Science*, capitalized and italicized too, like a cop pounced from a speed-trap, pulling them over to the side, badgering, hectoring, demanding—he was famous now, famous enough to be invited to talk to all sorts of groups, to chambers of commerce and rotaries and lions, to Sunday school classes, to cons in the pen, faggot Rush Street's boon companion, the guest of honor on Times Square (who'd cruised on the weekends: "I am Dr. Kinsey, from Indiana University, and I'm making a study of sex behavior. Can I buy you a drink?")—cooperation in the project, shooting for a hundred percent sample, turning the heat on, having them sing for his supper. Kinsey didn't accept fees for the talks he gave, and which he didn't prepare anyway, was paid off in low-down, intimacies, other people's sex lives like the open stacks in the IU library, assuring them of perfect confidentiality, on his scientific honor like a high horse, offering his objectivity, pledging all his scientific, nonjudgmental markers and swearing he would never betray them. Which he never did. Talking in code to his Bloomington associates. Wardell Pomeroy, who assisted him and took almost as many histories as Kinsey, has described their cryptic shoptalk: "I might say to Kinsey, 'My last history liked Z better than Cm, although Go in Cx made him very er,' Translated: 'My last history liked intercourse with animals better than with his wife, but mouth-genital contact with an extramarital partner was very arousing.' " Talking in tongues, parlor car stories like the periodic table of the elements, all the tender confidences of the nuclear age.

And the reports themselves as aseptic, as bland, the hot stuff cooled down into charts, graphs, the point something something decimals of neutrality, Masters and Johnson undreamed of yet, all *their* wired protocols of flesh, the special lenses uninvented, the down-and-dirty genitalia like locations, sets, special effects, the body's steamy skirmishes and star wars. (Dr. Masters himself the first to admit that if it weren't for Kinsey and Indiana University, Washington University would never have permitted Virginia Johnson and himself to have begun their astonishing investigations and observations of the physiology of sex—— the timid Alphonse and Gastonics of research, the *politics* of science, progress waiting on convention, red tape, green light and go-ahead while all that gets tested are the waters.) Published by the W. B. Saunders Co. of Philadelphia, medical textbooks to the trade. And the trade had never seen anything like it, 200,000 copies in hardbound the first two months after the publication of *Sexual Behavior in the Human Male* in January 1948, and a roughly equivalent number for the female volume almost six years later. All this a blow for the First Amendment, free speech good for business, freedom of the press climbing with a bullet. And maybe what he did for academic freedom and the First Amendment even more important than ever it was for love, the times easier now, more churlish but easier, less polite but easier, etiquette disappeared from the columns, and the streets too, I guess, and marriage-manual mentality all gone, sex by the numbers, but redress of grievance thriving, blooming, anger, outrage, and protest on the big board now and euphemism out of the portfolio altogether—it's a judgment call this business of influence—and though this was barely perceived during Kinsey's lifetime it *was* perceived, because that's what all the shouting was about, wasn't it, all that resistance? No in thunder just another weather forecast about your barbarians at the gate. So, it is to the everlasting glory of Indiana University and its president, Herman B. Wells, and its conservative trustees that they not only permitted Kinsey his research but stood foursquare behind it, continuing to pick up the check for at least a third of the Institute's expenses after controversy and criticism forced the Rockefeller Foundation to withdraw its support, the university hanging in there as friend of the court in a suit brought by the Institute—the Institute for Sex Research was incorporated in 1947, Kinsey transferring the ownership of his files and assigning all royalties from the publication of his books to the new corporation—against the government to reclaim "pornographic materials" meant for the Institute's library (which has what are probably the largest holdings of erotica in the world) but seized in 1950 by Customs. The suit, settled after Kinsey's death in favor of the Institute, had a dynamite impact, all landmark and precedent, on the freedom of scientific research.

But what did he do for love?

Well, that's harder because love had been doing o.k. It just hadn't known it is all, until Kinsey's flawed sample and scientific nonjudgmentals dropped by to reassure it.

For one, he discovered if not homosexuality then an incidence that until the publication of his books had been grossly underestimated. Kinsey had devised a "O–6 heterosexual to homosexual rating scale," which indicated that 13 percent of the male population was predominantly homosexual with an additional 20 percent sitting on homosexual fences; the figures for women were lower but still high enough to suggest that putting people in prison for what had been regarded as deviant behavior was not only impractical but unfair.

Genius is something in the air. It makes waves. Its waves are principles, all the connected dots and applied mathematics of being, some what's-good-for-the-goose-is-good-for-the-gander cosmology, and every good lesson democratic. In a peculiar and even farfetched way, then, the waves that Kinsey made go beyond the bedroom to, well, Death Row. When the Supreme Court ruled that the death penalty was unconstitutional not because it was cruel and unusual punishment but because it was a punishment unequally applied, it was using exactly the argument Kinsey had used when he questioned the rationale for treating homosexuals as sex offenders. Justice as quantity, liberty returned to its Nineteenth-Century, utilitarian underpinnings.

Because in Kinsey's book sexuality was not so much a physiological phenomenon as a sociological one. (He never heard of G-spots but knew vaginas like the back of his hand and showed—something else the fuss was all about—that women were lusty as sailors, as capable of orgasm, bringing the spilled beans of their fevers and kindling points.) He knew this, I think, all his "science" notwithstanding, that that DSc Harvard had given him and that had fooled him into thinking that those four million gall wasps in his collection, like all the pressed and faded roses of love, represented something more than they did. Because it's as if Kinsey had studied not two sexes but four—— upper and lower level males, upper and lower level females. People were stacked in these categories on the basis of their education; grade and high school were lower level, college upper level. (He interviewed blacks but left them in those separate-but-equal days to be considered in future studies. In a related way, though he was no bigot, he wouldn't hire an interviewer who had a hyphenated or Jewish name. He wouldn't hire foreigners or women or bachelors or people whose handwriting was not up to snuff, or anyone whose politics could be regarded as radical. He thought he was protecting the project, judgmental only here, at the base of things, assuming not *his* convictions but others', presuming their prejudices.) And his argument, generalized and oversimplified, goes, approximately, like this. The lower levels screw, the upper levels sublimate. Though Kinsey regarded all orgasms— which he called "total outlet"—as created equal whether brought on by intercourse, nocturnal emissions, masturbation, petting—fellatio was only a sort of heavy petting—getting it on with animals or any other of the assorted sodomies, and admitted the vast differences between the preferences and practices of individuals within a social group, he seemed to imply that blondes didn't have more fun—only more total outlet—than the sweating and swarthy of earth did, your huddled masses yearning to breathe heavily.

Petting, for example. Nowhere, he claimed, were the social levels farther apart: "The lower educational levels see no sense in [petting]. They have nothing like this strong taboo against pre-marital intercourse and . . . accept it as natural and inevitable and a desirable thing. Lower level taboos are more often turned against an avoidance of intercourse . . . against any substitution for simple and direct coitus. It is just because petting . . . substitutes for actual intercourse, that it is considered a perversion by the lower level."

They seem, Kinsey's LLMs and LLFs, to have been sexual snobs, put off, rather, by anything not the old in-and-out, not the old one-two, not the old biff-bam. Even the erotic stimulation provided by books or pictures did not, it would seem, sing to them. "The upper level male," Kinsey wrote in *Sexual Behavior in the Human Male*, "is aroused by a considerable variety of sexual stimuli," and then, in what itself may be one of the strangest and most frankly snobbish passages in the book, suggests that "The higher degree of eroticism in the upper level male may also be consequent on his greater capacity to visualize situations which are not immediately at hand." (A queer and clubby elitism here, a colorless—blacks were to come later—racism from the old freedom fighter.) But even the attitudes toward nudity along Kinsey's great chain of being were, well, revealing. About 90 percent of ULMs in his sample of 5,300 had sex nude, 66 percent of the men who go only through high school (MLMs?), but only 43 percent of those who didn't go past grade school. Kinsey's LLMs regarded nudity as "obscene," "deep kissing" as "dirty, filthy . . . a source of disease," "mouth-breast contact . . . perversions." Only 4 percent of the males who went no further than grade school and 15 percent of those who did not go beyond high school had ever had "mouth contacts with female genitalia" inside marriage, though 45 percent of those who went on to college did. "Lower social levels," Kinsey said, "rationalize their patterns of sexual behavior on the basis of what is natural or unnatural. Pre-marital intercourse is natural, and it is, in consequence, acceptable. Masturbation [though between 92 and 97 percent of the total sample had masturbated] is not natural, nor is petting as a substitute for intercourse, nor even petting as a preliminary to intercourse." Maybe because they knew where it had been, yet it's odd, a contradiction, that Kinsey's natural man should have been the squeamish one, hung up on fastidy and reserve. (But, come to think of it, it's true, that Kankakee whore wouldn't kiss me. It wasn't extra, it was out of the question.)

In the case of extramarital affairs the ULM had to play catch up. Among Kinsey's lower groups the extramarital experience was, at least in the first years of marriage, much higher than for the upper group. Forty-five percent of LLMs married before the age of twenty had affairs; by the time they were forty the percentage declines to 27 percent, by fifty to 19 percent. ULMs follow a different pattern, the lowest incidences being found in the youngest groups—— between 15 and 20 percent. This figure increases steadily till, by the time they were fifty, 27 percent reported having affairs outside marriage. Clearly, I think, lower level males did not go out of town much.

Perhaps because 75 percent of the sample in *Sexual Behavior in the Human Female* had gone to college—the national average was only 13 percent at the time—the second book had much less the notion of the Upstairs/Downstairs dichotomies about it and seemed to offer a story of progressive sexual liberation, not leaps and bounds but a sense of the steady-state evolutionary. Since many of the histories were taken from women born in the last decade of the nineteenth century— the oldest of these women would not even have qualified for Social Security when the book was published in 1953—the statistics reinforce this. Less than half as many women born in the late-nineteenth century had premarital intercourse as those born in the early twentieth; more than four times as many women born in the last century were not naked when having sex as those born in the twentieth. Tellingly, kiss and tellingly, of the 2,480 married women represented in the book, about a quarter of them had had extramarital affairs by the time they were forty, but the figure begins at 6 percent before the 1920s, rises to 9 percent in the 1920s, and jumps to 26 percent by the early 1940s. One-third of the women who'd had premarital sex had had it with from two to five partners. (In a recent *Playboy* survey the mean number of partners for women was 16.1, the median 7.8.) Do you know where your children are?

This concern with classification, while scrupulous, lends to the books, and even to their abstracts, an almost infuriating quality of chart, distracting as the proper conjugation of verbs, the correct alignments between articles and endings. One wants, that is, to speak the language, suddenly, all at once, simply to discover one's human place. And if Kinsey did not make that possible, then at least he created the conditions; he cleared the throat, say, and permitted the first halting conversations to begin. It wasn't enough, of course. It could never have been enough. We shall not ever, locked in flesh, discover the wavelengths and frequencies or learn the sexual forks or know what is expected of us. One wants the answer to one question—— how'm I doin'? One wants, that is, to measure dick. Because nothing alien is alien to *any* of us and sex is only the interesting fluids of the ego, the strange and lovely magnetism of the skin. It is that compulsive pushing of the centrifugals along the tumbling, degraded orbits of our lives.

MY
SHIRT
TALE

I REMEMBER WHAT IT COST ME IF NOT EXACTLY WHAT IT LOOKED like—— twelve ancient 1953 dollars, or doubloons, or whatever it was money was called back in those days. Twenty percent of our monthly rent, six movies for myself and my wife, something between a half and a full percent of a T.A.'s salary for teaching freshman rhetoric at the University of Illinois. So twelve bucks' worth of fiscal 1953 wampum expended in one fell swoop of shirt outlay.

Because a shirt is probably the only thing in which I look halfway decent. Wrapping myself in them as though they were flags, this purely personal patriotism, my indulgent streamers of self, my pretty banners of being. And of all the shirts from that decade, this is the one, though I don't remember it exactly, that I remember at all. It was yellow, not the bright, rich, improbable yellow of an egg yolk, but yellow enough, the yellow of a butter pat, yellow as cholesterol. And of a material and texture vaguely basted, and vaguely quilted, too, I think, as if the material had been directly sewn onto its tissue pattern—— a crinkly shirt, a seersucker shirt. It had shiny opaque buttons big as nickels and the color, I recall, of a blood blister on your finger. And a slim, purplish grid, precisely the color of the buttons, at its cuffs and up its front, fenced its wide yellow butter-pat fields and crops like aerial photography, a golden, glorious acreage.

And this next is tough to figure because I'm not, I think, the type. Though maybe I am. I eat the hard parts first, I mean. Observe the deferred appetites, keeping them like a kind of kosher, working my way from the radicchio and endives, the kales and cabbages, all food's sour foliage, past its blunt, pale vegetable instrumentality, its parsnips and turnips and eggplants, all the way through to my fried fats and favorites. But not the type anyway, so where did it come from? How did it get there? How, in me, arise, procedural as the first this/then/ that sequences in a mass, this lagging, red-tape heart? What, could I *be* the type? Not in my heart, of course. In my heart a big spender. Or where did those dozen dollars come from with which I bought it?

Putting it away once I had it, the shirt I mean, for a special occasion, on a sort of layaway, hope and expectation's dower.

Then, in June 1953, T. S. Eliot came to Champaign-Urbana to read his poetry, and I took the shirt out of my closet and wore it for the first time. Perhaps I thought he'd see it on me and make me a star. Though I'm not that type either, really, and don't do investments. If I make them at all it's in special occasions. (As dessert is a special occasion, as red meat is after supper's pale flora.)

You have to understand something. This was 1953, but only five years earlier I'd still been in high school. In certain psychic ways I still was. Now I must tell you something about the nature of courtship and show business in those days.

It was the Golden Age of Lip-Synch. And we can imagine how it must have begun.

Since the invention of the phonograph, all wars, for reasons of troop morale, have had a tradition not only of parodic cross-dressing, servicemen bereft of female companionship doing sexual burlesque for each other—think of "There is Nothin' Like a Dame" in *South Pacific*—but of cross-*singing*, too, an elaborate choreographics of gesture and mouth movement. I don't know why this was considered entertaining or even mildly amusing, but it was. During the war, and deep into the postwar years, it was a mainstay, a staple on variety shows and on all the amateur hours. On Dick Clark's "American Bandstand" recording stars lip-synched the words to their own records. There were offshoots and, no longer parody, the curious practice was raised to the level of a "talent" in pageants such as Miss Teenage America. One sees such things still, of course, but it's not like it was. Now it's only archaeology. There were giants in the earth back when I'm talking.

I've said I never understood the appeal of lip synch. In even its more dramatic avatars I didn't, where, like some one-man band, one person got to play all the parts, the percussion, the reeds, the strings, the brass, some Old MacDonald of an act, here a solo, there a chorus, ee-yi, ee-yi o! But, in ways I didn't understand at the time, I may actually have been inspired by such routines or, if not inspired, at least shaped, influenced at least, maybe even married.

For—it shames me to say it—back in high school, then, later, back in the earlier fifties, I used to sing to all my dates. I don't mean I lip-synched to the other guy's hits, or stood, proud as any Spaniard or Mexican, out in the elements beneath their windows or in their court-yards administering open, public Serenade to the girls. I *sang* to them, there on the dance floor, into their actual ears on the very first date. Nor did I merely move my lips. I impersonated Sinatra, impersonated Crosby, I did Dick Haymes to them and committed Perry Como. All the greatest crooners' greatest hits. It was, I thought, the way the sexes spoke to each other, pure mating ritual, purposeful as, oh, dipping a wing in dust and hopping about counterclockwise in the nest on your left foot, or swimming backwards, say, and rearing up on your dorsal to the fishy, liquid vertical before dumping your milt, by evolution sanctioned, by all the purring sacreds of biology.

Then I was a graduate student and T. S. Eliot came to town.

Yes, *that* T. S. Eliot. The one who changed my mating call. (Be-cause isn't that what literature is, finally, poetry only the upscale of all that lyrical moonery-junery in all those lyrics in all those dance tunes?) That T. S. Eliot, the special occasion on which my twelve-dollar shirt-cum-gonfalon had been waiting all along, without knowing it perhaps, but willing to bet you, dollars to 1953 doughnuts, that, like love, it would know it when it saw it and be, as they say, ready to wear. The red-letter day that was all it was waiting on until it could come out of the closet and shine, I thought, yellow for yellow and bright for bright against the sun itself.

And I say changed my mating calls because that's exactly what happened. I was a college boy now, a graduate student *nuch*, even a T.A., and changed my lyrics if not my tune, no longer so ready, as once I was, to drop "You sigh and then a song begins/ You speak and I hear violins/ It's magic" into my girlfriends' ears like so many coins in so many parking meters. (Well not so *many*, never so *many*. Damn few, really, when you come right down.) But changing my style and changing my ways.

"We," I'd tell them out there on the dance floors, "are the hollow men."

> *We are the stuffed men*
> *Leaning together*
> *Headpiece filled with straw. Alas!*

And, when I had their attention,

> *This is the way the world ends*

—I'd inform,

> *This is the way the world ends*
> *Not with a bang but a whimper*

—I'd whimper. Or suggesting, suggestively,

> *Let us go then, you and I,*
> *When the evening is spread out against*
>   *the sky*
> *Like a patient etherised upon a table;*
> *Let us go, through certain half-deserted*
>   *streets,*
> *The muttering retreats*
> *Of restless nights in one-night cheap*
>   *hotels . . .*

Urging them, pleading with them,

> *Oh, do not ask, 'What is it?'*
> *Let us go and make our visit*

Only hoping it served Eliot better than it served me. Then, recovering, telling them,

> *Because I do not hope to turn again*
> *Because I do not hope*
> *Because I do not hope to turn,*

courting them on a borrowed cynicism, on the other fellow's wearies and blues, as I'd—what?—lip-synched those fox-trots, more than, and more than now, too, actual mind-synching, actual soul-synching, getting down on what, Catholic convert or no Catholic convert, I never even realized was the other WASP's dime, doing a young man's inverted ventriloquism and following willy-nilly any old au courant fascism of style.

So there I was, into my hoarded, red-letter, special-occasion, secret rainy-day shirt reserves. And there was T. S. Eliot, into his. Into his, *really*. Looking, I mean, just exactly what you expected he'd look like, what he was supposed to look like, as certain monuments precisely look what you precisely think they're going to look like when you finally get to see them, their unmistakable, *sui generis* selves so identical to the head's forewarned, forearmed impressions of them you're *dis*-armed and actually experience a shock of recognition, a kind of primal, exponential déjà vu. Tall, but no taller than you thought he'd be, slender, but not so slender that it surprised you, in a dark wool suit no darker and no less dark than you'd anticipated. Wearing the familiar spectacles you'd assumed he'd wear, that made his famous, intelligent face look kindly as the picture of it you held in your head. T. S. Eliot doing T. S. Eliot, avuncular as a friend of the family in films. Me, on the other hand, hey, I could have been anybody. How had I ever supposed he might recognize me and make me a star?

An archivist at the University of Illinois reports that no one intro-duced Mr. Eliot, and while that seems difficult to believe, I have no memory of anyone introducing him, not even himself. That he made no commentary on the poems he read, other than to give us their titles, is certainly true, going from one to the next like a musician at a recital.

He read for fifty minutes. His voice neutral, serious, reasonable, understated, nothing at all like my own angry, spurious soul-synch.

But the only poem I absolutely remember him reading that night was "Journey of the Magi."

> 'A cold coming we had of it,
> Just the worst time of the year
> For a journey, and such a long journey:
> The ways deep and the weather sharp,
> The very dead of winter.'
> And the camels galled, sore-footed,
>   refractory,
> Lying down in the melting snow.
> There were times we regretted
> The summer palaces on slopes, the
>   terraces,
> And the silken girls bringing sherbet.
> Then the camel men cursing and
>   grumbling
> And running away, and wanting their
>   liquor and women,
> And the night-fires going out, and the
>   lack of shelters,
> And the cities hostile and the towns
>   unfriendly
> And the villages dirty and charging
>   high prices:
> A hard time we had of it.
> At the end we preferred to travel all
>   night,
> Sleeping in snatches,
> With the voices singing in our ears,
>   saying
> That this was all folly.

Nothing dramatic, nothing end-of-the-world here, just arranging the prosaic goods, unflamboyant as stock boys straightening clothing. He had knocked me down, the Lip- and Soul-Synched Kid, with a feather. I could have put myself under citizen's arrest, hauled myself up on charges, not for my callowness so much as for passing bad bills. But what good is crying over spilled youth? Most youth, unless you're very smart or very lucky, is spilled. You try to be better. Simply, you make an attempt to come into your own.

Mr. Eliot was signing books and people were clambering up on the stage with anthologies, their turquoise Harcourt, Brace *Complete Poems and Plays* extended, or with sheets torn from loose-leaf notebooks, from their homework. (I have an impression that he moved toward the apron and leaned into the footlights, stooping down, meeting his fans halfway, better than.) I asked Joan to get one of those autographs for me. Human stuff embarrasses her less.

It was, all in all, a grand evening, a splendid evening, just as special a special occasion as any nifty shirt—this was, and would always be, my T. S. Eliot shirt—could hope for. It was June. Almost certainly I would have worn it again, each time I put it on getting some extra, associative Proustian kick out of it, feathering myself in the true layered look, the one that goes back, I mean, the one that comes with nostalgia sewed on like buttons. (You have to come into your own, I said. I know, I know. But Rome wasn't built in a day. Why should your character have an easier time?) So I *must* have worn it again. I just don't remember.

Except for the last time. Another special occasion. A lollapalooza. The day I was inducted into the army in Chicago. Wearing it to Fort Leonard Wood on the train and, then, once I'd been given my uniforms, my fatigues and my khakis, bringing it with me all the way to Fort Carson, Colorado, where I did my basic training and where I was told to send home my civilian clothes because I wouldn't be needing them, and where, because I didn't know how to wrap a package, I finally removed it from my footlocker, where my C.O. had gotten tired of looking at it during inspections, and, Rome and my character still unbuilt, I threw it away.

SUMMER:
A TRUE
CONFESSION

I'M RECOLLECTING SUMMER HERE, INVOKING THE WRAITHS OF LIGHT and easy temperature, calling on soda pop, on ice cream, the 31 flavors like some Periodic Table of the Sweet, paging its avatars, the avatars of ice cream, the tasty geometry of the cones and cylinders, entreating its Fudgsicle felicities, its Creamsicle kicks—conjuring all possibility's erogenous zones, the regatta and sandlot, the campfire and day game, sweat and fireflies and feeling up girls, faces in the watermelon and all the heightened decibels of heat—the cicadas' sing-along and all the whistle, gruff, and flourish of traffic with the top down. The claims of machinery in open air.

I'm recalling the bright banging burst of fireworks exploding like bouquets of semiprecious stones, amethyst, sapphire, topaz, garnet— the gem boutonnieres. Commanding the spicy savories of hot solstice—— bratwurst, hot dog, coleslaw, beer. Remembering wicker, recalling bamboo, recollecting summer's swaying, loose, and ropy hammock style, the interlocking lanyard of the deck chair and chaise like furniture woven by sailors. The pinched stink of chlorine in the madeleine. All summer's ripish rounds like the treats of custody, of visitation—— a season like a Saturday, like a date with a dad. Its trips, I mean, to zoos and drive-ins, the littered life outdoors, stepping on candy wrappers, condoms, the sports pages like dry flora, everywhere setting off the sounds of localized fires like a kindled *shmutz*.

I'm singing, that is, of our astonishing, let-hung-out forms, of immodesty and surrender, of all our oils and fats and greasy glitter like a stored fuel. Of summertime's dangerously dropped guard.

Here's what happened:

The Virginia State Fair came to Richmond. This was 1956 and I was in the army and probably they were letting servicemen in free that night or discounting the admission, because I was wearing my uniform and so was Sherm, who, either of us, wouldn't have otherwise, and somehow I'd gotten separated from Joan and Sherm and Sherm's wife, Linda, and was in a far corner of the midway, some underpopulated, low-rent district of the fun fields, beyond even the last glancing illumination of the garish, kindled neon of the rides like odd, improbable lamps in questionable taste, the last blazing calliopedic centripetals and centrifugals of light. Beyond all altered gravity's—the Whip's, the Loop-the-Loop's—dizzying spheres of influence, and hard by the game booths, the pyramids of wooden milk, the ringtoss like a pegboard of missing keys, the circumferentials of all pitch-penny chance, the booths in the dark bright as stages.

"You," a voice said. "Hey, you. Soldier."

"Who? Me?"

"Of course who you. Sure who you. You see any other colonels in the area?"

"I'm not an officer."

"And too bad for our side that. So how you doing, sailor? How you holding up?"

"I'm fine."

"Glad to hear it. Not all of us can say the same. Come over and play this game with me. A quarter a pop."

"No thanks. I don't think so."

"Why?"

"Those things are rigged. I'd never win."

"Yeah, that's right. You got my number. You know what a shill is?"

"Sure."

"You're hired."

He handed me a dart.

"No," I said, "I told you."

"First game's free. Throw it."

"Where?"

"Where? At the target, in the air, at some tootsie's tush. What's the diff? It's rigged. You told me already."

"No," I said, "I better not."

"Geez, in carny thirty years, I run a game, and nobody comes. Let someone see you priming the pump, General. Be my hope for a better life. *Throw* the damn thing!"

I threw the dart. It wavered in a quadrant of cork.

"How do you like this," he called, "I got the Robin Hood of darts here. And an*other* winner!"

"Sure," I said I-wasn't-born-yesterday-wise. "What do I win?"

"Four bits," he said and put a half dollar down on the counter. I picked it up. "Hey," he said, "where you going? Hey *you!*" he said, raising his voice. "I'm running a business here! Hey," he shouted, "what do you think this is?"

"I'm a winner," I called over my shoulder, "I won this," and slipped the fifty cents into my pocket and went off to find Joan, to tell her the hustle I'd discovered.

"They'll break your bones off," she offered.

"Nah," I said, "it's foolproof. They let you win the first game. I take my prize and quit."

"Please," she said, wife-wise.

And I was right, even good at it now, my hick-innocent passerby look perfected by this time, my lonely-soldier-on-shore-leave aura not as studied as when I had found my calling, my who-me's more natural. Also, I had dropped the whistling, the more obvious blocking, all the la-dum-de-dum-dums of my plowboy distraction. Less scuffle, more scoot, no kicking up dirt, and my hands gone out of my pockets. A kid from Chicago who'd never even *heard* of the turnip truck. And cleaning up, I tell you. A prize in every box. If not the fifty cents of the initial bonanza—and compulsive gamblers are right, incidentally; it ain't what you stand to win, it's the action—then things, to me, on my roll, in the first ripening flush of my triumph over the system, even if the system were only the here-today/gone tomorrow trucks and jerry-built tents and ramshackles of mudshow, even if it were only the barker's promissory spiel, important stakes of high order because they represented some grand ineffable *gotcha!* for little guys everywhere, and maybe, just maybe, I was, back in that 1956 Virginia summertime, soldiering for the first time and seeing, for the first time too, no pun intended, *action*, the genuine article, the real thing.

Here, as best I remember them, in addition to the fifty cents, are the spoils of that war, those campaigns:

From Po-ker-eeno—a package of Camel cigarettes.

From the ringtoss—a ball-point pen.

From knocking over the top bottle of wooden milk—an ink eraser in a cellophane packet.

I also took away a ruler, a bag of marbles, a plastic doll.

And urged Joan off, and Sherm and Linda, too, who had come to watch me, pressing the cigarettes on them, the pen, the ruler, the eraser, the marbles, my doll. "Don't you see," I said, "it's not as if I even *wanted* this stuff."

And strolled off to work the next booth. Ahead of my time. The *Death Wish* guy, the subway-vigilante one.

"Soldier," called a voice. "You *soldier!*"

"Let me get this straight," I told him a moment later, "you let me play the first game free."

"Absolutely free," he said.

"And I'm under no obligation."

"Scot free. No obligation."

"Jeez, I don't know. I ain't ever heard of an arrangement like that. It sounds, you know, too good to be true."

"Don't worry about it," he said, "I'm market-researching Pingo in your area, and Uncle Sam lets me write free games off my taxes."

"And I keep what I win?"

"You have my word." He handed me a Ping-Pong ball. "Just toss it into the mouth of the whoosie." He pointed to a sort of funnel, the size and color of a galvanized pail. Complicated tubing bunched at the bottom of the contraption separated and fed into a group of lettered baskets on a shelf behind him at about the level of his waist. "Just toss it," he said. "Gravity takes care of the rest."

I stood at his foul line and took my free throw. The ball disappeared into the funnel, where I heard its tinny ricochet. It emerged into one of the clear plastic tubes, made a brief, intricate passage through the thing's intestines, and dropped into a basket.

"Number one-oh-two in basket 'F,' " he said and referred to a chart at the side of the booth. "One-oh-two. There, see it? One-oh-two in basket 'F.' Seven-and-a-half points."

"What happened?"

"I told you," he said. "You won seven-and-a-half points."

"What do I get?"

"Seven-and-a-half points. All right," he said, and extended a Ping-Pong ball, "it costs a quarter to play."

"No," I said, "forget it, I don't want to."

He took down an expensive portable shortwave radio from his shelf and placed it on the counter. "Ten points and she's yours."

"Nah, it'd never happen."

"You're one *tough* GI Joe, ain't you? OK," he said, "I shouldn't encourage this, but it's slow tonight and I'm giving you a *second* game on the house."

"Well," I said, "if it's on the house . . ." And won another point. "No," I said, backing off, "I see what's happening."

"It costs you a quarter to see what's happening. What have you got to lose?"

Because he was right. What *did* I have to lose? I was half a buck ahead, the Camels, the ball-point, the eraser, the ruler, the marbles, the doll. I paid my quarter and won an Add-a-Prize. He put a toaster down beside the radio.

I had eight-and-a-half points. I was a point-and-a-half away, not so much from the prizes, which even I knew by now I would never win, but from finding out all the ways I would never win them. Wasn't that worth a quarter? Wasn't such knowledge worth a quarter?

I won half a point.

On the next toss I didn't win anything. I was at nine points and holding.

Then I won a free game.

The free game won me another Add-a-Prize, a beauty, a seventeen-jewel wristwatch.

All right. I'll spare you the details. To tell the truth, I don't really remember the details. The details compounded. They were ad hoc details. Ad hoc and ad hominem. Ad hoc and ad hominem and Add-a-Prize details, too. By the time I was into him for $4.75—this was 1956; if $4.75 wasn't a night on the town it was at least two or three hours of it—the price of Ping-Pong balls had jumped to fifty cents. (He explained this, too. It was the cost of doing business, he said.

When the value of the prizes exceeded $500, it was only natural that the list price of a Ping-Pong ball had to go up. You had to pass along your expenses to the consumer or you could go broke. It was a law. It was Keynesian, Malthusian. It was on the Chart. He showed me. It really was. On the wonderful chart that codified the random and might have been a document of summerness and summertude itself, of the makeshift and make-do I mean, of high summer's open-air tree-house conditions and arrangements.) And these had joined the wrist-watch, toaster, and radio on the counter: a 35-millimeter camera, a Waring blender, a pair of binoculars with Bausch & Lomb lenses, and a $50 gift certificate for my lady from the Spiegel catalogue people of Chicago, Illinois.

Who'd caught up with me by now. Who'd caught up with me and was tugging on the sleeve of the uniform and begging me to come home with her as if we were characters in a saloon in a nineteenth-century melodrama. Which I wouldn't. (Because I was wrong. The compulsive gamblers are wrong. *What you stand to win* is *the action!* We *weren't* born yesterday. I was behind a high-tech, sky-high heap of 1956 treasure—and is *that* how they beat you I wondered, by piling prize upon prize until it gets too high to see over, let alone throw over, and you have to toss the Ping-Pong ball blind, is that how they beat you, by messing with your vision, by hobbling your eyes and turning it into an actual athletic contest with actual handicaps like golf or the steeplechase, is *that* how, will it say on the Chart?—holding nine-and-a-half points.)

"Come away," Joan pleaded.

"Stan," Sherm pitched in.

"Half a point," I told him. "I only need half a point."

"It's that last half point that's the hardest."

"Take Joan away," I said; "I've got to know how it comes out."

"Jerk," she said, "you *know* how it comes out!"

"*Then how they get it to come out that way!*"

I grinned at the guy. We were co-conspirators.

"Ball's in your court," he reminded me gently. I threw it and he added a big stuffed teddy to my prizes. I pushed fifty cents toward him through a space I cleared for it on the counter. He shook his head and pushed it back to me.

"What's this, mercy? I don't need it. Give me a ball."

"Sorry, pal," he said. "Balls are a buck. You've been wavering on the cusp of the eight-bit ball for some time now. The teddy bear pushed you across. Look at the chart."

"Sure," I said, "so that's how. OK. All right. You price us out of the market. You just bring us up to where it's too rich for our blood. I see. All right. That's what I needed to know. Thank you."

"Hey, where you going?"

"Didn't I tell you thank you?" I said. "I appreciate it. Really," I said. "I do. I'm grateful for the instruction." And started to walk away.

"Hey, soldier." No, I thought, he wouldn't. Maybe he means Sherm. He could even mean Joan. "Is this what happens?" he asked. "You turn tail and run?"

"Look, you beat me fair and square. You run a crooked game but you beat me fair and square. I'm not complaining, but I know when I'm licked. I'm not buying any more Ping-Pong balls."

"Right," he said, "I'm not selling any. I'm out of the Ping-Pong ball business."

Then he did something I'll never forget. I won't. Though I've never forgotten any of it. He reached into his pocket and brought out a wad of bills that could have been the actual weight and measure of money, as forty nickels, say, constitute a roll, or fifty dimes in any Savings and Loan or Federal Reserve Bank in the country do. I could only guess at the total, but as soon as I saw it I knew that this was the size a roll of bills came in. The rubber band that held it together, rust red as the eraser on your pencil, could have been issued by the Bureau of Engraving; even the amount, give or take the newspaper even I knew must have been there for bulk and ballast, the singles that probably hid behind the tens and fifties and twenties that salted it, would have been as fixed and set as the rate of exchange. I don't know. Say $600. That was the metaphor we used for it anyway.

"What." It wasn't a question.

"How much money do you have left?"

"What."

"In your wallet? That you ain't spent yet?"

He explained it to me. How it wasn't his business. How he worked for the guy. A rat. A thief. A bastard. A cheat. That for months he'd been thinking about it. How he could do the guy in. No, nothing violent. Not kill him. He didn't mean kill him. He didn't believe in violence. But pay him back. Dish out to others. What they dish unto you.

"Look in your wallet. How much money you got left?"

I didn't have to look. "Six dollars," I said.

"Give me."

"I told you, I quit."

"No," he said, "not the game. The game is finished. Give me your six dollars."

"Why?"

"To pay the guy back. The rat."

"Pay him back."

"Sure," he said. "To wipe that thief out. Listen," he said, "I give you your prizes. The short-wave, the watch, the big stuffed teddy— all of it. And the roll," he said, holding it out. "*All the money in the roll!*"

"And I don't have to throw any more Ping-Pong balls."

"No," he said, "the Ping-Pong balls are over."

"Not even if it's a free game."

"Of course not," he said. "We fix the bastard."

"I don't understand what you need the six dollars for."

"So when I tell the bastard how you came along and wiped him out and he asks me, 'O yeah, then where's the dough it cost him to play?' I can show him this six and the money you already lost and the cheat's got no comeback."

I held on tight to my six dollars. He extended his wad of bills.

"All right," I said, getting it straight, "I give you six dollars and you give me six hundred. Is that how it works?"

"That's right."

"Plus I get all the prizes."

"That's right."

"That I see on this counter. *And* the six hundred."

"That's right." He extended the money farther. It was practically under my nose.

"You swear?" I said.

"On my honor."

"You swear on a Bible?"

"Cross my heart."

"On your life?"

"On mine, on my kids'."

"I don't know," I said, "I still don't quite get it."

"What are you," he asked, steamed now, watching me narrowly, "one of these First-Game-Free freaks? You go up and down the midway taking us for our rulers and ink erasers, ripping off our cigarettes and marbles and ball-point pens, and making trouble?"

"People do this?"

"There are more things in heaven and earth than are dreamed of in your philosophy, Rube."

"All right," I said, "I—"

He ripped the six dollars out of my fist.

He handed me a Ping-Pong ball.

"But you said," I said, stunned, flummoxed, looking helplessly at the ball in my hand, rattling off the terms of our deal, and shouting how we had a verbal contract.

"Are you crazy? Do they take crazy people in the army now? What happened to section eights?"

"I'm telling," I said. "I'm calling a policeman."

"You're telling? You're *telling*? Sure, sonny, go ahead."

We were the same age. Only he looked his. As a matter of fact he looked like the guy in *Carousel*, what's-his-name, Billy Bigelow, and I looked like the stuffed teddy. "I am," I repeated, "I'm calling a policeman."

And I did. A state trooper. And told him my story as I guided him back to the booth, the two of us in uniform and one of us incredulous. And repeated it before the man who had taken my money, and Joan and Sherm and Linda, too, now, picking up my party, collecting them like Dorothy loose in Oz. Warming to my grievance. Hot on it. Outraged. *All* of them incredulous, the guy in the booth who ran up against suckers every day but maybe had never had to deal with a bad sport before or ever even *heard* of a whistle-blower. The trooper shook his head and told him to give me my six dollars back. Then both of them shook their heads, then all of them did, gnawing away at what they believed was some rich mother lode of the improbable like babes at tits.

Hey. Hey, you. This is my true confession. It was my summer and my sound-and-light show, and just because my guard was dropped that don't make it no open season or holy occasion or olly olly oxen free on fools.

THE
MILD
ONE

I AM NOT NOW AND NEVER WAS A MEMBER OF HELL'S ANGELS. Nor fitted my helmet out of Pots and Pans. Nor wore fascism's spooky zips, snaps, chains, and leathers, its hulking, spit-in-your-eye costume jewelry. Trying to prove *something* though, its tweedy, vitiate equivalent, maybe. I taught at the University of Wisconsin in Milwaukee the summer of '69. Where Richie went to school, Ralph Malph. Hard by where Arnold flogged hamburgers, Fonzie cool. In that schizoid summertime when Armstrong picnic'd the moon and Manson helter-skeltered Sharon Tate, and the entire UWM English department (or so it seemed to me, still nursing a myocardial infarct already eighteen months old) drove motorcycles and did taverns, not a half dozen among them seeming to have left actual houses, seeming instead to have been air-lifted off oil platforms or come down from watchtowers in forests, the lighthouse's tight, spiral staircasing. Sleeping in scaffolding, gantry, the snug cement cubbies along the infrastructure of municipal build-ings—— car barns, little rooms behind the steel doors in subway tunnels. They lived in tents maybe, or sleds on railroad tracks, in the wide cabs of trucks and long trailers on the littered ground of construction sites. Never admitting they had homes to return to, spouse-less, kidless, *echt* goyim, or no, not goyim, not anything religious, just guys off on a tear, boys being boys. (This is how they seemed to me, who envied them.) Men with expertise, throwing about the names of their bikes as if they were equipment in which they were checked out, rigs they were qualified to drive, the lengths of the fuses they were entitled to light, the candlepower of the acetylene they were certified to spark—— all the graduated tolerances and earned sufferances their table talk, like laborers gifted in band-saw, in trowelers and dozers and yard loaders, the teamsters' knacks, their competencies and aptitudes, metiers and flairs, green-fingered in blacktop and carpentry and all the alchemies of poured cement.

It was the summer I met sky divers, ice-surfers, triathletes, men who roller-skate sand dunes, characters engaged in improbable rides, their motorcycles only for openers. The summer I traveled man's-man circles on colleagues' long Leatherette bike backs, a sidekick sidesaddled as a Roman wife. And watched my pressure, took my pulse, timed my clotting factors, and counted to my age when I peed. I had this ritual: I'd start counting when my stream started and stop when it stopped. Unless the numbers added up to thirteen—forty-nine I was a dead man—I divided everything after thirty-nine, my age at the time, by two and added that to the total—fifty-eight I was history—to see how long I'd left to live.

Back in St. Louis I sprang for a motorcycle of my own—— a Honda 175 with an electric starter, though I made the purchase contingent on someone teaching me how to operate the thing, for I'd never actually *driven* a motorcycle. The man in the showroom, looking more academic than the profs in Milwaukee, was very cooperative and assigned someone to teach me until, he promised, we were all of us confident I could make it past the dozen or so lights, stop signs, and tricky left turns between the agency and home. I wouldn't, he said, be allowed off the lot otherwise. (Yeah, I thought, sure. I'd heard *that* one before, reminded of gentle, patient four-bit-an-hour ponies of my youth who'd taken mommy's money and run, leaped, roughed and tumbled too, or whose heavy necks I couldn't pull off the ground whenever they felt like licking the track or nibbling their shadows.) Only I couldn't quite get the knack of it, blowing the delicate tap dance required to shift gears, the precision heel-toe, brush-brush tensions, just using hand brakes to stop alien to a kid checked out in Basic Schwinn whose instincts demanded he stand on what weren't even pedals. (Because it's true. Once you learn to ride a bike you *don't* forget. Even if it ruins your efforts to learn anything else.)

I went back on my word and bought the thing anyway. It was important for me to have a motorcycle that year, even if the salesman drove it home while I, a passenger in a pal's car, held my helmet and lapped the field. And asked, "Get it on the kickstand? Good, let it stand there forever."

Copping surreptitious peeks when I passed a window. Checked out in little red wagon, scooter, sled, my very own Big Wheel, *vroom, vroom.* Till Joan spied me spying. "Have neighbors without heart problems move it into the living room. Use it as a planter."

I learned how to ride from the owner's manual. I'm not Rocky, a listless, up from-nowhere Before blossomed into a splendid, ameliorant After. There ain't montages in life. What would they show? Boning Up on Oil? Learning Tool Kit? Mulling Maintenance?

Hey, I was too scared of the thing to ever get any good at it. Or feel settle in my pants whatever altered, transfigured avatar of transubstantiate power those 175 cc's of engine were supposed to represent. But you know what? When I put on the helmet it covered my bald spot. Strangers threw me high signs, peace signs, V's for victory, occasional birds. Which, too unsure of my skills to take my hand off the handlebars, I rarely acknowledged, earning me points for my cool.

We sat on it, the in-laws, my kids, up on its back like people posing on ponies. When I sold it in 1974 it had less than twelve hundred miles on it. I'd tell you exactly, but it didn't add up to thirteen.

MY TUXEDO:
A MEDITATION

FORGET RELIGIOUS DIFFERENCES, POLITICAL. PUT BY THE SOCIAL notions, the racial and economic hang-ups. The fine distinctions aren't. Not the lump-sum bracket arrangements of the IRS, not the intellectual coordinates of the SATs or any of talent's false, misleading facets—— mechanical aptitude, the tenor voice. There are only two kinds of men finally. Those whose clothes fit and the other kind.

Sam, my clothes don't fit. My handkerchiefs are too small. My ties. One's shoelaces and eyeglasses. Sam. My shirt buttons won't hold a crease and my leather belts are rumpled. My canes, Sam. My scarves and my zippers. Sam, Sam, I don't look good in *furniture*!

Because there are certain bodies that slough clothes, that nudge the hang of a shirt off true, the line of a suit or a p.j. Something perhaps actually repudiate to fabric, fashion, some possibly haunted condition of raiment that billows the break in a trouser, the roll of a cuff—— ghosts in your shirts, phantoms in your pants. That revokes habiliment's grace periods and cancels all its five-year/50,000-mile whichever-comes-first warranties—— the old, splendid shine of the new, some glorious, chin-up, chest-out protective sheen of clothing's maiden voyages when we were kids, that almost cloaklike status of new duds that glowed on us spiffy as force fields. (A knife pocket in a boot, I remember. I remember my first long pants and recall a zipper on a windbreaker that ran like a sash from my waist to my shoulder, the forty-five-degree slant endowing me with, lending me, I mean, some sense of the unique that, paradoxically, sits inside the very idea of a uniform, exuding pride, patriotism, the swaggered vibes and wavelengths of mission, like the rakish tilt of a green beret or the colored neckcloths of special forces, say. Kids with messages on their T-shirts must feel this way.) And what looked good in the shop and at least offered a reflection in the department-store mirror, reduced, in daytime's available light and the one-on-one circumstances of the eye, not just to the out of plumb but to the shabby and old shoe, to all the played-out, sad-ass obsolescence of bus-depot style. And though worse things have happened at sea and I'm a baby to mention it, it's a deformity of sorts, a small sin against the self, to have, at my time of life, to continue to flaunt my playground ways, my low couture, my hick chic—— shirttails loose, flapping, rising like a sort of escaped weather from the back of my pants, the points of my collars rounded, curling in on themselves like petals spoiling, and the illusion, somehow, that I wear badly aligned knickers, collapsed socks.

It ain't just faulty body imaging or low esteem that's spooking me. Because the thing of it is, most people's clothes fit. Not well dressed particularly, not anything glass of fashion or mold of form, just those light, casual arrangements of the hand-in-glove—— extras in movies and athletes in outfields, salesmen on airplanes and fiddlers in dance bands, shoppers at K mart and people on picnics. Most folks' do. Housewives in *shmattes* and doctors in lab coats. Because a size is a statistic, a mathematical fact, men's and the tailor's historical weights and measures, scientific and fixed as a light-year, the mileage to London. (Because the real Industrial Revolution had nothing to do with steam, the railroads, smoke, soot, and time clocks, Birmingham's murk, Liverpools' *shumtz* like generalized climate, some Tropic of the Urban. It had nothing to do with internal combustion. The sweatshop was the true beginning of modern times; the sewing machine is at the core of civilization—— and the rack off which we buy our clothes at the bottom of things. The bespoke broken like a code, and Bond Street and Savile Row only expensive cottage industries now, mom-and-pop operations for tourists, the rich, the neighborhood changing and the march of empire spreading outward from the downtown department stores to the suburban malls, to all the aisles, bins, counters, and crabbed changing rooms of the ordinary.)

I am, I guess, unfit.

Or was, used to be.

A little over a year ago I was invited to *Esquire* magazine's golden anniversary do at the Four Seasons, Lincoln Center. Black tie, the invite specified.

Those tuxedos one rents are like costumes, trick suits, some break-away vaudeville of the haberdash. They are a sort of tailored palimpsest, cloth pentimenti, a scaffolding, a tux armature of seams and tucks and great squirreled-away swatches of excess material. Look inside one of those suckers—the pants, the jacket—and you'll find secret suits, smuggled suits, suits within suits, garment strata, actual strip mines of fabric, great Mesabi Ranges of worsted. One size fits all, at least potentially, and how that thing moved when I did is a mystery.

The fact is I looked fine. I wanted to buy it. It wasn't the price that put me off—though I was surprised they could ask that much to buy a suit that must already have paid for itself four or five times over—so much as some used-car notion of it I had, the sense, suddenly fastidious, suddenly nice, of buying somebody else's troubles. (Because isn't love the point of all this? Some romantic return on your invest-ment? This was a garment that had been out all night at proms: this was a suit that had stood up at weddings, that had fallen down drunk, that had ridden in the back seat of convertibles and maybe gotten lucky now and again and watched dawn come up perhaps over the points of interest. This was a suit, that is, that had been around the block a few times.)

And, anyway, where would I wear it? It could be another fifty years before *Esquire* had its next golden anniversary.

In Scarsdale my cousin's kid was getting married. Big German au-tomobiles in the circular driveway. Roses, orchids in the swimming pool like the floating gardens of Xochimilco. Would-be actors offering drinks, hors d'oeuvres on the lawn. Strolling musicians strolling and a full-piece orchestra in the white circus tent set up over the tennis court. Chefs in the mess tent and the caterer fussing. A New York State Supreme Court justice mingling, muttering the ecumenical vows like an opera singer vocalizing, doing soft scales.

And twice in ten months now the pleasure of my company requested if only I could come up with black tie, the snoot equipage and swank accoutrement of the social. I was on a roll whose idea of the high life was any party not specifically B.Y.O.B. Like someone, a young married, say, just learning the fundamentals, the ABCs of economic life, I determined to buy rather than rent. Not knowing I was in the vanguard of a trend, that this was the fashionable thing these days, unaware, I swear it, that yuppies were gathering, that tuxedos were in, or otherwise I might not have done it. (I remember my Nehru jacket, which I thought was beautiful. The first on my block and worn only once. I remember the white polyester double-knit dress shirt I bought, and that I also thought beautiful, a high-fashion breakthrough.) On all the cusps of the current, positioned as an ambusher and embarrassed, as ever, by home-court advantage, my unreasonable aversions and inverted prides. Because I had not yet come to understand the real meaning of the tuxedo.

Now, in recent years I have come to dread shopping, particularly shopping for clothes, all the little humiliations of purchase, the holographic views one catches of oneself in the three-way mirrors, those coming-and-going visions of the bald, diminished, frailing self that are really, God knows, the going-going-gone eyefuls and look-sees, telling as CAT scans, of old mortality and downscale being. I make no mention of that moment of truth when they take your credit card away to see if it will bounce and speak hardly at all of the flimsily curtained dressing rooms, their hard little benches, no deeper than bookshelves, where you don't so much try pants on as wrestle with leverage (like dressing, I imagine, in a closet)—— the gyms of the sidelined, say, the teensy locker rooms of the sedentary.

So, bamboozled by my body and the other panics, my customized, white-knuckled, fear-of-flying fear, and turning it, if you will, into a kind of trip to the dentist, I put off for as long as I decently could actually going out to buy the damned thing.

The whole business took maybe ten minutes.

I'd forgotten, you see, all I'd learned at the tuxedo rental joint seven or eight months before—— the great, one-size-fits-all tuxedo principles, the fact that tuxedos are the very medium of the tailor/salesmen in these places, that they do almost only one thing and one thing only, the way, say, oh, the lady behind the gravy-and-mashed potatoes station in the cafeteria lunch line ladles out little mountains of starch, then sets gravy in them like perfect puddles of landscaping, and, most important of all, the almost total absence of choice in these matters, decision surrendered, out of your hands, whatever of option remaining only the shape of your shirt collar, the detailing of your lapels, to notch or to shawl, or just a matter of color, the red cummerbund and tie or the black. (To notch, of course. To black. So no choice at all really. And even the accessories a package—— the tie and cummerbund, the onyx studs and onyx cuff links, the black suspenders, the pleated dress shirt. Less choice finally—oh, much less—than the mandatory options on new cars.) You try on the pants, you try on the jacket, a quick once-over with the tape, a few passes with the chalk, and it's come back Tuesday . . .

Once, maybe a decade before I bought one for myself, I wrote of a character in a book that he "stands tux'd, his formal pants and jacket glowing like a black comb, his patent-leather shoes vaulted smooth and tensionless as perfect architecture. He might be standing in the skin of a ripe bright black apple. He feels, in the inky clothes, showered, springy, bouncy . . . [can feel] his clean twin sheathing of tall silk hose, can almost feel the condition of his soles, their shade like Negroes' palms. He is accessoried. In his . . . white dress shirt his delicious burgundy studs are as latent with color as the warning lights on a dashboard. Onyx links, round and flat as elevator buttons, seal his cuffs, and dark suspenders lie on him with an increment of weight that suggests the thin holsters of G-men, and indeed there *is* something governmental in his dress, something maritime, chief-of-staff. The golden fasteners beneath his jacket could be captains' bars. A black bow tie lies across his throat like a propeller."

It was a fairly accurate description but it was a guess. What I'd missed was the proprietary condition, whatever it is that platforms the heart and smugs the senses of a man in such clothes and somehow lends a guy in a tux his surveyor instincts, like a fellow on horseback, something possessive in the feel of the thing, something hospitable and generous, father-of-the-bride, say, founder-of-the-feast. (Leader-of-the-band. Master-of-the-ceremony.) Something patrician, the long, deep bloodlines of first families and old money.

I didn't want to take it off. I *never* wanted to take it off.

And am working on my image, up to my ears, till I accustom my friends, in my new jerk status. (Hey, no pain no gain, Rome wasn't built in a day, and they laughed at Fulton.) Because I'm serious. If the suit fits—and it does, it does—wear it!

I'm breaking it in. Taking it to dinner parties.

"Look," Marilyn Teitelbaum said, laughing, the first time she saw me in it, "look at Stanley!"

"What the hell's he wearing?" her husband, Steve, wanted to know.

"Those things are in now," someone else said. "I just read in *Time*."

(I didn't know. We don't take the paper; I don't keep up.)

"You," said Naomi, "are a ridiculous human being."

"He looks all right."

"Sure he does."

"I'm not sure about the cummerbund," I said.

"The cummerbund?"

"It rides up."

"Have someone sew one of those hook-and-eye arrangements onto it."

"That's a good idea." I said. "They can do that?"

"They can put a man on the moon."

"He's trying to show us up. It's a stunt."

"No," I said, "I'm the guy who came to dinner. You can wear this anywhere."

"You could go bowling in it."

"You wouldn't look out of place at an accident."

"Or a prom."

"I think he looks like he's on a scavenger hunt."

(Yes, I thought. Exactly. A scavenger hunt!" Teamed up with heiresses, with ingenues yoked. To lark attached, to hoboes in Hooverville. A scavenger hunt! With milkmen at sunrise conjunct. In nostalgia dressed up and playing somebody else's decade, epoch, it ain't never too late. Cute as a dancer-till-dawn, as a drunk, as some playboy in love. Top-shod, top-hatted, silk-scarved. Black and white as a photograph, as a screwball nephew in a screwball comedy—— Cary Grant in Connecticut. Remember my even more formal, tail-coated, wing-collared uncles, their elaborate heavy clothes like the big leather furniture and burnished paneling of their exclusive clubs? See them, laughless, dour, skin-deep Scrooges? Watch the lifted sieges of their hearts taken by storm by orphans.)

Yes, Sam. *Yes!*

Because clothes do *too* make the man and appearance *is* reality, and sometimes all you need to be happy is the conviction that your togs fit, that you don't clash, that your threads, duds, garb, and trim, your gear and frippery are in good repair.

No? You think not? No? *Then why does a stain on your cuff ruin your evening? And how can a little spilled soup spoil your life?* Because we would be gift wrapped as packages! And come on to one another stylish and spiff, pristine and groomed as the close-order drilled, as hand-in-glove, bespoke, and customized, finally, as Goldilocks's just-right bowl and cereal, her chair and bed, compartmentalized and discrete as wallets, smitten by proportion, scale, and all the tongue-in-groove congruities, by the dress-parade possibilities of a perfect, human geometry!

And maybe *that's* the real meaning of the tuxedo. It corrects nature; it covers up flaw. It's designed, that is, to hide you. Like a kind of sartorial White Out, like a sort of male muumuu, its pleated shirt never looks wrinkled, its studs nail you together, its grosgrain stripes hold you upright, and its cummerbund turns on a dime, tucks hospital corners into your discordant, discrepant fabrics, the gap between your pants and your shirt. It papers you over, it bastes your body, it blind-hems your flesh and turns you seamless. Or the hiding aggressive, some sexist camouflage. Haven't I heard that men's evening clothes—the very term suggests a darkness—are the color they are the better to show off the brighter costumes of the women?)

Here's a brief, conversational history of the tuxedo.

About a century ago the jacket was designed by Henry Poole, a British tailor who adapted it—a tailcoat minus the tails—from a velvet smoking jacket he'd made for the Prince of Wales. It was then known as a "call" or "compromise" or "go-between" coat, and Poole convinced Evander Wall, an American client, that it could be substituted for the more formal tails. However, when Wall tried it out in the ballroom of Saratoga's United States Hotel, he scared the ladies, frightened the horses, and was asked to leave. In 1886 another American, Griswold Lorillard, wore Poole's new dinner jacket into the Tuxedo Park Club—he was one of your tobacco Lorillards and his pop founded the club, in Tuxedo Park, New York—and made the papers. (And that, incidentally, is how the pig got its curly tail.) It caught on but saw action mostly at stag parties and didn't become acceptable in mixed company until just after World War One, Armageddon being a great leveler. Affluence saw the return of full dress and the Depression the return of the shorter coat—— the old story of flush times' amplitudes and overloads, hard times' tightened belts. (Materialism not just a philosophical opinion about the universe but a theory of bolts and textiles, dry goods, piece goods, lengths, and stuff. A Dow Jones astrology—— its houses of fortune, its signs of luck.)

Bill and Mary Gass gave their annual New Year's Eve party. Steve, who'd expressed such astonishment weeks before when I'd shown up at his house in my tux, was in a tuxedo of his own. We were the life of the party. Or our clothes, our clothes were.

Jarvis Thurston was telling about the time he'd had to rent a tuxedo.

It was his senior year at Weber State College. He'd put the yearbook together, was the fellow in charge of all the nature passages, all that stuff on the seasons—autumn with its smell of falling leaves, spring with the buds and the sap, Jack Frost nipping at your nose. . . . He was valedictorian that year, too, and had, as part of the honor, as part of his duties, been chosen to escort the school's beauty queen to the big graduation dance, not just to squire her but to signal that the dance could begin by promenading with her down this long flanking lane of the Court of Love and Beauty—past the deans and professors, the alums and parents and invited guests, past the fraternity boys and sorority girls and all the graduating seniors for whom he and Miss Weber State College were surrogates—and inviting her to dance the first dance with him in full view of a considerable part of the population of the state of Utah.

Now, he wasn't too sanguine about a lot of this. A few things bothered him. For one thing, he'd always been a little nervous around beautiful women. For another, he was alarmed by all that ceremony. "You'd have thought it was a West Point marriage," he said. "Crossed swords, that sort of thing. We had rehearsals for the marching part, for the bowing and scraping, but I wasn't much comforted. Because the other thing was, I didn't know how to dance."

But he was the valedictorian. The fuss and the ceremony, the pomp and the circumstance, came with the territory.

Anyway, he got fitted for his tuxedo, the first one he'd ever worn, he said. He didn't know how to do a bow tie, he said. He said he didn't understand the accessories.

He was a nervous wreck, but everyone kept reassuring him he'd do fine, and he picked up his tuxedo the day of the dance and got suited up in plenty of time just to make sure, and all his friends in the boarding house were very supportive. They tied his tie for him and fixed his studs in place and did his handkerchief and fitted it into his breast pocket and told him how swell he looked in a dinner jacket. One of them even remembered about the corsage and rushed off at the last minute to get one for the beauty queen before the shop closed.

They kept up this cheerful pepper talk and reminded him that most of the things folks worry about, the awful things they think are going to happen to them, the faux pas and slip-ups, really never do.

They were very kind, he said. If it hadn't been for them he didn't think he could even have thought of going through with it. They not only stood by him, he said; they stood *with* him. Because he wasn't going to take a chance on wrinkling anything important by sitting down. "It was a lesson, I tell you." Jarvis told us, "in how nice people are."

An hour before the dance he called the beauty queen up and told her he had to cancel.

"That was the word I used, 'cancel.' I told her, you know, that it had nothing to do with her, that I'd voted for her myself. It was the dancing, I said. That just wasn't me. It was the dancing; I couldn't dance. I was *from* Utah. I grew *up* on ranches. If it'd been anything else, if I could do it on horseback, I told her, I could handle it."

That was better than forty years ago and he hasn't worn a tuxedo from that day to this. He says, "I've had my chances, of course, but I figure I disgraced the uniform and lost the right."

And maybe that's the meaning of the tuxedo, too. Not just to hide, not just to play the gigs of class or money, or watch the ladies or practice the trends but, from time to time, to show the flag—— of the civil, of the civilized, bound in the secular, civic glad rags and wraps of honor.

THREE
MEETINGS*

I MET HIM, OF ALL PLACES, IN WESTERN KENTUCKY IN THE, OF ALL seasons, summer of, of all times, 1941. I was curator of a highway zoo and snake show gasoline-station complex on U.S. Bypass 97 eleven miles west of Humphries. I don't flatter myself that Vladi stopped because of the wonders collected there. There was a gas war and Dmitri had to use the Men's. (Nor am I showing off when I use the pet name. A gracious and democratic man, Vladi instructed me to call him thus not five minutes after we had met.)

You know how it is with these highway zoos. The specimens are scrawny and seem somehow *sideshow*, freakish reductions, bestial lemons teetering on the brink of some evolutionary misstep. Well there's good reason, but it isn't what you think. You mustn't be too hasty to blame the curator. Nobby understood this. (Never a formal man, he instructed me to call him thus not ten minutes after we had met.) He knew the debilitating effect of the tourists on the fauna. It is the stare

*Originally appeared in *Tri Quarterly*'s Festschrift for Vladimir Nabokov, Winter 1970

they bring, a glazed gaze between boredom and boldness on them like pollen, like the greasy dust of the last state line, like fruitflies and parasites on the oranges and plants between Arizona and California. What can you do? You can't have them wash their faces first. It's a ruinous hypnotism, this wear and tear of the eyes. With their fixed look they can intimidate even the healthiest animal and over the course of a season actually impoverish it. (I've seen the rich oriental rug of a snake's second skin turn to a moldy scab under this gaze.)

I accompanied Boko through the menagerie—not one to stand on ceremonies, he ordered me call him after this fashion not seventeen minutes after we met—and watched as he grew sad contemplating my failing beasts. Every so often he would shake his head and punctuate his unhappiness with lush Cyrillic *tch tch's* that would have been beautiful had I not guessed at the torment behind them. When we had toured all the corrals and pens he looked significantly toward a woman tourist with New Hampshire plates who was depressing my porcupine.

"There's your trouble," he said.

"I know, but what can I do? It can't be helped."

"Have them wash their faces first," he said gently.

"That's brilliant. It just might work, Boko."

"More rasp on the *k* sound. It takes a strong *h*."

Struck by the incisiveness of his recommendation, I serendipitously offered to show him my butterfly cases. (I did not know who he was at this time, but there is something in a curator's temperament or even in a caretaker's or guard's that makes him always keep something special in reserve that the public never sees. This is universally true. Remember it the next time you visit the top of the Empire State Building or go out to see the Statue of Liberty. We don't necessarily do it for the tip, mind.) It was a standard collection made somewhat exceptional by the inclusion of two rare specimens—— the Bangelor Butterfly and the highly prized Lightly Salted Butterfly.

I could see that Bozo was very excited. "Where did you come upon this?" he asked animatedly and pointed with a shaking finger to the Lightly Salted Butterfly. "I have searched in Pakistan and sought in Tartary. I've been up the slopes of Muz Tagh Ata and down Soputan's cone. I have stood beneath Kile's waterfall and along the shores of Van. I must know. Where?"

"In the meadow."

He revealed who he was and gave me his card and said that if there was ever anything he could ever do for me I should look him up.

And that was the first meeting.

I saw him a second time in Venezuela after the war. We had met in Cair at a boatel, or marina, where we had both gone independently to be outfitted for an expedition up the Orinoco in search of the most fabulous and legendary creature in the entire species— the Great Bull Butterfly. (The highway zoo had failed due to the construction of a new interstate and a settlement of the gas war. With the acceleration of construction on the Federal Highway System many small curators were out of a job in those days. There is no more room for the little man, it seems. Many former highway zookeepers—those who have not been absorbed by larger institutions—have been driven by their love of display and the diminished outlet for their talents to exhibitionism and been arrested.) We decided to join forces. It was Uncle Volodya who suggested it. (Never an uncompassionate man, he had seen that the rasping *kh* sound was giving me the sore throat and permitted me to call him thus.) By now I knew his reputation and his great work in lepidopterology and would have been too shy to put forth the idea myself. I was sitting in the boatel sipping an Orinoco-Cola and reading.

"What are you reading?" Uncle asked. I hadn't noticed him but recoginized him at once. I didn't know if he would remember me, however, and so did not presume to remind him of our first meeting.

"Oh," I said, "it's a birthday card. Today is my birthday. Have you ever noticed how a birthday card always arrives on your birthday? Never a day early, never a day late? My people are in far-off Kentucky, yet the card was in this morning's mail." It was the longest speech I had yet made to him. He was clearly moved, and I have reason to believe that it was on the strength of this insight that he asked me to accompany him on the Great Bull Butterfly hunt.

We set out next morning and for the next five weeks assiduously traveled downstream, searching along the banks by day and camping by night. We encountered many strange and rare larval and pupal forms, together with some lovely eggal forms I had never before seen, but nothing approaching the mature imago we sought. Perhaps the natives were mistaken in their descriptions, I thought, never daring to voice my suspicions aloud, of course. Or perhaps, I thought racistically, they lied. Maybe the Great Bull Butterfly was a Wild Goose Chase. As I say, I never said this, but one night I was sitting glumly in front of the campfire. He noticed that I was not playing my saxophone.

"You're not playing tonight, Shmoolka. Why?"

"It's the reeds, Uncle," I lied. "I've worn out the last reed."

"That's not it. What? Tell."

"Well, if you must know, I think the expedition will fail. I think it's a cruel hoax."

"A hoax, Shmoolko?"

"We've been searching five weeks, and if you can't find a diurnal creature in broad daylight in five weeks—"

"*Diurnal be damned*," he shouted suddenly, falling unconsciously into his fabled alliteration. "You've given me an idea. What if— what if the Great Bull Butterfly is *nocturnal?* If he were, then of course we wouldn't have found him. Shmuel, I think that's the solution, I think that's it." Before I could even reply, he was on his feet and off into the jungle. He darted heedlessly across the path of a black cat and gave it bad luck. I followed breathlessly. We found it that night.

But, alas, we had been gone longer than we had expected. The bearers had run off. We were low on supplies. The trip back to Cair was upstream against a heavy current made more dangerous by the torrential rains. We had no more food. We had eaten my last saxophone reed the day before. I don't think we could have lasted another twenty-four hours, but we were found at the eleventh hour by natives— Uncle puts it at the eleventh hour; I don't think it could have been past ten-thirty—who fed us and promised to conduct us back to Cair the next morning. They knew a shortcut.

"Why are you so hung up on butterflies, Nuncle?" I asked at campfire that night after marshmallows.

"Shmuel, that's because they're a metaphor is why."

"A meadow flower?"

"A metaphormorphosis."

"I met a fire more for us? A meaty forest?"

"Call me Steve."

"But why *butterflies*, Steve?"

"Lepidopterology—don't you hear that word *leper* in there? They're the outcasts, you know. They're the exiles. Like me. Anyway, it wasn't always butterflies; for a time it used to be squirrels and dogs. Then for a while it was pinto ponies. But I've been east and I've been west, and I think butterflies is best."

"Could you speak about them?"

In the glow of the fire his face seemed serene and very sad.

"Like *ur*-airplanes they are," he spoke suddenly. "Lopsided glider things riding turbulence like snowflakes. Heroic, heraldic. Bug pennants, bucking, choppy flags of the forest."

"That's beautiful," I told him.

"Also, if you keep one in your pocket it's good luck."

"Call me Ishmuel."

And that was the second meeting.

SOME
OVERRATED
MASTERPIECES

T HERE'S NOTHING SO CONVINCING AS AN OPINION, AND AN ODD thing about words is the cockeyed weight they're permitted to bear, so that if I say something as flagrantly meaningless or flat-out arbitrary as, oh, he's the sort of person who parts his hair, I've not only suggested something negative about hair-parting but have made, too, an aspersion on character. He'll think twice before he parts it next time, I bet. And this goes double for written words. "He uses after-shave," I charge, "and his last three cars have been hardtops." "His wife," I continue mercilessly, "dresses the twins alike and pushes them about the streets in a perambulator like one of those wide-load house trailers!"

This isn't just a haughty aesthetic of the supercilious, it's the astonishing Law of the Unframed Indictment and is the critical equivalent of holding political prisoners without bringing charges. We condemn a thing simply by mentioning it.

Turner, I claim, evenly, uninflectedly as I can, paints elements, water and air in ratios seldom seen in life and got up in murk and slate fug like a foul mood. What's the difference, then, between a Turner and ordinary mall art? Why, merely the weather, only the

sobriety of his colors, as if genius were a question of the intervention
of light, like sun block, say. This time, though, by having introduced
a reason, however spurious, I seem to have taken higher ground. But
in questions of taste there *is* no higher ground. In matters of art and
cuisine, reasons are created equal. It's a perfect *democracy* of reasons
and, hey, I know what I like, isn't only a perfectly respectable argument
but an absolutely unanswerable one. There *is* nothing so convincing
as an opinion.

Am I Philistine? What, with *my* up-front heart? Philistine? *Me?*
With my sleeves and my hankies and all the other emotional ready-
to-wear in the wardrobe of my attentive sentiments? The sucker *I* am
for almost any statuary in the open air, in landscape, or any of the
kempt green gardens of the world? *This* pushover, never mind the
music or even only the tune it's playing, for the simple human har-
monics of any orchestra at work, *any* orchestra, any symphony or pit
band, any string quartet, jazz band, pick-up bluegrass rhythm jammers,
or even just any saw- or jug- or steel drum-and-washboard skiffle group!
The cooperation, I mean, the parade-ground synchronicity, whatever
the factor is that makes for the precision of the Rockettes, for example,
or the spontaneous applause every time the shuttle goes up— all
that concentrate timing, all that good will and get ready, get set, go
of the honed and attuned? What, *this* soft-souled, nolo-contendere,
hearts-and-minds pussycat? Anybody's fascist, this nose-led company
man, as willing—willing? *anxious*—to be stirred as sugar in tea, this,
what I'm saying, lawn-chair enthusiast for all the brass, fife, and oom-
pah-pah of high summer's slam-bang reviewing-stand occasions and
gazebo patrioticals.

But lesser art forms are all collective, I think. Which pretty much—
because I know what I don't like, too—puts opera's hyperbolic charms
and vocal circus in its place. Because art ought to be as one-on-one
as intimacy, something if not actually shades-drawn and pulled-curtain
to it, then at least discreet, and the last thing—saving architecture
perhaps, which, like that gazebo from which those marches occur, is
public, communal as wafering—art ought to be is stirring. And if Van
Gogh's painted room in Arles can command my tears, all I can tell
you is that those must be a different sort of tears, *vintage* tears, could
be, unlike my public performances in the sculpture garden as ripple
from champagne. Speaking of which, incidentally, with its taste like
a mixture of dishwater and sugar substitute, while not one of the

overrated masterpieces I mean to consider here, may not be a bad instance. It comes down to us through the bubbles' reputation. Though of course that's how everything comes down to us, history working its gravitational will through word of mouth.

Trust me. What I'm talking about has nothing to do with what's in and what's out, what's up and what's down—— prepositional aesthetics. There ain't any old Roman pleasure to it, the thumbs-up, thumbs-down joys. I don't lord it over, I don't set myself up. I already said, I know what I like. It's strictly personal. Because, for me, there has to be *something* personal or I won't play. And there is. Not envy, I *hope* not envy, or not envy exactly, and not sour grapes, *exactly* not sour grapes, with which I've no patience. Sour grapes are pathetic. Just something inimical in me to the overrated, the next guy's hype, a kind of rage like an allergy. It's a myth you don't feel your blood pressure. I *feel* my blood pressure. And, for me, the test of time is simply an adjustment of the systolics and diastolics, a small subsidence of the personal. John Gardner's dead, and how long can I reasonably hold a grudge against *The Bonfire of the Vanities?*

So this shall chiefly take place within the precincts of the safely historical, where bygones are bygones and even subjectivity has cooled to a temperature that can't be felt.

Take Leonardo da Vinci, for example, who, with his polymath imagination and sci-fi instinctuals, seems to have been to art what Jules Verne and H. G. Wells were to fiction. Indeed, though many of his designs and sketches seem plausible even today—his tanks and fortifications, his flying machines, catapults, machine guns, hoists, and gears—— all the heavy arsenal of his Armageddon heart—there's something comic about Leonardo, some after-the-fact humor laid on by perspective and hindsight, the joke, that is, of the primitive, like Fred Flintstone propelling his car by foot power, some principle of the dated operating here. And if this isn't fair, isn't, in fact, specious at the root, if it suggests that a principle of the dated is *always* operable, chipping away like a kind of erosion at what was once thought true and beautiful, the water, wind, and temperature of age, why not accept at the outset that *most* things left out in history like the open air oxidize, tarnish, become, finally, subject to the simple human joke of time? The moving finger writes, paints, makes, and having writ, painted, or made, moves on to the next thing. Because a lot of what we talk about when we talk about art is, well, fashion. Not so much in flavor-of-the-month ways as in retrofit or adaptive ones. Since nothing is made out of whole cloth and even genius is incremental, even, I mean, at its most perverse, when it's weighed down by the social or even only personal mood swings of the artist and is simply reactive. (It's impossible to imagine a giant of cubism, say, arising out of the neoclassical tradition.) Because there's something always at least a *little* nostalgic about even the greatest art. Not the *hommage* of a young film director to an admired, established elder, or even a sly joke or slipped-in referential, so much as the conventional givens of a particular medium, subject matter, or point of view, even if it's only the plain true fact of canvas.

Add to my charge against da Vinci that he was a "visionary," this intellectual rover and time traveler, and it's possible to see a kind of instability in him, a certain failure of *sitzfleisch*, an inability, that is, to sit still in his talent, almost as if he took too seriously the burden of being a Renaissance man or was the sort of guy who parted his hair.

Now, about this Mona Lisa.

See her there in her cat-who-ate-the-canaries, her smug repose and babushka of hair like a face on a buck. A study in browns, in muds, and all the purplish earthens of her jaundiced, low-level, f-stop light. See her, see her there, this, well, girl of a certain age, with a faint streak of bone structure blowing off her skin like a plume of jet trail all she has for brow. See her, see the rightward glancing of her color-coordinated eyes inside the puffy, horizontal parentheses of her lashless lids. See the long, low-slung nose dropped inches below the painterly rules of thumb. Now see her famous statelies, her upright, comfortable aplomb, her left forearm along the arm of a chair, her fat right hand covering it, as clubby and at ease as one foot crossed over another. Look at the background through the open casement, the queer to-pography like mounds of green volcanic vegetable, the strange striated water and all the wavy switchback of the road like something carved from earth by one of the maestro's anachronistic machines, a backhoe, say, some plow or grader of the yet-to-be.

Focus. *Focus!*

In and closer in to the central occasion of her odd, asexual face, in where the mystery lives, the secret agenda, in toward her giacondas, her giaconundrums, the hidden mystery of her guarded gingivitis smile!

Because I'm changing my mind here, a little I am, and thinking maybe it's Nat Cole's version I'm not that crazy about, his viscous syrups I'm thinking of, confusing the box-step cliché and sentimentals with the fact of her face. Because what levers our attention is that nose and those lips, and a truth about art is the company it keeps with the slightly askew, the fly in that woodpile of symmetry, mere balance in painting, equilibrium, a stunt of the "beautiful." What commissions the eye is face. No likeness hangs on the wall of hair, hands, breasts, behind, the soles of one's feet. Indeed, faces are the most private part. It's the face that draws the eye in the Mona Lisa, but I was only kidding about the mystery of that smile. There *is* no mystery. No one ever had to solve a face, and the notion of *this* face's enigmatics has always been a kind of anthropomorphism, only paint's pathetic fallacy, facial phrenology, a horoscopics by bone structure, an astrology of the eye, the palmistry of character, wrongheaded, literary, the racism of beauty, unreliable, finally, as any other pseudoscience, as if to say, oh, as if to say "Read my lips."

Next slide.

Georgia O'Keeffe was a painter who rarely depicted human beings. Her desert subject matter is, in a way, the flip, parched, only apparently sunnier side of Turner's wet coin—— blanched, bleached landscapes of polished, picked-clean death. This hermit—in New Mexico she lived at "Ghost Ranch"—this prospector type whose unpopulated, desiccated paintings, save for the fossils that appear in them, seem studies in an almost relished absence. The bones and white skulls in O'Keeffe's work signify not decay so much as the evidence of a fled, efficient hunger—— the art of the buzzard, the art of the scavenger hunt. Even her rather wonderful cityscapes (*East River No. 1; Shelton Hotel, New York, No. 1; East River from the Thirtieth Story of the Shelton Hotel, New York; New York Night*) are alternative versions of shapes found in the desert paintings—the mesa, canyon, adobe variations—seem deliberate, even perverse, essays in exclusion, as though both Nature and the man-made contain value only to the extent that they not only avoid but actually proscribe the human. (Only in *New York Night*, and only if you look carefully, can you make out, in the lower left-hand corner, any people at all, four stick figures of black paint rather more like exclamation points that human beings.) It's as if O'Keeffe were driven by some wilderness, Sierra Club will, vaguely snobbish, a restrictive, country-club vision. She's Edward Hopper without people, without even the saving grace of their dignified loneliness. She's interested only in shapes (my favorite O'Keeffe paintings, her *Sky Above Clouds* series, have always seemed rather like *New Yorker* covers to me), but where there is no "face" there can be no interest. Even her suggestive, almost gynecological and phallic flora (which almost never appear in bunches and are rarely "arranged") seem parodic, sterile, lush enough, but in their issueless isolation really only a sort of sexual floor plan.

Like other private artists she became her greatest achievement, a beautiful woman whose bone structure was her fate and who posed, in a literal sense, in her black clothes, white scarves, and black hats, paring herself down and paring herself down into a piece of art quite like sculpture, a leathery, unsmiling woman of manipulated style, editing herself and disappearing at last behind the very image of a collective, hermaphroditic animism, some perfected, deliberated simulacrum somewhere between ancient squaw and old manitou, a final, showy mysticism complete and functional as the bony infrastructure of those skulls she preferred to the faces that covered them. I think narcissism infrastructures the infrastructure here, the dangerous virus she contracted by being both a subject—all those portraits she permitted Stieglitz to make of her—and an arranger of subjects.

But it's hard to talk about art. Maybe there should be a law against it, some First Amendment gag order like crying Fire! in a crowded theater. Still and all, if one knows what one likes, well where's the harm, eh? And anyway this is the war news, day thirteen or fourteen into the Mother of Battles, though it seems longer, of course, deeper into time than anything I can remember—and I'm sixty if I'm a day— and I've seen, well, not a lot, but my share, more than, and what I haven't seen, like everyone else, I fill in the blanks, make an allowance, do the Kentucky windage adjustments, write off if not to experience then to helplessness and despair this, well, looting of end times everywhere, this breaking and entering the other guy's turf, with wiser heads figuring—this is a big benefit of the doubt I'm giving away here—that damn-near no one has led the right life. The Gulf's a floating filling station, Marines have died, civilians on all sides in God knows what apocalyptic positions fallen on what rubble and hoisted on what shrapnel, and I see that over on the "Home Shopping Club" Operation Desert Storm sweatshirts are going for $19.75, over four hundred sold and counting, and, Jeez, if the world made it, it would have been the millennium in nine years and, in another one-and-a-half, the semi-millennium of the discovery of the New World. Some millennium.

Some semimillennium. So it's pretty late in the day to be having any Mother of Battles. Ain't going to *study* no war no more! And I take it back about injunctions on art talk, prior restraint. Because maybe that's the only thing we ought to be allowed to talk about, stuff above our station, playing catch-up with culture, sucking up to civilization. And the point is, well, God bless the artists the point is. Here's to those with the paints, whether we know whereof we speak or not. Here's to artisans, folks who make violins, cast bells, throw pots, have perfected their pitch. Here's, I mean, to all those whose attentions are engaged in innocent acts, to everyone everywhere who doesn't know where the time has flown. To minders of their own determined business who wouldn't hurt a fly. Here's to occupational therapy even, to doodle and whittle, to whistle and hum and all the preoccupied instrumentals of the head and heart, the aye-lu-loo-lus and sweet-dream lullabies of softest yore. And to all those makers of those less-than-masterpieces who lend point to the sermon, and to dilettantes, oh, especially, Lord, to dilettantes, window shoppers on the artier avenues, friends of the museum, patrons of the symphony, pals of the zoo, to everyone every-where who's ever tossed a pledge to PBS, NPR, ladies and gentlemen of good will who keep the Sunday. So, waiting for the worst, hoping for the best, it's back I go to my own harmless knitting, an expert self-proclamated but innocent as any.

Now what *I* don't much care for is all the boring, adulatory religious art of dark old early times, the triptychs in their layered gilded frames like great wooden fanfares, I mean; the altarpieces; the madonnas with their malnourished, wizened bundles of infant Jesuses in fishbowl, space-helmet halos or under a rakish nimbus of beanies (not like Michelangelo's pink, meaty, muscular biblicals so oddly like Picasso's great fleshy giants and giantesses); all the annunciations running to-gether in our heads like a pony express of the holy; all the lugubrious figures making their there-there's of comfort over the spilled milk and blood of the major players on all that stained glass and shining wood; all that adoration in kings' caucus in the stable like so much political buzz, their baksheesh of gold, frankincense, and myrrh; angels in improbable, heavier-than-air wings; lashed, trussed, hangdog Jesus, pathetic, almost sheepish, shouldering a cross like a T-square, neither a Son of Man to inspire confidence nor a God to reckon with, looking nothing near what he's cracked up to be, looking confused in fact, lost, as if he'd rather be in Philadelphia—— all the stupefying *junk* I mean, in Europe raised to the level of an industry, complete with guides, *nuch*, scholars of the local (and here's to guides in billed caps, creased gray suits, and stuffed pockets), all those panels of unskilled, uninspired piety cartoons that looked at long enough bring on the headache and fog up the mind, and cause, as stated, to run together in the memory this blur of art, this crisis of criticism, this deferential politeness on all sides—*"Bella, bello,"* I assure the guide, *"molto, molti, tres molti bella"*—in my broken European, not only as if no one had ever been afraid of being caught short in church but as if tourists were as anatomically incorrect as all those God doll altarpieces.

And, God forgive me, *Hamlet* is an overrated play. Well, it's too long, but that ain't it, and too melodramatic, of course, *and* familiar, but that ain't it either. For one thing, the premise has always bothered me, or if not the premise then what triggers the play, bothered me, I mean, even back in those old new-critical days of my undergraduate youth when we fastened on the incest thing, or the question of the Prince's madness, ruse or consequence, or just plain dug H's brilliant, witty manic depression. He was, for most of us, our first psychological hero, more pyschological even than Ivan in *The Brothers Karamazov*, which we hadn't read yet anyway. Absolutely, Hamlet was our first interesting guy, a role model even, with his get-thee's-to-a-nunnery and all the tortured Ophelia bashing and secret titillation of the dirty private jokes, his breezy killer instincts, all the full-throated cynicism of his bullying intellect— role model, male bonder, man's man, prince's prince.

What puts me off, what I can't get past though, is, quite simply, Hamlet's father's ghost, to me as silly as that cadre of icons in all those triptychs on all those altarpieces, the angels and allegoricals, themselves a band of ghosts, sentimental and sweet-cheeked as zephyrs on maps. I am what I am and cut no slack for the times, the other fellow's world view. Besides, at its core *Hamlet* is a realistic play, and having truck with ghosts goes against its grain, botches the unity of its tone, and anyway the ghost's only a device to put the ball in play in the play. In a drama so dependent upon personality, this ghost is a stick figure. It has no character. Nor will it do to write the ghost off as a psychological projection. It comes with too much information for that. A forensic pathologist of a ghost, it fingers Claudius, fine-tunes the terms of its dispatch during its afternoon nap ("Cut off even in the blossoms of my sin,/Unhous'led disappointed, unanel'd,/No reck'ning made,

but sent to my account/With all my imperfections on my head"),
charges Hamlet to avenge it, and even dictates how Hamlet is to treat
his mother.

(And like where do *I* get off?)

Some soliloquies bother me—— all its vaunted To-be-or-not-to-
be's, a speech that I've never heard delivered by any actor, *any* actor,
who's not managed to make it sound silly. To be or not to be? That's
the question? Some question. Some answer: "To die—to sleep./ To
sleep—perchance to dream: ay, there's the rub!/For in that sleep of
death what dreams may come/When we have shuffled off this mortal
coil,/Must give us pause." This is an argument? Hamlet buys this?
And what flat-footed locutions: "Perchance to dream." "Shuffled off
this mortal coil." This isn't English, it's W. C. Fields impressions,
stretch rhetoric, but nothing compared to the barbarous poetry a few
lines down: "When he himself might his quietus make/With a bare
bodkin . . . " *Hamlet* is top-heavy with phrases like these, but finally,
it isn't the ghost and it isn't the overblown language that grate so much
as the flip side of this "interesting" man, for Hamlet's procrastinations
lie as heavily on the belly as bad food. One has the sense that Shakespeare, not Hamlet, is vamping till ready, that Hamlet's frozen will is
finally as much a device to stall the play as the ghost is to get it going,
because for all the brilliant facets of Hamlet's reckless character, his
too-fastidious duty pulls him down and locks up the play like so much
left luggage until, well, until we begin to suspect that will paralysis is
itself a device, that Hamlet, for all his thoroughbred, live-wire wit,
for all his charm and playfulness, is not so much the Dane as one of
those paid professionals at an Irish funeral, a bespoke whiner and
keener, the ultimate wailer and scold of fate. Brilliant along the bright-
est edges of its day, the play naps like the old king during the dead,
leaden center of its long, endless afternoon.

And get *these* to a nunnery:

Birth of a Nation, The Cabinet of Dr. Caligari (well almost every
silent movie ever made, including Buster Keaton's, including Charlie
Chaplin's). *Citizen Kane, Gone With the Wind,* that documentary
about the '36 Olympics, most "screwball" comedies of the thirties
(well, most black-and-white films generally). All the Marx Brothers,
all the Ritz Brothers, Judy Garland, Fred Astaire. No more "face" to
them than the dry, blanched bones of a Georgia O'Keeffe, mask all
they ever had for face, as customized as a clown's patented, painted

puss, Garland all pixie/gamine/urchin pout and phony hope, that mask
out on a ledge somewhere between outrage and melted love and on
a kind of red-alert verge of perpetual tears from the tip of her pigtail
in *The Wizard of Oz* to the top of her pompadour in *Meet Me in St.
Louis*, a face, like the clown's, made for black velvet, crying out for
it like a fix, and not much more face to her voice either if you want
to know, decibel for decibel its direct weights-and-measure vocal equiv-
alency, all vibrato and belt but slightly off-true, and Fred Astaire's
fixed puzzled-bumpkin expression more pleasant, perhaps, but as
locked-in as Garland's. Though maybe even more mpg for Astaire,
bang-for-the-buckwise, than J. Garland's overdrawn checks. (Am I
cranky, crotchety, under the weather? Are my shoes too tight, is cur-
mudgeon written all over me? Am I this old fogey, is my bite worse
than my bark? Or is this still the war news, something fed-up in my
bones with hyperbolicized attachment, the red rant of unearned, misunderstood praise?) So take *that*, Fred Astaire, with your vaunted grace
in your top hat, your white tie, and your tails, in your nightclubs, on
your patent leather, art deco floors, your decks like the seamless, level
tiles of toney beauty parlors, barbershops, and mens' rooms in the
basements of world-class hotels. Take that and *that* on your fey, heel-
toe, heel-toe bearings in your smug, noli-me-tangere aloofness and
look-ma-no-hands gravity denials, your tango indifference and vain,
vaguely threatening, predatory swoops and leaned inclinations as if,
Ginger Rogers or no Ginger Rogers, elegance were only a narcissistic
one-man show, *ur*-performance art, removed as the elsewhere-engaged
attentions of a juggler.

Though maybe all movies fall short of art with their soft blandish-
ments and easy endowments— sound, close-ups, an arch, arranged
lushness, perfect and unblemished as a gorgeous bay posed on a postcard. (Are my pants too small, is my hat off-plumb? Nah, nah, this
from a *lover* of movies, one of their easiest marks, privileged to get
out of an evening, watch the coming attractions, the trailers, who,
settled in his seat in the auditorium, sighs, remarks to the wife, "What
could be better?) Because the truth about art *is* the company it keeps
with the slightly askew, and the real stunt of the beautiful is not to be
too beautiful.

And Jasper Johns's flag series— *White Flag* like a plank floor, *Two
Flags* like a wall of carelessly mortared bricks, and, for my money,
the best of them, *Three Flags*, like a box for a board game. Well, I

say "for my money," but who's kidding whom here? All that dough and no Hawaii or Alaska? Jasper Johns in a fallen world an easier target than Astaire or Garland, than *Citizen Kane*, than *Gone With the Wind*, though richer people take him more seriously, a desecration not of the flag but of money.

(And once—this would have been in the middlish sixties, Baby Jane Holtzer was a Presence, People Are Talking About, Buzz Buzz and etcetera—I found myself in Frank Stella's East-something brownstone—uninvited, unintroduced, it being a whimsy intentionally inflicted or a perverse, acceptable usage among certain groups never to make a devoir, as if one's physical, accompanied presence in a place—He's-with-Me understood—were a sort of moral vouchsafe or silent parole, like an obscure but flashy idiom of behavior redounding not so much to the credit of the *schlepped* as the honor of the *schlepper*, but no crasher either, given carte blanche like any real guest, special roaming privileges like a range chicken, to mosey, take it all in. I've never forgotten my first impression. Which was, there, surrounded by the astonishing furniture in the setlike rooms—chrome and leather, glass and steel—and several hundred thousand bucks worth of Stella's frames and canvases, the paintings like patterns on bolts of fabric, the strangely shaped frames like exercises in bizarre carpentry, a realization that what I saw was visionary, but misunderstanding the vision, not recognizing in what was still merely the sixties that what I saw was basically only your expensive de rigueur restaurant decor of the seventies, eighties, and nineties, maybe even a first take on the higher mall motifs.)

(And another time, years later, in Paris at the Rodin Museum, Stella confounded, inverted, in a different mode, on a different scale, some metrics of the monumental, translated really, their differences all there was to run them together in my mind and, miles from the ornamental now, beyond decor or the Wagnerian either, the Tristanic and Isoldic, heroism's warp speeds, into cruel health like bloody organ meats on the redded-up floors of some human abattoir, those monumental sitters or loungers or drowners in their own stone, Rodin's more-than-solid citizens, who can't keep their hands to themselves, whose every pose—think *The Thinker*, think the vats and bone banks in *The Gates of Hell*, think *Adam*, think *Eve*, *The Crouching Woman*, *I Am Beautiful*, *The Prodigal Son*, *Nymph Kneeling*—suggests, whatever its title, not bodies so much as their functions. Rodin embarrasses finally. He embarrasses *me*. I get, I swear, the penis envy every time I see one of his improbably hung men, I want to sit in the laps of those ladies. Worse yet, and this *is* the war news, prefiguring, to me prefiguring—think of his statue of Victor Hugo—much of the totalitarian art of the last seventy-five years or so—Hitler's, Stalin's, Mussolini's—the romantic, muscular graffiti of all those death trippers.)

And, because a man's got to do what a man's got to do, *The New York Times Book Review*. Well it puts itself forward, bidding itself up and bidding itself up as the venue of masterpieces—— the bourse of books. (Next slide. *Quickly, quickly,* for God's sake!) Harvard. Grappa. Curries. The book of the month, the catch of the day. (Acquired tastes generally.) Rolls Royce automobiles, Rollex watches, airports, the configuration of jet planes, all coach-class seating and any lavatory on every airplane. Into design now but, like the toilets on those planes or the tourists in those churches, anatomically incorrect. Talkin' the truisms, talkin' areas that ought to be taken for granted by now, basic highway design, say, or form-follows-function footwear; talkin' the abhorrent, cryin'-out-to-be-filled vacuums. Like, why are the backs of TVs lopsided, or VCRs lost in a ganglia of connection? Why are cameras badly designed, unbalanced, weighted with topple and bristled with inexplicable dials and buttons as a camcorder or a fishing reel? (To my way of thinking, the last beautiful camera was the Speed Graphic.) How do you explain the anomalies? Why is it certain articles of men's clothing (their hats, for example—— I'm thinking of the fedora, I'm thinking of the Borsalino) make a higher fashion statement than women's? Can anyone here say why cutlery is more handsome than dishes, stamps more agreeable to look at than coins, coins easier on the eye than bank notes? (It's the focus of face, the joy of manageable scale.) Or why almost all jewelry, men's *or* women's, is unattractive? (Because it tries to mimic in metals or gems—in dead organics— natural forms, a vaguely frozen machinery of moving parts—— insects', the stars'.) And how, this late into time, this far into history, more than two dozen days now into the Mother of Battles (because I can't concentrate, because I'm too old to be a soldier and too far away to be bombed, and because there are no priorities like the priorities of life and death and I can't keep my mind on my business), does one explain the aesthetic downside of furniture?

Compared to many forms that lend themselves to art or craft— drama, the novel, painting, the composition of music, even the *inter-*

pretation of music, like, oh, say, singing the national anthem before the game, infinite other forms that seem to thrive, almost to wallow, in permutation, assuming new content, a mother lode of fresh ideas and differentiated styles as they're taken up by one artist after another— it's extraordinary how furniture is like most other furniture, as if furniture, alone among crafts, not only lived along the perimeters of some platonic ideal but had somehow actually managed to colonize it: an imperialism of the conventional. Except for a detail here, a detail there, inlay, marquetry, the pile-on of money, of pharaohs' or aristocracy's royal dispensations, a couch is a couch, an escritoire an escritoire. Beds resemble beds, tables and chairs are like tables and chairs. In domestic arrangements, form, bound to the custom cloth of human shape, really *does* follow function. The height of a table has to do with average lap tolerances. Chairs and beds are the hard aura of a strictly skeletal repose. Even so, something's busted, I think, in the imagination of the furniture designers—I except the art directors of certain major motion pictures set in Manhattan apartments; talkin' environment, the ecology of "life-style," of plot and character, what the principals look like against the bookcase, propped among the furnishings; one must learn the script of one's life and be able to afford it; because only in movies does furniture play well— all lamps and appointments, all cunning, edge-of-the-field doodad and inspired house-dower; one has at least the illusion one could live with this stuff, that it won't vanish in a season like a Nehru shirt—something stuck in the vision, some sorcerer's-apprentice effect, which permits to keep on coming and keep on coming with minimal variation, if any, what has come before. It isn't anything elegant as highest math happening here, just lump-sum arrangement, ball-park figure, bottom line. It's the fallacy of the assembly line, the notion that only costs get cut in such a wide sweep of swath. No, but really. *Isn't* it astonishing that personality, surely as real as the width of one's shoulders or the breadth of one's beam, should be so infinite but attention to body so meager and hand-to-mouth that—chairs, say chairs, I *know* about chairs—there's been less progress in the design of chairs than in the design of luggage. (I speak as a cripple full-fledged—chairs are a hang-up with me—but set that aside.) It's as if clothing came in a single size, pants like tube socks, every dress like a muumuu. And a rule of the chair seems to be that if it's beautiful it's rarely comfortable, if comfortable it rarely makes the cut to beauty.

Indeed, there are so few contemporary "museum-quality" chairs one can almost list them—— Marcel Breuer's side chairs, his "Wassily" chair like a leather-and-steel cat's cradle; Jacobsen's "Egg" chair; Thonet's bentwood rockers; Mies Van Der Rohe's "Barcelona"; Saarinen's molded plastic chairs on their round bases and tapered stems like cross sections of parfaits; all Eames's ubiquitous plastic like stackable poker chips or the pounded, hollowed-out centers of catchers' mitts, and as locked into a vision of the fifties as pole lamps, his famous lounge chair and ottoman that, like the Nehru shirt, have become a cliché. A spectrum of vernacular chairs—— soda-fountain chairs, directors' chairs, black canvas camp chairs, those crushed—almost imploded— white or charcoal leather pillow chairs like soft fortresses or marshmallow thrones; some of the new ergonomic chairs that sit on you as much as you ever manage to sit on them.

So I *know* about chairs and still have my eye out, never mind I'm sixty if I'm a day, for that evasive, lost-chord masterpiece of the genre, which, like love, I'll know when I see like a sort of fate.

Though maybe not. Not because I haven't the imagination to cut my losses, or even the courage to finesse my life and choose to sit out the close of my days in desuetudinous splendor, but because it may not exist. The chair, my gorgeous prosthetic of choice, may not have been fashioned yet. Because oddly, strangely, ultimately, chairs are all attitude, molds of the supine or up on pointe, aggressive or submissive as sexual position. Occupied or unoccupied either, they are shadows, ghosts, signs of the been-and-gone, some pipe-and-slippers choreography of spiritual disposition, how one chooses to acquit oneself, highly personalized as an arrangement of flowers, and oh, oh, if one but had the body for it one would live out one's days in Van Gogh's room at Arles, eating up comfort and beauty and having it, too, there in one last fell binge of boyhood in the cane and wood along those powder-blue walls of the utile, of basin and pitcher, of military brush and drinking glass, of apothecary bottles clear as gin on a crowded corner of the nightstand, to be there on the feather bed, on the oilcloth-looking floor amid one's things. All, as I say, you have to know is the script of your life. You wouldn't even have to worry whether you can afford it. What, this poor Goodwill stuff, these nitty-rubbed-gritty YMCA effects of the weathered and flyblown pastoral? I could pay out my life there gladly, not so much a hero as a loving dilettante of idyll, using only the plain equipment of beauty. Substituting "the hard work of freedom" with the even harder work of contemplation, giving way to quietude, calm, doing the doldrums in study's sargasso seas, all the light housekeeping of a stock-still ego laced with awe. There are worse character flaws than sloth. Nationalism, I think, patriotism, the too-forgiving love of tribe, maybe even of family itself. All the flaws of a restrictive loyalty, whatever makes us want to be part of a small idea, whatever makes us dangerous or allows us to entertain, even for a moment, the idea of a Mother of Battles. Much better to wait it out at Arles. Much better never to have seen the flashy dance steps from which we take our marching orders.

And it's the day before yesterday now. Joan and I are at the Shady Oak to see *Mr. and Mrs. Bridge*. And it's five o'clock on Presidents' Day, but that's only irony. It's the Rush Hour Show. Which is the one we always try to make. It's half price at Rush Hour but that's not the reason. We're old, we're old people, we get senior citizen whatever the hour. In spring and summer and some of the autumn it's still light when the movie lets out. It's important, that last bit of light. And anyway, though we know no one, we recognize everyone. Peers, birds of a feather, comfortable at the core as ourselves. We buy our tickets and go in. The lights are still up, enough to be able to see what I'm doing when I make the difficult transfer from my wheelchair to the theater seat. Joan folds the chair and parks it by the screen. "What could be better?" I ask automatically, but with absolute sincerity, as she slips in beside me.

The lights go down and something happens that has never happened before. They're playing "The Star Spangled Banner." It's for the war. An American montage like a little music video. American kids in American suburbs; transparent, billowy, slo-mo flag collages; purple mountains' majesty from one shining sea to the next, fields, fruit—all Ma Nature's starched summer dress whites. And they're standing, they're standing and singing! Card-carrying AARPers. It's like, well, it's like *church* is what it's like. They hold, some of them, their hands over their hearts. I mean there they *are*, singing, or perhaps just lip-synching in the dark in some key of the common denominator, ne-gotiating the difficult leaps and bounds of our national anthem. In the dark, singing to a screen as if it wasn't *Mr. and Mrs. Bridge* they'd come to see but *The Rocky Horror Picture Show*. And not to any orchestra but to a sound track! And the Shady Oak is automated, so not even to a projectionist but to a machine. Which, by default, makes

Joan and me the only audience at this odd performance. We're embarrassed, but what embarrasses us, I think, is to be so far out of the loop. Hey, there's *nothing* so convincing as an opinion.

We can't know this yet but G-Day is penciled in. Sunday, February 24, 3:00 A.M. Gulf time—two hours earlier at Arles—a ground war will begin that will last only 100 hours and make a name for this overrated masterpiece of a war. But still Saturday the 23, 7:00 P.M. Shady Oak time. When Rush Hour is winding down and the bigger spenders are lining up for the full-fare show. Who are on the cusp and, when the time comes, may or may not know just what it is they were standing for.

ABOUT
THE
AUTHOR

Stanley Elkin, winner of the 1982 National Book Critics Circle Award for fiction (for *George Mills*), is the author of fifteen other works, including *The MacGuffin, The Living End, The Dick Gibson Show,* and *The Franchiser.* Mr. Elkin, Merle Kling Professor of Modern Letters at Washington University, St. Louis, has received fellowships and awards from the Guggenheim and Rockefeller foundations, was nominated three times for the National Book Award, and is a member of the American Academy and Institute of Arts and Letters.